EXCURSIONS IN SOUTHERN SPAIN

40 Great Trips Through Andalusia

by David Baird

SANTANA BOOKS

Published in April 1996 by Ediciones Santana S.L.

Graphic design and typography by Bruce Williams, Mijas Costa 258 6653.

Printed by Grafícas San Pancracio, S.L.,
Pol. San Luis, C/.Oratova 17, Málaga.
Depósito Legal: MA-331/1996

ISBN: 84-921229-4-3

"David Baird reveals a hinterland of secret villages with stupendous restaurants, smuggler's routes and Europe's highest road. There's also sobering advice" - *Sunday Express.*

"Definitely one for tourers. Andalusia was made for touring and this is certainly a most useful guide" - *Sunday Telegraph.*

"Disarmingly honest . . . highly commended" - *Automobile Magazine, USA.*

This guide would not have been possible without the help of those who generously shared their intimate knowledge of the region. Their accumulated experience and their readiness to reveal their own favourite places - whether a scenic short-cut, a cultural highlight, or the most popular tapa-bar in town - made the research a pleasure. My sincere thanks to the staff of Lookout Magazine and fellow-contributors, to patient tourism officials, and to all those whom I met on the roads and byroads of Andalusia. Particular thanks go to Rafael Belmonte, Angela Pitt, Bartolomé Vergara, Victor Fernández, Manuel Domecq Zurita, Andrew Gaisford, Javier Hidalgo, Manuel Iglesias Fernández, David Hart, Antonio Jiménez, Manuel Pérez Regordán, Janet Mendel, Sonia Longman, Penny Ward, José Manuel Cabezas, and Bayard Osborn.

CONTENTS

Half-day excursions from the Costa

One-Day Excursions

One-day excursions *continued . . .*

Main and alternative routes to the cities of Andalusia

Side trips

USING THIS GUIDE

Welcome to Andalusia. This book - intended for both budget travellers and the well-heeled - takes you behind the Costa del Sol, to a region bursting with fascinating places to visit. It aims to make it easy for you to discover for yourself the attractions of this part of Southern Spain, famed for its exuberant people, its colourful customs and its spectacular scenery.

You will find information on the great historical cities like Granada and Seville. But this guide also takes you off the beaten track, to little-known villages, to unusual fiestas, to nature reserves and to unfrequented beaches - to places where many tourists never think to venture.

All this is detailed in 40 suggested excursions. Apart from background about the places visited, you will find highly practical information about possible overnight stops and where to eat. And at the end of the book we have included advice on driving hints, basic vocabulary and fiestas worth experiencing.

To simplify planning your excursions, the book has been organised into sections. First come half-day trips and day trips, which start from key points along the Mediterranean coast, from Málaga, Marbella, Fuengirola and Nerja. Then details are given of main and alternative routes to other towns and cities. Finally, 14 side-trips originating in those centres are described.

When following the excursions, you will come across some names printed in bold e.g. **SEVILLE**. This indicates that full information on these places is available at the end of the book in the Town and City Guide. The main tourist centres are listed, with details of their history, the most important sights, hotels, restaurants and other essential information.

TRANSPORT

While travel by car or motor-cycle is ideal to reach remoter corners, you can get around by public transport as long as you allow sufficient time to make connections. Trains, including the high-speed AVE between Seville and Córdoba, run between major centres. Buses are more frequent and usually cheaper. They are comfortable and usually airconditioned, but there may be only one a day to smaller villages. Cycling can be extremely strenuous because of the heat and the mountainous character of the country. Hitch-hikers need large doses of patience as they are often regarded with suspicion and lifts may be few and far between, particularly away from the coast.

VISITING HOURS

National monuments and museums are usually closed on Mondays. Apart from the important cathedrals, churches are usually only open for services, most often in the evening. However, ask around as the local priest or the caretaker may be available to give access. Citizens of the European Union have free entrance to a number of sights, where non-Europeans must pay.

INFORMATION

Addresses are given of tourist information offices, which can be found in most towns. They provide a useful service, giving out maps, brochures, booklets in several languages, and information about coming events. For basic tourist information (in Spanish, English, French and German) about Spain in general, including useful addresses and telephone numbers, you can call 901-300-600 between 10am and 8pm seven days a week. The call is charged at a reduced rate.

EATING OUT

While driving, keep your eyes open for a Great Spanish Institution, the "venta" or roadside inn. These are unpretentious places with very basic decor. Formica-topped tables and paper table-cloths are generally the rule. A television may be blasting away in one corner to keep diners properly entertained. Nobody pays any attention to it as they are too busy enjoying substantial meals at bargain prices. Written menus and wine lists are unknown in these establishments. They have not heard of credit cards. If you have difficulty in making yourself understood, ask to see what is cooking and point at what you want. Ventas are cheap and cheerful and well worth a visit, which is why you will find quite a number recommended in this book. If you cannot find a place billing itself as a venta or restaurant, look for a bar or mesón (a fancy name for a bar serving food). Most serve tasty *tapas* (snacks). Ask for a *ración* if you want a plateful. Tapas are usually available at all hours. Remember that Spaniards take meals late, lunch anytime between 2 and 5pm, dinner after 9pm.

Price Guide

Because there are constant fluctuations in prices and exchange rates, we have not specified exact prices of meals and accommodation. Instead, we give a rough guide.

At the end of each restaurant's rundown, you will see the letters B, M, E, or VE, indicating the price for one three-course meal, not including wine.

B - Budget, under 1,500 pesetas.

M - Moderate, in the 1,500 to 4,000 pesetas range.

E - Expensive, more than 4,000 pesetas.

VE - if you have to ask, the price you probably cannot afford it.

WHERE TO STAY

Standards of accommodation have improved considerably in recent years. If you find yourself in a small town or village at nightfall, beds are nearly always available at a small inn or in a private house. The rooms may be spartan, the bathroom communal and the water cold, but these places are usually spotlessly clean - and cheap. Many village pensions have been modernized and have en suite bathrooms, offering exceptional value. In addition, interest in rural holidays has led to many village houses and farmhouses being converted for tourist use. Inquire at tourist information offices and town halls.

A blue plaque outside hotels indicates the official rating. At the bottom end of the market, F stands for *fonda* (inn), P for pension, and Hs for hostal. Remember that hostal and hotel star ratings only take into account the amenities provided, not the quality of the service or atmosphere.

The Junta de Andalucía (the regional government) publishes a useful annual guide to all accommodation, including apartments and campsites. It is available free in tourist information offices.

Price Guide (for a double room)
In pensions and one-star hostals, expect to pay : between 2,500 and 4,000 pesetas.
Two-star hostals: up to 5,000 pesetas.
One-star hotels: between 4,000 and 6,000 pesetas.
Two-star hotels: up to 8,000 pesetas.
Three-star hotels: 6,000 to 10,000 pesetas.
Four-star hotels: 12,000 pesetas upwards.
Five-star hotels: from 15,000 pesetas.
Paradors (state-run hotels often in unusual locations such as castles and convents): from 10,000 pesetas a night.
Prices can vary with the season. Also rooms are often available at lower rates than those in the official guide, depending on demand.
Many hotels are part of the Bancotel, Ibercheque, and Hotelcolor systems, which offer hefty discounts. At travel agencies, you buy vouchers for at least five nights, handing these to the hotels on arrival. Advance booking is essential.

LET US KNOW

Our aim is to keep this guidebook as up to date as possible. We welcome your help. If you come across any changes, if you discover a restaurant worth recommending or a hotel with a special appeal, please let us know. We shall take it into account - and give you a mention - when preparing the next edition❑

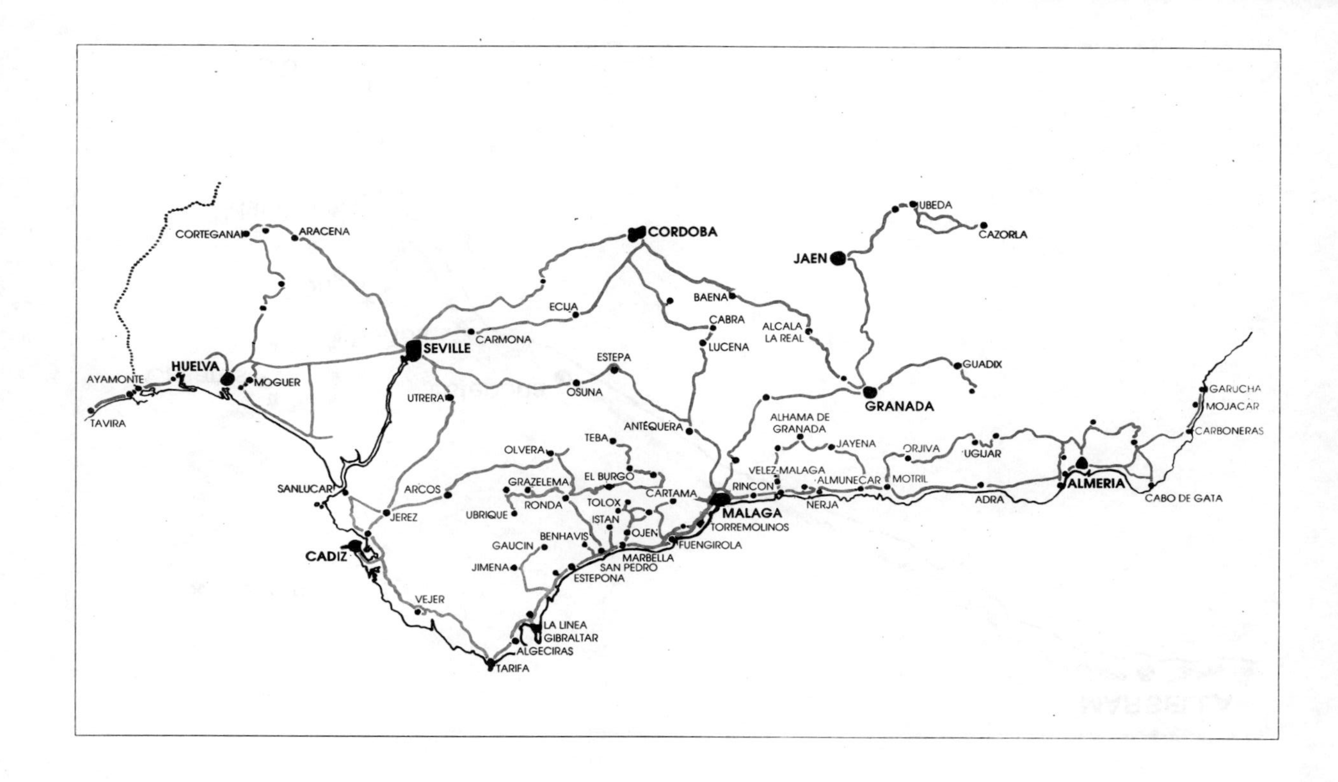
CORTEGANA
ARACENA
CORDOBA
UBEDA
CAZORLA
JAEN
BAENA
ECIJA
CABRA
ALCALA
LA REAL
CARMONA
LUCENA
SEVILLE
GUADIX
ESTEPA
HUELVA
AYAMONTE
MOGUER
OSUNA
GRANADA
UTRERA
TAVIRA
ALHAMA DE
GRANADA
ANTEQUERA
GARUCHA
MOJACAR
CARBONERAS
JAYENA
TEBA
OLVERA
ORJIVA
UGIJAR
VELEZ-MALAGA
GRAZELEMA
EL BURGO
ALMUNECAR
MOTRIL
ALMERIA
ARCOS
RINCON
SANLUCAR
CARTAMA
CABO DE GATA
ADRA
RONDA
TOLOX
NERJA
MALAGA
UBRIQUE
JEREZ
ISTAN
TORREMOLINOS
OJEN
BENHAVIS
GAUCIN
FUENGIROLA
CADIZ
MARBELLA
SAN PEDRO
JIMENA
ESTEPONA
VEJER
LA LINEA
GIBRALTAR
ALGECIRAS
TARIFA

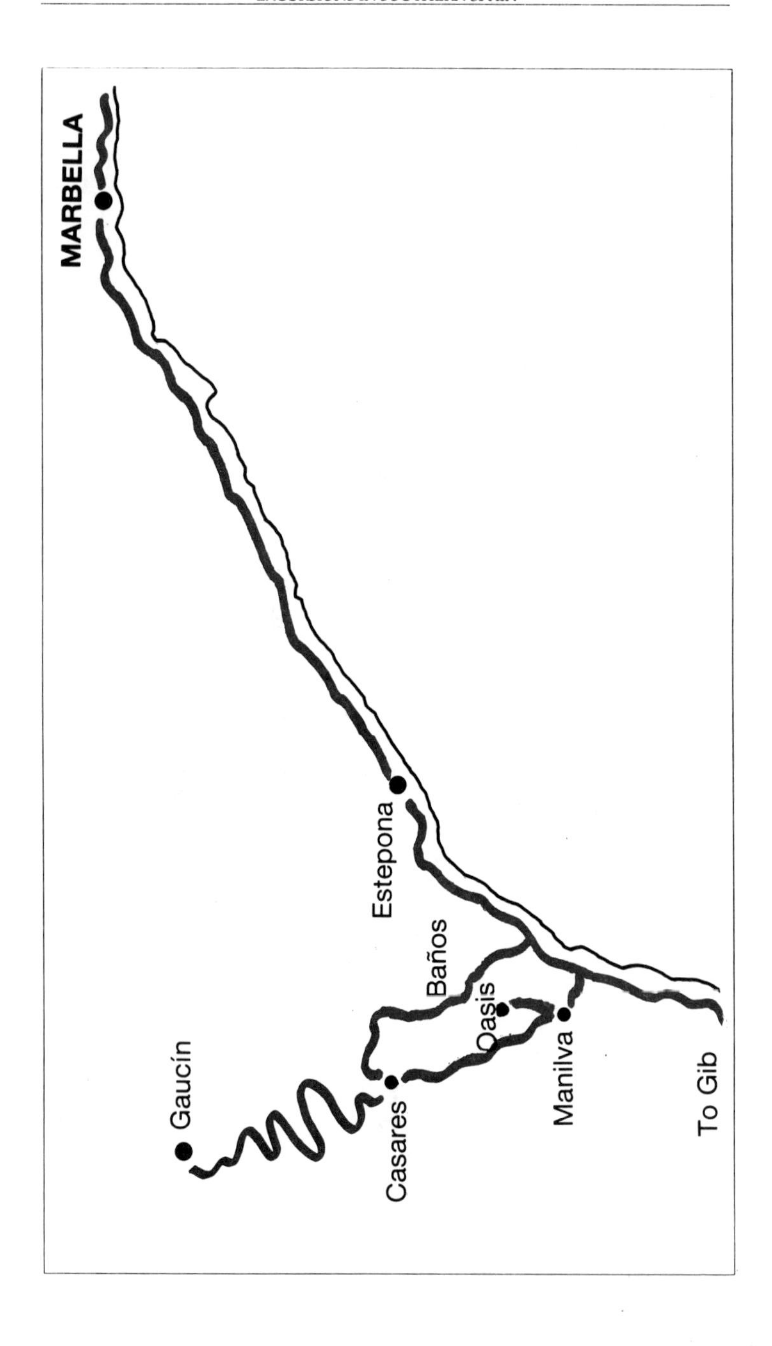
MARBELLA
Estepona
Baños
Oasis
Manilva
To Gib
Gaucín
Casares

Excursion 1- Tranquil Oases:

Marbella-Estepona-Casares-Manilva-Marbella
Distance: 70 miles (110km)

Escape from the coast to one of Andalusia's most spectacularly-situated "white villages", to craggy, hawk-patrolled mountains, and to a tranquil valley where Caesar himself once came to bathe his wounds. This route can easily be covered in half a day, but you may well decide to extend it so that you can linger over lunch or relax in Roman baths.

Heading west on the N340, you pass an area of the coast which has seen frenetic construction in recent years. One new urbanisation succeeds another.

After **ESTEPONA**, however, the developments begin to thin out. A pleasant place to stop for a coffee is at one of the quayside cafes at the Puerto de Estepona. This poor man's Puerto Banus is not so flashy as its Marbella counterpart. Even so, when you survey some of the craft riding at anchor, you may reflect that poverty is strictly relative.

Three miles (4km) from Estepona lies Costa Natura, the first purpose-built nudist pueblo in Spain. Inquire about temporary membership if you are interested in an all-over tan.

Soon you cross the boundary of the Casares municipality. About six miles (9km) from Estepona, after passing the Hotel Piedra Paloma, you glimpse the square outline of the Arroyo de Vaqueros tower on the beach. Turn right to Casares, passing through a shady eucalypt plantation. Suddenly the brash commercialism of the coast falls away. There are no billboards and only a few distant villas dotting the hills.

Cattle graze on the bare hills. Vines march up slopes to your left. The road begins to twist upwards, crossing an arroyo choked with oleander. It passes the Venta Villa Garcia and Venta Victoria, as we snake upwards past cork oaks and fire-seared pines in the foothills of the Sierra Bermeja.

Topping a rise, nine miles (14km) from the coast, abruptly

we encounter Casares (pop. 3,000), a village created for picture-postcard manufacturers. It looks as though somebody has played dice with hundreds of white cubes. They spill away below our feet, over a rocky saddle then up the facing slopes to jostle the battlements of an Arab castle. It is a view that few visitors can resist capturing on film.

Several restaurants serving local dishes offer this panorama from their dining rooms. La Terraza (Ctra de Casares km 12. Tel: 95-289 40 40. Open: 11am-4pm, 8-11pm. Winter 11am-4pm. Closed Monday. Amex, Master, Visa. M) has such dishes as *gazpacho casareño* (a hot soup) *codornices en salsa verde* (quail in green sauce). Craftwork is on sale on the ground floor. Another possibility is Curro (Barriada Los Ponis, tel. 95-289 52 05. Master, Visa. B) where you can sample conejo a la casera (rabbit).

Further along, on a right-hand bend, is the Laura restaurant (Tel: 95-289 40 24. No cards). Walk through the bar and past a display of pottery to reach the eating area, which looks out on village and castle.

A sharp left-hand turn carries you down into the village. During peak tourist times, you will have to park your car at the entrance to the pueblo. Otherwise, you may find a place on the Plaza de España, with its taxi-drivers, bars and pensions. White doves flutter about the central fountain.

To one side, against the wall of the Virgin of Rosario chapel stands a statue of Blas Infante, regarded as the Father of Andalusia. He was a notary, born in Casares, who led an Andalusian nationalist movement, until he was executed by Franco's rebels at the start of the Civil War. The town hall plans to turn the house where he was born, number 51 Calle Carrera, into a museum and cultural centre.

Just up from the square is La Chuleta, a restaurant located in an immaculately-maintained old house with small intimate rooms. Londoner Robert Mays, his Filipino wife Imelda (no, not **that** Imelda), and son Joemarie run this friendly establishment. They offer such dishes as shoulder of lamb with rosemary and spare ribs in honey (Villa, 25. Tel: 95-289 40 03. Open 1-5pm, 7-10.30pm, lunch only in winter. Closed

Wednesday and one month February-March. Master, Visa. M)

Keep climbing the narrow street and eventually you come out on top of the town, 1,400 feet above sea-level. Here is the old fortress, with a television reflector now attached to its square tower. Nearby is the derelict church, sacked during the Civil War, and Casares cemetery. And here is one of the *great* views.

A fresh breeze usually blows over the heights. Look out for peregrine falcons and kestrels riding the wind and gaze out towards the coast, the Rock of Gibraltar and the mountains of Morocco. You will understand how difficult it must have been to conquer this strongpoint in ancient wars. Waves of invaders broke against this gaunt, rocky pinnacle.

Casares history goes back at least 3,000 years. One version has it that it was named after Julius Caesar. Pedro the Cruel seized the fortress from the Moors in the 14th century and, after an unsuccessful 16th century revolt by the Moriscos, hundreds of rebel prisoners were hurled from this crag into the ravine. From all accounts, some nasty things also happened more recently, during the Spanish Civil War.

Continuing on the road that loops around Casares, you quickly come to a T-junction. To the right, eight miles (13km) away, lies Gaucin. Turn left to run down to Manilva and the coast.

You have excellent views of Casares and its crag as you descend through open country along a road which seems to have ice-cream foundations, for it crumbles away in any storm. A long rocky ridge accompanies you to the left and then Manilva appears, vineyards running up to its walls.

Just before Manilva, where trucks rumble out of a quarry to the left, a sign points to the Roman Oasis and a road leads steeply downhill to the Manilva River. At the bottom turn left along a dirt track towards the Baños Romanos.

After less than a mile, just before reaching a chapel there is an open grassy area on the right where it is advisable to park. Continue on foot to the baths. The smell of rotten eggs tells you you are getting close.

The baths have been sadly neglected. Ugly concrete covers the original roof over the spring and a surrounding wall is daubed with graffiti. But look in through the entrance and you will see clear water flowing from beneath archways built by the Romans 2,000 years ago. When Julius Caesar was in the district in 61BC, he is claimed to have cured a skin infection in these sulphurous waters. They are pleasantly cool to bathe in, but the odour may linger longer than you would like.

Back along the track, park your car near a pool in the river, a favourite swimming spot for local kids. A plank bridge leads to the Roman Oasis restaurant and bar, set amid vineyards. This is a very, very relaxing spot, shaded by trees, where fans twirl languidly and hammocks await the weary.

A chirpy English proprietor who escaped from Puerto Banus runs the Oasis. Specialities include a salad with caviar and heart of palm ingredients, English Cheddar cheese, barbecued meat, roast lamb and some 50 brands of port wine (Tel: 908-1514 66. Open: June-September 10am until late, and possibly April-May lunch only. Closed Wednesday and winter months. Master, Visa. M).

If you can drag yourself away from your hammock, continue through Manilva (pop. 4,500). This area produces delicious eating grapes and every year in the first week of September a riotous wine festival is held.

You can sample the product at the local bars. Bodega Agustín, last on the left leaving town, serves a pleasant sweet wine and a dry white, at bargain prices.

There are good views of coast and mountains as you run down the ridge to reach the N340 near the sandy Sabanillas beach. A little to the right is the Puerto Duquesa and to the left it is a 25-mile (39m) run back to **MARBELLA**❑

Excursion 2 -The Quaintest Pueblo:

Marbella–San Pedro-Benahavís-Marbella
Distance: 25 miles (40km)

This is an easy half-day trip to a little village which not so long ago was a sleepy rural community and has blossomed into an upmarket offshoot of the Costa with some good-value eating places.

A mile or so west of San Pedro de Alcántara on the N340, you cross the Guadalmina river and enter the municipal area of Estepona. A right turn takes you five miles (seven kilometres) to Benahavís.

You pass the greens of Atalaya Park golf club on the left and follow the Guadalmina valley. It is a typically rural scene with glimpses of grazing horses, rocky outcrops, gnarled fig trees and plantations of fast-growing eucalypts. The valley narrows into a gorge, the river tumbling along below limestone buttresses.

Then you turn a corner and Benahavís appears, spruced up, cobbled, whitewashed, almost too good to be true. There are still goats grazing on the surrounding hills and traces of the bucolic past, but heavy development has transformed Benahavís. Today there are more foreign residents than Spaniards among its 2,000 inhabitants.

The humble old pueblo has been converted into a sort of Andalusian-style Beverly Hills. It's been done in such chic good taste it almost hurts; indeed, the quaintness can be overpowering.

The main street, Avenida de Andalucía, is newly cobbled and lined with bars, restaurants and shops, catering to the many visitors from the coast. A side street to the right leads to the Plaza de España, a pleasant little square, and to the town hall.

On the square are two restaurants with the same name, Las Cañas, serving more or less the same dishes. One is run by Miguel, one by Eugenio, brothers who went their separate ways. Fortunately there appears to be enough business for

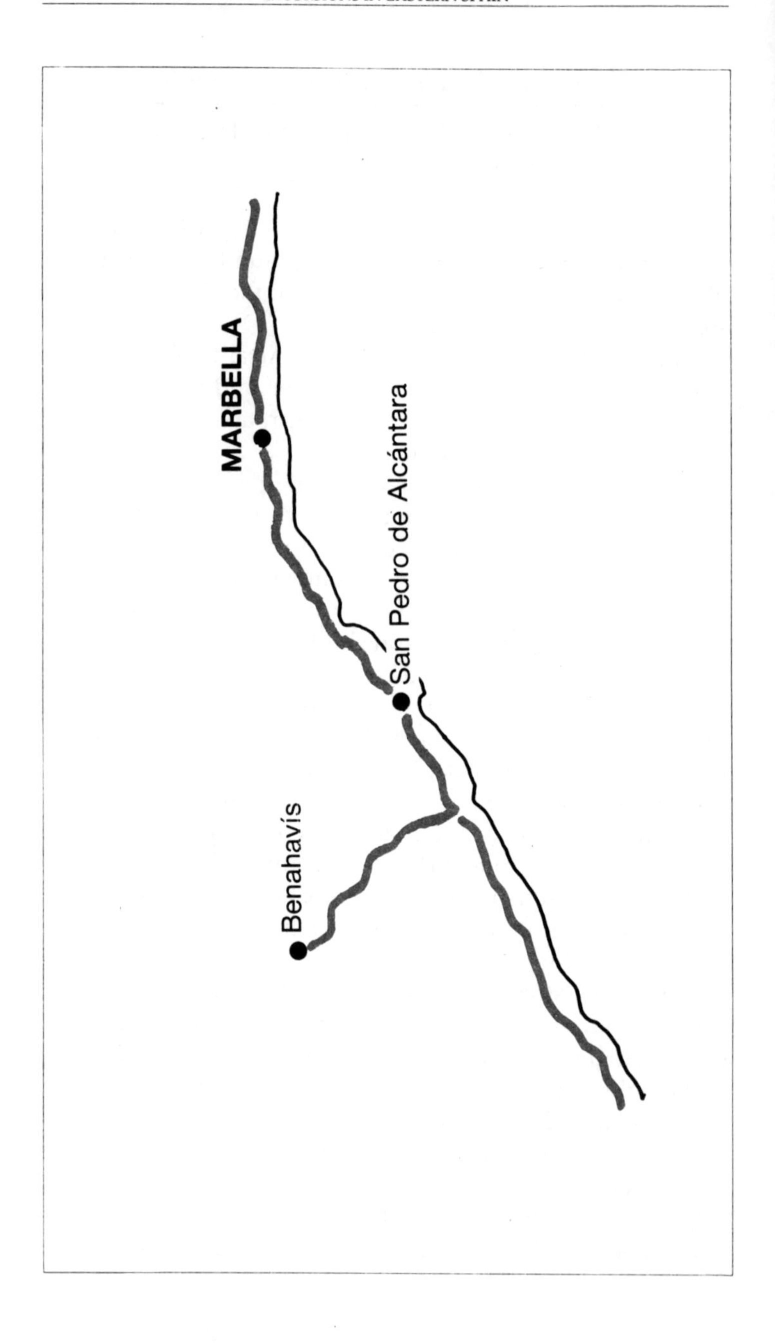
MARBELLA
San Pedro de Alcántara
Benahavís

everybody.

Continue down the main street and you come to La Aldea, a mini-pueblo created by wellknown British sculptor David Marshall. Old doors and grilles, numerous antiques and marble fountains have been used to create the illusion of Old Andalusia.

Marshall's spacious art gallery, with many of his imaginative works in metal, is a focal point. Nearby is a wall plaque unveiled by Nobel prize-winning writer Camilo José Cela who took time off from writing bestsellers and giving his testy opinions on television talk shows to open the complex.

The words are by Cela: *"Aqui escuchó el rumor del agua, el trino del ruiseñor y el melodioso canto de la odalisca, el hijo del guerrero Havis, el moro que reinó en el castillo de Montemayor y se pasó cien años peleando, amando y componiendo versos en el corazón."*

"Here the son of the warrior Havis heard the murmur of water, the cry of the nightingale, and the odalisque's melodious song, Havis, the Moor who ruled in Montemayor castle and passed 100 years, fighting, loving and composing verses in his heart."

Wander through the streets and you will come across a sculptor's studio, shops selling leatherwork and handicrafts.

"Típico" architecture, i.e. wooden beams and white walls, are a feature of the many restaurants. They attract large numbers of visitors from the coast because they are much cheaper than San Pedro and Marbella establishments.

There is little to choose between them, as they are virtually all family-run, with very similar menus. English is spoken everywhere.

You can enjoy grilled meat in the patio of the Lindaraja Restaurant (Calle Higuera, 2. Tel: 95-285 55 65). La Sarten (Avenida de Andalucia. Tel: 95-285 55 75) is also worth trying. For something more exotic, visit Las Griegas (Marbella, 8. Tel. 95-285 54 65) which - as the name implies - features Greek dishes. Sunday is a big day in Benahavís. Monday finds many places closed.

Benahavís is a sanitised version of a true pueblo. But some relics of the old Spain do hang on in the lower part of town. There, on Calle Málaga, you may find the Bar Ramírez, noisy and cheerful. The customers are mainly masculine, domino experts slapping down their pieces and billiards-players lining up the next shot through the cigarette smoke❑

Excursion 3 - To Istan's Green Valley:

Marbella-Istán-Marbella
Distance: 26 miles (42km)

Only a short distance from the topless beaches, the all-night discos, the luxury yachts and the millionaires' palaces along Marbella's Golden Mile, the mountain village of Istán remains remarkably unchanged - on the surface, at least.

Starting from **MARBELLA**, this is an easy half-day tour, offering fine views and rural tranquillity.

As you drive west along the N340, keep an eye out for the Marbella Club and Puente Romano, both on your left.

On the right you see the mosque, the first to be completed in Spain since the Moors were ejected 500 years ago

Just after, four miles (six kilometres) from Marbella, turn right to Istán. You pass close to the palace walls of the King of Saudi Arabia and cross over the Marbella bypass.

You pass the Sierra Blanca sports centre and clubhouse and the road winds up the Río Verde valley, leaving the coastal bustle well behind.The valley falls away to your left, green and lush, planted with citrus fruit and avocado orchards.

Four miles (six kilometres) from the turn-off on the N340 you sight the Presa de la Concepción, a formidable dam blocking the valley. A road leads down to the dam but it is closed to the public.

This is a good place to halt and admire the view. The reservoir shimmers in the sunshine. Gorse and juniper, thyme and rosemary clothe the hillsides. In spring wild flowers abound.

Istán, within whose boundaries the reservoir lies, proudly claims: "We supply all the coast's drinking water." Unfortunately the prolonged drought of the 1990s meant that often even Istán could not satisfy the needs of the coast.

Since water started backing up behind the dam in 1972, local folk say the climate has changed. Winters are warmer, summers more humid.

As you continue the drive on a road rebuilt after sections

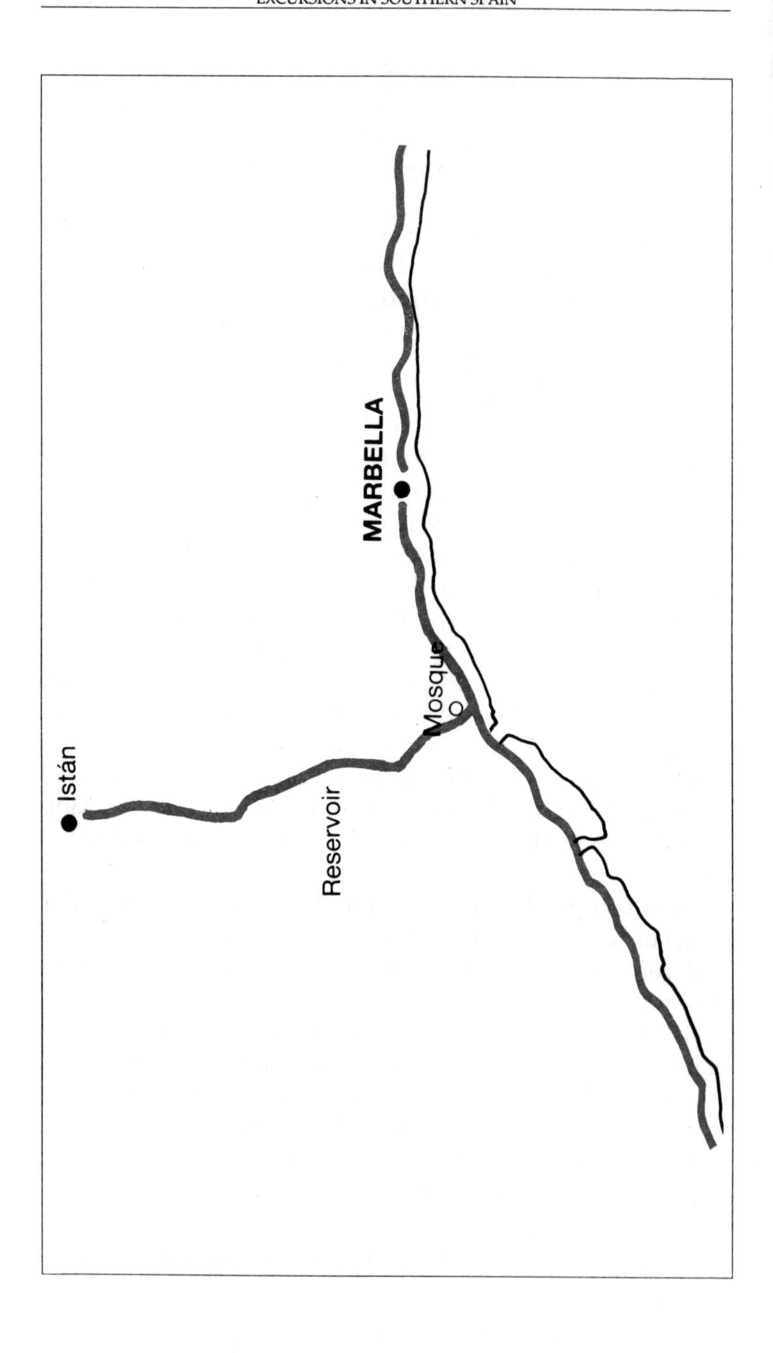
Istán
Reservoir
Mosque
MARBELLA

were washed away in 1989's record rains, you will see the Sierra Blanca rising to your right. It towers more than 4,000 feet above Marbella.

Ten miles (15 km) from the coast you round a bend and there lies Istán (pop. 1,600), a surprisingly unspoilt pueblo riding a ridge. It lies where the road ends, at 1,000 feet above sea-level, on the edge of the Serrania de Ronda hunting reserve. Beyond, the Río Verde valley cuts through the sierras, uninhabited but for birds of prey and wild goats.

Avenida Juan Carlos 1 leads into the village. Park your car on or near the esplanade at the entrance. You can look out over the valley's orange and lemon trees from a number of points in the village.

Walking is the only way to explore the narrow streets and byways of a village that dates back to the ninth century. Just beyond the esplanade to the right you will hear a familiar Istán sound, running water.

Water spills from a six-spouted fountain and under some arches water burbles along a trough, serving as a washplace. Not far away is the church square and down a side street the town hall.

A striking tiled mural on the stairs of the town hall tells something of village history. The Arboto fort at Istán was a strongpoint around which swirled scenes of bloody strife more than 1,000 years ago during Omar Ben Hafsun's rising against the mighty Caliph of Córdoba.

The ruins of the fort have yet to be found although a Moorish tower exists within the village. Ask for the keys at the town hall. The tower, with a typical Moorish archway, stands amid weeds and fig trees, hidden away in a side street behind a green door.

Not until 1485 did Istán fall to the Christians and new settlers arrived from Castile and Murcia. Because many people came from El Cristo de Panocho, a village in Murcia, to this day Istán inhabitants are known as "panochos".

In Moorish times the mountains above Istán, on the slopes behind La Conca, which frowns down on Marbella, are said to have been covered with vineyards. Until recently at least 40 families lived from their flocks of sheep and goats. But now four-fifths of the village workers drive down to the coast every day where they have jobs in tourism or construction.

Istán is sleepy during the week, when the "panochos" are glued to their television sets - a new transmitter installed in 1990 finally allowed them to pick up clear signals.

But the village is much visited at weekends. It really wakes up between September 28 and October 1 when the annual fair in honour of San Miguel is held, with a romería to a shrine three miles (four kilometres) away.

A passion play, using a 200-year-old script, is staged in the church square on Holy Thursday and Good Friday, starting around 4pm.

Istán has no restaurants, but many bars serving bargain tapas and platefuls of food. On the square you find the Bar Troyano. Then there's the Bar Sud Americano, Bar Barón . . .

Two of the village specialities are *sopa de maiz* and *sopa de tomate.* The latter is more nutritious than you might expect. It consists of layers of bread with fried onion, tomatoes, and sardines, topped with boiled eggs.

One of the villagers may rent you a bed for the night, but Istán will finally have a hotel when work on a new structure on the hillside overlooking the village is completed.

When you leave Istán, take your time on the winding road and be extra careful when you hit the N340 - after the easygoing pace of the interior, the high-speed coastal traffic can come as a jolting surprise.

A curiosity in the area of Istán is the so-called Castaño Santo (holy chestnut). This goliath of a tree has a girth of 13.5 metres and it takes nine adults linking hands to encircle it. It is claimed to be the oldest tree in Málaga province, dating back at least 700 years.

It gets its name from an incident five centuries back when a monk fleeing Moslem persecution hid beneath it. Its special qualities were underlined more recently when a forest fire devastated the area but left the holy chestnut untouched.

To see the Castaño Santo you do not visit the village of Istán but penetrate the mountains by a totally different route along the Río Verde valley. The excursion takes about three hours and can be done on bicycle or by car, although a four-wheel-drive is recommended.

From the highway at Puerto Banús, follow signs to Nueva Andalucía and La Quinta Golf. On reaching La Quinta you cross a small bridge over the river and take a forestry road to the right, following the river bed. After leaving the golf course behind, the track crosses the river once more and you see two tracks. One continues along the river. Ignore this and take the right one up the hill, following it for about eight miles (15km) when you see a track descending to the right.

Leave your car here as a chain restricts entry. Follow the main path 200 metres to the giant chestnut. The tree is on the Finca Hoyo del Bote and the owner of the property requests visitors to respect the environment❑

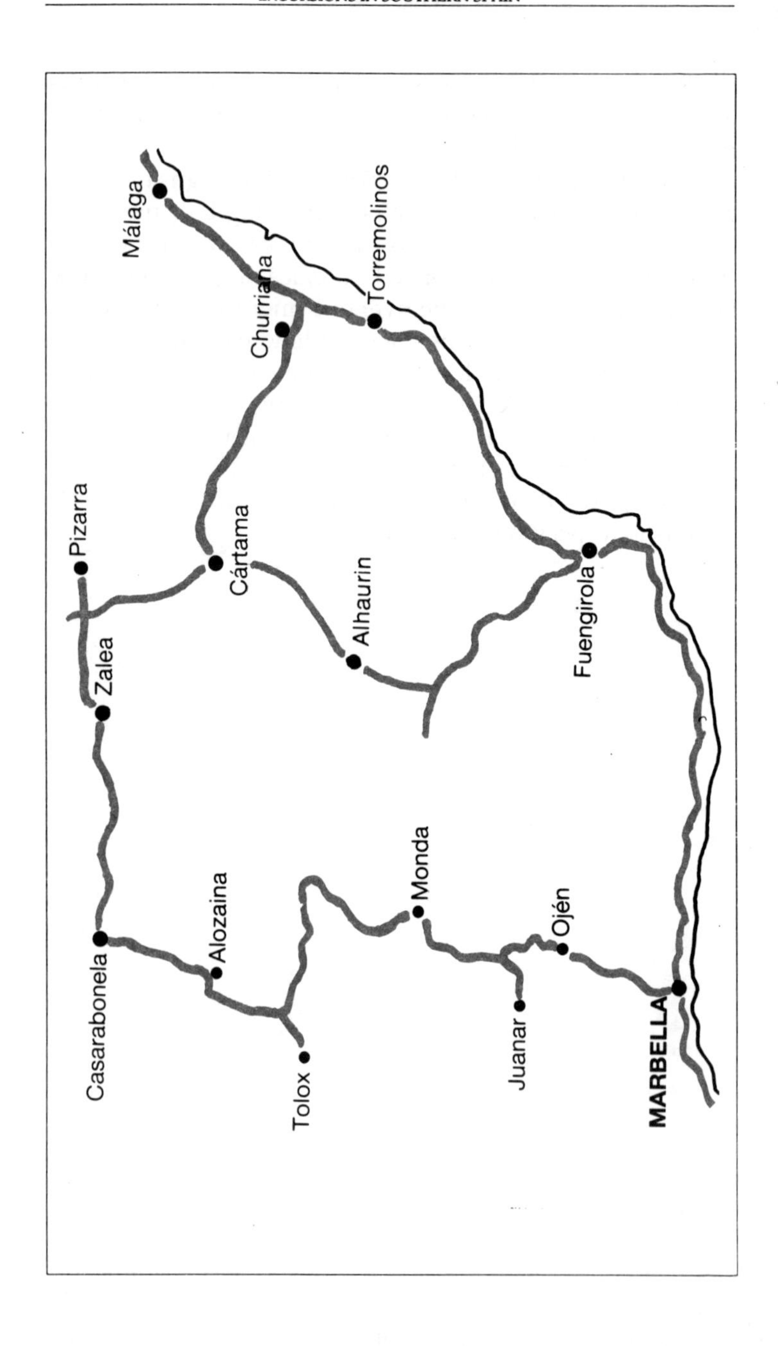
Málaga
Churriana
Torremolinos
Pizarra
Cártama
Alhaurin
Zalea
Fuengirola
Monda
Alozaina
Ojén
Casarabonela
Tolox
Juanar
MARBELLA

Excursion 4 - Taking the Cure

Marbella-Ojén-Monda-Tolox-(Alozaina-Casarabonela-Fuengirola)-Marbella

Distance: 62 miles (100km), returning via Casarabonela and Torremolinos 100 miles (160km)

This is your chance to explore the mountains that loom dramatically behind Marbella. You will find a royal hunters' hideaway, health-giving waters and - maybe - wild goats.

The half-day tour can easily be extended into a full day with some further exploration of the villages and mountains of Málaga province.

The old route C337 hairpins inland and sharply upwards from the rear side of **MARBELLA** towards Ojén. But a modern highway, branching off the Marbella bypass, now speeds the journey to Ojén and Coín.

Six miles (9km) from Marbella, the village of Ojén (pop. 2,000) stands sentinel at over 1,000 feet above sea-level over the green valley of the Río Real. Dive down into its narrow streets from the main road, park your car near the Plaza de Andalucía and take a stroll.

On the Plaza de Andalucía, two palms stand guard outside the old church. On the church wall, a plaque carries an impassioned appeal against "bad and barbarous war". Children splash water at the nearby fountain. Somebody is always whitewashing. Despite its nearness to the coast, Ojén retains its character.

Just around the corner is the Cafe Bar Felix Marín, the archetypal village bar. Old codgers ponder the past. Dominoes are slapped down. And the prices are a little different from those reigning in tourist haunts just down the road.

In the past Ojén was famed for its fiery fennel-flavoured *aguardiente.* You will not come across it now, but there are several bars where you can enjoy tapas and you will pass several ventas on the highway.

Continuing on C337, we climb over a pass and shortly after it a left turn takes us four miles (6km) up a lonely valley to the

Refugio de Juanar. This is a comfortable hotel. Once a hunting palace stood here, owned by the wealthy Larios family (Calle Larios in Málaga is named after a Marqués de Larios), who entertained guests like King Alfonso X111.

Surrounded by trees, the low buildings offer tranquillity in an ideal setting, with plenty of outdoor activities if you are looking for them (Sierra Blanca, Ojén, (Málaga). Tel: 95-288 10 00. Three stars. Special rates for longer stays. No dogs).

Cherry blossom greets spring visitors. One visitor was de Gaulle, who spent a while here in 1970 when he was writing his memoirs. On cold days a log fire burns in the lounge, where goat and deer horns hang on the walls. Partridge and roast kid are usually on the Refugio menu.

Hunters come here in season in quest of Spanish ibex, the wild mountain goat, for Juanar lies in the 23,000-hectare Serranía de Ronda hunting reserve. Trails lead off into the Sierra Blanca, to Istán and Ojén, if you want to do some hiking. Forests of pine, oak, chestnut and eucalypt clothe surrounding slopes and observant walkers may sight anything from wildcats to eagles. Early morning and evening are the best times.

Walk along the bumpy track from the Refugio, to reach a Mirador (lookout point), just over a mile away. This is the closest you can get to flying over the Costa del Sol without stepping into an aircraft. Standing 3,000 feet above the azure Mediterranean, the lookout point offers a breath-taking view of Marbella and the Mediterranean - and on clear days the mountains of Africa.

Back on the main road, the scenery grows wilder as you penetrate the sierras, until Monda (pop. 1,700, alt. 1,200 feet) appears, squeezed into a valley. Monda is a nondescript sort of place, topped by a renovated castle (see Excursion 10).

Ask for the road to Guaro. This runs north to join the C344, the Málaga-Ronda road. Turn left on the C344 and within five miles, before it crosses the Río Grande, a side-road to the left takes you to the secluded village of Tolox. A handy venta stands at this junction.

The Tolox road rounds a curve and abruptly you have a splendid view of the village. Tolox's buildings are glued to a steep hillside, each one seeming to balance perilously on the shoulders of the one below it. After three miles (5km), you enter the village (pop. 3,500, alt. 1,170 feet).

Keep left rather than entering the village centre. You pass a riverbed where donkeys and mules are likely to be grazing, then the road, shaded by gums, coils up a delightful valley.

At the end lies a sand-coloured building with a green-tiled roof, the Balneario de Fuente Amargosa (open from mid-June to mid-October), standing above a river tumbling over rocks. This spa's waters pour out at a temperature of 21 degrees Centigrade. Their radioactive qualities are said to be beneficial for those who suffer from breathing ailments, kidney stones, bronchitis, catarrh.

It is a popular spot and accommodation includes a one–star hotel, the Balneario de Tolox (Extramuros s/n. Tel: 95-248 01 67).

Above the Balneario the statue of a wild goat perches on a rock, a reminder that the adjacent hunting reserve is one of the last refuges of the *Capra hispanica.*

Eucalypts throw shade over a flat promontory above the murmuring river waters, an ideal spot for a picnic.

It is not always so quiet in Tolox. During the San Roque fiesta in mid-August, thousands of rockets are launched when the saint is carried in procession.

From Tolox you can return to Marbella, or reach the coast via Coín and Mijas. But, if you want a longer excursion, continue towards Ronda. We come to the attractive village of Alozaina (pop. 3,000), which has a 14th-century castle. Fill up at the petrol station as they are few and far between. If you feel like refreshment, turn into the village. On the esplanade where a weekly market is held, the Bar Nuevo offers seats outside in the shade.

The C344 continues towards **RONDA** through rugged country, but we branch off towards Casarabonela and Alora. The road wriggles along below the Sierra Prieta, offering views of mountains and across to the Guadalhorce valley.

Turn left to climb to Casarabonela (pop. 2,800), a snowdrift of a village lodged below woods and sierra. It too has remains of a Moorish fortress, plus traces of two Roman roads, to Ronda and to Málaga. A Moorish-style archway gives entrance to Casarabonela, where swifts practise aerobatics about the blue-and-white-tiled steeple atop the parish church tower.

On the way out of Casarabonela, on the road to Venta del Carmen leading to El Burgo and Ardales, there is a handy two-star hotel, the Alcaparaín (Avenida Federico Muñoz, 14. Tel. 95-248 0900), with views over the valley.

Orange trees flourish on the well-watered terraces below the village. Back on the MA403, we run downhill to the Guadalhorce river in its fertile valley, flowing with the dark green of citrus orchards.

Two miles (3km) before Pizarra, a right turn takes you across Arroyo de las Cañas towards Cártama. The white houses of Pizarra are glimpsed across the river (see Excursion 13).

The broad road swoops along through irrigated farmland. Side-tracks branch off to orange groves. It is easy to get lost on these tracks as there are virtually no signposts. By the wide riverbed of the Río Grande there are shady spots for picnics.

Joining the Coín road, the MA422, near Cártama, you have several choices to regain the coast. A left turn takes you to Cártama, Churriana and **MALAGA**.

Alternatively, a six-mile (10km) road cuts across the farmland, known as the Hoya de Málaga, to Alhaurin el Grande. A mile or so beyond Alhaurin you reach the Puerto de los Pescadores and join the MA485 to Mijas and **FUENGIROLA**❑

Excursion 5 - White Villages

Fuengirola-Mijas-Benalmádena-Arroyo de la Miel-
Torremolinos-Fuengirola
Distance: 25 miles (40km)

This half-day trip takes you on a scenic drive above the coast via two archetypal *pueblos blancos*.

Look for the Mijas and Coín sign on the Fuengirola bypass on highway N340 and turn inland. The road winds steeply upwards past a succession of villa developments to reach, after five miles (8km), a village that for many visitors typifies the Spanish pueblo.

Tourism and the real estate boom have brought dramatic changes to Mijas. Not so long ago it was a poverty-stricken agricultural community; now it is one of the wealthiest communities in Spain.

Only a few thousand people live in the old village, but the municipal area covers 148 square kilometres. Mijas territory includes the workers' suburb of Las Lagunas near Fuengirola, the fishing beach of La Cala and more than 170 urbanizations.

Although the officially registered population is 30,000, a more likely estimate is at least 75,000, of whom two thirds are believed to be non-Spaniards. More than 60 nationalities live within the Mijas boundaries and no less than 84 per cent of the building land is foreign-owned.

Despite the influence of mass tourism, however, the village itself retains a picture postcard appeal. A splash of dazzling whiteness on the mountainside 1,300 feet (428m) above sea-level, it commands a magnificent panorama of the coast.

Turn right on the bypass just before entering Mijas. This takes you above the town for the best views. On the hillside above the village is a shrine known as the Ermita del Calvario, built in 1710 by Carmelite monks. A pilgrimage to the shrine takes place during Holy Week.

Driving into the village itself, fork left and park in the main square near the grandiose town hall. Nearby is perhaps the best-known local tourist attraction - the burro taxis. The dozy

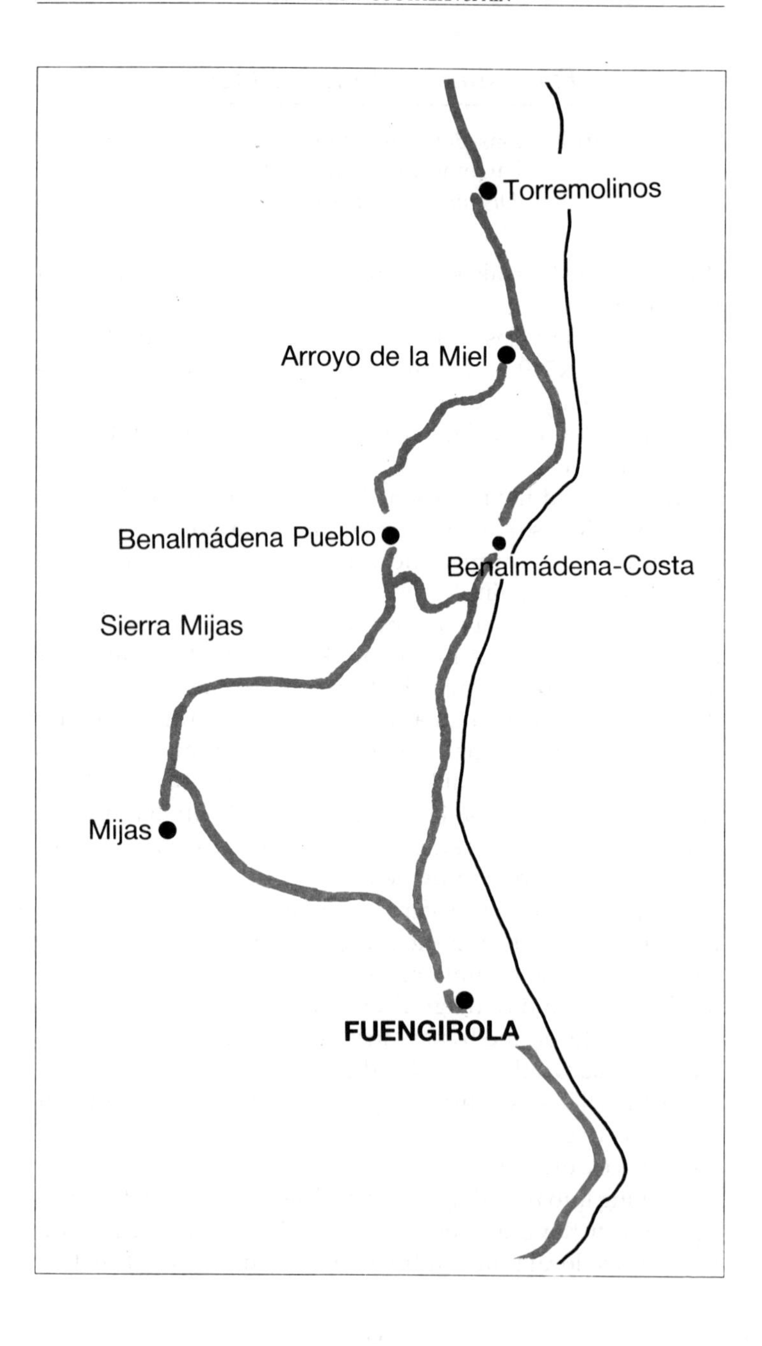
Torremolinos
Arroyo de la Miel
Benalmádena Pueblo
Benalmádena-Costa
Sierra Mijas
Mijas
FUENGIROLA

donkeys and their crusty owners wait patiently, ready to take visitors on a jog around the town.

Walk up to the Ermita Virgen de la Peña, a shrine which shelters a sculpture of the Virgin believed to date back 1,000 years. Further along, passing the remains of old walls, are gardens offering stupendous views of the coast. You can visit the church of Inmaculada Concepción, with its Mozarab tower. It is built on the site of a ninth-century mosque. Near the church is an outdoor auditorium and an unusual square bullring.

Mijas was one of the fortresses of Omar Ben Afsun when he defied the Caliphs of Córdoba and established his own kingdom in the ninth century. When the Moors lost control of the settlement after the fall of Málaga in 1487, the mijeños were stripped of all their possessions and ejected. Their lands were handed over to nine Christian families.

For tourist information, inquire at the town hall (95-248 59 00), where there is also a department for helping the many foreigners resident in the area. Tourism influence is so heavy around the square with dozens of souvenir shops that Mijas has come to epitomize the stereotyped Tourist Spain. Ironical, when you consider that the thousands of visitors come here to see the Real Spain.

In fact, it exists, just around the corner. If you take a short stroll, you find streets that appear little different from those in any typically Andalusian town. Old women in black add yet another coat of whitewash to already immaculate walls and geraniums bloom brightly in window boxes. Dominoes are slapped down in traditionally smoky, noisy bars where package tourists rarely enter.

In La Alcazaba commercial development, off the Plaza de la Constitución, is recommended El Mirador restaurant (Tel. 95-259 01 78, open 1-4pm, 6.30-11pm, closed Mon. Amex, Diners, Master, Visa. M). The owners, from Valencia, make authentic paella and other specialities include leg of lamb and good desserts.

Drive back out of Mijas towards Fuengirola. Opposite the service station, a narrow, sinuous road, the MA408, goes left towards Benalmádena. Follow this as it twists and turns, offering good views of the hills dropping away towards the coast. Once there were vineyards here, now hillsides are carved away to slot in villas, each with its sea-view, azure swimming-pool, boungainvillea and green lawn.

One mile (1.5km) from Mijas look for a sign on the left indicating Cantera Los Arenales. A road snakes up through pine forest to a television transmitter and the top of Mijas mountain. The route up can be a little hair-raising, so drive with extra care. But the views of the coast and of the city of Málaga are magnificent.

Continuing down the MA408, you pass the Buena Vista villa development, then twist downwards towards the N340 autoroute. You can stop for a drink or a meal at a venta which has been serving travellers since 1840.

However, El Higuerón has changed considerably in recent years. This popular whitewashed restaurant (Autopista Costa del Sol, Salida 217. Tel 95-256 82 00. Open 12am-12pm. Amex, Master, Visa. M) has doubled and trebled in size. It stands high above and from its glassed-in terraces diners enjoy magnificent views of the coast. *Fabada asturiana* is among the specialities.

Just beyond El Higuerón, the road passes under the four-lane coastal highway and runs past olives, gnarled carob trees, and luxury villas to **BENALMADENA**.

Just before entering the village, a road zig zags down to the right to reach the coast at Torremuelle. Buses stop below the village to allow passengers to take a stroll through the pueblo.

A few hundred yards down the Torremuelle road stands the Castillo Colomares, a fantasy castle in brick, stone, and concrete. The prow of a ship, pillars, and domes create the sort of vision that a Moorish Gaudí with a brainstorm may have dreamed up. It is now the scene of daily falconry demonstrations. Vultures, owls, hawks and eagles swoop over the crowd (Castillo de Aguilas, Banalmádena Pueblo, tel. 908-95 25 64. Open 11am-pm, 3.30-6pm. Closed Mon).

Returning to the pueblo, you can park your car on the road above it. It is a typical village of narrow streets which are easier to walk than drive. Although the coastal area of this municipality has sprouted high-rise blocks and grown into the brash tourist resort of Benalmádena-Costa, the original mountain village retains its traditional architecture and atmosphere.

Immaculately-whitewashed and cobbled, it looks down with tranquil dignity on all the fuss taking place down below it. You have an excellent view towards the Mediterranean from the Jardines del Muro and there are open-air cafes where you can pause for refreshment. Casa Fidel (Maestra Ayala, 1. Tel. 95-244 91 65. Open: 1-4pm, 7.30-12pm. Closed Tues. Amex, Diners, Master, Visa. M) offers national and international dishes.

On the highway is the Archeological Museum, which has some remarkable examples of pre-Colombian art, as well as a number of artefacts found locally (open 10am-2pm, 4-7pm, closed Sat, Sun). Excellent reproductions are on sale. The museum was started originally with the collection of Felipe Orlando, a Mexican painter, poet and philosopher who settled in the village.

Benalmadena's tourist office is not in the pueblo but on the coastal highway (Avda Antonio Machado, 14. Tel: 95-244 24 94).

Leaving the pueblo, you pass Benalmádena's bullring and the International Cemetery. The road winds down towards Arroyo de la Miel, a workaday community where many of the Spaniards employed in tourism on the coast live.

On the outskirts of Arroyo, to the left, is the vast Tivoli pleasure park (for information call 95-244 18 96), which features everything from an open-air theatre to a "montaña rusa" (a roller-coaster).

Continuing east, the highway reaches the **TORREMOLINOS** bypass. From here it is a brief drive back to **FUENGIROLA**, either by the N340 along the coast or by the autovía (take the bypass exit to the Palacio de Congresos and continue past the Palacio to a junction)❑

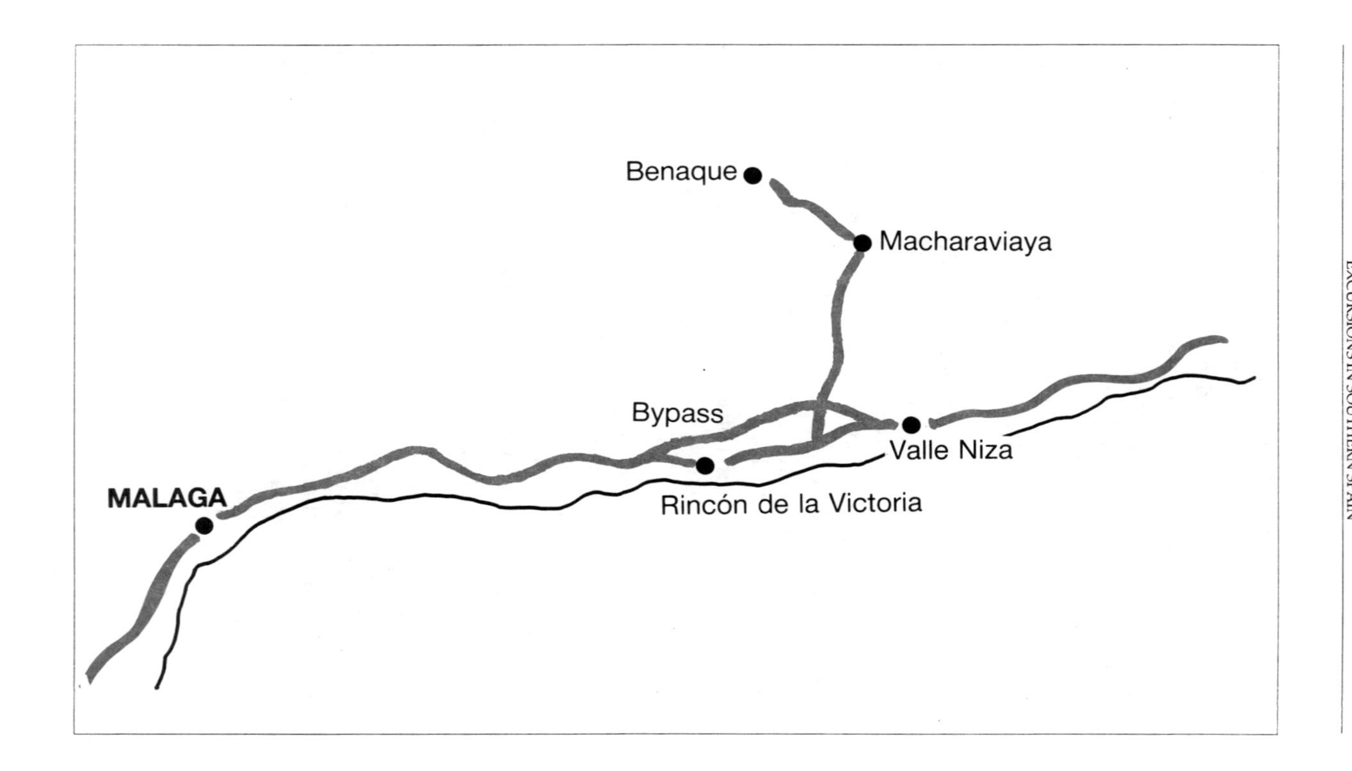
Benaque
Macharaviaya
Bypass
Valle Niza
MALAGA
Rincón de la Victoria

Excursion 6 - To Little Madrid

Málaga-Rincón-Macharaviaya-Málaga
Distance: 32 miles (52km)

East of Málaga stretches a part of the Costa del Sol which remained undeveloped while the Torremolinos-Marbella strip was booming as a tourist destination.

Now this wedge of Málaga province, known as the Axarquia, has been discovered. **NERJA**, Torrox and Torre del Mar attract thousands of visitors. But inland lies an enchanting area of mountainous country and ancient, sunbleached villages where the 20th century has delayed its arrival.

Dozing blissfully, Macharaviaya seems no different from its neighbours. But it has a special claim to attention. Once it was so famed for its progress and prosperity that it was dubbed Little Madrid.

After two centuries of slumber, the four-lane bypass which curves through the hills around Rincón de la Victoria, just east of Málaga, has brought the tiny community a little closer to the outside world.

This is an easy half-day excursion from **MALAGA**, a trip for searchers after tranquillity and those with a taste for nostalgia. From the old coastal highway east of Rincón, it is six miles (9km) to the village. If you are coming from Málaga, it is quicker to follow the Rincón bypass on the Almeria highway, N340. After the bypass has swooped around the hills inland, you will see the Machariaviaya exit.

After passing the Añoreta golf course you are suddenly back in Old Spain. The narrow road climbs and twists past olive and almond trees until you begin to descend and sight the hamlet of Benaque, where Salvador Rueda, an acclaimed poet, was born in 1857.

Macharaviaya lies closer at hand, tucked into a fold at your feet, its parish church towering over the humble village dwellings.

There is not much happening in the main street. Traffic is

sparse. But take a good look at that church. It was in a lamentable state but has been restored, although without much aesthetic regard.

For such a small community, this Neo-classical building with its 63-foot nave is overpowering in its size. Four pillars adorn the main entrance, above which is a coat of arms topped by a crown. Valuable paintings once adorned the interior, but they were destroyed in the Civil War.

To visit the church and pantheon underneath it, ask for Amparo who lives nearby, at a house above the main street. She has the key. The pantheon contains the remains of the Gálvez family, who two centuries ago transformed the fortunes of Marchariaviaya. Soldiers, diplomats, adventurers, they became the favourites of King Carlos 111 and enforced his will in the New World.

In the gloomy, damp-streaked vault, with its six alabaster sculptures, look for the grey marble tomb of José de Gálvez , the most prominent of four brothers. His ashes are contained in a large urn.

José rose to become Marquis of Sonora and Minister of the Indies. He played a big part in expelling the Jesuits from Spain's American colonies and moved swiftly to block the Russians moving into California.

His nephew Bernardo fought the Apache Indians, became governor of Louisiana and defied the British in the American War of Independence. Galveston is named after Bernardo and a United States order known as Los Granaderos de Galves still pays tribute to him for his help in beating the Redcoats.

The Gálvez family did not forget their birthplace. They rebuilt the church and packed it with treasures, including it is said six Murillo paintings. You will not find any of them there now, as the building was sacked during the Spanish Civil War.

A factory employing 200 people was established to manufacture playing cards and it enjoyed the monopoly of their export to the New World. Traffic bustled along the new carriage route from the coast to the bustling community with its fine paved streets and bubbling fountains.

Little Madrid's heyday 200 years ago ended with the passing

of the illustrious Gálvez family and it sank back into obscurity. But its links with the United States can be read in the street names, Pensacola, Mobile, New Orleans. It is twinned with Mobile.

Refugees from city life have refurbished some of the houses. Potters and painters have moved in to Macharaviaya, so close to the United States and so far in temperament from the Costa. Official population is barely 360.

For snacks and meals pay a visit to the bar La Candela. You reach it by taking the right-hand street at the entrance to the village.

Return to the coast via the same route or, if you are in more adventurous frame of mind, follow Macharaviaya's main street downhill and out of the village. It curves left then sharp right down to the river, deteriorating into a dirt track.

This meanders past fields of crops, along a valley side, passes a hamlet and finally runs uphill to a junction with a paved road. Turning left will take you to the village of Cajiz, turning right brings you back to the coast at Valleniza, near Benajarafe❑

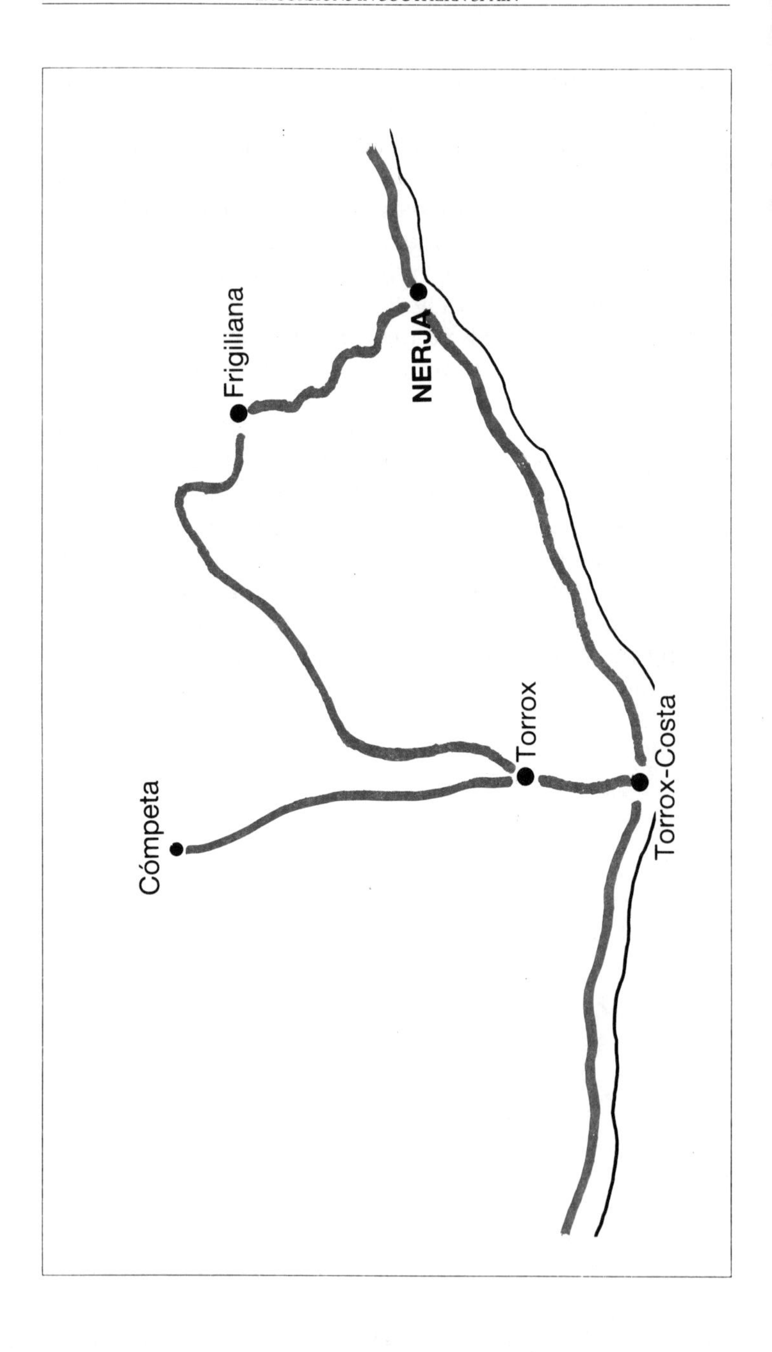
Frigiliana
NERJA
Cómpeta
Torrox
Torrox-Costa

Excursion 7 - To the Costa's Prettiest Village

Nerja-Frigiliana-Torrox-Nerja
Round trip: 20 miles (32km)

Vine-and-olive-clad hills, mountains which really do look like the edge of a saw (sierra), and impeccably-whitewashed villages make any visit to the interior of the Axarquía, the eastern corner of Málaga province, worthwhile. This half-day journey calls in on two typical villages.

Driving east on the N340 from **MALAGA**, ignore the right fork to enter **NERJA**, drive past a nightmarish-looking piece of statuary entitled The Abduction of Europe, and 200 yards along turn left to Frigiliana on the MA105.

The road runs erratically uphill, past fields of sweet potatoes and recently-planted avocado orchards, towards the sharp-toothed mountains of the Sierra Almijara.

Frigiliana (pop. 2,100) is only four miles (6km) from the coast, but - at 900 feet above sea-level - it retained the character of a typical agricultural village, at least until recently. With its cubist architecture and mosaic-cobbled streets, it has won both Spain's national and Andalusia's regional prize for the best-preserved and beautified village.

It owes its unspoilt beauty to a far-sighted mayor who some years ago ruled that all building must be low-rise and in traditional Andalusian style. However, Frigiliana's fame has spread and the increasing number of tour groups plodding the streets is inevitably changing the character of the place.

Park your car near the bus stop and the Cuartel (Civil Guard barracks) and walk into the old section of town. If you climb up the stepped streets of the Barrio Alto and take a path that curves around the hillside, you reach the site of a Moorish fort which commands magnificent views of sea and mountains.

All that remains are traces of old walls, for Frigiliana castle was razed 400 years ago after a major battle in the War of Granada. Moriscos (Moors converted to Christianity) made their last stand here against Philip 11's forces but were finally crushed. One of the Frigiliana streets is named after Hernando El Darra, the Morisco leader.

Twelve ceramic plaques dotted about the village recount the epic tale. One reports that the Axarquía was populated by "slight, strong men of such great spirit that in the old days the Moorish kings regarded them as the most valiant, daring and effective in the Kingdom of Granada".

Several crafts shops have opened, but the pioneer establishment is the popular La Cesta, in the main street, a few steps from the church square and the town hall. La Cesta stocks an unusually wide range of authentic Spanish handicrafts, including pottery, leatherware, and weavings, plus batik paintings and tapestries. Local wine and honey are available, too.

Entering Frigiliana from Nerja, you see the Bar/Restaurant Orihuela on the right. It has excellent baby goat in almond sauce and several other good-value dishes.

Below the church square is La Fuente, with a sunny terrace at the rear, where you can enjoy typical local dishes. Tucked discreetly away behind the church is the family-run La Bodeguilla, with tables outside and home cooking.

For fine views with your food, climb to the Barrio Alto, the upper part of town where there are two bar/restaurants with terraces, El Jardín (English-run) and the Mirador (South American).

Every family makes the heady vino del terreno from sun-dried moscatel grapes and is proud of their brew's quality. You can buy genuine virgin olive oil from the Ingenio, the large building near the Civil Guard barracks, and also molasses, canned here in the last molasses factory in Europe. The Ingenio, once owned by the Count of Frigiliana, retains the old sugar milling machinery, now incorporated into a bar-museo.

From the bypass which runs below the village a new paved road curves away up the mountainside. It leads to Torrox, nine miles (14 kilometres) away. You pass two ventas offering meals and fine views near Frigiliana.

On your right at first is the mass of El Fuerte, a 4,000-feet-high mountain covered with scrub, esparto grass and gnarled trees, where the Moriscos (Moslem converts to Christianity) took refuge from Philip 11's forces during their 1569 rebellion.

Men and women hurled rocks down on the advancing soldiers from these heights. Look for a cliff of reddish bare rock. Here, it is said, many Moriscos leaped to their deaths rather than be captured.

In pre-Civil War days, the path that ran around El Fuerte and headed into the mountains was busy every night with traffic as muleteers urged their animals on towards distant Granada. They had to reach the markets in that province by morning to sell fresh fish from the Mediterranean.

The Frigiliana-Torrox road is an unforgettable scenic drive - particularly in February and early March when the almond blossom is out - as the road swoops along ridge crests, the sierras soaring to the north. To your left, steep hillsides clothed in vineyards and olive trees plunge towards irrigated fields and the sea.

Whitewashed cortijos are scattered about, many of them now being rebuilt as new owners take over and irrigation schemes bring such exotic sub-tropical fruits as avocadoes, custard apples and kiwi fruit.

Think twice before using the Frigiliana-Torrox road at night. Sharp curves and steep drops are common, crash barriers few.

The road swings toward the coast before looping over a ridge to reveal the town of Torrox, straggling over a ridge below. You descend, cross a narrow river bridge, and approach the town.

Be careful here not to veer left into Torrox itself. Drivers have been lost for days as they struggled to squeeze through the narrow streets. Instead keep right on the road around the top of the town. Beyond the rooftops, you glimpse plastic-covered fields and upended matchboxes, the apartment blocks at Torrox-Costa.

Turn left after you pass a school and drive around the edge of Torrox. Where this bypass swings sharply right to head towards the coast, good tapas are available in two bars, Stop and El Rubio. You can park your car near here and stroll up to the market and the pleasant square outside Torrox town hall, where there are pavement cafes.

Just above the square is the 18th century parish church. The old town retains its traditional air with narrow, winding streets and occasional mules and donkeys plodding by.

On the Sunday before Christmas, Torrox celebrates its *Día de las Migas,* when thousands arrive to eat migas (a leaden concoction of flour or bread crumbs fried in olive oil), drink the powerful local wine, and enjoy fandangos, verdiales and other folk music.

"The Very Noble and Very Loyal Town of Torrox", important as an agricultural centre (pop. 10,000), is said to have been the birthplace of the great Moorish leader, Al-Mansur.

Continuing to the coast, you reach Torrox-Costa (tourist information, Avda Esperanto, Bloque 79. Tel: 253 02 25).

Near the lighthouse, traces of a large necropolis, baths, a villa and ceramics ovens testify to the presence of a major Roman settlement between the 1st and 4th centuries. Garum, the smelly fish delicacy beloved by the Romans, was produced here.

On the beach, 3,000 men were put ashore in 1569 to march against the Morisco stronghold at Frigiliana. Now the beach is a favourite with German visitors and a pleasant spot to enjoy a meal and a drink at one of the many chiringuitos (beach restaurants).

NERJA is five miles (8km) to the east, along a coast road running between rock faces and a number of sandy beaches. Along the coast you will notice a series of watch towers, built to give warning when Barbary pirates were approaching❑

Excursion 8 - Gourmet Surprise

Nerja-Almuñécar-Salobreña-Motril-Gualchos-Castell de Ferro-Nerja

Distance: 78 miles (125km)

An easy half-day excursion from **NERJA** or **ALMUNECAR** takes you along a coast with some of the Mediterranean's most spectacular scenery, then inland into the hills to a ridge-hugging cluster of whitewashed houses, where an agreeable culinary surprise lies in wait.

The N340 weaves eastwards, skirting steep cliffs and tiny coves. Soon you see the dazzling white bulk of Salobreña (see Excursion 22) and its impressive fortress, rising above a flat delta with waving fields of sugar-cane.

Follow the signs into Salobreña and up to the castle. It is a good walk, or - if you have steady nerves - a testing drive up along impossibly narrow streets with dog-leg bends.

At the top of town steps lead to the Castillo (open 10am-2pm, 4-6pm, later in summer, small entrance fee), where you can wander through pleasant gardens and gaze from the walls at the snows of the distant Sierra Nevada or over the rooftops towards delta and sea.

The castle history is explained in a display in a tower. The settlement here dates back to the Bronze Age. The Moors built an important fortress, often used as a prison. In 1408 as Muhammad V11, the sultan of Granada, lay dying, he feared that his brother Yusuf would take the throne instead of his son. So he sent an emissary to kill Yusuf, imprisoned at Salobreña.

The story goes that Yusuf was playing chess with the castle warden when the assassin arrived and asked if he could finish the game. It was still proceeding when news arrived that Muhammad had died and that a new ruler of Granada had been proclaimed - Yusuf 111.

Between the 15th and 17th centuries the castle was a vital point in defending the coast against Turkish and Berber pirates. Later it fell into ruin and has only been restored, extensively, in

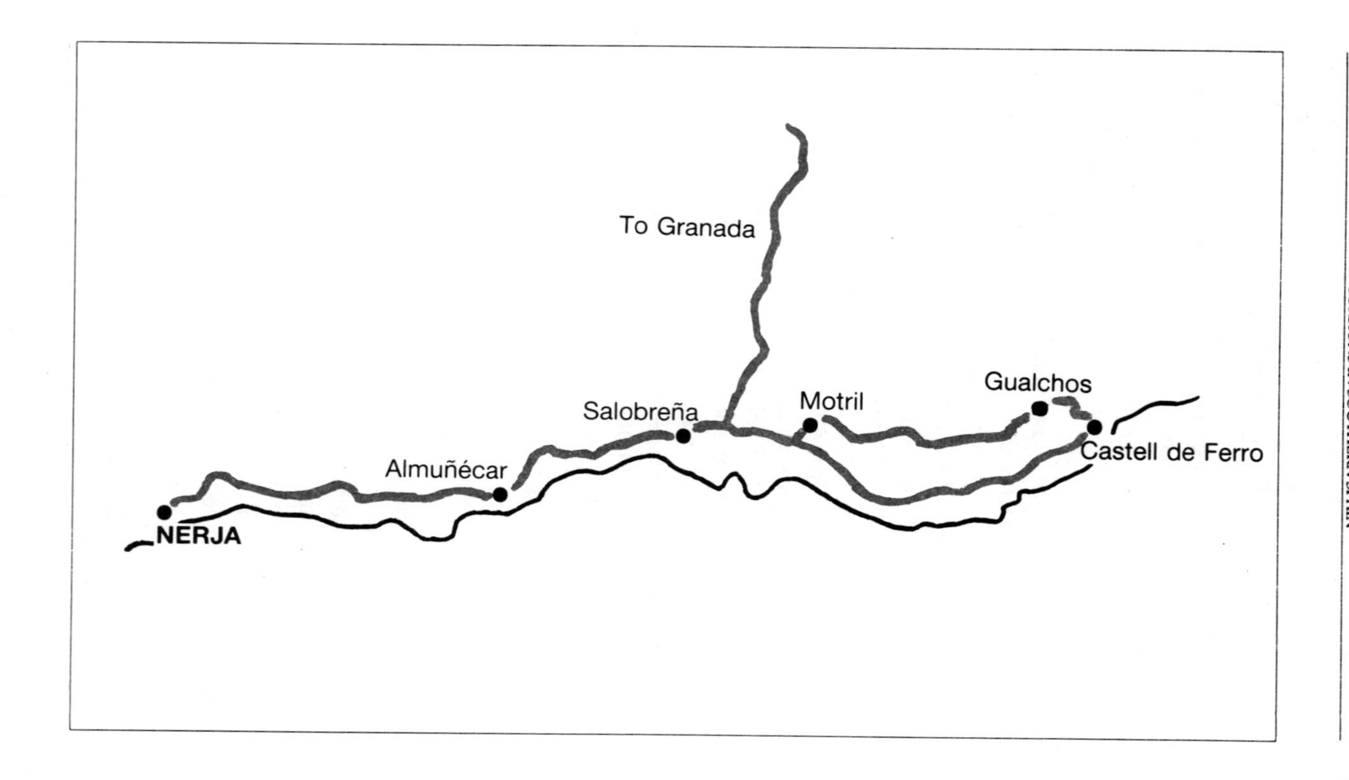
To Granada
Gualchos
Motril
Salobreña
Almuñécar
Castell de Ferro
NERJA

recent times.

The parish church, a little below the castle, built on the site of a mosque, has a Moorish-style arch at its entrance with green and gold tilework above.

Salobreña has a long sandy beach, split by a large rock which juts into the sea like a basking whale. The restaurant here, El Peñon (Playa del Peñon, tel 958-61 05 38), is recommended, particularly for fish dishes. In summer diners on the terrace are entertained by daredevil local youths leaping into the sea from the rocks.

If you have time only for a snack at Salobreña, call in at La Bodega, a bar and restaurant on Avenida de Motril, not far from the eastern exit from the N340. It serves good tapas and local wine, including mosto from Itrabo, one of the villages a short distance inland.

The tourist information office is nearby at Plaza Goya (tel. 958-61 03 14).

Back on the N340, turn left at the sign for Motril and in the town follow the signs for Almería, turning left at the petrol station on the eastern edge of town, then almost immediately right on the Gualchos road.

Motril, with mostly modern uninteresting buildings, attracts few visitors, although its beaches - several kilometres away - are popular in summer. A boom in sugar-cane in the 18th and 19th centuries won the town the nickname "Little Cuba" and a rum distillery still operates.

The Baroque-style Ayuntamiento, dating from 1631, has two fine Mudéjar coffered ceilings. Nearby is Encarnación church, Mudéjar with later additions.

After a plague decimated the population in the 16th century, the Iglesia del Carmen, with a beautiful cupola, was built to commemorate the 500 victims on the site where they were buried.

A sanctuary to the Virgen de la Cabeza stands on the hill where Zoraida, mother of Boabdil, last king of Granada, once had a fortress-palace. A week-long August fair pays homage to the Virgin and she is carried in procession in January when Motril gives thanks for being spared from an earthquake.

Along the Gualchos road, you are getting well and truly off the beaten track although only a few miles inland from the Costa de Granada. You pass the Instituto de Formación Profesional, a large modern building, after just over a mile (2km). Soon the road swings left and you see the Mesón Puntalón, which specializes in baby goat and chicken wings.

The scenic route loops 10 miles (17 kilometres) over the hills. To your right shimmer acres of *plasticultura* (crops growing in plastic greenhouses) and beyond, the glittering sea. To the left rise the slopes of the lower Alpujarras with two white domes on the heights signalling the presence of an off-limits defence installation, a satellite-tracking station.

A side road leads to the Sierra de Lújar, sheltering the sleepy hamlet of Lujar. Almond trees splash the hills with pink and white in early spring. In Arab times there were no doubt plantations of mulberry trees as silk weaving was important.

When you get to Gualchos (1,200 feet above sea-level), leave your car at the entrance to the village near a corner bar. It is much simpler to walk from here on.

Wander through the maze of corkscrewing narrow streets and you encounter a sleepy little plaza. Dogs doze in the sun and locals gossip in the corner bar.

Rival villages mutter - clearly without foundation - that Gualchos folk are fig-splitters, implying that they are so mean that they would rather cut a fig in two than give a fraction more weight than a customer is paying for.

The inhabitants, some 600 of them, don't mind that so much. But what really rankles is that a few years back upstarts from the neighbouring community of Castell de Ferro on the coast stole the town hall and the village has never been able to get it back.

In past centuries Gualchos was a safer place to be because of the danger from pirates. But that threat has disappeared and municipal administration was transferred to Castell, which has been developing faster thanks to a modern invasion, of tourists.

In the early 1600s pirates actually seized Gualchos and held it to ransom. Only a rich aristocrat's willingness to pay up allowed the population to go free.

Last century vineyards brought prosperity, until the dread phylloxera wiped out the vines. Today, like many villages, Gualchos appears asleep.

You can get simple refreshment in the local bars or, if you investigate what lies behind a plain brown door on one corner of the square, you will find more imaginative fare.

The discreet entrance leads to a village inn with a difference. Beneath a beamed ceiling in an airy room diners tuck into fricassé of rabbit with mustard sauce or pork fillets served with honey and leeks.

Clients call from Paris and further away to reserve rooms and food at La Posada, a small hotel and first-rate restaurant (Plaza Constitución, 9 y 10 Gualchos (Granada), tel. 958-65 60 34, open 1-3.30pm, 8.30-11pm, closed Mondays. Master, Visa. M-E). Gualchos may be hard to find, but it is definitely on the international gourmet map thanks to the efforts of José María Gonzalez Zubiaurre, a native of Santander who runs La Posada.

José, trained in Geneva and Paris, cooked in British restaurants. He returned to Spain to convert a big, rambling house into a nine-room hotel. The antiques and decoration give it a country house atmosphere.

The house next door, a former inn, was taken over and transformed into a comfortable bar and restaurant, preserving the old style.

Restaurant and hotel are closed in December, January, and February, and also during September's four-day San Miguel fair, celebrated with cacophonous enthusiasm in Gualchos.

If you want to overnight in the tranquillity of La Posada, reserve in advance. Clients are expected to take half pension.

From Gualchos, a seven-kilometre road winds down to Castell de Ferro. The intensely-cultivated valley bottom below the village was once regarded as an arrow pointing at the heart of the Alpujarras because it gave easy access to invaders from the sea.

It was to guard that strategic route that the Castell (castle) was built on a hilltop near the coast, first by the Romans, then by the Moors. There it is still, standing guard over the N340 and the growing town of Castell de Ferro, which is popular with Spanish holidaymakers.

From Castell, it is 14 miles (22 kilometres) back to Motril, passing Calahonda, with its spectacular cliff dominating town and beach❑

Excursion 9 - Toehold of Empire:

Marbella-Estepona-La Línea-Gibraltar-San Roque-Castellar-Sotogrande-Marbella

Distance: 106 miles (170km)

A ghost town girdled by medieval walls and one of Britain's last colonies await you on this day trip to two unusual corners of the Iberian peninsula.

West of **MARBELLA**, the N340 is busy with traffic serving the tourist developments and running to and from the busy port of **ALGECIRAS**. Sandy beaches, rocky headlands, and marinas lie along the seaside.

Inland, hills roll away to distant sierras. Innumerable villas dot the slopes. Golf courses and real estate developments appear at every turn. **ESTEPONA** retains some of its fishing town atmosphere, but tourism is the big industry all along the coast.

The scenery grows wilder and greener as you go west, towards the Straits of Gibraltar and the Atlantic. The silhouette of the Rock, often girdled with cloud, looms on the horizon. As you approach the Guadiaro river, you will see the pleasure port of the Sotogrande complex (polo, golf).

After about six miles (10km) a left turn takes you to La Línea de la Concepción and Gibraltar. The road brings you in through the back areas of La Línea (pop. 60,000), not a particularly pretty sight, and then runs along La Atunara, a long sandy beach where attempts are being made to upgrade the area with new apartment blocks.

Go slowly as - even in broad daylight - you may bump into tobacco-smugglers carrying ashore their latest cargo sneaked in from the Rock. Smuggling has always been a popular pastime around Gibraltar.

Where fishing craft are drawn up stands a large and excellent fishfood restaurant, La Marina (Paseo Marítimo, La Atunara. Tel: 956-10 15 31. Open 1-5pm, 7.30-12pm. Amex,

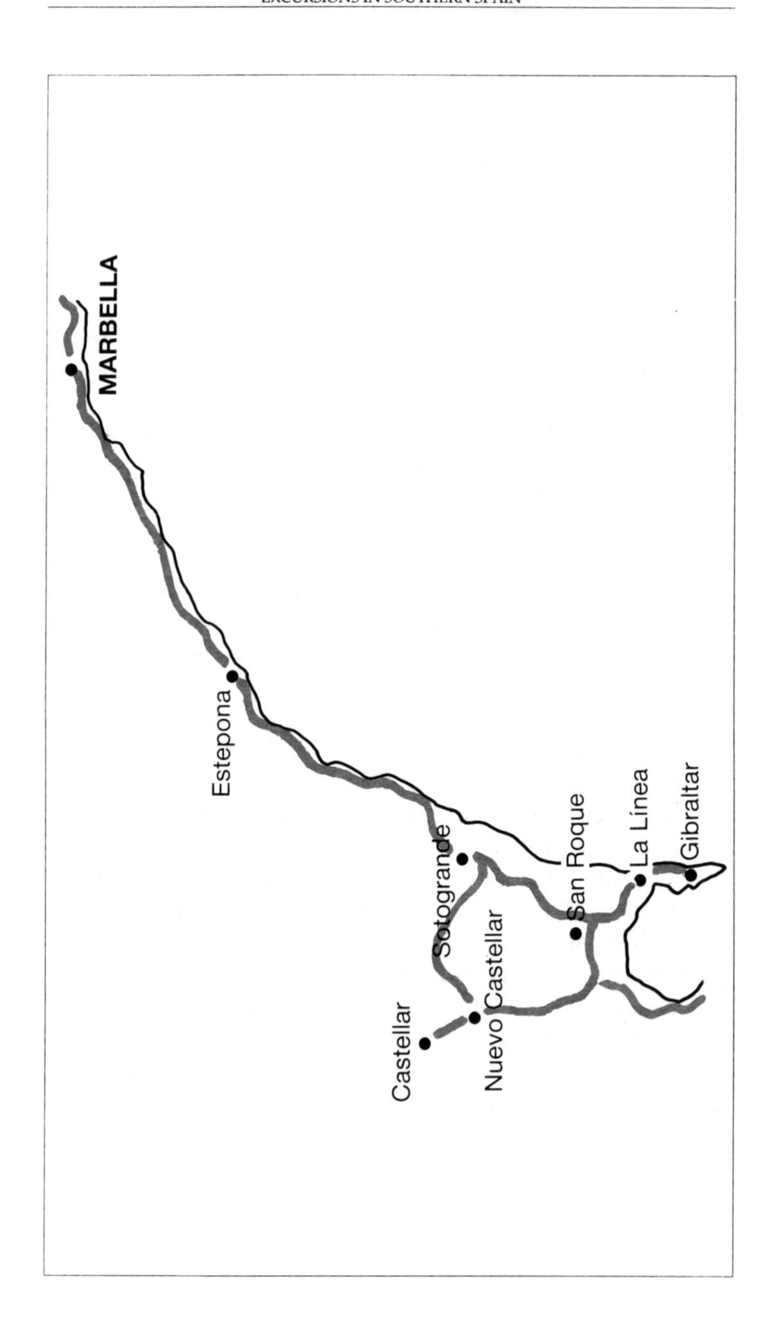
MARBELLA
Estepona
Sotogrande
San Roque
La Línea
Gibraltar
Castellar
Nuevo Castellar

Master, Visa. M). If you do not want a full meal, go into the bar and order some *raciones* (platefuls) or tapas of fish.

Further along is another restaurant, the smaller El Mirador. This stands close to a big football stadium, built as a grandiose gesture by General Franco after he closed the Gibraltar border to all traffic in 1969. The move was an attempt to force Britain to negotiate the return of the peninsula to Spain but failed abysmally. It also had a dire effect on poor old La Línea.

This town grew up in direct response to Britain's seizure of Gibraltar in 1704. Three forts were built by Spain's King Phillip V on this sand-spit and it became known as La Línea de Contravalación de la Plaza de Gibraltar. When the border was closed, thousands of La Línea residents were thrown out of work as they provided much of Gibraltar's labour force. Many of them went to England to seek employment.

With the border open again, many La Línea habitants once again work on the Rock. Every day many Gibraltarians flock over the border to buy fresh fruit and vegetables and on Wednesday mornings La Línea has a popular flea market held near the frontier.

Ignore any youths who attempt to flag you down as you approach the border and park in the authorised area where you are required to buy a ticket for display in your windscreen. Do not leave anything of value in your car as La Línea is notorious for its drug addicts who need cash to feed their habit.

There is only one good reason to take your car into Gib - to fill up, as petrol is considerably cheaper in the colony. But you may have to queue to enter, inside the tiny territory parking is extremely difficult, and when you leave you may have to queue again. This happens during rush hours when both Spaniards and Gibraltarians return to their homes in Spain, but also whenever the Spanish authorities want to put the screws on the colony by insisting in agonizingly lengthy security checks on all cars entering their territory.

Formalities to enter **GIBRALTAR** are minimal. Winston Churchill Avenue runs up to the border. If on foot, take a taxi or one of the cheap town buses which run from the frontier across the airstrip and to Casemates Gate, the main entrance through the old ramparts. From there it is a short stroll up Main Street, crammed with shoppers looking for bargains in establishments selling everything from videos to exotic perfumes. In fact, prices in Gibraltar are not necessarily lower than in your home country. Check prices carefully and do not be carried away.

Shabby in parts, Gibraltar is trying to refurbish itself and big new commercial projects are taking shape. It can be a claustrophobic place, but it certainly has a unique atmosphere. Indian shopkeepers, Orthodox Jews, robed Moslems, sun-blistered tourists, British soldiers, pin-striped bankers, pram-pushing mothers mingle in Gibraltar streets, patrolled by helmeted Bobbies who speak Spanish as fluently as English. There are numerous English pubs selling draught English beer.

Metal wall plaques tell the story of this often-besieged fortress. The Trafalgar Cemetery shelters the graves of sailors who died in the Battle of Trafalgar. Just above the cemetery, in the Charles V Wall, built in 1552, is Prince Edward's Gate. The gate was cut in 1790 and named after the fourth son of George 111 who was serving in the colony at the time. Later he fathered the baby who was to become Queen Victoria.

A plaque by one of the sentry niches recalls that an inscription here used to read: "God and the soldier all men adore in time of trouble and no more, for when war is over and all things righted, God is neglected and the old soldier slighted."

Fewer military are in evidence today as Britain reduces its garrison and Gibraltar places more emphasis on becoming an off-shore financial centre. Something else has changed too. Over-fed by some of the 3.5 million tourists who annually visit Gibraltar, the colony's pack of monkeys (properly called Barbary macaques) has been falling in numbers.

Legend has it that when they die out, Gibraltar will no longer be British. During World War Two, Churchill ordered that the number should never fall below 35. To protect the Queen's Gate troop they have been confined to a special park, guarded by a warden. You can still see them by taking the cable car up the Rock, but there is now an entrance charge.

For eating in Gibraltar, see details at the back of the book.

After leaving the Rock, follow the Algeciras road along the edge of the bay. A large anchor stands at the entrance to the palm-lined driveway to Los Remos, a restaurant in a colonial-style house, built by the British financier who created the Algeciras-Ronda railway. Rated one of the best eating-places in Spain, it offers sumptuous and expensive dining, featuring imaginative fish dishes (Finca Villa Victoria, Ramal San Roque-La Línea km 2.7. Tel: 956-10 68 12. Open 1-4pm, 8.30-12pm. Closed Sunday lunch summer, Sunday dinner winter. Amex, Diners, Master, Visa. E).

For something less luxurious, try one of the restaurants in El Campamento. After passing Campamento, a turning to the left will take you towards Puente Mayorga, an oil refinery and the ruins of Carteya near the Guadarranque rivermouth.

Founded by the Phoenicians, Carteya was a Roman colony from 171BC and for a time was the most important port on the coast. Remains of a quay, an amphitheatre and aqueducts survive, although materials were carted away to build nearby San Roque (pop. 21,000).

This town was constructed by Spaniards who fled from Gibraltar in 1704 when the British occupied it and the parish records and flag brought from the Rock are preserved here. The flag is said to have been embroidered by Juana, later known as La Loca, daughter of the Catholic Monarchs.

The old quarter crowns a hilltop. Drive up the narrow streets to the parish church Santa María la Coronada. Nearby is the Mirador Domingo de Mena, from where you have a good view of the Rock. Unfortunately, you also have a view of the oil refinery and urban sprawl around Algeciras bay.

Near the church is a beautiful 18th-century house accommodating the Don Benito restaurant (Plaza de Armas, 12. Tel: 956-78 07 78. Open evenings. Closed Sun, Mon. Master, Visa. M). It features international dishes and good service.

From San Roque, return to the Algeciras highway and after two miles (3km) turn right up the C3331 which runs along the irrigated Guadarranque valley.

After six miles (10km) a left turn takes you up the sinuous road to Castellar de la Frontera, past slopes thick with holm and cork oaks, ash and oleander. Wild boar and deer roam these woods. After passing the Venta Jarandilla - check whether they have venison or wild boar on the menu - we swing upwards past steep hillsides with knife-edges of rock erupting through the topsoil. The Guadarranque reservoir appears below on our left.

Castellar's ramparts loom above boulder-strewn slopes. Goats graze the area, stripping leaves from trees and sometimes trotting across the rooftops of the houses hiding behind the rocks. A colony of young Britons and Germans - regarded as "hippies" by the locals - has moved in.

Leave your car below the castle entrance, where a bar awaits your custom. From here, 800 feet above sea-level, you look towards the Strait and Gibraltar crouching on guard. To enter Castellar, you walk up a ramp and through archways. Until recent times, the gates to this seemingly impregnable stronghold were closed every night and the villagers retained their feudal condition.

Built in the 13th century, Castellar fortress was fought over for centuries. It was finally captured from the Moors in 1434 by Juan de Saavedra, lord of neighbouring Jimena de la Frontera. A nephew became Count of Castellar, to be succeeded later by the Duques de Medinaceli who ruled over La Almoraima, covering 40,000 acres (16,000 hectares) and claimed to be Europe's largest estate.

The hardness of the life here finally persuaded the authorities to offer the 2,000 inhabitants land and housing below in the valley in 1971. Nearly everybody decamped and Castellar became a ghost town. Many of the houses are in disrepair, doors and windows bricked up. Some have been bought by foreigners, but in one corner a few old folk still hold out, tending their flowers and vines.

Attempts are being made to restore Castellar and return some of the lost glory to the castle, once a ducal residence. Meanwhile, you will not be the first if, as you pace silent streets occupied only by stray cats, you experience a distinctly spooky sensation.

The road runs beyond Castellar but is virtually impassable,

so we return the way we came.

Turning left on the C3331, you pass La Almoraima, an unusual hotel. An Oriental-looking tower rises above well-kept gardens, lawns, tennis courts and swimming pool. Constructed as a convent with the money obtained from fines levied on the unfortunate Castellar folk by their feudal lords, it later became a hunting lodge for the Medinaceli family. Four-wheel-drive vehicles and horses are available for excursions (Casa Convento de La Almoraima, tel: 956-69 30 02).

A little along the road on the left stands the Venta La Cantina (closed Mon), where there is cheap eating - good stew - and a nasty-fanged boar's head leers over the toilets.

Orange plantations and cork oaks are cultivated around here. Nuevo Castellar appears on the right. This is the somewhat soulless, rectangular new town to which the Castellar community moved. But on one day of the year it is filled with picturesque movement.

In the first week of May thousands arrive to pay homage to Santa Cristo de La Almoraima, a much venerated image of Christ on the Cross, transferred from the Almoraima convent chapel to the new village church in 1972. A colourful procession takes place, with scores of mounted pilgrims, and later a flamenco competition.

Behind the new town, the CA513 meanders over the hills to Sotogrande. This area is rich in wild life, not least in a company of apes, which escaped from a safari park and have eluded all attempts to recapture them.

At Sotogrande you reach the N340 and turn left for the run back to **MARBELLA**❑

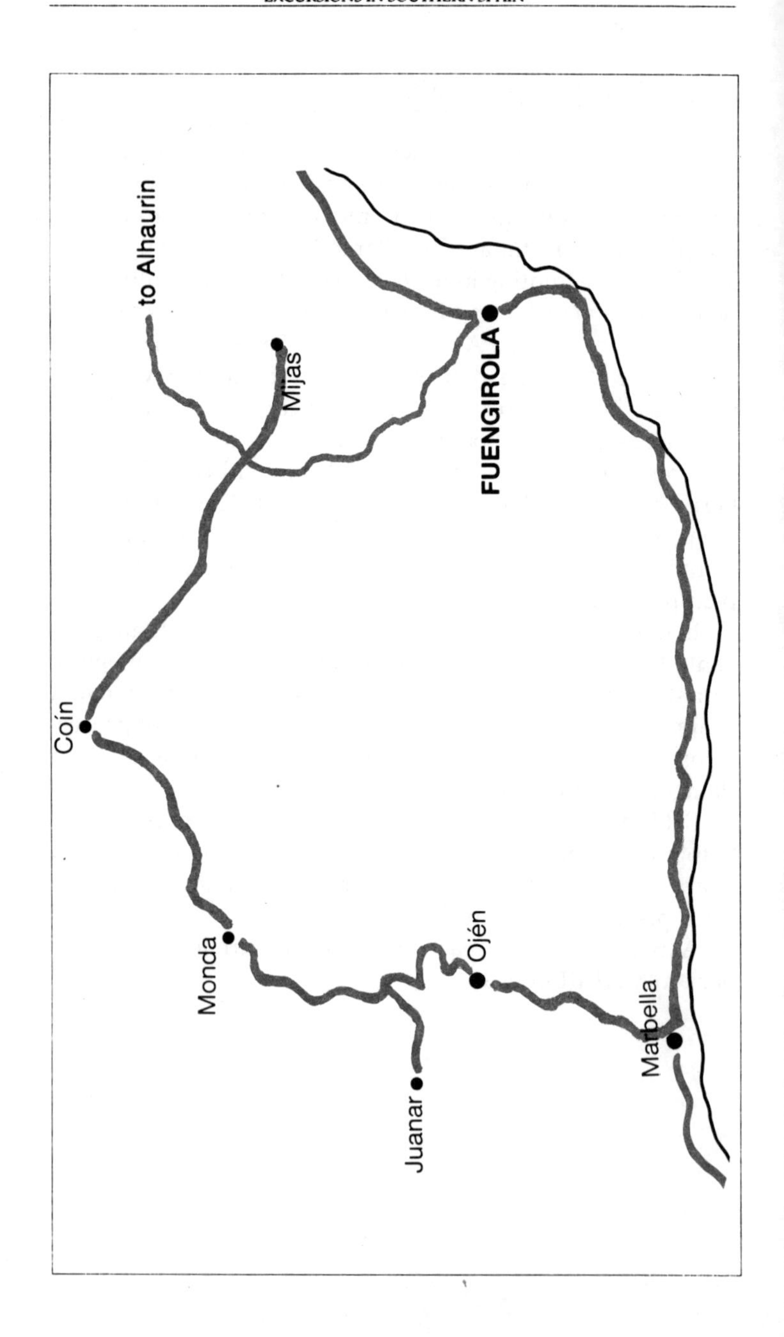
to Alhaurin
Mijas
FUENGIROLA
Coín
Monda
Ojén
Juanar
Marbella

Excursion 10 - The Back Country:

Fuengirola-Coín-Monda-Ojén-Marbella-Fuengirola
Distance: 62 miles (100km)

Only a few minutes drive from the coast, untouristy villages nestle amid ruggedly beautiful landscapes. This day trip, starting in **FUENGIROLA**, takes you to some of the more interesting places in The Back Country.

Heading along the N340 on the Fuengirola bypass, direction Marbella, keep an eye open for signs on your right to Mijas Golf and the Hotel Byblos. Take this exit. Initially you bump through suburbs in course of construction near the Fuengirola river. Several ventas are dotted about, including Las Fuentes on the right and La Morena on the left, both known for grilled meat.

After four miles (6km), manicured emerald lawns on your right indicate you are passing the golf course and Hotel Byblos.

A little later a left turn leads across the riverbed to Entreríos, a lush valley of avocados and citrus fruit.

Continue on our road, which offers a convenient short-cut into the interior, bypassing Mijas. It scythes upwards through pleasant rolling country, passing dry hills and scattered farmhouses.

The 3,700-foot-high Sierra de Mijas soars to the right, the Cerro del Aguila to the left as we reach the Puerto de los Pescadores, the Alhaurín golf course, and a crossroads midway between Mijas, five miles (8km) to the right, and Coín. If you drive straight across the intersection, you reach Alhaurin el Grande a little over a mile away.

What looks like a medieval castle breaks the skyline to the north. It is actually a carefully disguised water tower on the La Mota estate.

Cheap and cheerful meals are available from Venta Los Morenos (closed Thursday) on the junction. It has a terrace at the rear and swings for children. Looking down on it from above the crossroads is El Balcón, a German-run restaurant

(Tel: 95-249 11 94. Open lunch only. Closed Mon & Aug. Master, Visa. M).

A pine-bordered track between El Balcón and the Alhaurín road leads to Finca La Mota, a laidback restaurant in a 300-year-old farmhouse, ideal for a relaxed meal of barbecued spare ribs or roast lamb (Tel: 95-249 09 01. Open 12.30-4.30pm, 7.30-11pm. Amex, Master, Visa cards. M). La Mota, under American-Scottish management, also has bedrooms, some with fourposters.

Continuing along the Coín road, you swing through moorland. A turn to the left dips down through pinewoods to Barranco Blanco, a very private German development in a verdant valley. Further along, also to the left, along a dirt track, lies Coín Film City, studios originally built for a controversial, ill-fated BBC TV series called Eldorado. The studios are surrounded by a high fence, but may be open to visitors on conducted tours (call 95-245 34 18).

Continue to the workaday community of Coín (pop. 20,000). A new highway is due to pass by the town and curve through the mountains north of Málaga, forming an arc between Marbella and Vélez-Málaga.

Meanwhile, Coín (pop. 20,000) jogs along as an agricultural centre, making few concessions to tourism. Once known as "The town of the 300 orchards", its fertile, well-watered countryside produces large amounts of fruit, particularly oranges and lemons.

It is built on the site of the Roman settlement of Lacibis. The Moors founded Castro Dazcuan here in 929. Where they prayed to Mecca is now the site of Santa Maria de la Encarnación church. Several buildings date from the 16th century, including a Mozarabic tower.

Local legend has it that when the Catholic Kings laid siege to Coín, Christopher Columbus was among the royal followers, no doubt raising smiles with his dreams about voyaging around the world to discover a fabled land.

As you enter Coín, you weave past the market, a good spot to buy vegetables and fruit by the crate. On Sunday mornings farmers sell seedlings and plants outside the market.

In the centre of town, follow signs for the C337 to Monda and Marbella. The road struggles through the town's old quarter. It is not advisable to drive into the narrow side-streets unless you enjoy finding your way through a labyrinth.

Two miles (3km) from Coín is the English-owned Santa Fe restaurant and pension (Ctra de Monda, km 3. Tel. 95-245 29 16). It is located in a beautiful old house with swimming pool and tennis court. Five rooms are available. The restaurant is open for lunch, except Tuesday, and dinner Friday and Saturday (no cards).

You pass a fertile vega, with irrigated fields and orange and lemon plantations, and then the road curves over hills, where in spring old cortijos appear like snowflakes on a green carpet and pink and white rock roses speckle the verges.

As the mountains loom closer, Monda (pop. 1,700, alt. 1,200 feet) appears, tucked into a valley. It is an insignificant sort of place, but it does have a claim to fame - in the year 40 BC Roman armies fought a mighty battle near here. Julius Caesar crushed Pompey's forces and went on to conquer the rest of the empire.

That is the story. Unfortunately, historians claim that the battle of "Munda" took place elsewhere, possibly near Ronda or Montilla.

On a crag above Monda stand the remains of a castle. The original fortress was pulled down in 1570, after the ill-fated Morisco rising. Arévalo de Zuazo expelled the inhabitants of Monda and handed over all they possessed to eight Christians.

A German aristocrat set about rebuilding the castle in the early 1970s, but a change of official mood halted the work. He was followed by English owners, who in 1996 openned to open a 26-bedroom luxury hotel.

Around the castle crag, you may see hawks and other birds of prey wheeling. Below, outside the village, real estate developments are taking shape. A new highway speeds traffic up from the coast at Marbella.

Remote Monda, once a hippy hideaway, is being jolted into the 20th century. The village itself, however, has a dozy atmosphere. Old men seek the shade around the Plaza de la Constitución. On Mateo Macias street, named after a respected former mayor, La Vera bar and pension offers simple meals and beds.

Continuing towards Ojén, the road enters wilder mountain country. A convenient spot to stop for lunch is the Venta Pula, with reasonably-priced meals. You can eat outside, on a terrace shaded by vines.

A little further on, a right turn leads four miles (6km) up an uninhabited valley to the Refugio de Juanar, formerly a hunting palace and now a comfortable hotel, offering tranquillity and outdoor activities in an ideal setting (Sierra Blanca, Ojén, (Málaga). Tel: 95-288 10 00. See Excursion 4 for more details).

Back on the main road, we continue up and over the Ventorillo del Puerto and run down to Ojén (pop. 2,000, alt. 650 feet), commanding the intensely cultivated Río Real valley. Time may not have stood still in Ojén, but considering its closeness to the coast it is remarkably unchanged.

Treading its narrow, cobbled streets, edging past whitewashed walls and gushing fountains, you gain the true flavour of an Andalusian pueblo (see Excursion 4 for more details).

The old road to **MARBELLA** corkscrewed down six miles (9km) to the coast, but access has been smoothed by a new highway❑

Excursion 11 - To the Eagle's Eyrie

Málaga-El Burgo-Ronda-San Pedro-Málaga
Distance: 150 miles (240km)

Dramatic mountain scenery is a feature of this drive which takes us from Málaga to remote villages in the Serranía de Ronda, once the haunt of smugglers and bandits, and then back to the coast at San Pedro de Alcantara.

Driving west along the N340 from Málaga Airport towards Torremolinos, swing right along the C334 to Churriana and Alhaurín de la Torre.

To the right there are views of the intensively-cultivated farmland of the Guadalhorce valley as we pass Alhaurín de la Torre (pop. 11,000). Many Málaga families have built villas amid the citrus and avocado plantations and at weekends the ventas (inns) along this route do roaring business.

The scoured bulk of the Sierra de Mijas rises between us and the sea as we approach Alhaurín el Grande. The outskirts of the town are modern and unlovely, but then we wind up through the pleasant old town, past a church square where veterans gossip and gaze.

Alhaurín (pop. 16,000) has the remains of a Roman aqueduct and traces of Moorish settlement. El Encarnación church stands on the site of an old Arab fort.

From here to Coín (22 miles, 36km from Málaga) the sheltered plateau produces bounteous crops, particularly of tropical fruit. The highway skirts Coín itself - look out for ceramics workshops - and heads up a narrow valley, thick with citrus trees, into the heart of the sierras.

A left turn near a bridge over the Río Grande leads to the village of Tolox (pop. 3,100). A venta stands at this junction. Tolox is three miles (5km) from the highway and beyond it lies a popular spa, open from July to mid-October (see Excursion 4 for more details).

Continuing towards Ronda, we pass Alozaina (pop. 3,000), a prize-winner for its prettiness but with another attraction. It has one of the few petrol stations around here. Turn into the

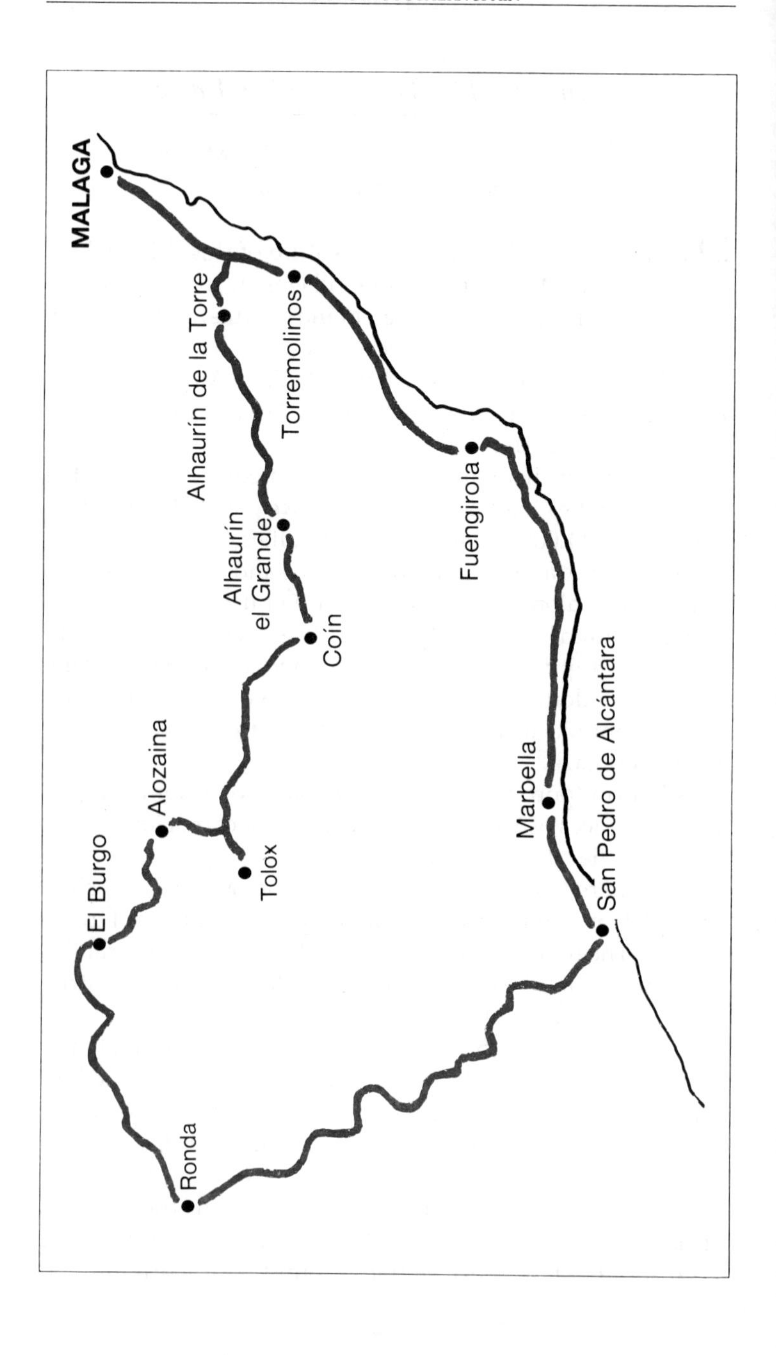
MALAGA
Alhaurín de la Torre
Torremolinos
Alhaurín
el Grande
Fuengirola
Coín
Alozaina
Tolox
El Burgo
Marbella
San Pedro de Alcántara
Ronda

village to the esplanade where a weekly market is held. The Bar Nuevo offers seats outside in the shade.

The country grows ever wilder as the C344 weaves upwards through pine plantations towards the Sierra de las Nieves. Just after the Jorox pass, at 1,800 feet above sea level, pause for breath and admire the panorama.

Crags and chasms run into the misty distance, while close at hand several cortijos and terraces of citrus orchards have been squeezed into a cleft.

An old watch tower stands above the road as you skirt Yunquera and below it on a crossroads is El Castillo, a bar and restaurant (Open all year. Tel: 95-248 04 28). It is a typical venta, with a characterful waiter and a television in one corner so that diners are not bored. Try the potaje, a rich mixture of beans, black sausage and other ingredients. It is extremely good value.

We climb up over Las Abejas (the bees) Pass. To the left rises the Sierra de las Nieves, dominated by the 6,200-foot Torrecilla peak and the home of the rare Spanish pine. To the right soar the rugged slopes of the 4,900-foot Sierra Prieta.

It is not surprising that in the past this area was a refuge for outlaws. Around here Pasos Largos (Big Steps), a murderous poacher known as the Last of the Bandoleros, was hunted by the Civil Guard in the 1930s. He was born near the next village, El Burgo.

El Burgo (pop. 2,200) sits in an amphitheatre of mountains. Approaching from the eastern flank, you see its church jutting above a hillock thickly clothed with cactus. Remains of an old Roman road and a Moorish castle are to be found here, but at the junction with the Ardales road stands a more bizarre sight, a 20th century "castle". This one, constructed of breeze blocks, is the scene of barbecues and other merry-making.

Skirting pine forest and rocky buttresses, we reach the Mirador del Guarda Forestal. Park the car and walk up this crag, topped by a limestone statue of a forest guard and a boy. The view down to El Burgo and over the sierras is tremendous, the air like champagne.

The Ronda road runs west, over the 3,600-foot-high El

Viento Pass and then across a grassy plateau dotted with rocks and grazing sheep. Shortly we approach **RONDA**, once the centre of a separate kingdom and still with an independent air.

You can park your car near the bullring, regarded as one of the most beautifully-proportioned and also one of the oldest, and explore the town. Just up the Espinel pedestrian street, on the left, is a photography shop displaying some interesting pictures taken when Ernest Hemingway visited to see his friend matador Antonio Ordoñez fight.

Several bridges span the gorge, the topmost one being the 200-year-old Puente Nuevo. On the other side is the old section of town, known as La Ciudad, where Gothic, Renaissance and Mudéjar churches and palaces have resisted the elements and long-forgotten wars.

If you stay the night, you will find that once the tourist buses have left Ronda reverts to its true self, a genuine Spanish town which has not yet changed its customs to suit tourism.

The C339 will take you swiftly back to the coast. This highway is an impressive piece of engineering as it weaves daringly through stunningly rugged country, descending from over 2,000 feet to sea-level in 30 miles (49km). Often mists will shroud this road when the sun is shining on the coast, and caution is advised.

About seven miles (12km) out of Ronda a bumpy track meanders off to the left. This eventually leads to a forest of pinsapos, the Spanish fir found nowhere else in Europe. It prefers cold, damp places more than 3,000 feet above sea-level and this area in the Sierra of the Snows is ideal in that respect.

The highest peak is Torrecilla, soaring 6,200 feet. It lies within the 58,000-acre Serrania de Ronda hunting reserve, an uninhabited area of crags and chasms where wild goats roam and eagles and vultures wheel overhead.

As the highway zig-zags down, on a clear day you will catch sight of the Rock of Gibraltar crouching in the sea to the southwest.

A pleasant place to stop for refreshment and a meal before hitting the coast at San Pedro is the Venta Al-Cuz Cuz, near the Madroñal development❑

Excursion 12 - Smugglers' Route

Marbella-Estepona-Jimena-Gaucín-Ronda-San Pedro-Marbella

Distance: 125 miles (200km)

Armies, outlaws, contraband-runners have all trekked up from Algeciras Bay to Ronda. This is one of Spain's most scenic routes, climbing more than 3,000 feet above sea level through wild sierras.

The journey can be covered in a day, although it would be better to plan on staying overnight in one of the villages or in Ronda.

Head westwards on the N340, the main coastal highway, from **MARBELLA**. After 30 miles (48km) you enter the province of Cadiz and approach Sotogrande. Before reaching that luxury development and before the Guadiaro river you will see a right turn to San Martín del Tesorillo. The CA513 follows the river, crosses it to look in on San Martín and then follows a tributary, the Hozgarganta. Ten miles (16km) after leaving the N340, you reach the C3331.

Turn right and drive up the flat river valley, reaching Los Angeles, a cluster of houses, cork-processing factories, and a station on the Algeciras-Ronda rail line. A 15th century Franciscan monastery here shelters the Virgen de Los Angeles carved - according to legend - by St Luke.

Brown cattle graze on adjacent grasslands and above you see Jimena de la Frontera, straggling down the hillside below the silhouette of its ruined castle. Jimena was in the frontline of the battle between Castilian forces and the kingdom of Granada for two centuries.

At the entrance to town, inhabitants take their evening stroll on the Paseo. This is a broad esplanade with an old tower rising from it, where on Fridays stalls are erected for the weekly market.

Expatriate Brits have settled in force at Jimena. One of their meeting points is the upstairs bar of the Hostal Anon (Consuelo, 34. Tel: 956-64 01 13), up one of the narrow, twisting streets near

Ronda
Algatocín
La Sauceda
Gaucín
MARBELLA
San Pedro
de Alcántara
Jimena
de la Frontera
Manilva
Sotogrande

the entrance to town. This rambling, English-run establishment, converted from six houses, offers clean, reasonably-priced rooms. Its restaurant features steak and kidney pie (open 1-3pm, 8-11.30pm, Master, Visa).

If you are in no mood for expatriate chit-chat, head for one of the local bars where there are budget-priced tapas.

If you continue up the Hozgarganta valley from Jimena, you enter notorious bandit country, a sparsely-inhabited area, of rocky outcrops, and oak-clad slopes. You are in the depths of Los Alcornocales nature park, covering 68,000 acres (170,000 hectares), the most extensive Mediterranean woodland in Europe. Deer, mongooses, wildcats and birds of prey inhabit the park, which receives heavy rainfall.

Amid the woods, some 15 miles (24km) from Jimena - in the remotest corner of Málaga province - is La Sauceda, a settlement abandoned and now converted into a recreational zone with a campsite and 27 spartan cabins for rent. A guardian mans a *casa forestal* (tel. 95-215 02 02).

In the past the area's inaccessibility attracted outlaws, rebels and smugglers. In 1923 a chapel, a school and mills were built, although many of La Sauceda's inhabitants had no documentation. In the Civil War, they refused to submit to Franco's forces and the village was bombed. The people fled to the hills and their houses were destroyed.

A little further along the road, towards Arcos de la Frontera, is a bleak and lonely little venta at the Puerto de Galis, serving tasty meals. It was a traditional meeting place for outlaws.

Reverting to our main route, from Jimena the road to Ronda lies along the C341, where once your fellow-travellers were likely to be tobacco-smugglers coming from Gibraltar. At first you have orange groves for company, but once in Málaga province the road climbs into wilder country. Cattle with nastily-pronged horns peer out from amid the oak trees.

About two miles before Gaucín (6.2km from the Gaucín petrol station), look for a sign on a yellow pillar. A track to the right leads to La Almuña, the second house on the right, a rambling cortijo with wonderful views. With six bedrooms only, it is run in informal country-house style by an English mother and daughter. A swimming pool, tennis court and horses are on hand. (To book, call 95-215 12 00 or write to Diana Paget, La Almuña, Apartado 20, Gaucín).

You round a curve and Gaucín spreads itself out for your admiration. A 13th-century castle spears the skyline. It was in or near the castle that Guzmán El Bueno, hero of Tarifa, died in battle with the Moors in 1309.

In San Juan de Díos street, at Number 8, an old-style fonda, the Nacional, is open for business, but only for meals (tel: 95-215 10 29). It has been catering for weary travellers since 1868. Last century, when it was known as the Hotel Inglés, it welcomed many a British military type travelling between Gibraltar and Ronda.

Ask to see the original registry. This has been so thumbed that a photocopy has been made. It includes the remarks of both testy and well-pleased visitors - "capital cooking and the best wine we have had in Spain".

The castle is open for visits, mornings being the surest time to find the caretaker there. Within its walls is a church where the much-venerated Santo Niño Dios is kept. This image of the Holy Child is carried in procession through the village in the first week of September every year.

You can eat at the Fonda Nacional and at El Pilar restaurant, on the main road which skirts Gaucín. El Pilar, near the petrol station, has a terrace with good views.

From Gaucín you can return to the coast down the MA539, which loops around the Sierra Bermeja to Manilva 15 miles (24km) away (see Excursion 1). But the most scenic part of the C341 lies ahead. It runs along the ridge between the deep Guadiaro and Genal valleys. Across the valley you glimpse splashes of whitewash, villages cleaving to the mountainside amid forests of chestnut, pine, fir and oak trees.

At the Puerto del Espino, well over 2,000 feet up, television and telecommunications antennae stand over the road and the crossroads where Venta Solera stands. A side road wriggles down towards Cortes de la Frontera. It crosses the Algeciras-Ronda railway, a brilliant piece of construction built in the 1890s by English engineer John Morrison, backed by a wealthy financier, Sir Alexander Henderson. The halts along the line have similar architecture to those of rural English stations.

Just before Algatocín on the Ronda road, a municipal pool has been built on the mountain side, should you feel like cooling off. This village, framed by cherry blossom in February, appears in danger of sliding into the abyss below. From it, a road serpentines down steeply to the Genal river then climbs past Jubrique and over the Sierra Bermeja via the Peña Blancas pass to Estepona, 28 miles (45km) away. It is a little-travelled road through wild country, where anti-Franco guerrillas roamed during the 1940s.

Stern barriers or rock rise to the left of the C341 and to the right you will notice hills densely covered with chestnut trees. Turn right to tiny Benalauría to enjoy honest country cooking at a pretty eating place called La Molinera. Negotiating the narrow streets should improve your appetite.

A little further along the C341, you sight Benadalid, with its unusual cemetery located inside the walls of the old fort.

Shortly before Atajate, a side road leads to Jimera de Líbar and the Pileta cave (see Excursion 27). Herds of goats are about all that can find sustenance on the bleak, stony hills as we climb up to the 2,350-foot-high pass of Encinas Borrachas (Drunken Oaks). Olive groves and cornfields appear as we descend towards **RONDA**, riding high above its chasm in an amphitheatre of mountains.

If you are not visiting Ronda on this trip, turn right at the entrance to the old town on the C339 to San Pedro de Alcántara. This excellent highway descends from over 2,000 feet to sea-level in 30 miles (49km). Mists will often obscure the route in autumn and winter so caution is advised.

Tortuous country roads wander off on the right to remote villages such as Cartajima, Igualeja, Pujerra and Juzcar where harvesting the chestnut crop from the surrounding forests is one of the biggest events of the year.

About seven miles (12km) out of Ronda a bumpy track to the left leads to the Sierra of the Snows and a forest of Abies pinsapo Boiss, the Spanish fir found nowhere else in Europe. It prefers cold, damp places more than 3,000 feet above sea-level.

In these sierras - highest peak, Torrecilla (6,200 feet) - lies the 58,000-acre Serrania de Ronda hunting reserve. Wild goats roam over the crags and ravines. As the highway zig-zags down, on a clear day you will catch sight of the Rock of Gibraltar crouching in the sea to the southwest❑

Excursion 13 - Málaga's Lake District

Málaga-Alora-El Chorro-Lakes-Teba-Carratraca-Málaga
Round trip: 100 miles (160km)

Spectacular mountain scenery, a delightful lakeland picnic spot, and a colourful dash of history makes this a trip for all seasons.

If starting from west of Málaga, head towards Málaga airport and after passing **TORREMOLINOS** take the turn off the N340 towards Alhaurín de la Torre and Coín. Look for the signs for Churriana. Turn right as though heading for that community, but immediately fork left towards Cártama.

Alternatively, from Málaga centre drive west and follow signs for Campanillas and Parque Technológico. A four-lane highway, the MA401, whisks you out of the city. After crossing the Río Guadalhorce, the highway intersects the road from Churriana.

On the left, on the old Churriana road, you glimpse El Tintero, a popular venta where diners flag down one of the dozens of waiters to sample whatever he is carrying. Barbecued meat is a speciality and the prices are surprisingly low. Access has been made a little confusing because of slow progress on the Cártama bypass.

At a T-junction, you can head right across a bridge spanning the Guadalhorce to reach Estación de Cártama, then turn left on the MA402 towards Pizarra.

Alternatively, turn left on the MA422, skirt Cártama and turn right towards Carratraca. A fine new road runs up the Guadalhorce valley, green with thousands of citrus and avocado trees, while sun-bleached, eroded hills lie beyond.

After five miles (7km) you cross the Río Grande, a trickle of water despite its impressive name. There is a good eucalypt-shaded picnic spot - plus indications that some previous picnickers have yet to learn about environment protection.

About nine miles (14km) from Cártama turn right to reach Pizarra, a cluster of white below grey and ochre rock faces. The

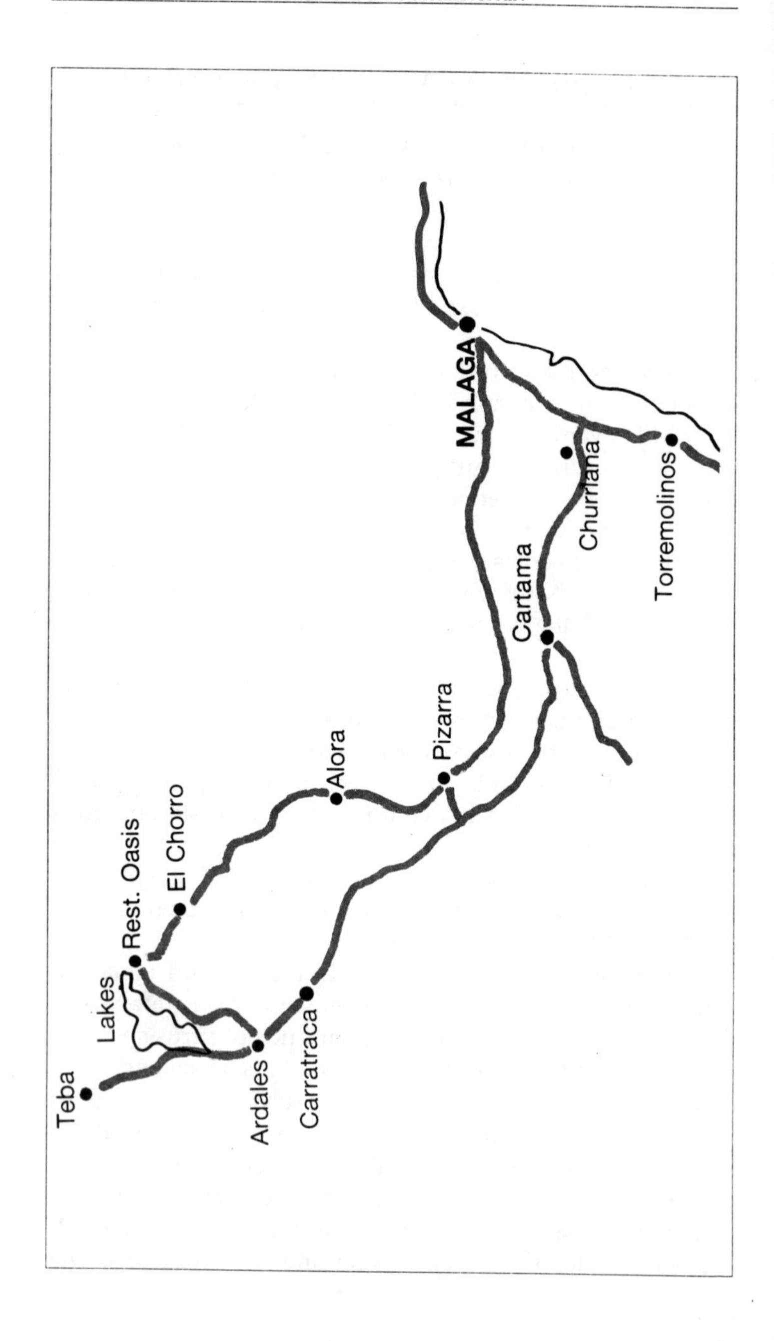

MALAGA
Churriana
Torremolinos
Cartama
Pizarra
Alora
El Chorro
Rest. Oasis
Lakes
Teba
Ardales
Carratraca

village has nothing special to offer, except an unusual municipal museum. You find this just over a mile (2km) south on the MA402 towards Málaga.

Look for the Casa Blanca, on the right (open 10am-2pm, 4-8pm, closed Mon), which houses 5,000 items collected over 20 years by American artist Gino Hollander. Exhibits include Iberian ceramics, Roman glass and antique furniture.

Continue north up the C337. The ochre ramparts of Alora castle can soon be seen to your left. The houses of this agricultural community (pop. 14,000) roller-coast up and down the slopes near it.

Before crossing the river, the C337 branches right, through lonely sierras to Valle de Abdalajis and Antequera. We swing over the river and scale the heights of Alora. On the outskirts of the town, take a right towards El Chorro.

From here on the driving gets serious as the road narrows and twists and turns. The abundant water encourages the cultivation of a variety of crops and tropical fruit.

Then the mountains close in until we are passing through a steep-sided chasm, the river Guadalhorce tumbling along below us. Watch for sudden dips in the road.

A solid barrier of rock looms ahead, apparently blocking the valley. Here you find one of the most spectacular sights in Andalusia. The Guadalhorce river slices through the Garganta del Chorro, a gorge with sheer, 600-foot high walls.

Turn right over the dam below El Chorro. The road winds up to a station on the Málaga-Córdoba line. Before it reaches the station a track goes off to the left.

Follow this if you are in adventurous mood. A path winds along the hillside to reach the rail track. You pass across the railway bridge to gain access to the Camino del Rey (the King's Path). King Alfonso X111 is supposed to have taken a walk along here in 1921 when he opened the Guadalhorce dams.

He could not have suffered from vertigo. The catwalk clings like a fly to the rock face and vaults the gorge by way of a bridge. It is in a dangerously bad state, although there are plans to repair it.

Near the station are a bar and restaurant and La Garganta

apartments in an old flower mill, offering stunning views. A dirt track zig-zags up the hill and after a thousand metres or so you reach La Almona, a fine old farmhouse whose British owners rent out self-contained rustic cottages, with use of a pool. There are good hiking and climbing possibilities in the area.

From El Chorro the narrow road, edges crumbling, climbs past pines and eroded rock. Shortly after passing a shrine in honour of the Virgin of Villaverde, patron of Ardales, and the Bar La Hermita, you take a left turn into ancient history. A four-mile (6km) road soars up to 2,000 feet and a flat-topped mountain where 1,000 years ago Bobastro - capital of a rebel kingdom - was located.

Omar Ben Hafsun is said to have used this as his base in his wars with the Caliph of Córdoba. You can see why. It is virtually impregnable. Remains of old walls can be found, as well as caves inhabited in Moorish times. A modern curiosity is the large reservoir which occupies part of the summit; its waters tumble down the mountain to generate power for Málaga. Look for a sign indicating the Mozarab church. A walk of a few hundred yards from the road takes you to this unique structure hewn from the rock.

Continuing on the main road, we reach a T-junction. Ahead lie the emerald waters of Lago Turón, one of the three Guadalhorce lakes which provide water for Málaga province.

Turn right to wind along through pine forests with the lake glinting on your left. Fishing for barbell, carp and bass and boating are popular here. Soon you encounter an information office for the Parque Ardales, a campsite, picnic tables and El Mirador Restaurant. This is an ideal spot to enjoy lunch in the shade as the breeze sings through the pines.

The road runs through a tunnel under the restaurant. Just before the tunnel a track runs up to the right. Take this for the best view over the lakes from the hill just above the restaurant.

If you continue along this track as it winds down for just over a mile, you reach a power station. A path runs to the left below the station, skirting a small dam. Follow this to encounter the northern section of the Camino del Rey.

The path enters the Gaitanes chasm, through which cascades a torrent formed by three rivers. As the gorge grows steadily narrower, the path becomes a footway high above a dizzying, two-mile section, ending up at El Chorro. It can be traversed but it is perilous.

Returning to the lakeside road, continue until you cross a dam. A small restaurant serves good home cooking here.

Turn right to explore further the lake area and hydraulic works. Two hundred yards along on the right you come to the highly-recommended Restaurante El Oasis (Pantano del Chorro, Ardales. Tel: 95-245 81 02. Open 1-12pm. Visa accepted).

A bull's head broods down from one corner as diners tuck in to excellent roast lamb or rabbit. Service is fast and friendly, but the restaurant can be crowded on weekends.

Return over the dam and head towards Ardales, a typical sierra village of 3,000 inhabitants. The Puente (bridge) de la Molina has been in use since Roman times. The Mudejar parish church dates from the 15th century and dominating the labyrinth of interlocking houses is the usual Arab fortess.

A ten-mile (15km) excursion to the north of Ardales, skirting the lakes and broad ploughed acres, brings us to the town of Teba, straddling a rocky outcrop. An unusual story of Scottish heroism is linked to Teba (pop. 4,500).

Drive up to the ruins of La Estrella castle and pause in the town at the Plaza de España. A monument of white Scottish granite commemorates the heroism of a warrior who fell in battle here in 1330.

Following a deathbed request from Scotland's King Robert the Bruce, Sir James Douglas - known because of his dark complexion as the Black Douglas - agreed to take Robert's heart to the Holy Land. En route, he became entangled with King Alfonso X1 of Castile's wars with the Moors.

In the siege of Teba, he was surrounded and, after defiantly hurling the casket containing the royal heart at the Moorish horsemen, he was cut down. Lord Selkirk, representing the Douglas clan, unveiled the memorial in 1989.

Pig-breeding and leather manufacture are modern sources

of income in Teba and neighbouring Campillos. On the Campillos-Antequera highway you will find several large showrooms offering leatherware. Los Chopos (Ctra N342, km 140, tel. 95-272 27 70), a modern two star hotel on the highway, is handy for tired travellers seeking a meal or overnight stay.

Retracing our steps to Ardales, we head south on the Alora road. Just off this is the Cueva de Ardales, also known as the Doña Trinidad Cave after a wellknown Málaga figure last century, which has spectacular stalactites, Paleolithic drawings and traces of Neolithic man. It is difficult to find, but guided visits can be made, limited to 15 persons daily. Call Ardales town hall (95-245 80 87) for details.

A short drive through the olive and almond trees brings us to "the Diamond of Málaga", Carratraca, a spa which in its heyday last century attracted everybody from Lord Byron to Alexandre Dumas. The waters of the stone-built balneario, open from June to mid-October, are rich in minerals and are beneficial for skin troubles, nervous diseases and a variety of other complaints.

When the beautiful Empress Marie Eugenie, wife of Napoleon 111 and Countess of Teba, visited, three gambling casinos were flourishing in Carratraca. Things are quieter today.

But the inn King Fernando V11 ordered built for himself and his courtiers in 1830 (though it is not clear if he ever stayed there) still stands. It is called the Hostal El Príncipe, a creaky, rambling place with enough character to satisfy the most romantic (Antonio Rioboó, 9. Tel 95-245 80 20. Rated one star).

If you are in the area during Easter Week, do not miss El Paso, the Carratraca passion play, enacted by about 140 villagers - one-seventh of the population - in the bull ring on Good Friday and Easter Saturday. Remarkably, this popular event owes its origins to a Canadian, Vancouver-born James Blaine Rutledge who dusted off an old text and organised the first Paso in 1975.

From Carratraca, route MA 441 rocks and rolls around the dry hills to Alora. But a more comfortable, direct ride back is offered by the new road which runs towards Pizarra and Cártama.

You can vary your return to the coast by taking the MA422 to Coín and **MARBELLA** or the road from Cártama to Alhaurín El Grande, then to Mijas and **FUENGIROLA**❑

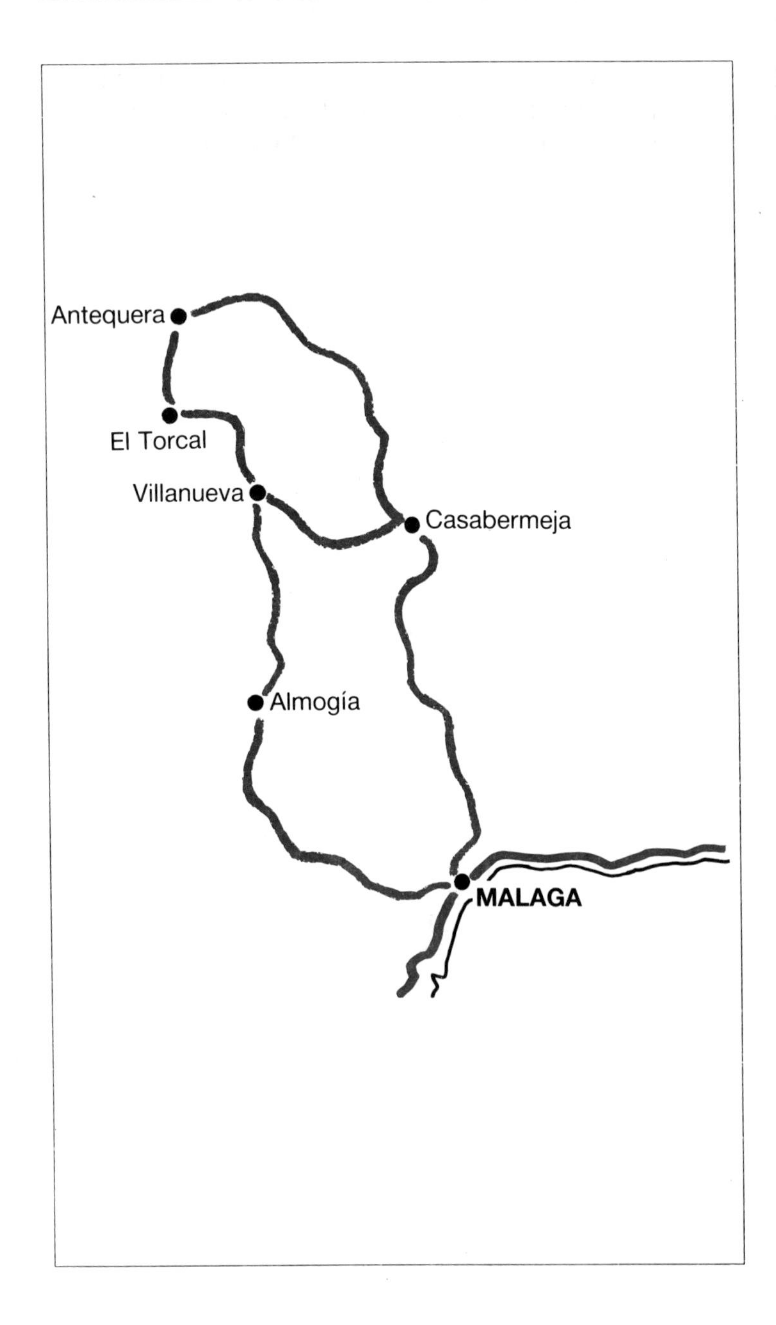
Antequera
El Torcal
Villanueva
Casabermeja
Almogía
MALAGA

Excursion 14 - Mysteries of the Past

Málaga-Almogía-Torcal-Antequera-Casabermeja-Málaga
Distance: 66 miles (105km)

Take the high road from Málaga to visit remote villages, the magical landscape of El Torcal - and one of antiquity's great mysteries. You can spend one or two days on this trip which includes truly dramatic mountain scenery.

The first part of the route is comparatively little travelled. It starts in Málaga. Follow signs for the Carlos Haya Hospital, then Universidad Laboral. If you drive up the Avenida de Carlos Haya, running northwest from the Alameda and city centre, you pass the hospital on your right, and join route MA 423 to Almogia.

Initially, traffic is heavy through this suburb. Villas sprawl over the low hills. But soon you leave the city bustle and run up a valley where algarrobo trees, cactus, almond and olive trees clothe the slopes.

Many ventas (inns) dot the route. They are crowded at weekends but peaceful enough midweek. You can sit on a terrace and enjoy simple, bargain-priced food with cheerful service.

The road swings over a bridge across the Campanillas River. It twists upwards, offering magnificent views over the countryside. Sixteen miles (26 kilometres) from Málaga, the village of Almogía (pop. 4,100) appears on your left, a Moorish tower standing above the houses tumbled over a ridge.

Park your car in the main square overlooked by the Ayuntamiento (town hall). The Bar Central is close by if you are in need of refreshment.

A stroll through the streets will give you glimpses of pensioners dozing in doorways, girls working away at sewing machines in a cottage industry turning out lacy women's underwear, housewives whitewashing. Look for Calle Winters (Winters Street). Believe it or not, Almogía is twinned with the town of Winters, near Sacramento, California.

For the best view of town and country, trek up the concreted track which leads up the hillside to the ruined tower, topped by a television antenna. A number of foreigners have fled the coast to live in or near tranquil Almogía.

Be on your guard for mules plodding along as you continue north. The road, now MA 424, winds through sparsely populated country which finally opens out into an open landscape of cornfields, emerald green in spring. In the distance, above the white outline of Villanueva de la Concepción tower the ramparts of El Torcal.

Wind and water have carved Torcal's 1,200-hectare area, a nature park under the protection of the regional government, into all manner of bizarre shapes. It is possible to envisage the rocks as turrets, reptiles, or animal forms, particularly at twilight. You can enjoy beautiful views over the mountains towards the blue-hazed coast.

At El Torcal's entrance an information centre has details about the geology and history of this area. Paths are marked through the labyrinth for walks of one to three hours, though not all the paths are always open. Don't get caught by the dark as you could spend an eerie and uncomfortable night amid the rocks.

El Torcal lies off the Villanueva-Antequera road, the C3310. You can cut short your trip here by returning to Villanueva. From there a good road runs 10 miles past fields and almond orchards to Casabermeja, on the main Málaga-Antequera highway. This road is a new one and may not be marked on all maps.

Alternatively, drive a further nine miles north to **ANTEQUERA**. It is a scenic route and there are several ventas (inns serving meals) along the way.

As you drive down into Antequera, look over the rooftops and beyond and you will see an unusual-looking outcrop known as the Peña de los Enamorados.

From this angle it appears to offer the profile of a human face, gazing up at the heavens. Legend has it that a Moorish damsel fled to this peak with her Christian lover when their families opposed their union. At the top, they embraced and then plunged together to their deaths.

Antequera's main street - busy with traffic and shoppers - is named after Infante don Fernando, who paved the way for Castile's ousting of the Moors by crushing their army in a battle at a neighbouring chasm, known as the Ass's Mouth.

If you climb up to the Moorish fortress commanding the town, you will pass through the impressive 400-year-old gate, the Arco de los Gigantes. Beyond lies a national monument, the 16th-century Colegiata de Santa María la Mayor, with a Renaissance facade and interior.

Addicts of religious architecture have plenty of scope in Antequera, for although the town has only 28,000 inhabitants it boasts 24 churchs plus several convents. Several of these sell cakes made by the nuns, including the Belén convent, open 9.30am-12.45pm and 4-6.45pm.

The local tourist information office is in the Palacio de Najera, which also houses the municipal museum. Outstanding exhibits include a fine carving by Pedro de Mena of Francis of Assisi and Efebo, a delightful bronze statue of a boy. Efebo, dating from the first-century AD of the Roman era, was unearthed at a local farm.

Roman settlement left many traces around Antequera and evidence of earlier civilisations are still coming to light. Whatever you do, don't miss Antequera's greatest mystery, the dolmens. There are three of these well-preserved burial sites, constructed around 4,000 years ago by a people of whom we know very little.

The Cueva de Menga, with the Cueva de Viera nearby, is on the edge of town, near the petrol station on the Granada road. See if you can figure out how the massive stone slabs, the heaviest weighing 180 tons, were transported here, apparently from the Cerro de la Cruz, one kilometre away.

To visit the Romeral dolmen, drive further out of town to the junction with the old Málaga- Cordoba highway. Turn left, cross the railway line, then take the first turn left on a rutted track, following the signs. A cement factory grinds away and to your right is the mound of the dolmen, surrounded with cypresses.

If you do not see the guardian at first, wait a few minutes

and he will appear and open a gate to give access to Romeral. Unlike the other dolmens, this one - dating from 1800 BC - is circular with a slate cupola. Objects of value entombed with the dead were found under the slab lodged in the wall of a smaller inner chamber.

From Antequera, highway N331 winds up steeply towards Pedrizas pass. Look back and you will see the mosaic of fields forming the Vega, the fertile plain where everything from sunflowers to asparagus flourish.

Halfway back to Málaga, Casabermeja (pop. 3,000) tumbles down the hillside towards the road. This village was founded by Queen Isabel's decree in the 16th century.

It gained brief notoriety in 1840 when farmers ran the biggest landowners out of town and declared the place a republic. Forty horsemen and 40 infantry sent to crush the rising were repelled, but a full-scale army soon put paid to the republic.

The parish church stands at the foot of the main street - Calle Real, which climbs straight to heaven. The continuation of the main street runs down to the gates of Casabermeja's pride, the cemetery. It is distinguished by some elaborate Moorish-style cupolas and rows of tiled tombs.

Immediately below, traffic thunders along the main highway. It will whisk you the 15 miles (25 kilometres) back to **MALAGA** in a few minutes❑

Excursion 15 - Route of the Wine

Nerja-Torrox Costa-Cómpeta (Archez-Algarrobo) -Canillas de Aceituno-Vélez-Málaga-Torre del Mar-Nerja
Distance: 56 miles (90km)

This excursion takes you to wine-producing country and some of the remoter villages behind the coast in the Axarquia region, which lies east of Málaga near the borders of Granada province.

From **NERJA**, take the Málaga road past cliffs diving down to the sea and sandy beaches. The journey starts at Torrox Costa, where tower blocks line the sea and a lighthouse stands on a rocky peninsula near Roman remains.

Turn inland at El Conejito traffic lights on the N340 and follow MA137 to Torrox.

The road winds past developments and plastic-covered fields carved from the hillsides, where tomatoes, beans and melons ripen when Northern Europe is suffering snowstorms. You pass the 16th-century Convento de las Nieves, on the right just after a series of bends.

Park on the bypass that circles around Torrox to the left and stroll up to the town hall plaza where there are pleasant spots to enjoy coffee in the open air (for more information on Torrox and Torrox Costa, see Excursion 7).

Follow the bypass around the western side of Torrox and take the 10-mile (15 kilometre) Torrox-Cómpeta road. It threads up into the hills along a river valley.

Outside many cortijos you will see earth-covered beds, always facing the sun. These are where every autumn moscatel grapes are laid out to dry to prepare some of the most delicious raisins you will ever taste.

Grapes are also sun-dried before they are pressed for wine-making, so that the sugar content is greater and thus the alcohol level is higher. All the villages of the Axarquia produce the typical Málaga wine, very much in fashion a century ago until phylloxera struck. Usually it is sweet, but drier vintages are

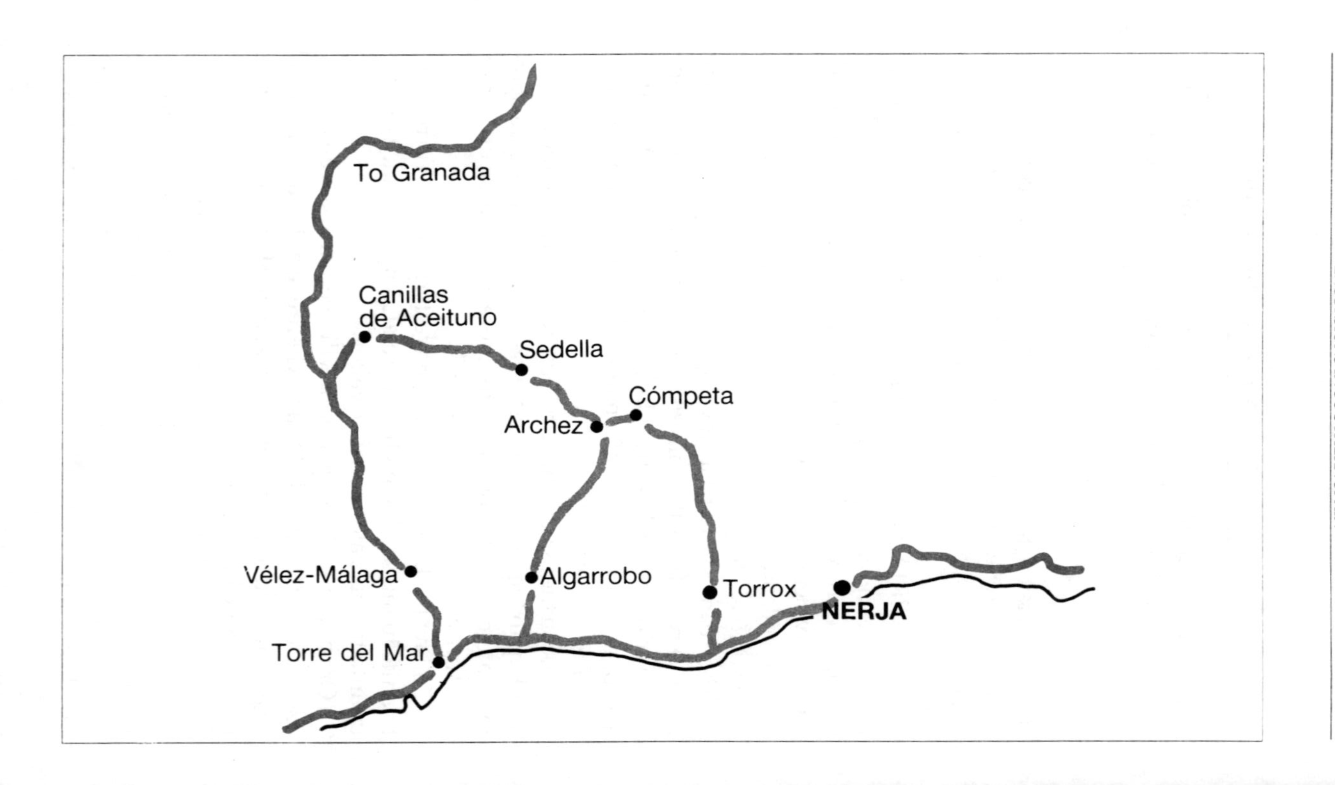
To Granada
Canillas
de Aceituno
Sedella
Cómpeta
Archez
Vélez-Málaga
Algarrobo
Torrox
NERJA
Torre del Mar

made too.

If you walk though this countryside and meet one of the farmers, inevitably he will invite you into the farmhouse to try some *vino del terreno* and test your reaction to the18 per cent alcohol brew. In some of these cortijos the grapes are still crushed in the age-old way, by hours of treading.

You may also be offered chorizo. Be warned that this fatty sausage can blitz unaccustomed stomachs.

Cómpeta has the widest fame for its wine - it holds a wine fiesta every August 15 in the main square - but every village is convinced that its own product is as good or better.

About two-thirds of the way to Cómpeta, you will sight an array of flags advertising the Pavo Real restaurant. English and Dutch-run, this attracts many expatriates who live in the area. It is worth stopping if only to try the pea soup, a thick nourishing brew which is a meal in itself.

White-bleached Cómpeta (pop. 2,300) spills attractively down its hillside, the domed brick tower of its 16th century parish church jutting above the tiled rooftops. Despite its distance from the coast, Cómpeta has become a home from home for many Britons and Danes. Scores have bought abandoned farmhouses on nearby hillsides and renovated them, often installing large cisterns to catch rainwater.

On a ridge overlooking the village is Villa Chile, originally built by a returned migrant. It is now an English-run restaurant, open for lunch Wednesday to Sunday. More rustic fare is available from Bar Marcos, on the main road below the village, recommended for hearty home cooking.

Swing right up a steep street to enter the village. There is a car park on the way up. Check out Cerámica La Posada, the showroom on the left on the way from the car park to the church plaza. The friendly proprietors stock their own imaginative, high-quality stoneware. English is spoken. Just opposite is La Buena Uva, a bodega where wine used to be made. The press is still there, but now it is a pleasant bar.

Bar Perico in the plaza, dominated by the church, is a favourite meeting place, as is Franquelo's, another bar just below the plaza. They both serve meals at reasonable prices.

The village, with its steep crook-leg streets and alleys, is pleasant to walk through and easy to get lost in, especially if you have been sampling the wine.

If sleep is coming on, Cómpeta has Los Montes, a simple, one-star hostal overlooking the church square (Plaza del Generalisimo, 2 Cómpeta. Tel: 51 60 15). A new establishment, Hostal de la Mina, is due to open in the heart of the mountains along a hair-raising track; inquire at the town hall.

Further inland lies Canillas de Albaida (known to the Arabs as "the white one"), where a road plunges into a gorge then climbs to meet the Archez-Salares track.

From Cómpeta you have a choice of routes back to the coast. The more direct one is a 12-mile (20-kilometre) run, via MA 111, to Algarrobo Costa, near Torre del Mar, passing vineyards, almond and olive trees along a scenic valley. Just outside Cómpeta, a monument from the Franco years stands at the side of the road. It pays tribute to an 18-year-old law student "vilely assassinated by the Marxist hordes on this spot on January 8, 1937."

You pass Sayalonga (Mudéjar parish church and an unusual circular cemetery) and Algarrobo, where a stroll through tortuous streets brings you to the Ermita de San Sebastián for a good view of the village.

Two kilometres from Algarrobo on MA111 towards the coast are two ventas specializing in grilled meat. El Cochinillo (open 1-4pm, 7-11.30pm, closed Monday) is on the highway. Fifty yards down a dirt track lies Mesón Los Lobos (lunch and dinner, open weekends and holidays, closed May), an attractive place with big earthenware plant pots at the entrance.

A little further down the road turn left towards the Residencia Trayamar, a mansion housing nuns, and the Necrópolis de Trayamar. Park your car near the entrance, then follow the dirt track lined with cypress trees.

You pass an alberca (water tank) on your left. Next to this is the necropolis, inside a rectangular building, but first you have to collect the key from a farmhouse down the track on the right.

The excavated Phoenician tombs dates back to the 7th century BC. A moth-eaten information sheet behind cracked glass - vandals have broken into the necropolis - relates that some finds were made in 1930 and more were discovered by Madrid's German Archeological Institute in 1967.

Amphoras and priceless jewellery, including a beautiful gold pendant, have been removed to museums in Málaga and Madrid.

An alternative, longer route to the coast from Cómpeta takes you through the mountains and then down to Vélez Málaga. You will really feel you have hit the back country as you roller-coast through the sierras past a series of remote white villages.

Roll the village names off your tongue. . . Salares, Sedella, Canillas de Aceituno, all hotbeds of rebellion in the 16th-century Morisco war and still with a Moorish air about them.

Take the MA111 towards Algarrobo and, three miles (4km) from Cómpeta fork sharp right into the valley to Archez. A sign indicates the Ruta del Mudéjar, or should do so - a local joker has blotted out part of the "R" in Ruta to make it a "P".

Archez, a dozy huddle of houses, is worth a halt because of its church tower, a 14th century minaret with beautifully ornate brickwork. Just outside the village, turn right, up and over the hill towards Salares.

If, instead, you carry straight on along the MA119 - a road of a thousand curves leading to Vélez Málaga - you reach the hamlet of Daimalos and a spring with magical powers. A legend from Moorish times relates that the water of the Fuente Perdida can restore a man's sexual power and a woman's fertility.

Continuing on the MA119, just before the village of Arenas take a precipitous three-kilometre track (not for nervous drivers) up to Bentomiz castle. Almond and olive trees grow within the ruined walls and there are stupendous views, making it an ideal picnic spot. A huge bell of solid gold reportedly once hung in the castle. When the Christians were about to conquer the fortress, the Moors hid the bell in a tunnel - treasure-seekers are still looking for it.

Forgetting about dreams of gold, we return to our original route and take the road to tiny Salares, also boasting a fine minaret, and Sedella. On the right rises the great bulk of Maroma, at 6,600 feet the highest peak in Málaga province. Often clothed in snow in winter, it marks the boundary between Málaga and Granada provinces.

There is a good view of Maroma from Casa Pintá (tel. 95-250 88 77), a modern two-star hostal, with attractive arches and tiles, on the outskirts of Sedella. Five double rooms are available and the restaurant specializes in chivo al ajillo (garlic-flavoured kid). The swimming pool is in use from June to September.

Almond and olive trees dot the slopes and citrus orchards occupy more sheltered spots around Canillas de Aceituno (pop. 2,700). A footpath weaves up to the summit of Maroma from Canillas, but it is a strenuous all-day hike and walkers should be properly equipped - hailstorms are not unknown on the heights in early summer.

The MA125 executes a few hair-pins before finally dipping down to the C335. Turn left towards **VÉLEZ MALAGA** and the coast. A new road speeds you along the intensely cultivated Río Vélez valley to Vélez (pop. 52,000), administrative centre of the Axarquia zone, 22 miles (36km) from Málaga.

Although modern buildings surround the town, you will still find the atmosphere of old Spain in the narrow streets hugging the hill below the fortress.

Waving fields of sugar cane cover the Vélez river delta around neighbouring Torre del Mar, a dirt-poor fishing village until in the 1960s it was hit by high-rise madness. Fortunately, this unplanned instant resort has had a much-needed facelift.

The seafront, with a long beach of gritty, greyish sand, has been transformed by a fine promenade, with gardens, palm-trees, and open-air cafes.

On the Málaga side of town, Avenida Antonio Toré Toré (named after the builder responsible for much of the damage) leads to the beach. Pizzerias seem to have been breeding on this avenue; two of the best are Cosa Nostra (Edificio Ibiza, open 12-4pm, 7-12pm, closed Wed), decorated with a rare selection of dolls, and Italia (Edificio Hamburgo, open 12.30-3.30pm, 7-12pm, Master, Visa, closed Mon & mid-Nov to mid-December, tel. 95-254 04 48), with some authentic Italian culinary touches.

Torre del Mar has a selection of reasonably-priced restaurants. Seafood fans flock to Bar La Cueva (Paseo de Larios, near the Post Office. Open 12-4pm, 7-11pm). The decor is starkly functional, but the bar is always crowded because of the excellent value offered by the *raciones* (platefuls) of a wide variety of fresh fried fish served at the counter.

Driving back to Nerja, you pass the fishing and pleasure harbour of Caleta de Vélez. Overlooking Caleta and the coast is Villas del Mediterraneo (Avda de Sierra Nevada, s/n, tel. 95-251 13 76), a luxury three-star aparthotel, with well-equipped two-bedroom apartments and villas. It offers exceptional value off-season, but prices double and treble between July and September.

At La Mezquitilla, look for a monument near the fishing boats drawn up on the beach. It commemorates the return of Miguel de Cervantes to Spanish soil after years of captivity in North Africa. He is said to have landed on this beach❑

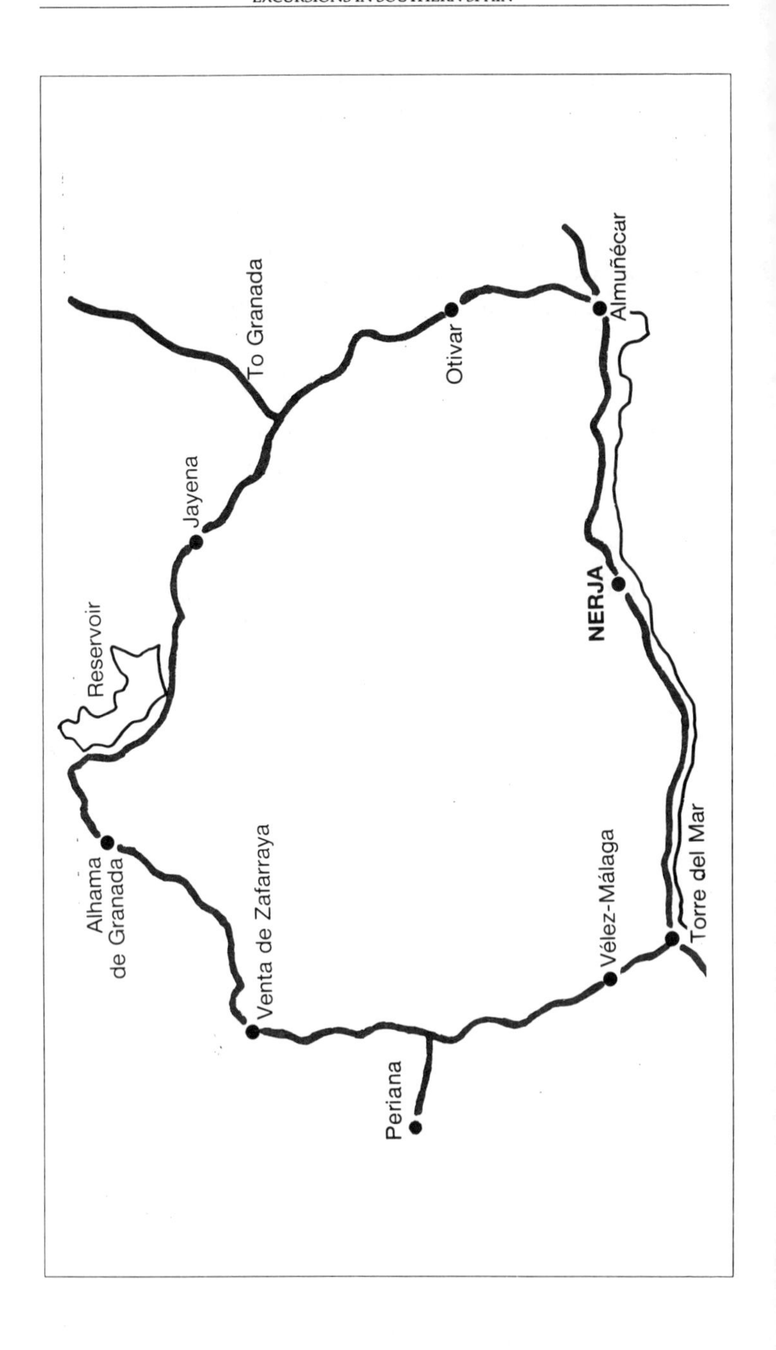
To Granada
Otivar
Almuñécar
Jayena
Reservoir
NERJA
Alhama
de Granada
Venta de Zafarraya
Vélez-Málaga
Torre del Mar
Periana

Excursion 16 - To the Hot Springs

Nerja-Almuñécar-Otivar-Jayena-Alhama de Granada-Ventas de Zafarraya-Vélez-Málaga-Torre del Mar-Nerja
Distance: 106 miles (170km)

This is one of the most spectacular roads in Andalusia. It takes you up into the sierras of Granada province and to the hot springs near the old town of **ALHAMA DE GRANADA**.

Driving east from **NERJA**, head along the coast on N340 into Granada province. Branch right at the traffic lights to enter **ALMUÑÉCAR**. Look for the signs to Otivar. A left turn takes you under the N340 via an underpass to drive up the Río Verde valley.

The narrow road winds past lush plantations of custard apple trees, avocadoes, medlars and pomegranates. The sheltered conditions allow all manner of exotic fruits to flourish, even paw-paws and mangoes.

Shelves have been cut in the surrounding hillsides to allow more trees to be planted and drip irrigation to be installed. Drought and the farmers' ever-increasing need for water has provoked fierce conflict with neighbouring communities over water rights.

Look for a sign two kilometres from Almuñécar indicating Torre del Monje, Columbario Romano. A steep, stony path past cactus and barking dogs leads to a columbarium, a small square tower inside which are niches where the Romans stored their loved ones' ashes.

Further along, on a right-hand bend at Torrecuevas (3km, 2 miles, from Almuñécar), you will see the arches of an aqueduct built by the Romans and still in use.

After the village of Jete, the road climbs the valley side to Otivar (pop. 1,200), nine miles (14 kilometres) from Almuñécar. They still remember the Napoleonic Wars here. A plaque outside the town hall commemorates the courage of a former mayor who stubbornly resisted French invaders.

The quiet streets have evocative names, suggesting past feuds and passions. Look for Calle Beso (kiss street) and Calle

Engaño (swindle street).

On the highway running above the village centre a series of restaurants, balanced on concrete stilts over the abyss, do good business. They offer filling country fare at astonishingly low prices and many people drive up from the coast for lunch. Specialities include *morcilla* (black sausage), mountain ham, and a delicious *pollo a la manzana* (chicken cooked with apple). Vino de la Costa, served in earthenware jugs, washes it down.

A little beyond Otivar, a side-road zig-zags up to Lentegí, a hamlet lodged like an eagle's eyrie 2,000 feet above sea-level in the Sierra del Chaparral. The pace of life in Lentegí makes Otivar seem like Piccadilly Circus.

Cars park on the Plaza de España near the church. Nearby, the Cueva del Trabuco bar - look for the shotgun - is built under the rock. Another bar, the Piedra Dura, is down a few steps from the plaza.

Climbing again on the main road, you pass occasional abandoned farmhouses on rosemary-and-thyme-covered slopes. Once they were clothed in pines, but many have disappeared in disastrous forest fires. The road slices through rock and hairpins upwards to Mirador de la Cabra Montés, a remote petrol station eight miles (13km) from Otivar, a worthwhile halt to revel in the splendid views back towards the coast.

You may even glimpse the *cabras* (wild goats), hawks and eagles which inhabit these lonely sierras.

North of this point the road levels out briefly, then gets really serious. After passing over a narrow saddle between two valleys, it scales the face of a sheer cliff. Hacking out this section must have been a tremendous task. Down to the left you will see hundreds of newly-planted young trees.

Soon the road reaches a plateau, passing a farm school and Mesón Los Prados, useful for a snack if it is open, and undulating through pinewoods. Seventeen miles (28km) after Otivar, take a left turn in the pinewoods to travel westwards towards Jayena and Alhama de Granada.

If, instead, we stuck to the Granada road, we would soon reach a rolling plain of barley and wheat with the snow-tipped

Sierra Nevada shimmering over all. This is a particularly breath-taking sight in springtime.

This road joins the thundering traffic of the Motril-Granada highway at the Suspiro del Moro (Moor's Sigh) pass, so-called because Boabdil, the last Moorish King of Granada, paused here for a final look at the city from which he had been ousted by the Catholic Monarchs. "Go on, weep like a woman for that which you failed to defend like a man," sniffed his mother.

Few vehicles trundle along the recently-constructed road to Jayena. We pass through this village, and its neighbours, Fornes, and Arenas del Rey. On one hand is the Embalse de los Bermejales, a large reservoir. To the south the sharp peaks of the Sierra de Almijara rise more than 5,000 feet high.

Fields of corn, dotted with scarlet poppies in spring and early summer, lap the roadside, where wild flowers abound. Poplar trees, whose leaves shine like gold coins in autumn, line the river winding down from the sierras towards **ALHAMA DE GRANADA**.

A mile before the road from Arenas (GR141) reaches the Alhama-Málaga road, a swimming pool at the Pato Loco restaurant and bar offers an enticing opportunity to cool off. The pool is in use from June to September. In summer you will find the local youngsters splashing about there or in Alhama's municipal pool.

In the past, Alhama (2,800 feet above sea-level) was important because of its strategic location on the route from Granada to Málaga. It lies on the edge of a spectacular chasm formed by its river. Drive into town and park on the main square near the market.

Good drinking water bubbles from the fountain outside the Iglesia del Carmen. Rafael, the veteran caretaker, will appear to guide you around the church. Opposite is what remains of Alhama's castle, sealed off by a high wall and incorporated into a private house.

A short stroll away are the Tajo (gorge), the tourism office (in a former jail), and the main sights, including the parish church which shelters embroidery said to have been executed by Queen Isabel. "You can see it's hers because it is not very good - well, a queen can't be good at everything," explains a local.

Just out of town along the Granada road turn left and drive down a side-road which cuts through a chasm to the Balneario Alhama de Granada, built over 12th-century Moorish baths. The water, gushing from a spring at a temperature of 47 degrees C, is recommended for rheumatism, breathing problems and kidney illnesses.

From Alhama it is 12 miles (19 kilometres) on C340 over the oak-dotted hills to Ventas de Zafarraya. A handy place for refreshment en route is Los Caños de la Alcaicería bar and restaurant, on a 90-degree bend. The service is friendly and there is a swimming pool. A bull's head and newspaper reports on the walls reflect the fame of a local landowner, known as El Caballo Andaluz in his days as a *rejoneador* (mounted bull-fighter).

A fertile valley, hemmed in by rocky heights, leads to Ventas. This was always an important way station for muleteers and stage coaches, for it stands at the head of a pass formed by a narrow gap in the mountains, known as the Boquete de Zafarraya.

Often the pass is shrouded in mist when the sun is shining brightly on the coast. Scenery and climate change quickly as you descend into Málaga province. Occasionally you will glimpse tunnels and an old track where a railway once ran from Málaga up to Ventas de Zafarraya.

As the C335 swings down the valley in wide curves, you will see crumbling walls crowning a hilltop. These are the ruins of Zalia, a Moorish fortress.

A little below the ruins, a turn to the right leads along the C340 to Periana (8km) with fine views over the Viñuela reservoir towards mountains and the coast. Compared to its neighbours, Periana is a youngster, being founded in 1761 and rebuilt after the devastating 1884 earthquake.

It is wellknown for the quality of its olive oil - follow the green signs indicating the way to the Cooperativa - and its apricots. But the area planted with apricot trees has been seriously reduced by drought.

A *villa turística* (tourist village), financed by the Junta de Andalucía, was due to open in 1995 four kilometres from the village near the old rail line to Ventas de Zafarraya. This hotel's bungalows offer comfortable accommodation to those eager to enjoy tranquillity, walks and mountain air.

A delightfully scenic road continues beyond Periana to Ríogordo and Colmenar (see Excursion 21).

Continuing on the C335 towards Vélez, you see a turn to the left to Puente Don Manuel and - way up on the side of the Sierra de Tejeda - Alcaucín (meaning "the arches" in Arabic), a particularly picturesque village. The murder in the 16th century of the Alcaucín innkeeper and his wife by outlaws provoked such cruel Christian reprisals that the local Moriscos (Moorish converts to Christianity) rose in revolt.

If you need an overnight halt, the low-rise, one-star Hotel Romero at Puente Don Manuel (tel. 95-251-08 04) offers modern, reasonably priced rooms (heating, TV) and a restaurant.

The C335 runs swiftly down towards Vélez-Málaga, passing citrus orchards, palm trees, and whitewashed dwellings framed by hibiscus and geraniums. Recently improved, the road bypasses the many hamlets and the village of Viñuela but passes close to the main dam of the Viñuela reservoir.

Seven other dams, plus a network of tunnels and aqueducts, channel water into the reservoir to meet the needs of the Axarquía. A fine road to the right, the A352, runs across the dam to Los Romanos and Riogordo. It is part of a new highway designed to link Marbella and Vélez-Málaga via the interior.

On a side-road above the reservoir stands an impressive-looking ochre and white building, the new Hotel Municipal de Viñuela (tel. 95-251 90 02).

The road follows the intensely-cultivated Vélez river valley and the air grows steadily balmier. At Trapiche, a right turn takes you along the MA159 to Ríogordo (see Excursion 21).

When you reach **VÉLEZ MALAGA** and the bustling highway to Torre del Mar (see Excursion 15), you know you are back on the coast❑

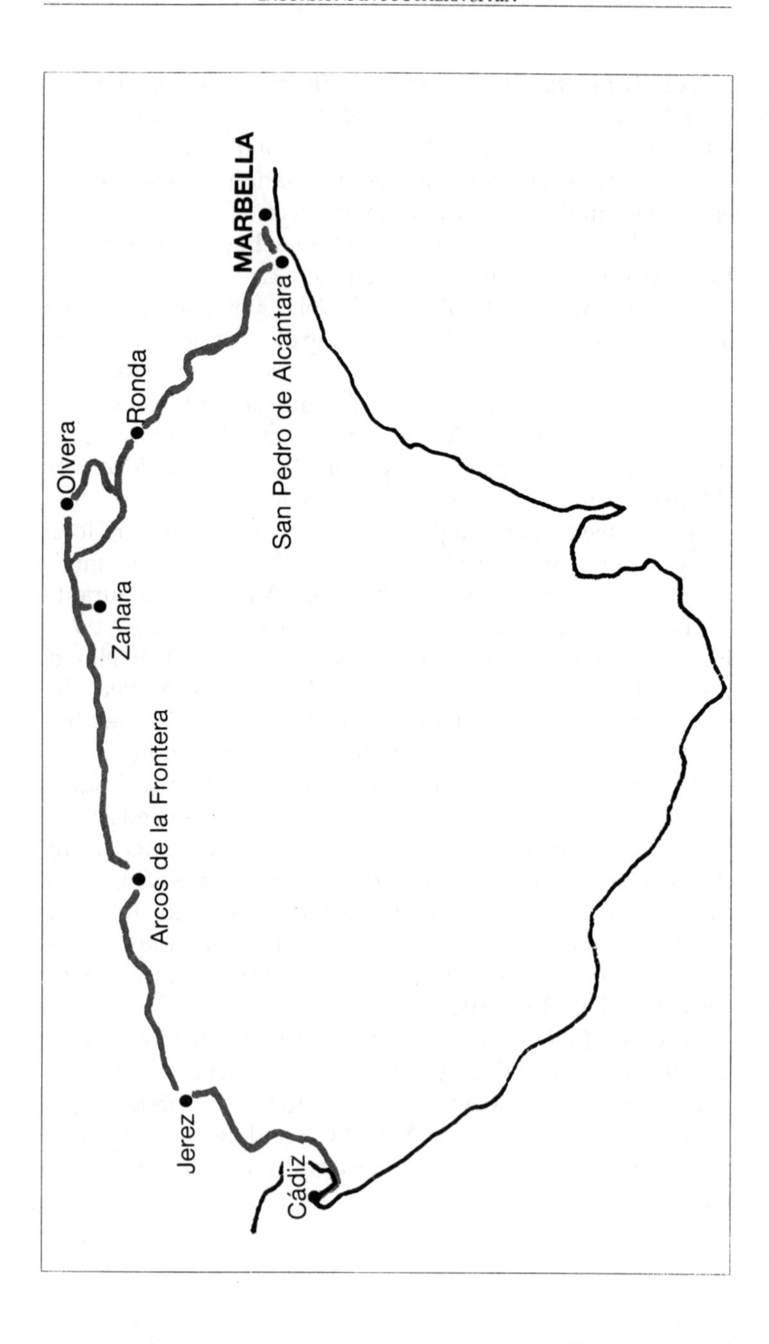
MARBELLA
San Pedro de Alcántara
Ronda
Olvera
Zahara
Arcos de la Frontera
Jerez
Cádiz

Excursion 17 - To the Cradle of Bullfighting:

Marbella-San Pedro-Ronda-Olvera-Zahara-Arcos-Cádiz
Distance: 144 miles (230km)

Just inland from the Costa del Sol lies some of Spain's wildest scenery and most spectacular towns. It is worth several days' exploration. But if you have limited time, this route gives you the chance to enjoy some of the most interesting aspects en route to **CADIZ** and **SEVILLE.**

The drive takes you to sherry country and the Atlantic coast via a town which should be on everybody's must-see list - Ronda, the cradle of modern bullfighting, perched on the edge of a 600-foot chasm.

Drive west from **MARBELLA** on the N340, turn right to bypass San Pedro de Alcántara and follow the signs for Ronda. Highway C339 soon begins to climb sharply as it swerves past upmarket villa developments. Pines clothe the lower slopes of mountains which rise abruptly to bleak heights as we pass the Puerto de Alijar.

Built in the 1970s, this road makes clever use of the terrain to avoid very steep gradients as it coils upwards to more than 2,000 feet above sea level. To the right rises the massive bulk of the Sierra de las Nieves. The highest peaks are Enamorados, 5,800 feet high, and Torrecillas, 6,200 feet. Forests of the rare pinsapo, or Spanish fir, are to be found in the rugged fastnesses of this range. A track to the right, seven miles (12km) before Ronda, leads to these woods.

To the left, wooded hills stretch away to the Sierra Bermeja behind Estepona. This area is virtually uninhabited, except as we near Ronda, where a string of remote villages nestle amid chestnut-clad slopes.

Approaching **RONDA**, 30 miles (49km) from San Pedro, the road reaches a plateau. The city of Ronda rises from a rocky bluff above the surrounding countryside.

For a good view of Ronda's most famous feature, continue into the town centre. You cross the Puente Nuevo, a bridge crossing El Tajo, the 600-foot deep gorge that splits the town in two.

A bypass avoids the town centre and takes us along the Seville road, the C339. The road crosses the railway line to Algeciras and the Río Guadiaro. Look for a sign, on the right seven miles (12km) from Ronda, pointing to Acinipo. This road will take you to the ruins of a Roman town, also known as Ronda La Vieja (open 10am-6pm, Fri-Sun 9am-7pm. Closed Mon pm).

It is worth the trip if you are a fan of Roman theatres, and also for magnificent views as the ruins are on a lofty ridge. This is one of the spots where Julius Casar and Pompey are said to have fought the Battle of Munda around 45BC.

If time is pressing, return to the C339 and continue northwest along a recently-improved highway to join the N342 to Jerez

Alternatively, drive on past the Roman ruins into Cádiz province and to the El Gastor-Setenil road. Turn right to visit Setenil, one of the strangest and most claustrophobic towns in Andalusia. The houses are wedged into a crevice and many have roofs of solid rock. The two-star Hotel El Almendral (956-13 40 29) offers rooms on the Setenil-Puerto del Monte road.

From Setenil, a country road leads 15 kilometres northwest to Olvera, on the Antequera-Jerez road, the N342. As soon as you see the town climbing up its ridge, surmounted by castle and church, you see why somebody once wrote: "Olvera, one street, one church, one castle . . . but what a Street, what a Church, what a Castle!"

The town (pop. 9,000) presents a majestic skyline as it rises above the surrounding fields. A long street runs straight up towards the 12th-century Arab castle. María, the caretaker, lives at No 2 on the nearby Plaza de la Iglesia - unless a new access has been completed, she will beckon you through her living room and patio to climb up to the castle.

The panorama from the battlements is tremendous, but don't go up if you have no head for heights.

You look down on Encarnación church, built over a mosque in the 14th century and rebuilt by the Duque de Osuna two centuries later with two imposing bell-towers. There is a Gothic baptismal chapel.

Olvera has a modern two-star hotel, the Sierra y Cal (Avenida Nuestra Señora de los Remedios, 4. Tel: 956-13 03 03). Rooms have bathrooms, telephones and heating and there is a restaurant. The hotel looks out at a splendid view of the town.

The disused railway line between Olvera and Bornos has been converted into a "green trail", a 40-mile (65km) track for the use of hikers and cyclists.

Head west on the N342 towards Jerez. You pass the junction with the C339 from Ronda and Algodonales, to the right. Branch left to drive five miles (9km) to the picturebook pueblo of Zahara de la Sierra. The road crosses a dam retaining the Guadalcín reservoir and weaves up towards Zahara's clustered dwellings. A tower sprouts melodramatically from a crag above.

Back in 1481 Muley Hacen, Moorish King of Granada, stormed Zahara and killed the Christian soldiers. This provoked the wrath of the Castilian warlords and helped ensure the fall of Granada itself.

Walk up to the much-restored tower above the village for fine views of olive groves, bare hills, and Olvera in the distance.

Zahara has a two-star hostal, Marqués de Zahara (San Juan, 3. Tel: 956-12 30 61), if you are inclined to pass the night in this village of 1,700 inhabitants. It is spartan but clean, with hot water and a restaurant.

Next to the hostal is Zahara's information office, open daily in the mornings (956-12 31 14). It can organize horse-riding, mountain biking and other activities. Ask there about visiting the Garganta Verde, a spectacular gorge. Numbers are limited to 30 a day to avoid disturbing the griffon vultures *(buitres leonados)* there and during the nesting season permission to enter is required.

The Garganta lies five kilometres south of Zahara off the CA531. A road-side sign warns that it is a "very tough" two-kilometre excursion; in fact, the first 500 metres is not too difficult, leading to a chamber in the rock known as the Ermita. However, traversing the rest of the narrow gorge is for experienced, rope-equipped climbers only.

If you continue on the CA531, it soars and loops dramatically over the mountains as vultures circle above to reach Grazalema (see Excursion 27).

Back on the Antequera-Jerez road, the N342 performs a few wriggles, then straightens and flattens along the Guadalete valley. Just beyond Villamartin appears the large Bornos reservoir, followed by the smaller Arcos reservoir and beyond, the arrogant outline of **ARCOS DE LA FRONTERA**, lording it from the summit of a rocky buttress. In good years (recently drought has shrunk the lake) you can boat and swim in the Arcos reservoir.

As you climb through the narrow alleys and tortuous, claustrophobic streets of Arcos, you have the sensation of entering a truly medieval town. The streets lead steeply upwards to the Plaza del Cabildo and a mirador looking out over the Guadalete River gorge. The Parador is one side of the square, the Ayuntamiento on the other against the castle ramparts. Also on the square is Santa María church; climb the tower for a dizzy view.

Arcos was in the forefront of the Moors v Christians wars and thus gained the "de la Frontera" (of the frontier) tag.

Semana Santa is particularly spectacular as the religious images are squeezed through the streets, the climax coming in the early hours of Good Friday. Locals claim that the house walls lean inwards in the hope that they will be touched by the passing crosses. On Easter Sunday a bull is released to chase the more daring through the old quarter.

Leave Arcos on the Jerez road, N342. If you want the best picture-taking point, turn left on the Paterna road and you gain a fine view of Arcos perched over the gorge.

Continue towards Jerez. Nearing that town, you see a hotel and Mesón La Cueva on the right This modern building, good for a halt for tapas, stands over a cave once used as an inn, near the tower of Melgarejo castle. It is said that the innkeepers, after accidentally killing a drunken customer, chopped him up and tossed the pieces into the well in the cave.

Close by is the Jerez motor-racing circuit and near that the Hotel Montecastillo (tel. 956-15 12 00), a modern luxury establishment overlooking a golf course designed by Jack Nicklaus.

The first vineyards herald your entry into sherry country. **JEREZ** and its bodegas are worth at least a day of your time (see Excursion 28).

If you are not visiting Jerez, look for the Seville-Cádiz autoroute which crosses the Arcos road. It is a toll road but brings you swiftly to Puerto Real, 16 miles (26km) away. From there you drive past shipyards and across the bridge that flies over Cádiz Bay.

Ahead of you, on a narrow peninsula, lies **CADIZ**, the oldest city in the Western World❑

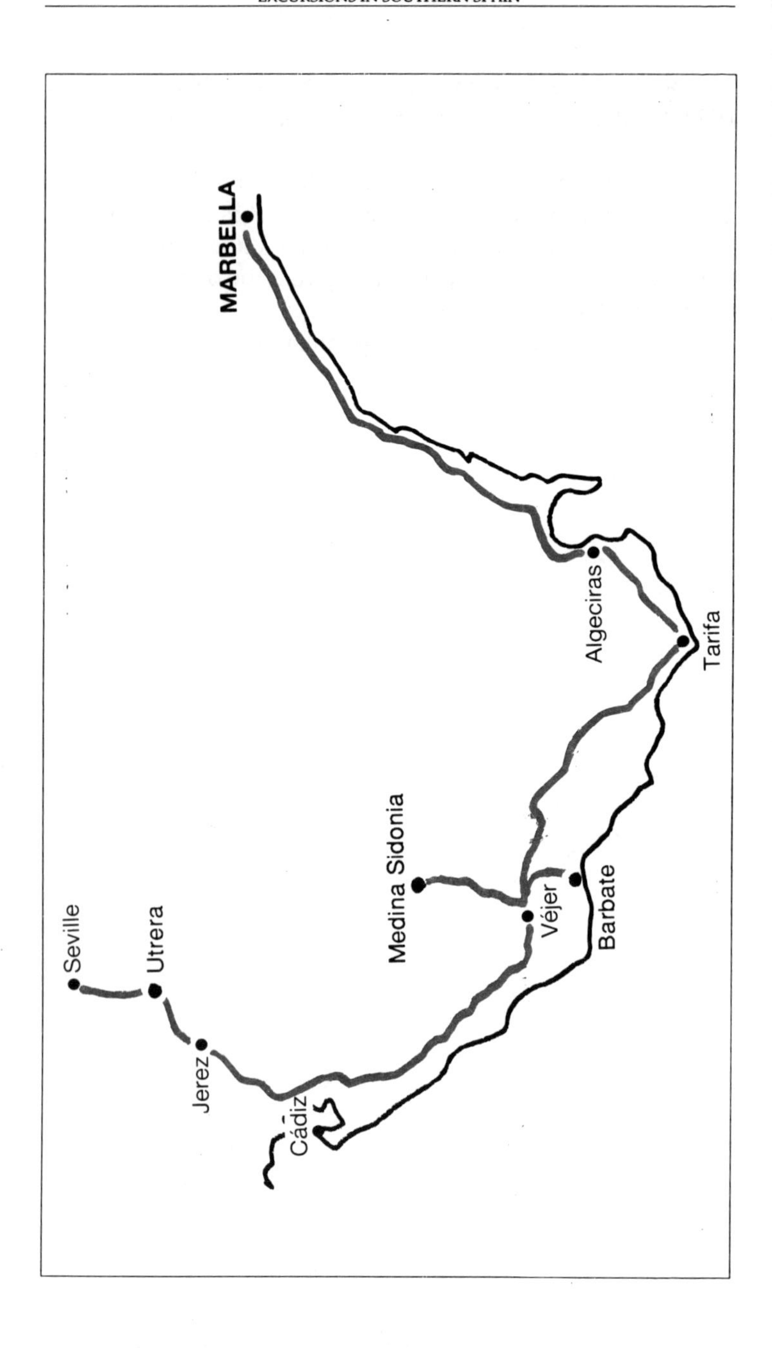
MARBELLA
Algeciras
Tarifa
Medina Sidonia
Véjer
Barbate
Seville
Utrera
Jerez
Cádiz

Excursion 18 - Surfers' Paradise:

Marbella-Estepona-San Roque-Algeciras-Tarifa-Vejer-Cádiz-Jerez-Utrera-Seville
Distance: 200 miles (320km)

Glimpses of the Rock, superb sandy beaches, a Roman town, a city founded 3,000 years ago, and sherry country lie on this route that takes you along the Mediterranean and Atlantic coasts to Seville.

Beaches, rocky headlands, marinas and innumerable tourist projects border the N340 between Marbella and Estepona. Golfing is a growth industry.

Nearing the Straits of Gibraltar and the Atlantic, the landscape grows wilder and greener. The Rock, often girdled with cloud, looms on the horizon. After the Río Guadiaro and Sotogrande, look for a turn to La Línea if you want to visit Gibraltar (see Excursion 9 for full details about this zone).

The N340 skirts San Roque on its hilltop and curves around Algeciras Bay, not a pretty sight thanks to attempts to create jobs through industrial development.

If you wish to spend the night amid more gracious rural surroundings, turn right on the C440. After three miles (4km), you reach Los Barrios. Here stands the Casa de las Doncellas, where the mayor locked up all the nubile local girls during the Peninsular War to protect them from the marauding French soldiery.

The C440 continues north to the white towns of Alcalá de los Gazules and Medina Sidonia, but we turn left at the end of an avenue of palm trees in Los Barrios and drive three miles (5km) westward. Just after El Molino, a restaurant in an old mill, turn right to Monte de la Torre, a 1,500-acre cattle farm amid cork oaks. A wing of the fine Edwardian mansion has been converted into flats for renting. Bed and breakfast is also available. Reserve accommodation in advance through Sue and Quentin Agnew,the estate managers (Aptdo de Correos 66, Los Barrios, Cádiz, tel. 956-66 00 00).

Continue on this side road to return to the N340 on the

outskirts of **ALGECIRAS**. As the jumping off point for Africa, the town mixes the colourful and the sleazy. Hydrofoils and slower-moving ferries leave frequently for Ceuta and Tangiers.

During the Second World War, spies of all nationalities put up at the Hotel Reina Cristina in Algeciras so that they could survey traffic through the Strait and at the same time keep an eye on their rivals.

The highway climbs 1,000 feet up to wooded hills and rolls along high above the Strait. This is a military zone. Pastures dotted with trees fall away to where Atlantic meets Mediterranean. A little below the Puerto del Cabrito, a mirador (viewing point) makes a handy stop. A steady stream of merchant vessels pass through the Strait, the hills of Africa looming closely in the background.

Just before Tarifa, the twirling blades of hundreds of windmills, generate power for the national electricity grid. The coast you are approaching, the Costa de la Luz, is noted for its windy conditions.

Windswept **TARIFA**, protected by ancient walls, is only 30 minutes away by hydrofoil from Africa. On clear days you can see Tangier gleaming white across the Strait.

Above Tarifa's ivy-covered entrance arch piercing the walls, a ceramic plaque reads: "Very noble, very loyal and heroic City of Tarifa, won from the Moors in the reign of Sancho 1V The Brave on September 21, 1292".

This is where the Moorish invasion of the Iberian peninsula began back in 710. Tarif Ben Malik came over for a reconnoitring trip, landing on the Isla de la Paloma (now occupied by the military). The next year an army led by al-Tarik arrived at a deserted peninsula, now known as Gibraltar (from Jebel al-Tarik, the mountain of Tarik), and 700 years of Arab and Berber domination began.

Tarifa's 10th-century castle, standing proudly above the harbour, was the scene of a legendary act of heroism - or foolishness, dependingon how you view it - in the 13th century when it was besieged by the Moors.

They threatened to cut the throat of the Christian leader Guzmán's young son unless he surrendered. Defiantly, he tossed them down a dagger to do the job with. Impressed, the Moors reportedly spared his son. After that he became, incredibly, Guzmán The Good. The tower from where he threw down the weapon is still there and a large white statue of Guzmán el Bueno stands on the nearby palm-shaded esplanade. He holds a dagger and looks pretty bad-tempered. You can contemplate him and his paternal love while enjoying a snack at the outside tables of the Restaurant Alameda close by.

When the Levante wind blows, there is a sinister feeling by night about the empty narrow streets of old Tarifa, so long just a bleak garrison town. But that relentless wind has brought new prosperity, attracting sailboarders from all over Europe and - in season - converting Tarifa into a sort of mini-Hawaii.

Shops with names like Hot Stick, Cocktails, and Cat Fun line the main street and sails flutter like brightly-coloured butterflies off the vast stretch of Los Lances beach. Tanned windsurf fanatics crowd into the campsites and hotels near the pine-fringed beach and by night live it up in the bars and discos of Tarifa's old town.

Nine miles (15km) north of Tarifa, a left turn from the N340 takes you five miles (8km) to the beautiful little bay of Bolonia, site of a Roman settlement. Visits can be made to the ruins on the hour from 10am to 6pm (to 5pm Sept 16-June 30) from Tuesday to Saturday, on Sundays and holidays mornings only. For information call 956-68 85 30.

This was once Baelo Claudia, where salted fish and garum - a thick paste made from fish entrails - were prepared for export to other parts of the Roman empire. Temples, streets, a forum, theatre and marketplace are visible. After you have visited the ruins, plunge into the sea off the white-sand beach and then relax over a cold beer at one of the beach bars before heading north towards Cádiz and Seville.

Brown, long-horned cattle crop large open pastures, fenced in with crooked sticks. Egrets peck calmly around the cattle and a stork may flap lazily by. Turn left along a quiet country road to Zahara de los Atunes, a windswept, strangely remote fishing village which has experienced a development boom in recent years thanks to its endless sandy beach.

Hotels have popped up everywhere. The Gran Sol (tel. 956-43 93 01), one star but two star prices, occupies prime position on the beach. It is opposite the almadraba enclosure, a place with thick crumbling walls where men and equipment employed in tuna-fishing used to shelter. Doña Lola (956-43 90 09), in the same price range, is at the entrance to town. Pozo del Duque (Ctra Atlanterra, 32. tel. 956-43 94 00), three stars, is a flashier alternative. Or there is a first-class campground. A popular bar with terrace is Casa Juanito, along an alley to the left after crossing the bridge into town.

From Zahara it is seven miles (10km) through uninhabited country, some of it used by the military for weapons practice, to Barbate. This is a somewhat bleak fishing town, with many modern buildings, but it has a new promenade and cleaned-up beach.

Take a walk out around the breakwater and you may come across a Japanese or Korean factory ship with the crew busily slicing up freshly caught tuna. Tuna-fishing has been big business here since Guzmán el Bueno, whose descendants became the Dukes of Medina Sidonia, was granted the fishing rights.

A mile or so off-shore an *almadraba* is set up. Huge anchors retain a wall of netting which funnels migrating bluefin tuna into a killing zone. When the boats come home around midday, in spring and early summer, you will see fish weighing up to 300 kilos being offloaded. Tuna steak is on many local menus and along the main street, Avenida del Generalísimo, slices of *mojame* (salted tuna) are on sale.

Two eating possibilities are Restaurante Torres (Ruiz de Aldas, 1. tel. 956-43 09 85. Closed Mon & Nov. Amex, Diners, Master, Visa. M), specializing in tuna dishes, and - tucked discreetly into a side street - the Gadir (Padre Castrillon, 15. Tel: 956-43 08 00. Open 1-4pm, 8-12pm. Closed Mon, winter months. Amex, Visa. M) a Basque restaurant with excellent seafood.

A road curls up through pinewoods behind Barbate, dropping down after five miles (8km) to Los Caños de Meca. The good beaches attract crowds in summer, including nudists and a posse of gays. Windsurfers find excellent conditions. Sand drifts over the road to a lighthouse on a headland on Cape Trafalgar, near which took place the famous Battle of Trafalgar in which Nelson routed the Franco-Spanish fleet on October 21, 1805, only to succumb to his wounds.

Unlike Zahara, laidback Los Caños has yet to be blitzed by developers. There are several campgrounds. A little away from the beach, the Alhambra (Ctra Caños de Meca 9.5km. tel. 908-65 45 44) is a pleasant little one-star hostal, with flowers, greenery and Moorish arches. It has a restaurant and is open all year.

Turn inland from the sandy, pine-covered coastal strip to reach Vejer de la Frontera (the "Frontera" dates back to the time when this was frontier territory in the wars between Moors and Christians). It can also be approached directly from Barbate through productive, well-irrigated farmland.

From a distance Vejer's forested slopes look like they are capped with snow. It is one of the most beautifully-located *pueblos blancos*. Old windmills are silhouetted on the hill behind the town.

Approaching up the road from the Trafalgar direction and the N340, park your car on the left near the esplanade which looks out over rolling countryside. A wall plaque proclaims:"Vejer! If you were a woman, I would fall in love with you."

The town hall has made an effort to conserve the traditional character of Vejer and even the video shop sign is in olde worlde style. Wander through the impeccably whitewashed streets and if you feel like staying the night, consider the Hospederia del Convento de San Francisco (Tel: 956-45 10 01).

This is a 17th-century Franciscan convent, restored at great expense. A Roman mosaic adorns the reception wall and some religious murals have been uncovered in the cafeteria. An experienced family of hoteliers runs the hotel and restaurant, which features nouvelle cuisine (open 1.30-3.30pm, 8.30-11pm. Diners, Master, Visa. M-E).

A cheap alternative to the Hospederia is La Posada (Los Remedios, 21. tel. 956-45 02 58), a two-star hostal looking out over the countryside.

Below the village, by the Barbate river at La Barca de Vejer, just off the N340, is Venta Pino, a determinedly rustic establishment noted for its food, but at non-rustic prices (Amex, Diners, Master, Visa. M-E). Opposite you find Cava Real, a bar/ restaurant offering Asturias products, including cider and pungent Cabrales cheese.

From Vejer, you can make a detour through bull-raising country to Medina Sidonia, an archetypal white, hilltop town 16 miles (26km) north via C343. The town is attractive but lacks vitality, perhaps because it is surrounded by large estates and there is little work. The ducal family of Medina Sidonia no longer has any local connections (see Sanlúcar, Excursion 28).

From the ruins of the Arab fort there are fine views. Nearby is the Gothic-Renaissance church of Santa María (La Coronada), with a outstanding Baroque altarpiece. The gossip centre is the spacious Plaza de España, with a handsome town hall. From Medina Sidonia you can join Excursion 28 (Sherry Triangle) at Jerez, passing the 10th century Arco de la Pastora as you leave town. Or you can head north to Arcos de la Frontera to join Excursion 17.

Ten miles (16km) up the coast from Vejer stands Conil de la Frontera, a fishing community popular with Spanish holidaymakers and Germans, who have established themselves in adjacent villa developments. The one-star Oasis hotel (956-44 21 59) on the beach looks as though it needs a refurbish, as does the beach itself.

You are approaching sherry country. Although Chiclana is not officially part of the sherry zone, it produces similar wines. To buy some from the barrel at a reasonable price, turn first right after the N340 crosses the river bridge and you will come across a bodega.

There is not much to delay you in Chiclana otherwise. A road leads five miles (8km) to La Barrosa beach, where a major tourism complex has taken shape, with a golf course and three expensive hotels. Nearby is the former tuna-fishing settlement of Sancti Petri and offshore the waves break over rocky, low-lying Sancti Petri island, where once a Temple of Hercules stood.

You can sample excellent seafood, with a glass of Chiclana wine to wash it down, in local restaurants. El Santuario de Las Carnes (San Antonio, 15. tel 956-40 42 64. Closed Mon), located in an old bodega, specializes in grilled meat.

Drive on towards Seville and the salt-beds and fish farms edging Cádiz Bay. Four miles (6km) from Chiclana lies a T-junction. A right turn takes you directly to Puerto Real, a dismal industrial town. If you turn left, the highway bypasses San Fernando, important as a Spanish naval base, and runs along a narrow causeway to **CADIZ**, squeezed into a narrow peninsula.

Before entering the city, turn right over a bridge that takes you across the bay past shipyards towards Puerto Real. The Cádiz-Seville autopista, a four-lane tollway, starts here and will speed you the 58 miles (93km) to Seville.

Alternatively, head for **PUERTO DE SANTA MARIA**. The scenery is flat and uninteresting, but the Puerto's sherry bodegas and fish restaurants lie ahead.

This is one corner of the Sherry Triangle (see Excursion 28), formed also by **JEREZ DE LA FRONTERA** and **SANLUCAR DE BARRAMEDA**. Follow the N1V past grapevines rolling towards the horizon, bypassing Jerez and continuing north-east along the N1V.

After 36 miles (53km) branch right on the N333 to the village of El Palmar de Troya. Just before it rises a massive domed structure surrounded by high walls.

Appearances of the Virgin here in 1968 and other miracles led to the creation of a bizarre sect headed by "Pope Gregorio XV11". This blind "hammer of heretics" named Franco a saint and has followers in North and South America.

Minibuses arrive daily at the grandiose concrete basilica from Seville, bearing cardinals, bishops and heavily veiled nuns, for a 6pm mass. This is an astonishing performance during which dozens of priests perform elaborate rituals and genuflections before more than 30 altars. To get past the dour guardians at the steel entrance gate you must have arms and legs well covered and women must wear skirts, "respectable" underwear, and head scarves.

You can return to the N1V to reach Seville or continue along N333 over featureless terrain to workaday Utrera (pop. 44,000), noted for its olives and flamenco (the *Potaje Flamenco* held in June is a major flamenco festival).

Worth looking at are the recently restored Moorish castle, the Gothic Santiago church, the 14th century entrance gate Arco de la Villa, the 15th century Santa María de la Mesa church with a splendid facade, the Ayuntamiento, built in 1730 with a rococo facade, and the pleasant Plaza del Altozano. Locals recommend La Brasa restaurant (Rubén Dario, 11. Tel. 95-486 00 33. Closed Thurs.)

From Utrera, the excellent C432 leads to **SEVILLE**, 22 miles (35km) away❑

Excursion 19 - Flamingoes and Ducal Palaces:

Málaga-Estepa-Osuna-Seville
Distance: 140 miles (220km)

All roads lead to **SEVILLE**. This one is the direct route from **MALAGA**, cutting up through the mountain ranges lining the coast and crossing the broad plain to the south of the Guadalquivir river. It passes flamingoes' breeding grounds, Andalusia's cookie capital and a town packed with striking evidence of past grandeur.

From Málaga follow the signs for Granada and Seville and head north up the N331. The road was expanded to four lanes in time for Seville's Expo 92.

An early start is advisable to avoid the worst of Málaga's morning rush hour.

On the left you pass the great wall of the Limonar dam and climb up into the mountains. One or two old steam-rollers have been mounted on pedestals to remind drivers of past construction feats through very difficult terrain.

With a four-lane highway all the way from Málaga to Seville, the journey takes less than two hours non-stop. However, we shall be dawdling on this trip to enjoy some of the worthwhile sights.

After several tunnels, we pass on the left the village of Casabermeja, the elaborate tombs of its cemetery hanging threateningly above us. Approaching the Puerta de las Pedrizas, you see a huddle of houses below to the right. This is Villanueva de Cauche, until recently a strange feudal anachronism.

The whole place belonged to the Marquesa de Cauche. Owners of houses built on her land paid an annual rent of one hen, or two hens if they had a patio. In 1989, the Marquesa agreed to sell out to the tenant farmers for a nominal sum.

After a right fork to Granada, the Antequera and Seville road undulates along between cornfields and bare rocky peaks until it descends quite abruptly offering a panoramic view over the fertile plain around **ANTEQUERA**.

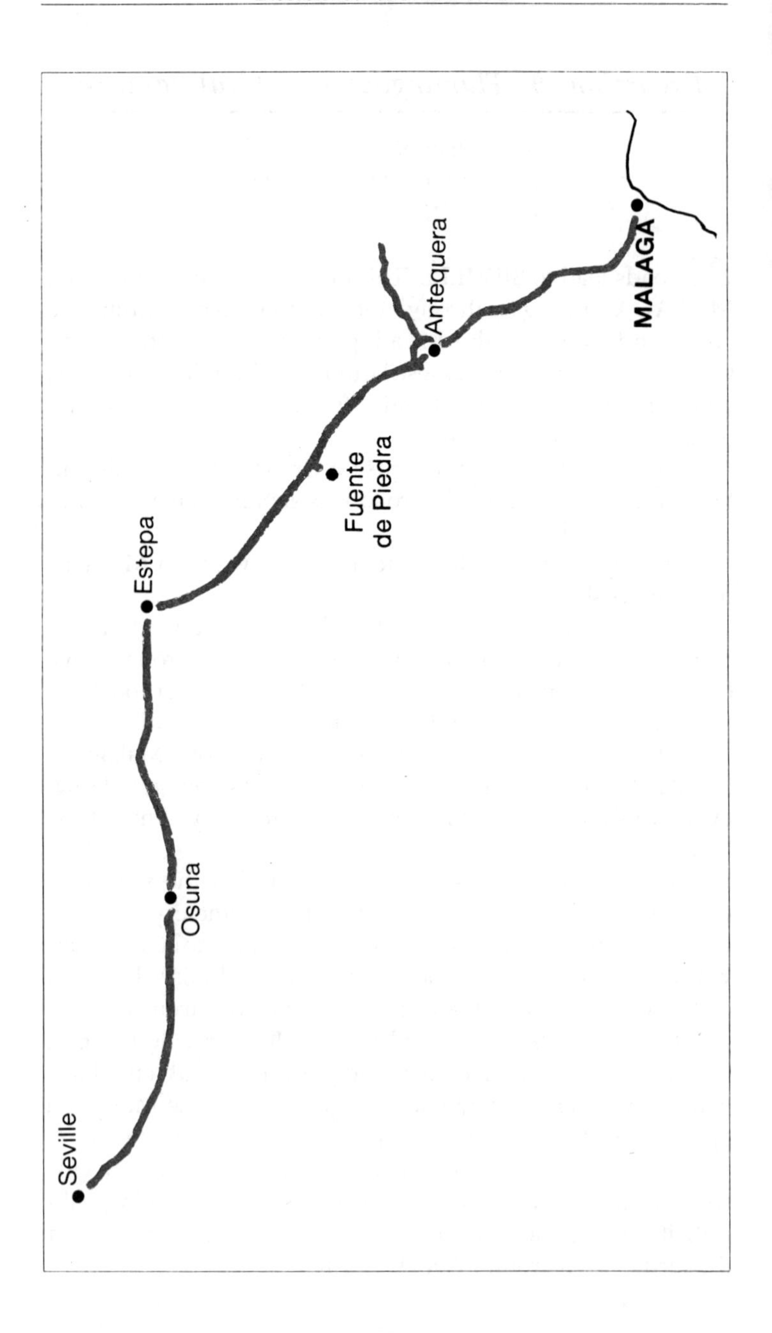
Seville
Osuna
Estepa
Fuente
de Piedra
Antequera
MALAGA

The main highway loops around that town to join the A92 heading northwest towards Seville.

A right turn on MA704 brings you to Mollina, around which most of the grapes for Málaga wine are grown. You can buy several excellent wines from the Tierras de Mollina bodega, which has ultra-modern installations at number five on Calle Fuentepiedra.

At Fuente de Piedra, a little further up the A92, ornithologists can make an interesting detour. Turn into Fuente and take the road towards Sierra de Yeguas. Just before a bridge over a railway line a dirt road on the left leads to the *Centro de Recepción* for the Laguna de Fuente de Piedra. The 3,500-acre Laguna (lake) and the Camargue in France are Europe's most important breeding areas for flamingoes.

In spring and early summer thousands of flamingoes make their home here. Evening is a good time to watch them drifting over the lake and occasionally taking flight. The lake itself is sealed off, but the AMA (Agencia de Medio Ambiente) centre (tel. 95-211 10 50) will give you information and advise where you can get close enough to have a good view with binoculars.

Back on the Seville road, we cross the border into Seville province. Approaching Estepa on its hill, there are wide vistas of olive groves and cornfields. This is La Campiña, an area of large estates, landless peasants, historic towns, and broiling heat.

The autoroute swings around the town, but the old N334 enters through a modern section with ugly new buildings. Approaching Christmas the air is sweet and heavy as the many factories move into high gear to produce tons of *polvorones,* sweet, crumbly cookies. This is a major industry in Estepa and many travellers stop to buy boxes of the various types, including *roscos* and *mantecados.*

Ostippo to the Romans, Istabba to the Moors, Estepa (pop. 10,000) is worth a halt. Climb up through the old part of town, traditionally Andalusian with its close-packed whitewashed houses, tiled roofs and ironwork balconies. Crowning the heights above ancient walls is a complex of convents and churches.

The 16th-century Santa Clara convent has a beautiful patio shaded by a palm tree and its main retable mixes Baroque and Plateresque styles. Knock on the convent door if you wish to buy some of the delicious sweets made by the nuns. The fortress-like Santa María church next door, built on the site of a mosque, has a 15th-century Gothic interior.

Just below is the Balcony of Andalusia, a great viewing point for the patchwork panorama of La Campiña and the roofs and steeples of Estepa, including close at hand the elegant, free-standing 160-foot-high Torre de la Victoria, a national monument. Opposite the town hall (which contains the tourist information office, tel: 95-482 10 00) on the Plaza del Carmen your eyes will be dazzled by the Baroque facade of the Carmen church.

An old refrain warns *"Si llevas dinero a Estepa, que ni el alcalde lo sepa* (If you take money to Estepa, keep it quiet - even from the mayor)." But you will find today's townspeople friendly and helpful. In ancient times they gained fame for their heroism when the town was captured by the Romans in 27 BC. They set fire to the town and died in the flames rather than go into slavery.

Estepa's restaurants and hostals are concentrated on the Avenida de Andalucía.

Some nine miles (14km) northwest of Estepa, via SE 735, lies the village of Marinaleda, the very name a rallying call to those demanding agrarian reform. Villagers decide important issues at communal meetings and their crusading mayor has frequently staged occupations of large estates with landless labourers. Note the revolutionary names of the streets.

West along the A92 through big sky country, we pass in early summer a countryside ablaze with wild flowers; rapeseed and sunflowers spread yellow carpets over the land. But by high summer the land is burned brown by the relentless sun.

Turn off the highway to enter OSUNA, a small town of 17,000 inhabitants but with abundant evidence of past grandeur. Old palaces with noble facades dot the streets dating from the times when the Dukes of Osuna ruled here and spent lavishly.

At the top of the town is the former university, founded in 1549 by the first duke's father. It is now a secondary school.

Next to it stands surely the most outstanding building, the Colegiata de Santa María de la Asunción, an immaculately-restored Renaissance church with a beautiful columned patio, magnificent Mudejar ceilings of tiles and wood, and ornate altars (there are five works by Ribera). Look for the life-sized polychrome of the Virgin and Child in the sacristy. Her stomach hinges open to reveal a storage place for the host.

Beneath the church is the pantheon still in use by the Osuna family. If you are surprised by the smallness of the niches, it is because only the bones are stored here.

Fourteen nuns, in white robes with black cowls, live at the Monastery de la Encarnación, located just below the Colegiata. The 16th century building, now a museum, has many religous treasures, including polychrome carvings and rich brocades made by the nuns.

Some of the most impressive house facades, including that of the Counts of la Gomera, are on San Pedro street. Afternoons are probably best for taking pictures here, when the ornate designs are highlighted by the sun.

Stews and *ardoria*, a type of *salmorejo* (made of bread, olive oil, vinagre, tomato and salt and served cold), are typical local dishes.

From Osuna, it is a fast run across the wheatfields of La Campiña to Seville, which can be reached in under an hour.

A short detour to the north on SE701 brings you to Marchena, an ancient town on a fertile valley. Its Arab walls date from the 12th century and it is dotted with fine old churches. Marchena enjoyed a golden age more than 300 years ago, when it was under the sway of the Dukes of Arcos.

Or turn left at La Puebla to drive 12 miles (20km) on SE451 to Morón de la Frontera. Standing on a hill, Morón has the ruins of a Moorish fortress with the Gothic-Renaissance San Miguel church below and steep streets. Nearby is a United States Air Force base. Rejoin the A92 at El Arahal.

Twelve miles from Seville, the highway skirts Alcalá de Guadaira, a name derived from the times of Moorish settlement when it was known as Al Kalat Wad Aira. About the only reason to stop here is to view the impressive castle, with seven of its 11 towers surviving, built in the Almohad era.

Passengers wanting to retain their romantic illusions should close their eyes for the final run from Alcalá into **SEVILLE**. The highway is lined by a depressing jumble of warehouses, apartments and other characterless buildings.

Drivers are advised to put all items of value out of sight, as a popular pastime among some Seville youths is to wait for visitors' cars at traffic lights on this road, grab anything they can and take off on motorcycles.

Don't get caught. It could spoil your stay in one of Europe's most fascinating cities❑

Excursion 20 - Land of the Caliphs:

Málaga-Antequera-Lucena-Cabra-Montilla-Córdoba
Distance: 110 miles (175km)

CORDOBA, once the most important city in Europe when it was the centre of an Arab kingdom, is easily reached from **MALAGA**.

Road improvements, including doubling the width of the highway for much of the route, have considerably reduced driving time - unless you choose to linger as we pass through an area producing some of Andalusia's best wine.

Take the four-lane N331 to Córdoba from Málaga. On the left you pass the Limonar dam as the road climbs into the mountains. One or two old steam-rollers have been mounted on pedestals to remind drivers of past construction feats through very difficult terrain. This road cuts through the rocky barrier that shields the Costa del Sol from the more severe climate of the interior.

After several tunnels, we pass on the left the village of Casabermeja and directly above the highway the Oriental-style tombs of its cemetery. After a right fork at the Puerto de las Pedrizas, where the N321 heads east towards Granada, the Córdoba road undulates along between cornfields and bare rocky peaks until it descends towards **ANTEQUERA**.

You have a panoramic view over the fertile vega (plain) around Antequera. The N331 loops around that town and runs north past broad fields before rising into hillier country as it passes into Córdoba province.

Pause to enjoy the view as you approach Benamejí. A bypass jumps across the valley, but the old road passes over a handsome bridge across the Genil River and winds up the other side to the village. The houses of Benamejí balance spectacularly on the brink of the eroded valley. In heavy rains the earth cracks and dwellings have toppled over the edge.

Unlike most of the towns in this area, the streets of Benamejí are broad and straight, laid out in an orderly grid by Hernan Ruiz, a noted Córdoba architect also responsible for the bridge

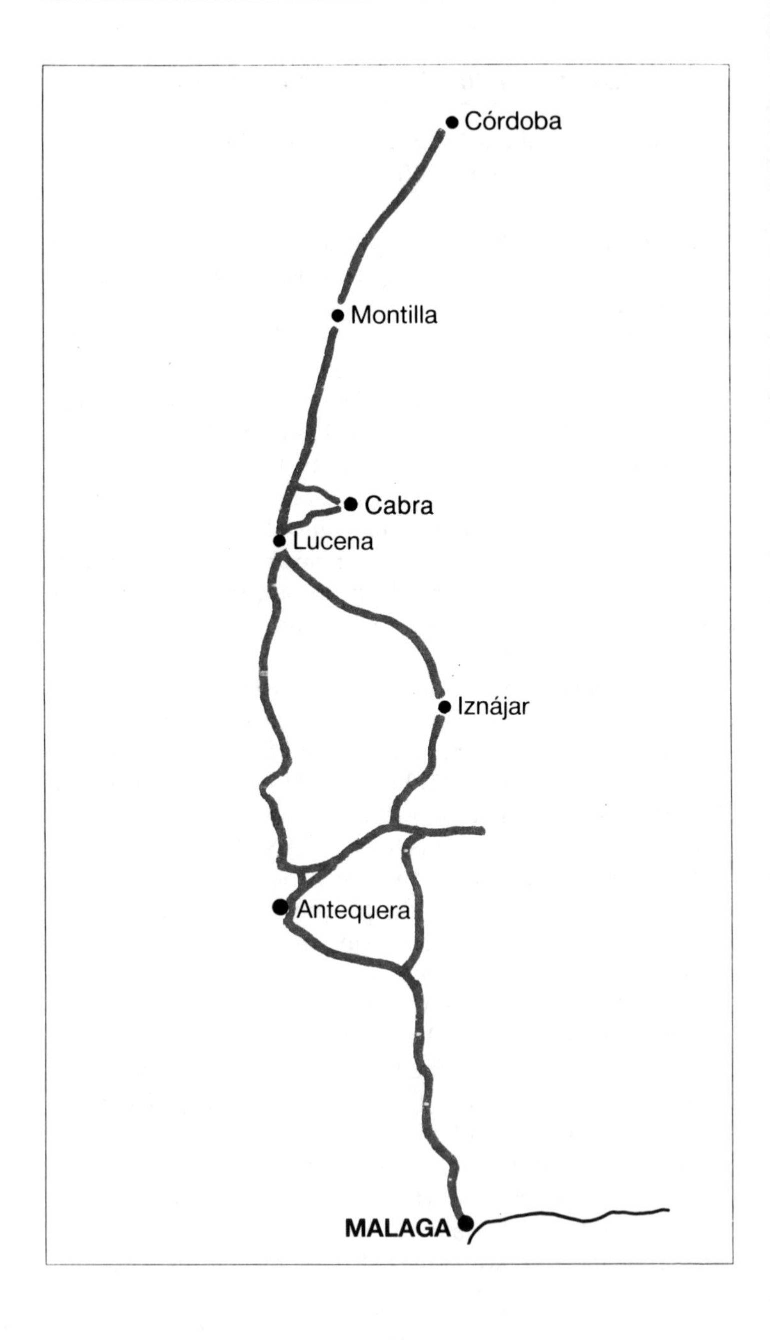
Córdoba
Montilla
Cabra
Lucena
Iznájar
Antequera
MALAGA

over the Genil.

Olive groves and fields of grain stretch on either side as we pass Encinas Reales and head for Lucena. Furniture factories and showrooms offering gleaming brass and copperware, a famous local product, are sprinkled along the highway. Several potters also work away at their wheels in Lucena (pop. 32,000), turning out *botijos* - the earthenware drinking vessels - and other traditional pots.

Under the Caliph of Córdoba, Lucena, with its prosperous community of Jewish merchants, enjoyed virtual independence. The site of the mosque and an academy of Talmudic studies is said to be Santiago church, a national monument. In the last days of the kingdom of Granada, the Moorish king Boabdil was imprisoned in Lucena's Torre del Moral.

Three miles (5km) from town the sanctuary of the Virgin of Araceli occupies a 2,800-foot-high hilltop, from where there are excellent views of the surrounding countryside. In April the Virgin is carried down to the church of San Mateo amid great emotion and excitement and on the first Sunday in May the Fiestas Aracelitanas are celebrated to pay due homage.

From Lucena, you can side-track on the C327 to Cabra, at the geographical centre of Andalusia and with architecture reminiscent of the Moors. Near the castle is Asunción church, built in the 15th century over a mosque. It has magnificent Baroque choir stalls and an altar of red and black jasper.

The Mesón del Vizconde restaurant (Martín Belda, 16, tel. 957-52 17 02, open 2-4pm, 9-11pm. Closed July. Amex, Diners, Master, Visa. M) enjoys local renown. It has fast, friendly service, decor in Sophisticated Rustic, and such specialities as *perdiz acebollada* (partridge with onions) and aubergines stuffed with salmon.

Out of town on the Priego de Córdoba road is La Fuente del Río, a pleasant tree-shaded picnic and swimming spot. Off the C336 to Priego is the Virgen de la Sierra shrine, a hilltop temple that attracts many pilgrims, including gypsies attending the Romería de los Gitanos in June.

From Lucena, the N331 proceeds north. A lofty clock-tower pierces the sky above Aguilar, standing above the undulating landscape of sunbaked earth, olives and vines marching into the distance. Thread your way through Aguilar's narrow streets to the unusual eight-sided plaza of San José, on which stand the Ayuntamiento and El Tuta tavern, where you can try the local wine. Nearby is the Torre del Reloj, a fine brickwork structure built in 1774.

Lucena to Montilla is the heart of the officially denominated region of Montilla-Moriles wine, which is produced in exactly the same way as sherry but so far lacks sherry's international reputation.

In the solera system, new wine is blended over the years with older wines as it is decanted through a series of barrels. In this way the final result - whether it be dry fino, nutty amontillado, aromatic oloroso, or ultra-smooth Pedro Ximénez - always has the same quality and characteristics.

At Montilla, turn off the main highway and then right into the town. The largest bodega, Alvear, is a few hundred yards along, facing a park. You can visit the winery between 9am and 1pm, but call previously to arrange a time (957-65 01 00). You will get to sample the wine and you can buy it at good prices at the shop to the left of Alvear's main entrance. One wine unlikely to be on sale there is Solera Fundación. This highly-prized dry amontillado is 200 years old.

Pérez Barquero (Avenida Andalucía, 27. tel. 957-65 05 00) also welcome visits if you call first. Their amontillado and oloroso are among the highest rated of Montilla wines. Live several other Montilla bodegas, they also produce a less alcoholic white table wine.

Long narrow streets penetrate the heart of Montilla (pop. 22,000), birthplace of the great warrior El Gran Capitán but with few outstanding sights. The public library is housed in the building where Garcilaso de la Vega, a Spanish Inca, laboured over his translations and works on the Inca empire. Ask for La Casa del Inca (Capitán Alonso de Vargas, 3. Open 10am-1.30pm, 5-9pm).

Montilla has several tapa bars and restaurants. Typical local dishes are available at Las Camachas (Ctra Córdoba-Málaga km 45, tel. 957-65 00 04. Amex, Diners, master, Visa. M).

For an overnight stop, the most comfortable spot is the three-star Hotel Don Gonzalo (Ctra Madrid-Málaga km 447. Tel: 957-65 06 58). It has a swimming pool, an important point in the heat of summer.

North of Montilla, the vineyards become sparser and you enter country sown with sunflowers, grains, and more sunflowers. If you are a ceramics freak, turn left to the town of La Rambla where dozens of family firms turn out brightly decorated jugs and vases. Makers of the more restrained traditional styles are a dying breed.

Head back to the N331 to reach Montemayor, a sleepy town with a 16th century parish church. Beneath the church is the Museo de Ulia, a museum of artefacts, mostly Roman, found in the area. The priest, Pablo Moyano, has the key as it is his personal collection. Behind the church is an esplanade with a fine view of country and castle, the latter owned by the Duquesa de Frias.

From Montemayor, it is a run of 22 miles (35km) along the N1V to the Guadalquivir River and **CORDOBA**.

Note: Between Antequera and Lucena, a recommended detour offers interesting landscapes along a slower, less-travelled route.

At the Puerto de las Pedrizas, instead of continuing towards Antequera take the N321 towards Granada. After 14 miles (22km) the Seville highway, the A92, merges from the left at Estación de Salinas. Turn left and then take the first right turn signposted to Iznájar and Rute.

Just up this road, the C334, a sign on the right points to La Bobadilla. A private road leads a mile through olive groves to this ultra-luxury hotel ensconced in gardens in its private valley. It features a wide range of sporting activities and an outstanding restaurant. Prices are to match, but the Spanish king could just be sitting at the next table. (Finca La Bobadilla, Ctra. Loja-Sevilla, desvio Las Salinas. Tel: 958-32 18 61)

If your pocket cannot stretch to such luxuries, continue north. The C334 winds through beautiful rolling country until you sight a vast expanse of blue water, with the castle-capped town of Iznájar bestriding a rock above it.

This is the Iznájar reservoir, more romantically termed the Lake of Andalusia. It blocks the course of the Genil River, which springs from the Sierra Nevada, to form a 20-mile-long lake with a capacity of 98 million cubic metres.

It is worth driving to the top of the town (pop. 6,000) to drink in the tremendous view and enjoy the perpetual breeze. You will find yourself on the Cruz de San Pedro street, which ends at a flowered cross on a balcony overlooking the lake. On a neighbouring hillock the old Moorish castle frowns down on the humble rows of houses.

At the lakeside a side-road leads a mile to Valdearenas beach. There is a camping area and the chance to picnic, fish, water-ski.

Continuing the nine miles (14km) to Rute, the road pursues a lofty course above the lake, offering long vistas of shimmering water and olive-clad hills. Broom, giant fennel, snap dragons and sage clothe the roadside.

Rute (pop. 10,000), benefitting from the good water from the hills behind it, has developed a wellknown aniseed liquor industry. The anise comes sweet or dry. The sweet is very sweet and highly potent. The dry, or *aguardiente,* is around 55 per cent alcohol, so watch out.

Rute has a two-star hotel, the María Luisa (Ctra Lucena-Loja, km 22, tel. 957-53 80 96), a modern three-storey establishment with gardens, pool and jacuzzi.

From Rute to Lucena, an improved road runs 14 miles (22km) through pleasant hilly country with the Virgin of Araceli sanctuary crowning a hill to the west. At Lucena you join the N331 to Córdoba❑

Excursion 21 - The Old Road to Granada:

Málaga-Colmenar-Alfarnate-Riofrío-Loja-Granada
Distance: 80 miles (130km)

Warring armies found it hard going trying to assault **GRANADA**, high in its mountain stronghold. Modern roadbuilders have made the journey from the coast much simpler. The direct route, via the N331, the N321 and then the A92, is a four-lane autoroute for most of its length, speeding you the 77 miles (124km) in under 90 minutes.

Along the Old Road to Granada it is a different matter - and much more interesting. This route wriggles and winds through fascinating scenery, visits bandits' haunts and drops in for lunch by a teeming trout stream before eventually pointing you towards the Sierra Nevada and the Alhambra.

Alternatively, you can branch back to Málaga via the fast modern highway and make this a pleasant round trip.

The old road, the C345, leaves Málaga on the Camino de Colmenar, a continuation of Calle Cristo de la Epidemia, passing the San Miguel cemetery on the left. Look for signs to Colmenar and Loja.

The road spirals upwards, at two points running through a tunnel and doing a 360-degree loop to pass over itself. This area is part of the Montes de Málaga, until a century ago renowned for their vineyards. Málaga wine, sweet and potent, was internationally popular. But the dreaded phylloxera, a small bug, killed off the vines and delivered a deadly blow to the Málaga wine industry from which it has never fully recovered.

There are many spots where it is worth halting to look back to Málaga and the coast far below. Ventas dot the route. At weekends, particularly during the winter months, thousands of malagueño families trek up here to enjoy long, noisy lunches.

Málaga folk say the further you travel from the city the better the food. Los Olivos and El Boticario are two recommendations, but don't look for much sophistication in venta atmosphere. They offer cheap and cheerful eating in vast, stark dining rooms. The hubbub is part of the fun. A popular dish is

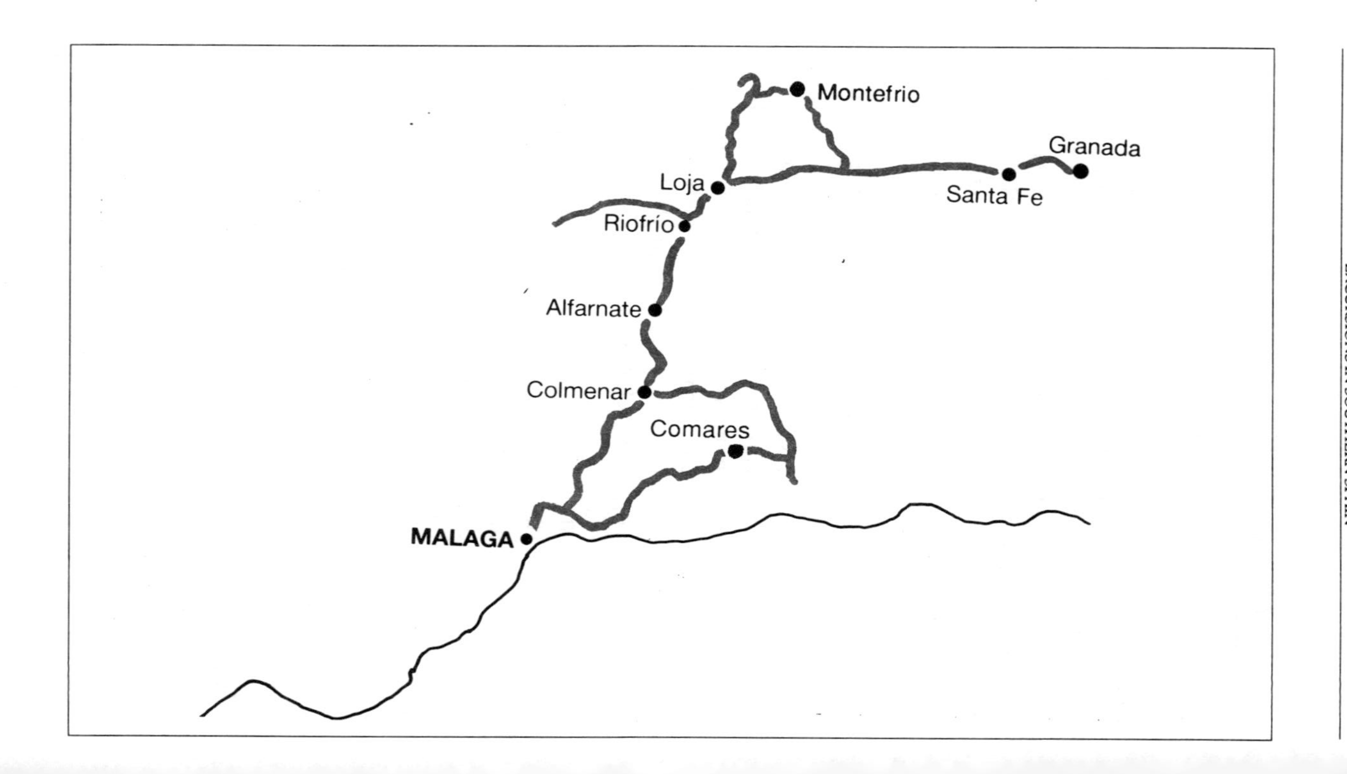
Montefrio
Granada
Loja
Santa Fe
Riofrío
Alfarnate
Colmenar
Comares
MALAGA

the *plato montes,* a gut-filling, cholesterol-heavy plateful of fried peppers, chips, sausage, egg and other ingredients, washed down with *vino del monte,* Málaga wine from the barrel.

We pass along the edge of the 4,900-hectare Montes de Málaga nature park. Carpeting the rolling hills are pines, oaks, olives, carobs, cypresses and poplars, and many shrubs, from spiny broom to asparagus ferns.

Walkers can trek the network of trails through the Montes, maybe catching sight of foxes, badgers, wild cats, chameleons and other wild life. Short-toed eagles, barn owls, kestrels, and partridge are among the bird species.

The road climbs upwards on the Cuesta de la Reina and storms over the Paso de León, 3,000 feet above sea-level. Near the Fuente Reina venta, a turning to the left leads to a recreation area known as Torrijos.

Here there is an old farmhouse, with ancient wine-pressing equipment. There are plans to create a museum. Meanwhile, to gain access, ask AMA, the Andalusian environmental agency (tel. 95-222 58 00) for permission to see the "museo etnológico".

Just after the pass, you can make a detour to one of Andalusia's most dramatically situated villages. Turn right on the MA113, which zig-zags back to the coast via Olias, and then branch left to Comares.

Spreading like a snowdrift over a mountain peak at 2,100 feet above sea-level, surrounded by olive groves, almond trees and vineyards, this village is known as the Balcony of the Axarquía.

Two towers remain of the Moorish fortress, near to the cemetery, with its tombs five decks high.

By tradition (and depending on the parish priest), on Sundays and holidays the church bell is tolled 30 times. This dates from the Reconquest, when 30 Moslem families converted to Christianity and were baptized in the street known as the Calle del Perdón.

Ask in the village about visiting the Mazmúllar cistern. A yard-wide hole in the hillside leads to a gallery of interesecting passages, forming nine compartments with domed ceilings. This was apparently built by the Moors around the 12th century to store water.

You can refresh yourself and try the tapas in the bar on the plaza, or try one of the nourishing stews at the Atalaya (tel. 95-250 92 08), a new one-star hotel with just six bedrooms.

From the village a recently-improved road snakes down the hill to join the MA 159. Turn right to head towards **VELEZ-MALAGA** and join Excursion 15 or 16. Turn left to return to the old Málaga-Granada road, following the fertile Río de la Cueva valley. A good spot for a snack is the Bar Ortega. It lies off the road to the right, five miles (8km) before Ríogordo, a quiet village which attracts thousands of visitors to its Holy Week presentation of a passion play.

You end the detour when you join the C345 again at Colmenar, amid spacious vistas of cornfields and bare, eroded summits. The name Colmenar (meaning "beehive") is said to derive from the local people's enthusiasm for beekeeping. It is a typical white village, the parish church tower rising above the jumble of tiled rooftops.

Legend has it that the Ermita de la Candelaria was constructed by Canary Islanders in thanks for being miraculously saved when a storm threatened their boat off Málaga, though why they came so far inland is a mystery.

After Colmenar, swing right on the MA115, which weaves upwards through craggy country, past a massive black rock known as the Tajo de Gomer. At a junction, where roads lead off to Alfarnate and Alfarnatejo, stands the Venta de Alfarnate, a beamed and whitewashed structure that has accommodated travellers for centuries (tel. 95-275 92 35, open 11am-7pm every day).

This venta claims to be the oldest inn in Andalusia, dating back to 1691. At weekends it is usually crowded with trippers, local girls hurrying between the tables to serve smoked pork and baby goat stew. Those with mega-appetites should order *huevos a la bestia,* a mighty dish of local specialities.

On the walls are newspaper cuttings recalling the history of the Venta, including an amusing tale about a visit by one of last century's most notorious bandits, El Tempranillo. His most famous saying was "The king may reign in Spain, but in the sierra I do."

There were certainly plenty of cut-throats about this area in the past and, during the 1940s, leftwing rebels roamed these mountains in a vain bid to challenge Franco's regime.

From the venta the road climbs again to Los Alazores pass, 3,300 feet up, and once past the border of Granada province becomes the GR115.

We follow the cultivated valley of the Río Frio, the Sierra Gorda soaring 5,400 feet to our right. Olive and almond trees clothe the slopes.

It is time for lunch and Riofrío is nearby. Ignore a sign indicating Estación de Riofrio. Instead, where the GR115 joins the main Antequera-Granada highway, turn left. A short distance along you will see a sign to the right, which leads you under the highway to Riofrío itself, a hamlet with almost as many restaurants as dwellings.

Near to the river where trout idle in the clear water stands a fish nursery with thousands of hatchlings growing fat in the tanks. Trout is the speciality in the pleasantly rustic eating places all around. Prices are very reasonable and you can buy fresh trout to take home.

If time is running out, it is a fast run (43 miles, 69 km) from Riofrío back to Málaga along the A92 and N321.

Continuing towards Granada, you sight the town of Loja (pop. 20,000), straggling below the highway and across the Genil river. It stands on a narrow section of the river valley, a strategic spot on the Málaga-Granada route.

The Moors knew it as Medina Lauxa, until they were ousted in 1486. Walls and towers of their fortress remain. Several convents and churches, including San Gabriel built in 1552 to the plans of Diego de Siloé, are worth visiting. Just east of the town are the Los Infiernos, where the Genil cascades through a narrow gorge.

From Loja, you can make a detour to the spectacularly situated village of Montefrío. Take the N321 north and after 17 miles (28km) branch east, reaching Montefrío after 10 miles (15km). Tourist information is available at the 18th century Ayuntamiento (tel. 958-33 63 35).

High on a crag at one end of the village is the Renaissance church of La Villa (open 10am-1pm, 4-7pm, if closed, for keys call Alfonso Mazuela, 958-31 00 38), built over an Arab fortress.In the centre of town rises Encarnación church (open 10am-1pm, 6-8pm). Unusually for Andalusia, this is in the Neo-classic style to the plans of a famed architect, Ventura Rodríguez. Scores of swifts and swallows have made their nests below the vast cupola.

To the east, the Baroque church of San Antonio, once part of a Franciscan convent, has a Plateresque facade and an 18th century cloister

On a bend as you leave town on the Illora road is Mesón Coroniche (tel. 958-33 61 46, closed Mon), recommended for its kid and the pork products, for which Montefrío is noted. Three miles (4km) further along the road lies a prehistoric burial ground, at the Peña de los Gitanos (open 9am-2pm and usually in the afternoon).

To return to the A92, take the tortuous C335 south over the mountains. The A92 flattens out to cross the Vega of Granada, the fertile plain which runs up to the gates of the city and to the foothills of the Sierra Nevada, whose snows can be seen from some distance.

Armies of poplars march across the plain, planted with tobacco, potatoes, maize and other crops. Just after Granada airport, Santa Fe (pop. 11,000) lies to the right of the highway, seven miles (11km) from the city.

On this spot the Catholic Monarchs camped with their army in 1491, when they were laying siege to the Moorish Kingdom of Granada. The story has it that a royal maid left a candle too close to a curtain in Queen Isabel's tent and flames swept through the campground. King Fernando thereupon ordered a proper town built and Isabel chose the name, which means "holy faith".

Here in Santa Fe the capitulation of Granada was signed in November, 1491, and here the monarchs finally relented and agreed to back Columbus's voyage of discovery, the queen proclaiming that she was ready to pawn her jewels to pay for it

The story is more romantic than the place. Santa Fé is a

prosaic town if ever there was one, with little to remind you of its illustrious beginnings. Four impressive gates admit entrance to the town. Three are said to be original, although most of Santa Fé crumbled in an 1806 earthquake.

There is a bloodthirsty touch in the large central square, but you have to look for it. Opposite the town hall stands the parish church, atop the facade of which, below a cross, is the severed head of a Moor (carved in stone).

GRANADA is waiting, just down the road❑

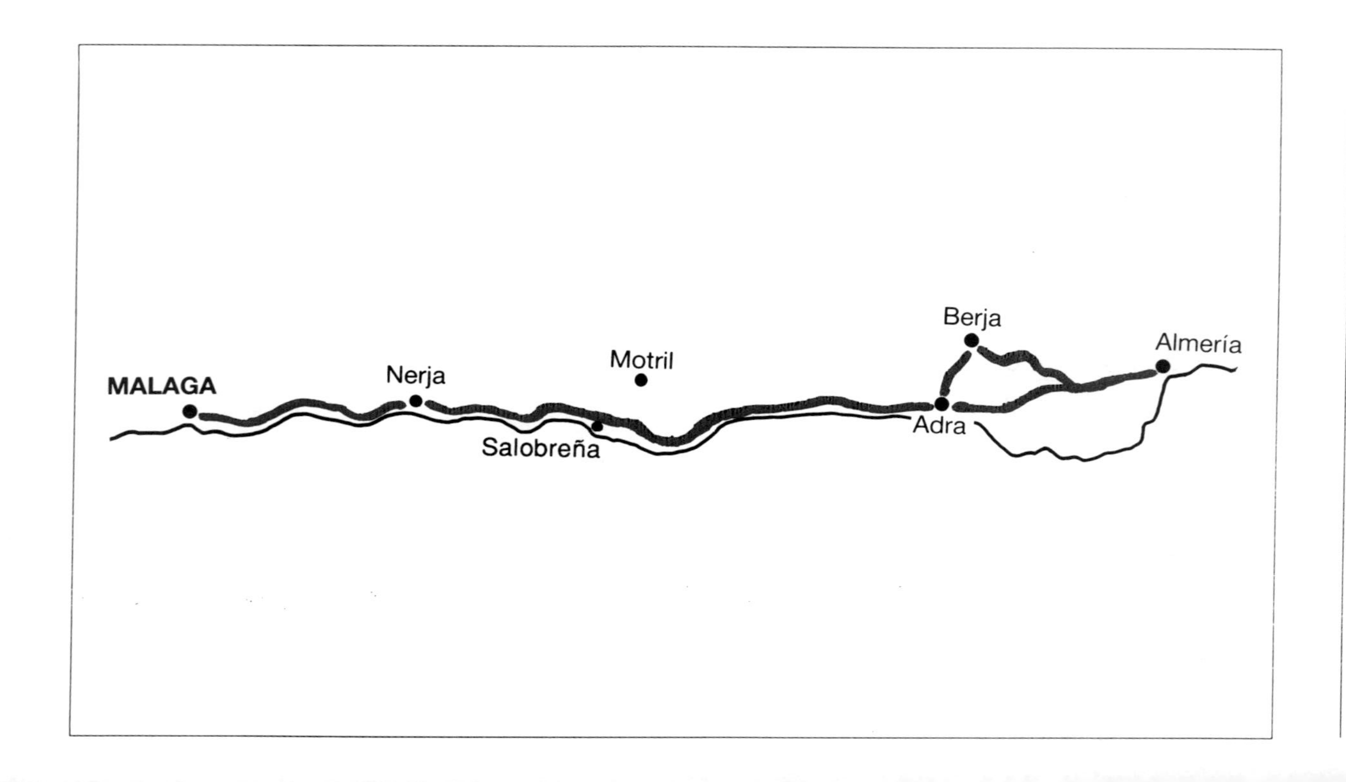
MALAGA
Nerja
Motril
Salobreña
Berja
Adra
Almería

Excursion 22 - Beyond the Costa Tropical:

Málaga-Nerja-Almuñécar-Salobreña-Adra-Almería
Distance: 137 miles (220km)

Spain has many Costas and the most direct route between Málaga and Almería passes through several of them. It is particularly scenic as the mountains plunge steeply to the sea.

The journey used to be an exhausting one, along the narrow coast road, the N340, which swerved alarmingly around tight curves with the Mediterranean looming below.

But a four-lane highway - completed in parts, in construction in others - makes it a faster, more relaxed drive. It can be covered in three hours or less, but there are a number of points where it is worth pausing.

The N340 passes first through the Costa del Sol Oriental, which - as the name suggests - is the section of the Costa lying to the east of Málaga. Until recently this was less developed than the Málaga-Marbella stretch, but that is changing fast.

The first 40 or so kilometres are unexciting. A bypass speeds you past Rincón de la Victoria, a nondescript dormitory town and beach resort popular with malagueños. The only important sight is Cueva del Tesoro, with stalactites, stalagmites and an impressive chamber with pools (open every day 10am-2pm, 3-6pm, varies in summer).

To visit the cave and see if you can locate the gold allegedly once hidden there by five Moorish kings, don't take the bypass but filter right through La Cala del Moral and, before reaching Rincón, turn left following the signs.

Strip development mars the coast towards Torre del Mar, an unlovely maze of high-rise apartment blocks. However, the seafront has been transformed by a fine promenade and gardens. Just inland is the old market town of **VÉLEZ MALAGA** (see Excursion 15 for more details about Torre del Mar, Torrox and the coast in between).

The coast grows more interesting near **NERJA** (pop. 13,000), which is rapidly becoming a year-round resort. It is famous for its palm-fringed promenade (excellent for people-watching) known as the Balcony of Europe and for the Cueva de Nerja, two miles (three km) beyond, near Maro.

The cave, occupied by humans 20,000 years ago, was discovered by boys playing on a hillside in 1959. Only the most blasé can fail to be impressed by its immense chambers and spectacular stalagmites and stalactites. Look for the world's biggest known stalactite, 195 feet by 58 feet, in the Sala del Cataclismo. An international music and dance festival is held in the cave every July.

See the Town and City Guide for more details of accommodation and restaurants.

Beyond Nerja, we leave Málaga province and the Costa del Sol becomes the Costa de Granada. The first section is also known as the Costa Tropical because of the abundance of such fruits as chirimoyas (custard apples), avocadoes, and mangoes, produced in the sheltered climate.

This stretch has the most dramatic scenery on the coast. Mountains leap abruptly into the sea and tracks and footpaths twist down to secluded coves. Crumbling watch-towers stand guard for pirates. Where they once landed armed to the teeth, now you may stumble across naked sunworshippers.

A right turn leads along the old coast road to Cerro Gordo, a towering rocky headland. Climb the path behind the Mirador restaurant (tel. 958-34 90 99, closed Mon, lunch in summer) to visit the watch-tower and enjoy magnificent views.

Continue to La Herradura. Its name comes from the beautiful horseshoe bay, backed by the Punta de la Mona, where expensive residences hide among the trees. Scuba divers can take advantage of facilities at the pleasure port of Marina del Este. Somewhere offshore there are said to lurk the wrecks of 25 galleons.

ALMUÑÉCAR (pop. 17,000) is a favourite holiday spot for Spanish families, most of whom rent or own apartments in the blocks along the beaches. It is pleasant to stroll through the old part of town, a warren of streets, many for pedestrians only. Finally you emerge on a promenade with a line of cafes and sunny terraces.

Known as Sexi to the Phoenicians, the town has remains of

an old Roman aqueduct. La Mazmorra tower, constructed on Arab ruins over Greek and Roman foundations, frowns down on the town.

Almuñécar has several worthwhile restaurants (details in Town and City Guide).

East of Almuñécar, one of the coast's most striking sights comes into view. The Arab citadel of Salobreña - its fortress jutting above white dwellings - floats amid the green ocean of swaying sugar cane covering the fertile Guadalfeo delta.

Plunge into the town's narrow, claustrophobic streets to visit the castle which has an unusual story attached to it (see Excursion 8 for fuller details). Or relax a while on the long beach, divided by El Peñon, a large rock. Tourist information is available at Plaza Goya (tel. 958-61 03 14).

Beyond Salobreña, the highway sweeps straight across the plain, bypassing workaday Motril (pop. 45,000), important as an agricultural and administrative centre (for more information see Excursion 8). The road passes nondescript Torrenueva before climbing again along the precipitous coast.

Calahonda, guarded by an impressive cliff face plunging into the sea, and Castell de Ferro, with its ancient castle, are two pleasant spots to halt for refreshment.

About three miles (5km) after Castell, look carefully and you will see a sign to the left for Polopos. If you want a quick excursion to a typical village tucked away in the great mass of the Sierra de Contraviesa, take this narrow road which rises steeply past almond trees and bare hillsides. The views are tremendous.

Above the village, turn right on the C333 which runs back to the coast at La Rábita, via Albuñol (this area of the Contraviesa produces an unsophisticated but appetising wine).

The beaches along this coast are not too attractive as they are of grey, slaty shingle. Terraced fields rise up the hillsides, many of them now covered with glittering plastic as new cultivation techniques are introduced.

Humble hamlets like La Mamola and Los Yesos dot the N340 before a bypass swings you around La Rábita. This was built after the great 1973 disaster when a cloudburst sent a wall of water rushing down the nearby riverbed and straight through the town, resulted in heavy damage and loss of life.

Entering the Costa de Almería, i.e. Almería province, you bypass the fishing and agricultural centre of Adra (pop. 20,000). It is rather dreary, a suitable spot for the last days on the peninsula of Boabdil, kicked out of his kingdom of Granada. He brooded here before finally taking ship for exile in Africa.

Just beyond Adra you can make a detour up the C331 to Berja, gateway to the Alpujarras region. The town has some fine old houses and grape-growing is important.

The AL401 runs back via Dalías to El Ejido on the coastal highway. A bypass will take N340 traffic around El Ejido (pop. 38,000), sparing travellers a close-up of one of Spain's ugliest towns - and one of the most prosperous.

This was one of Spain's poorest areas, but today El Ejido claims to have more banks per head than any other town - there are a dozen or so along the main thoroughfare. Its headlong growth comes from the boom in growing flowers, fruit and vegetables under plastic. More than 30,000 acres (12,000 hectares) of rocky wilderness have been converted into a colossal greenhouse.

Driving past the endless plastic, you may not be pleased aesthetically but you cannot help but be impressed. Irrigation, fertiliser and a layer of sand to retain moisture are employed to produce hundreds of thousands of tons of produce every year, most of which is trucked off to Northern Europe.

Just outside El Ejido, a right turn leads to the sea and the green oasis of Almerimar, a carefully-planned development complete with a 1,100-berth marina and 18-hole golf course. The Golf Hotel Almerimar (Urb Almerimar, El Ejido. Tel: 950-49 70 50) has comfortable four-star accommodation.

From El Ejido it is 21 miles (34 km) to **ALMERIA**, first crossing flat desert, with plastic greenhouses and nondescript ribbon development. The fast approach is via a new highway that soars high over the rocky barrier before Almería and will eventually link up with a bypass leading to the N344 to Murcia.

Sticking to the old road, you pass a turn to the right leading three miles (5km) to Roquetas de Mar, Almería's biggest seaside resort (see Excursion 38). Then you reach Aguadulce, a characterless high-rise resort with little to detain you.

From there, the old road tunnels through cliffs before emerging to a view of the provincial capital, dominated by its Arab fortress❑

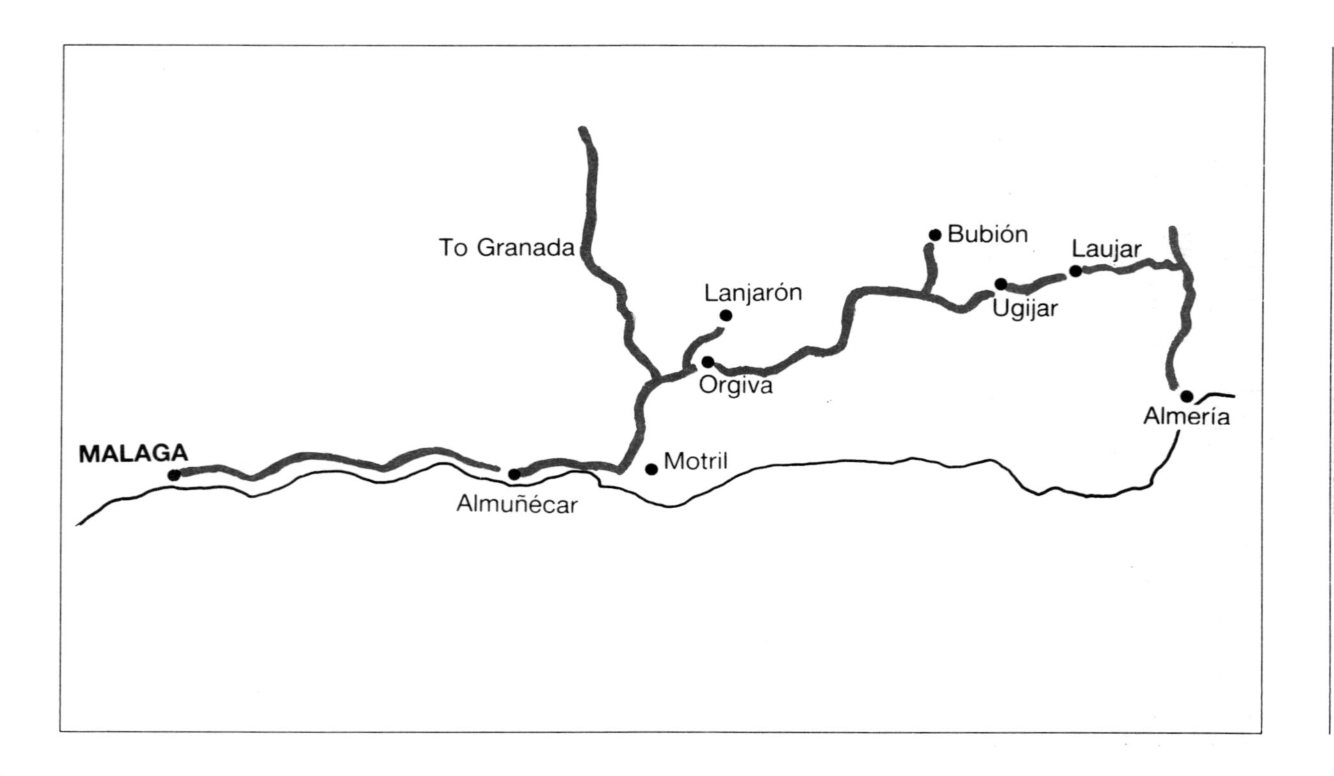
To Granada
Bubión
Laujar
Lanjarón
Ugijar
Orgiva
Almería
MALAGA
Motril
Almuñécar

Excursion 23 - To the Moors' Last Stronghold:

Málaga-Almuñécar-Orgiva-Bubion-Trevelez-Ugíjar-Laujar-Almería
Distance: 175 (280km)

This route demonstrates that the longer way between two points is often the best one. While the easiest and fastest drive from Málaga to Almería lies along the coastal highway, one of Andalusia's most fascinating corners awaits discovery if you detour inland and travel via the Alpujarras. Including an hour for lunch and occasional stops, it is an eight to nine-hour drive to Almería on this somewhat tortuous route.

Driving east from Málaga on the main highway, N340, follow the signs for Almería. Just after Salobreña and shortly before Motril, 60 miles (96 km) from Málaga, the highway crosses the Guadalfeo River.

Turn left on the Granada road, N323. Soon you are passing through a mighty sheer-sided chasm.

After 10 miles (15 km), leave the N323 by branching right across the river, then swinging left to head for Orgiva on the L451, passing a new dam project designed to solve some of the coast's water problems.

Suddenly the heavy traffic is left behind and you are plunging into the world of the Alpujarras, the last refuge of the Moors when the Catholic Kings conquered the Kingdom of Granada in 1492.

Across the Guadalfeo valley to your left rises the great mass of the Sierra Nevada. On its south-facing slopes the Moors instituted ingenious irrigation systems to use the abundant water and grow all manner of fruit and crops. Silk-weaving was an important industry.

Hoping to be left in peace by their conquerors, thousands of Moors converted to Christianity. But these Moriscos, as they were known, suffered continual persecution and finally rose in rebellion in the 16th century. A bloody war ensued in the Alpujarras before the Moriscos were crushed and ejected from their lands.

Only recently have better communications brought the region into closer contact with the outside world.

The splashes of white on distant hillsides are villages founded centuries ago under Moorish rule. Even today dwellings are built in a style similar to that of the Berbers in North Africa, with stone walls and flat roofs of slate and rubble.

The L451 continues east, joining the much-improved C332 to Cadiar, but we turn left across the Guadalfeo to Orgiva. On your right as you approach the town is the Hotel Taray (Ctra Tablate-Albuñol km 18.5, Orgiva, tel. 958-78 45 25). Set amid 15,000 square metres of garden, this three-star hotel is built of traditional Alpujarras materials and has a restaurant, pool, and riding facilities.

Orgiva (pop. 5,000), is the main administrative centre of the region. In the main street you will find several cafes. Check your time with the clock in one of the twin towers of the 16th century church. The previous timepiece, stored in one of the towers, achieved notoriety

The town hall bought it back in 1887 but neglected to pay for it. When the old bill came to light, the shame-faced Ayuntamiento coughed up the 4,000 pesetas owing. But they were 102 years late so they had to pay the clockmaker's 83-year-old grandson.

Expatriates of all nationalities have settled in the Alpujarras, from New Agers and hippies to those just fleeing the ratrace. A fair cross-section attends Orgiva's Thursday morning market when they emerge from their hideaways.

Just beyond Orgiva, at the cross-roads known as El Empalme, stands the Alpujarra Grill (tel: 958-78 55 49), a two-star hotel and useful spot for a meal.

Turn left on C333 for a detour, passing orange groves and olive trees, to Lanjarón six miles (10 km) away. Lanjarón (pop. 4,200) is famous for its waters. Scores of snow-fed springs bubble from the mountain here and each has particular curative properties.

Millions of litres of water are bottled for distribution throughout Spain and thousands of visitors arrive between June and October to take, under medical supervision, bubble baths, water massages and other treatment to improve their health. For information contact the Balneario (Avenida de Andalucía, 1. Tel: 958-77 01 62).

Lanjarón, which lies 30 miles (46 km) from Granada, has quite a few hotels, but many open only from June or July to September, as is the case with the three-star Miramar (Avda Generalísimo, 10. Tel: 77 01 61).

If you turn right at El Empalme, you loop upwards on the GR421 to the higher slopes of the Alpujarras. In spring the white of the almond trees matches the snow on the high peaks. In summer you may catch sight of farmers threshing in the centuries-old way with a mule pacing around a circular stone threshing ground.

Soon you reach Pampaneira, first village of the picturesque Poqueira valley, the most visited place in the region. It is so popular that it can get over-run at weekends.

Three villages are slotted into the valley sides, Pampaneira (pop. 364), Bubión (pop. 335) and at the top Capileira (pop. 605). Far above the valley is O Sel Ling (Place of Clear Light), a meditation centre given its name by the Dalai Lama when he visited.

Hiking opportunities abound and facilities are available for horse treks, mountain biking, and paragliding. Handmade rugs and blankets in traditional Alpujarras style are on sale in many craft shops.

Restaurants offer typical hearty country food at budget prices. Pork, ham and blood sausage, specialities in the Alpujarras, feature in the belly-filling *plato alpujarreño*. Vino de la Contraviesa is served in pitchers. Pink and potent, it comes from the Contraviesa range between the Guadalfeo valley and the Mediterranean.

Pampaneira, closed to traffic but with a large car park at the entrance, has an information office for the Sierra Nevada nature park (tel.958-76 33 01). Mesón Belezmin, in Plaza de la Libertad (tel: 958-76 31 02), offers pleasant outdoor eating on its roof terrace.

In Bubión, Restaurant Teide (tel: 958-76 30 37), on the main road has expanded and lost some of its charm. Penetrate the winding alleys of Bubión's lower quarter where you find the cosy Restaurante Alfajia (tel. 958-76 32 56, open 1-3.30pm, 8-11pm. Closed Mon in summer, Sun night, Mon and Tues in winter. No cards. B). Montse and Gina offer cous cous, vegetarian dishes, and cordero al horno al gengibre (roast lamb with ginger) at good prices.

Unthinking development has not improved Capileira, but it still has delightful views. The Pedro Antonio de Alarcón museum, showing typical artefacts of the region, is located in a typical Alpujarras house (open 11.30am-2.30pm, closed Mon).

Mesón Alpujarreño (Parra,1. Tel: 958-76 30 06, closed Sun night & Mon, no cards) is a cosy family-run spot, with such luminaries as Felipe Gonzalez and poet Rafael Alberti among earlier clients.

A spectacular road, the highest in Europe, climbs above Capileira and runs over the mountains to Granada (see Excursion 36, for full information).

Several hostals offer basic accommodation, but the most comfortable place to stay, as well as being a good place to eat, is the Villa Turística (Barrio Alto, Bubión. Tel: 76 31 11). Built in traditional style, each unit has kitchen facilities and provision for a log fire. Reserve for holiday periods and weekends.

As you continue east along GR421, you pass fields teetering on the edges of dark ravines and groves of chestnut, oak and walnut trees. Between Pitres and Pórtugos, five miles (7 km) from Pampaneira, stands the Virgen de las Angustias chapel. Below it is Fuente Agria. Visitors come specially to fill containers with the naturally carbonated water, rich in iron, gushing from six spouts.

At Pitres, Pilar Montoro runs an immaculate little hotel and restaurant, the Posada-Mesón San Roque (Calle Cruz, 1, tel 958-857486, two-star price range) with rustic flagged floors and typical Alpujarra architecture.

The road runs up a valley to Trevélez (pop. 800), claiming (at 4,840 feet) to be Spain's highest village. In airy sheds, thousands of hams are cured here in the shadow of loftiest peak on the peninsula, Mulhacen (11,420 feet).

Cafes and pensions congregate around the village's lowest

quarter, blighted by modern construction. Climb the winding streets to the upper barrio, where you can sit on the terrace of La Fragua restaurant and one-star hotel (San Antonio, 4, tel. 958-85 86 26) while enjoying some of that cured ham.

Near Trevélez, legend has it, Aben Humeya, leader of the Morisco rebellion in 1568, buried his treasure in a cave. And somewhere near the next village, Juviles, three black diamonds were concealed in a secret palace by Muley Hacen, Moorish ruler of Granada. Keep your eyes open as anybody discovering these diamonds is destined to be crowned King of Granada.

We join the C332 from the little market town of Cadiar, where Aben Humeya was crowned king of the Moriscos. Cadiar has the basic, bargain-priced Hostal Montoro (San Isidro, 20, tel. 958-75 00 68). Continue to Yegen, lying below the road, surrounded by fields of maize and peppers and shady apricot trees.

It has changed a good deal since the English writer Gerald Brenan walked in - there was no road then - and settled in 1920. He vividly recounted his experiences in his book "South from Granada". A plaque marks the house he lived in, paying rent of 120 pesetas a year.

Further east lies Válor (pop. 1,100), said to be the birthplace of Aben Humeya. Every year during the mid-September fiesta, the villagers stage an uproarious Moriscos v Christians battle in the main square to a thunder of shotguns. The play dates from the early 17th century.

Just after Válor, a road branches left to Mecina Alfahar and Laroles. From there you can climb the 6,800-foot Puerto de la Ragua and drive down to **Guadix** (see Excursion 37).

Continuing on C332, we run down a valley to the market town of Ugíjar (pop. 3,100). Plain but comfortable rooms are available at the Hostal Vidaña (Carretera de Almería s/n. Tel: 958-76 70 10), which also has a reasonable restaurant.

Soon we cross the Alcolea River and enter the Alpujarras in Almería province. The scenery grows increasingly arid as we drive east.

Vines flourish around the green oasis of Laujar de Andarax (pop. 1,900), where Aben Humeya was done to death by treacherous followers.

Stop at the Plaza Mayor and refresh yourself at the fountain, next to which a plaque bears an eulogy to the town's water. The lines were written by Francisco Villaespesa, a native son who achieved fame as a poet and dramatist. A nearby cafe, the Bar Rodríguez, sells the local wine.

To the left of the town hall, General Mola street leads towards El Nacimiento, the spring. This is a pleasant picnic spot, although a succession of dry years means you may see little water.

Hostal Fernández (General Mola, 4, tel. 950-11 31 28) offers immaculate, comfortable accommodation to commercial travellers, stray tourists and other intinerants. The friendly female proprietor also serves good-value meals.

Eastwards, the scenery has a bleak grandeur as you follow the Andarax valley with the bulk of the Sierra de Gador to the south.

Canjáyar (pop. 2,100) is spectacularly situated on steep slopes. It has a large church dedicated to the Santa Cruz, a much-venerated cross, and a colourful night procession is a feature of the annual Fiesta de la Santa Cruz, in the second half of April.

Ohanes, a lonely village off the C332 to the north, is particularly famed for its eating grapes and an unusual custom. On April 25, young men lead eight bulls through the streets and persuade them to kneel in obeisance before the image of San Marcos.

As the road begins to descend towards Almería, you see terrace upon terrace of vines, growing tall along wire frames to allow easier picking of the luscious eating grapes.

Soon after the spa of Alhama de Almería you join N324, the Almería-Guadix road which passes the prehistoric settlement of Los Millares (for more information on this section, see side trip from Almería, Excursion 38).

At Benahadux, you reach the Almería-Murcia highway. It is a seven-mile (12 km) drive to **ALMERIA**❑

Excursion 24 - Into the Frying Pan:

Seville-Carmona-Ecija-Córdoba
Distance: 86 miles (138km)

Two of Andalusia's most interesting old towns lie on the direct route between two of the region's most important cities, a route that takes us through an area known for good reason as "the frying pan".

Take the N1V highway to Córdoba and Madrid out of Seville. Once free of the urban sprawl this rolls across La Campiña, a vast plain watered by the Guadalquivir and its tributaries and a battleground in centuries past for a succession of conquerors.

The fields seem to stretch into infinity, forming a vivid pattern of ochres and greens. Wheat, sunflowers, oranges, olives ripen under the strong sunshine.

CARMONA (pop. 24,000), one of Spain's best-preserved old towns, stands above the plain, 20 miles (33km) from Seville. This was a strategic spot in Roman times and many traces remain.

As you enter Carmona, in the newer part of town, a sign to the left indicates the *Necropolis romana.* This is a remarkable funeral ground, excavated by British archeologist George Bonsor between 1881 and 1915.

It has 900 family tombs dating back to 200 BC, including the Servilia, the size of a patrician villa, and the elaborate Elephant Tomb, with the statue of an elephant at its entrance.

Driving on you reach the walls, pierced by one of Carmona's four Roman entrances, the Seville Gate. The battlements can be visited at weekends. It is a lung-and-legs-testing climb, but there is a fine view over the old town.

Carmona's fourth gate was discovered by chance in 1986. Wandering through the town, you will come across the others, as well as noble residences, ancient churches and convents. Not surprisingly, the town itself is a protected national monument.

Even if you are not staying overnight, visit the Parador, a

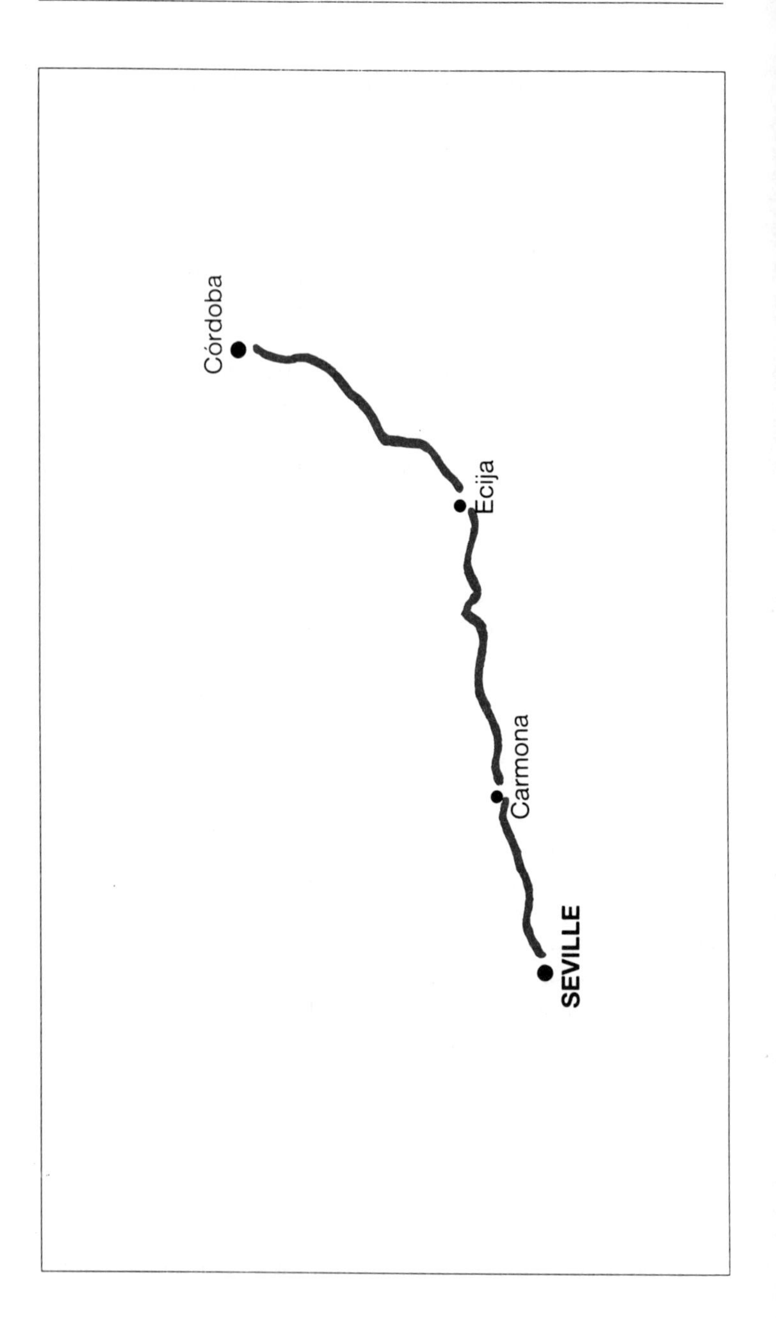
Córdoba
Ecija
Carmona
SEVILLE

state-run hotel located in the castle once occupied by King Pedro the Cruel. It has spacious public rooms and a beautiful Arab patio. From the terrace atop the ramparts you have a breath-taking view over the Campiña.

From Carmona, you can switch to Excursion 25 by taking the northbound C432. Passing cereal crops, sugar-beet, asparagus and orange orchards, you cross the river and join the C431 at Lora del Río, 17 miles (27km) from Carmona.

For this excursion, however, we continue east. It is an easy drive from Carmona across the plain to Ecija, 34 miles (56km) away, passing large estates but no settlements of any size. The run gives an idea of Andalusia's agricultural wealth. Grain crops flourish and - here and there - fighting bulls too. The home of the much-feared Miura bulls is off to the left, north of La Campiña.

Spring is delightful in this area. Poppies splash crimson over the verges and crops stretch away in a sea of green. But in summer farm workers begin their day at 6am and head for home by midday. The sun hammers down with rare intensity and temperatures soar to 45 degrees C and higher.

Not for nothing was the siesta invented here. You are in the Frying Pan of Andalusia. By September, when the fields are burned to dust, the locals are praying for rain.

Under the clear blue skies, the 11 towers and 15 belfries of Ecija (pop. 35,000) shimmer as in a mirage. The "City of Towers", on the banks of the Genil river, owes its origins to the Iberians. Romans, Visigoths and Moors passed by, but most of the town's monuments date from the prosperous 18th century.

Churches, some in ruins, appear at every corner, often with tiled belfries. That of Santiago (open in the evenings for mass) is approached through a pleasant arched patio shaded by orange trees. It has an outstanding Gothic retable.

Lined with old buildings, the Plaza de España - popularly known as El Salón (the lounge) - is a favourite spot for strollers and flirters. Around the large central fountain water spouts from pots borne by four female sculptures. Imagination took a holiday, however, when somebody named the establishment in one corner the Bar Gasolina.

Park your car in the Plaza de España. Information pamphlets with maps are obtainable from the tourism office in the town hall (tel. 95-590 02 40), which shelters a second century Roman mosaic.

A side street from leads to the Palacio de Peñaflor. It has an unusual curved facade with frescos. Only the patio and ground floor are open to visitors (10.30am-1pm, 5-8pm. Closed Saturday and Sunday).

Just opposite, a range of typical Seville pottery is on sale. And around the corner, opposite the Valdehermoso palace with its Plateresque facade, you will find the Bodegón del Gallego (Arcipreste Aparicio, 3. Tel: 95-483 26 18. Open 12.30-5pm, 7-12pm. Closed Sun pm, Mon pm in Aug, July. Amex, Diners, Master, Visa. M-E).

This pleasantly furnished restaurant features meat roasted in a wood oven and an unusual mixture of Galician and international dishes.

Another palace is hidden away in the warren of narrow streets. Ask for "La Comandancia" and you will eventually find yourself before the splendid marble front and colossal entrance of the 18th-century Palacio de Benamejí, a national monument.

It is occupied by the military. Ask permission to enter from the soldier on duty (open 10am-7pm). He will show you, on the right, an arched stable with stone drinking troughs and several old carriages and a well-proportioned inner patio.

Ecija - pronounce it "Etheeha" with the emphasis on the first letter - is noted as a military equestrian centre and herds of army horses graze in the surrounding area.

Northwest of the Ecija, the N1V enters Córdoba province and passes through La Carlota. A monument stands here marking an attempt 200 years ago to settle North European immigrants in Andalusia. It was an experiment initiated by King Carlos 111.

Thousands of German and Flemish settlers were lured by promises of 80 acres of land plus two cows, five ewes, five goats, five hens and a sow. Nobody mentioned anything about the Frying Pan of Andalusia, however, and the colonists seemed to have had a hard time in their new towns.

The monument, erected in 1967, renders homage to those who made it possible for "men of diverse nations of Europe, attracted by Andalusia's legendary fame, to transform these sterile and desert lands into industrious towns".

From La Carlota, the highway scales the hills of sunflowers and cereals and runs down into the Guadalquivir valley where the Great Mosque of **CORDOBA** waits to greet the tired traveller, as it has for a thousand years❑

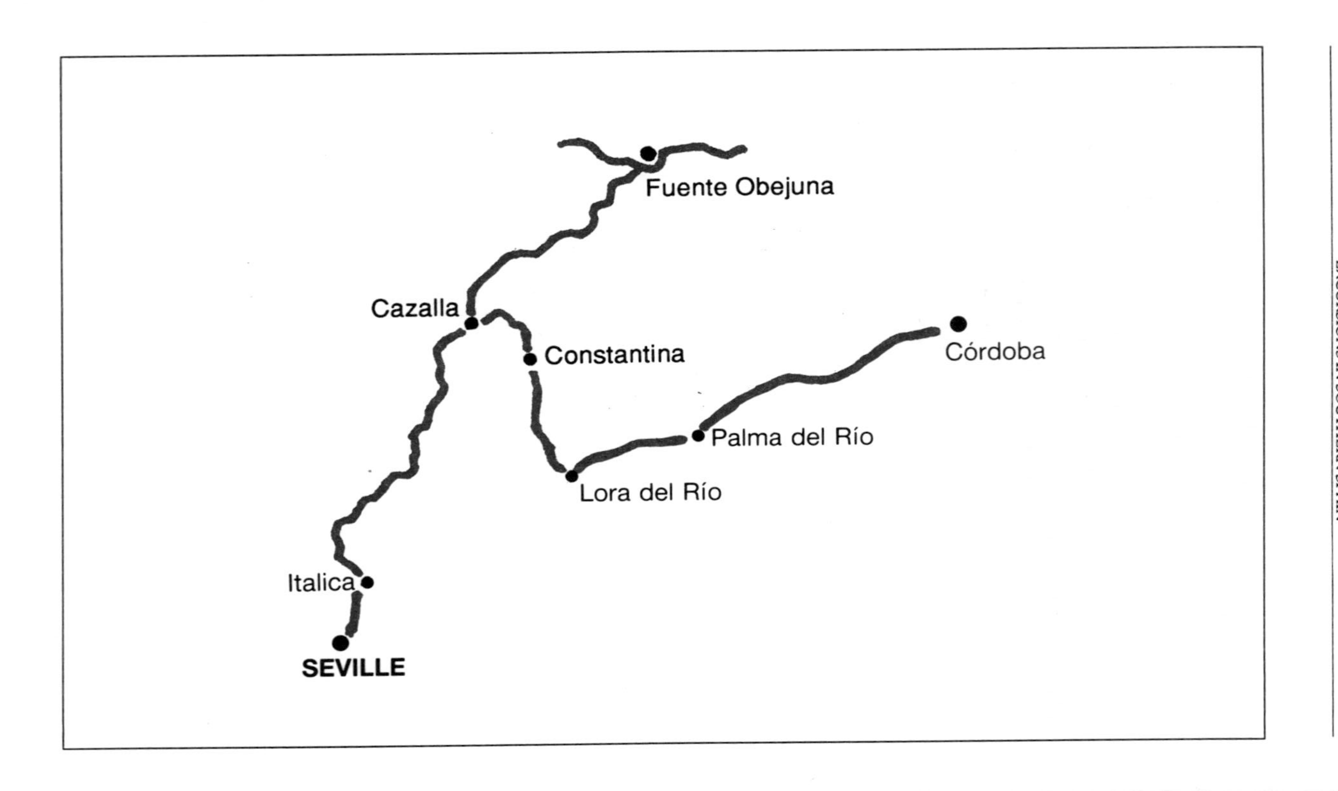
Fuente Obejuna
Cazalla
Constantina
Córdoba
Palma del Río
Lora del Río
Italica
SEVILLE

Excursion 25 - Following the Great River:

Seville-Itálica-Cazalla-Palma del Río-Córdoba
Distance: 137 miles (220km)

Less heavily travelled than the main highway via Ecija, this route from Seville to Córdoba follows the Guadalquivir River and includes a detour through the Sierra Morena, a wild area rich in game.

Leaving Seville, you can take the opportunity to visit the Roman ruins of Itálica by following the Huelva highway across the Guadalquivir then turning right on the Badajoz road, the N630.

Near Santiponce the ruins of streets and and an amphitheatre sprawl across a hillside (open: 9am-6.30pm. Sundays 9am-3pm. Closed: Monday). There is a good view from here of the Guadalquivir plain. The emperors Trajan and Hadrian were born in Itálica.

A little further up the N630, a right turn leads towards La Algaba, the C431 and Alcalá del Río. You can follow the C431 all the way to Córdoba, although the first few miles are of minor interest.

For a more scenic journey, head for the hills, turning left near Alcalá del Río and following the C433 to Cazalla de la Sierra. The country grows wilder as you penetrate the Sierra Morena.

You enter the Sierra Norte nature park, with scrub-covered hills and forests of holm oak and cork oak, sheltering Iberian pigs - valued for their hams - and deer and boar.

At El Pedroso, a halt on the Seville-Zafra rail line, you can eat heartily at the basic bar-restaurant Los Monteros (mushrooms and venison may be available in season). Head east from here on the SE190 if you want information from the Oficina del Parque Natural, El Robledo, Ctra. Constantina, tel. 95-488 01 10.

Continuing on the C433, between El Pedroso and Cazalla you encounter the imposing brick facade of an abandoned bodega, El Galeón. Weeds grow about its 114 huge vats where wine once matured.

When 70 local distilleries were making anise and cherry liqueur, the product was so famous that in parts of Latin America anise was referred to as "El Cazalla".

But the phylloxera bug destroyed the vines and olive trees replaced them. Only three Cazalla brands of anise are left, with an uncertain future

Cazalla de la Sierra, a sleepy white town of 5,000 inhabitants, 590 metres above sea-level, was the summer residence at one time of Spain's Felipe V, lured here no doubt by his passion for hunting. Now it is a favourite bolthole for sevillanos, looking for peace and fresh air.

The most impressive building is the fortress-like Consolación Church. Part of it is 14th century Mudéjar and a series of lofty pillars date from the 15th century.

Three kilometres east of Cazalla, along a dirt track off the C432 to Constantina, in an area where Pedro the Cruel is said to have hunted with the Black Prince, lie the ruins of a 500-year-old Carthusian monastery. Follow the signs for La Cartuja and the Villa Turística.

An English adventurer bought the monastery in 1973, but later it passed to a Spanish company. Carmen Ladrón de Guevara has restored much of the old structure and established an art gallery and a charming small hotel (Hospedería de la Cartuja, Ctra de Constantina, Cazalla de la Sierra, (Sevilla). Tel. 95-488 45 16. Three-star price range).

Birdwatching, riding and art courses are among the activities available.

You can also stay at the Villa Turística nearby (Ctra de Constantina, km 3.5, Cazalla de la Sierra, (Sevilla). Tel. 95-488 3310. Three-star price range). The 39 stone cabins blend reasonably with the landscape, not so the intrusive pool and restaurant.

Continue to Constantina (pop. 7,000), whose name comes from Constantine the Great; in Roman times the local wine, known as cocolubis, was famed throughout the empire. Silver and iron were once mined here. Below the remains of a Moorish fortress tumble the whitewashed houses and narrow alleys of the Barrio de la Morería.

(You can extend your tour of the Sierra Morena by taking the SE163 north and turning northeast at Alanis on the tortuous C421 to Fuente Obejuna in Córdoba province. This town owes its fame to a 15th century rising, recorded by the playwright Lope de Vega in his bestknown work. In 1476, angry townsfolk killed a local tyrant, hacking his body to pieces in the main plaza. Interrogated later about who was guilty, the people replied as one: "Fuente Obejuna, señor!". And nobody was punished. Fuente Obejuna has a one-star hotel, the Comendador at Luis Rodríguez, 25, tel. 957-58 22 11. Beyond lies the Valle de Los Pedroches, a plateau of oaks and granite. A mighty 15th century tower dominates Belalcázar, birthplace of Sebastián de Belalcázar, conqueror of Nicaragua. Outside Pozoblanco, the only town of any size, is the two-star San Francisco, tel. 957-10 14 35.)

From Constantina we head south on the C432 18 miles (29km) to Lora del Río (pop. 19,000), not the most exciting place but the centre of a rich agricultural area. We follow the C431 eastwards along the Guadalquivir, known to the Moors as Wadi al-Kabir, the Great River. Slow and muddy here, it irrigates the big estates that border the river.

Fifteen miles (24km) from Lora we cross the border of Córdoba province and turn right across the river, past the thick green foliage of orange orchards, to enter Palma del Río.

Vestiges of 12th century Moorish walls remain, but Palma is more celebrated as the birthplace of one of Spain's most controversial bullfighters, El Cordobés.

As a poor, barefoot youngster, he used to creep out into the fields around Palma on moonlit nights to practise fighting the bulls. Later when he returned he could afford to treat the whole town to drinks. Fighting bulls are still raised in the area, but Palma (pop. 18,000) wears a more prosperous air now.

Stay the night at the Hospedería San Francisco (Avenida Pio X11, 35. Tel: 957-71 01 83). A 16th-century monastery has been converted into a hotel, using Roman columns and hand-painted tiles. It resembles a small parador, but with more taste and lower charges.

To mark the fact that Fray Junipero Serra probably called here before going off to spread the faith in the New World, the rooms are named after Californian missions.

The restaurant, once the refectory, is something of an oasis in this part of the world and the Basque chef has gained renown, particularly for his game dishes (Open 1.30-4.30pm, 8.30-12pm. Closed Sunday night and first two weeks of August. Amex, Master, Visa. M-E).

A drive up into the hills from Palma takes you to a typical sierra village, Hornachuelos, and into wild country. Go carefully - especially at dawn or dusk - to avoid colliding with deer.

During winter months visitors come from all over Spain and Europe to take part in expensive monterías, in which stags are driven by dog-packs towards the hunters. Some 6,000 deer and thousands of boar are bagged annually in Córdoba province.

If you are in the mood for solitary meditation and tranquillity, you can stay at the Santa María de las Escalonias Monastery, near Hornachuelos (advance booking necessary, tel. 957-71 45 22). This converted cortijo has only three - suitably austere - double rooms and two singles. Silence is the golden rule in the monastery.

Near the river, tobacco, cotton, and asparagus flourish. The cotton is planted in early spring. In October and November expect to see what looks like drifting snow alongside the road. It is in fact stray cotton, as the bolls fall from trucks carrying away the harvest.

The highway is straight and fairly level as we pass Posadas, but then it curves upwards and one of the most striking castles in Spain appears. The battlements of Almodóvar del Río, dating from Moorish times but restored early this century, tower over river and plain. To visit the castle, call 957-63 51 16.

Almodóvar (pop. 7,000) once belonged to the Order of Calatrava. La Taberna (Antonio Machado, 20, tel. 957-71 36 84. Closed Monday and August. Amex, Master, Visa. M) in the centre of the town offers typical Córdoba dishes.

From here it is 15 miles (25km) to **CORDOBA**. Shortly before reaching the city, a left turn will take you up to Medina

Azahara, the palatial 10th-century residence where thousands of dancing girls and serfs once attended to the needs of Abderraman 111.

But you will have more time to examine that at your leisure if you follow Excursion 32 to the Ermitas in the sierras above Córdoba❑

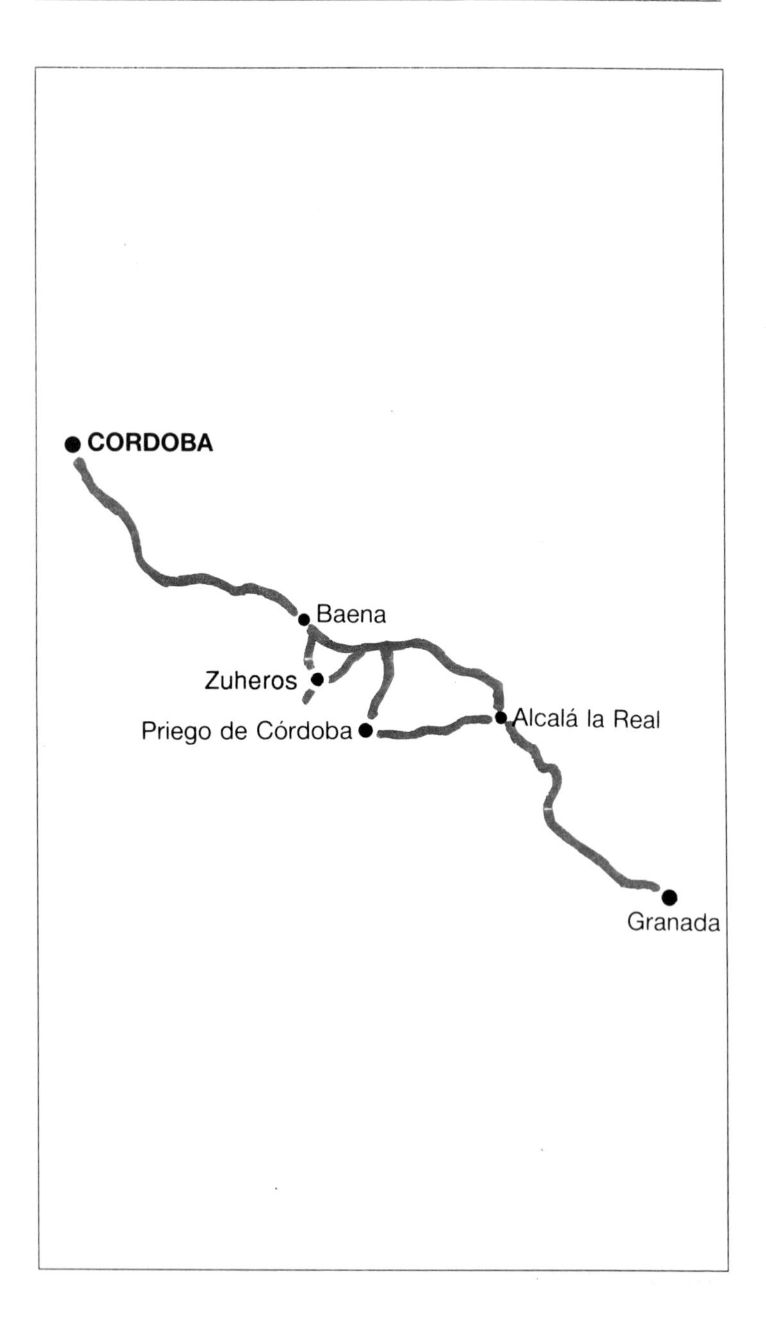
CORDOBA
Baena
Zuheros
Priego de Córdoba
Alcalá la Real
Granada

Excursion 26 - The Sunflower Route:

Córdoba-Baena-Priego de Córdoba-Alcalá la Real-Granada
Distance: 112 miles (180km)

This route heads directly for Granada with a short detour to visit one of Andalusia's prettiest and least-spoilt towns.

Take the N432, which runs southwest from **CORDOBA** along the Guadajoz River through undulating, treeless country. In spring and early summer this is a blazing yellow carpet of sunflowers and dark-green foliage, interspersed with the lighter green of ripening wheat.

By late summer it has been charred brown, with goats wandering over it, seeking stray bits of vegetation in the dusty, heat-cracked soil.

This is Córdoba's Campiña region. It has a feudal air about it, an impression confirmed by the sight of Espejo (pop. 5,000), with its medieval fortress dominating town and surrounding vineyards. The castle belongs to one of Spain's largest land-owning families, the Dukes of Osuna.

In comparison, Castro del Río (pop. 7,800) presents a non-descript aspect. Ask at the town hall if you want to see the room where Cervantes, during his tax-collecting days, was tossed into jail for a week for overstepping the mark.

Fields of garlic, artichokes, wheat and barley flicker past. Approaching Baena, 43 miles (62km) from Córdoba, olives take over. The quality of Baena's olive oil was already a byword 500 years ago. You can buy some direct from a local firm, Abasa, on Ctra Fuente Dueña.

A dazzling snowdrift drifting down its hill, Baena (pop. 19,000) has notable examples of Gothic and Renaissance art. On the top of the town you will find Santa María la Mayor, dating from the 16th century. Nearby is the Madre de Dios convent church with its marble altar. The Dominican nuns make cakes for sale, which you receive via a torno (a turntable which ensures you do not see the nuns). The hours are 8am-2.30pm, 4-7.30pm.

One side of the Plaza de la Constitución is bounded by the

brick facade of the new town hall, another by an old arcaded building. Once a tax office, then a Civil Guard barracks, the latter now shelters a good tapa bar and restaurant, the Mesón Casa del Monte (tel. 957-67 16 75. Master, Visa. Closed Mon). In the brick-arched dining room, you can sample *revuelto de la casa* (scrambled eggs with asparragus, broad beans, and onions) while drinking the local sherry-type wine. Ask for the excellent *fino Cancionero,* aged eight years in the barrel.

Honest food at reasonable prices is also available at the Iponuba restaurant (Nicolás Alcalá, 9. Tel: 957-67 08 99. B). The modern, brick-fronted building also houses the two-star Hostal Iponuba (tel 957-67 00 75). A venta, the Huerta de San Rafael, offers a shady spot to take refreshment, five miles (8km) east along the N432.

Easter Week processions are deafeningly impressive in Baena, as the whole town trembles to the thunder of 7,000 drums.

About two miles (3km) along the N432 out of Baena, look for a new road to the right leading to Zuheros. It passes a hamlet named Marbella before you take a minor road that winds up towards Zuheros, dramatically situated on a spur on the edge of the Sierras Subbéticas nature park, an area of limestone crags, oak trees and wild life.

Weave your way through the whitewashed village to the parish church and jutting arrogantly above it the battlements of a 16th century castle. Down an adjacent street is an immaculate two-star hotel, the Zuhayra (Mirador, 10. Tel. 957-69 46 93) with restaurant.

But Zuheros is bestknown for its Cueva de los Murciélagos (cave of the bats), reached by a road that curves way above the village and offers views of the Bailon river gorge. Not explored until 1937, the cave was inhabited in Neolithic times and wall paintings remain.

As a maximum of 150 persons are admitted daily to the cave, call 957-69 45 45 (9am-2.30pm weekdays) in advance. Individuals are admitted on weekends and holidays (11am-1pm, 4-6pm, 6-8pm in summer). The visit includes admittance to the castle and a museum with ceramics, arrow heads, and other artefacts.

From Zuheros, head east to Luque, its castle dominating the town, then along a backroad to Fuente Alhama on the CO231 to join the N321, turning right to Priego de Córdoba.

Old watch towers crown one or two of the hills to the right. We squeeze through Las Angosturas, a narrow ravine, and head across an irrigated plain towards **PRIEGO DE CORDOBA**.

Priego is a snugly prosperous town with a magnificent heritage of fine buildings, many dating from the 18th century when its silk industry flourished.

From the town hall square (Plaza del Ayuntamiento) wander up Calle del Río, a curving street lined with noble mansions with imposing front doors and ironwork. The tourism office is in Number 33, the house where Niceto Alcalá-Zamora, president of the Second Republic, was born.

The street ends at the Fuente del Rey, a king among fountains. Built between the 16th century and 1803, it has 139 spouts gushing into three pools, with Neptune in the centre.

To explore the rest of the town, head for the Barrio de la Villa. On the edge of this medieval quarter is the parish church of La Asunción, a Baroque monument. The extravagant sacristy chapel is a mind-blowing piece of Baroque art.

Behind the church is a labyrinth of immaculately whitewashed, astonishingly narrow streets. Geraniums and petunias run amok on balconies and on patio walls. Eventually, like a cork popped from a bottle, you burst out on to the Adarve, an iron-railed promenade where lovers flirt and you can gaze out at the surrounding countryside.

Along the Adarve you come to the tree-shaded Plaza de Columbia and if you wander further through the streets of Priego you encounter other magnificently adorned churches, such as the over-the-top Baroque of La Aurora. Every Saturday midnight the cloaked Hermanos (brothers) de la Aurora walk thorough the streets singing in praise of the Virgin and collecting alms.

Another brotherhood of the Aurora sings in the strees of Carcabuey, perched on a hump five miles (8km) west of Priego.

From the Ayuntamiento the stepped Castillo street and Virgen street lead up to the castle. Near it is a hole in the ground, a vaulted Roman dungeon. Between dungeon and castle rises a monument to 20th century sensitivity - a lofty electricity pylon.

Dozens of cats stand guard over the castle chapel sheltering Carcabuey's patron saint, the white-robed Virgen del Castillo. Eleven crutches by the altar and many ex votos testify to the Virgin's powers.

From Priego the new, well-paved C336 cuts through hills and olive groves to rejoin the N432 at Alcalá la Real (pop. 20,000) in Jaén province. The Fortaleza de La Mota presents a superbly dramatic outline above the town.

Drive up to it for fine views and to explore the collection of historic buildings which are being restored. La Mota castle was built by the Moorish kings of Granada in the 14th century to stave off the advancing Castilian armies and rebuilt in the 16th century.

Within the walls, on the flat hilltop more than 3,300 above sea-level, are two churches. Santo Domingo de Silos is 14th century Gothic-Mudejar-Renaissance and Santa María la Mayor, designed by Diego de Siloé, was almost completely destroyed by war but has been restored.

Alcalá lies 32 miles (52km) from **GRANADA** across hilly country of cornfields, bleached earth and olive trees. Rocky outcrops jut from the landscape. As the N342 begins to descend, you catch your first glimpse of the snow-capped Sierra Nevada, floating like a mirage above the haze.

The road dips towards Pinos Puente and the Vega of Granada spreads before you, a fertile plain of poplar plantations and patchwork fields. Five hundred years ago the armies advancing on the last stronghold of the Moors had the same breath-taking view❑

Excursion 27 - Old Crafts and Prehistoric Paintings:

Ronda-Grazalema-El Bosque-Ubrique-Cortes de la Frontera-La Pileta-Montejaque-Ronda
Distance: 82 miles (130km)

Start early. The distance may be small, but this route takes you over the Serranía de Ronda and Cádiz, an eagle's eyrie if ever there was one. Splendid mountain scenery, the wettest place in Spain, and unique traces of prehistoric man lie on the way.

Follow the Seville road, the C339. Ten miles (16km) from **RONDA**, take the C344 to the left towards Ubrique and the heart of the Grazalema nature park. The narrow but well-paved road passes through cornfields and then winds through miles of holm and holly oaks into Cádiz province.

At the next road junction, a left takes you to Ubrique. Turn right to Grazalema, claimed to be the wettest village in Spain. Clouds moving in from the Atlantic collide with the peaks above Grazalema, depositing their loads on the area.

Grazalema (pop. 2,300) has long been famous for its handwoven woollen goods. The craft was in danger of dying out but has been revived.

Look for the petrol station with roses growing before it. Just after, turn right up the hill to the Nuestra Señora del Carmen factory (tel. 956-13 20 08), where high-quality blankets and ponchos are turned out on 200-year-old looms. The shop is open 8am-2pm and 3-6:30pm, Monday to Friday. The same hours apply to the factory-museum, except that it is closed on Friday afternoon. Shop and factory close at weekends and in August, but a shop on the village plaza selling the same products remains open.

Grazalema is a classic white village, with cobbled streets, tiled roofs and ironwork balconies. A bull chases through those streets every mid-July during the Lunes del Toro fiesta (the first Monday after the Virgin of Carmen fiesta).

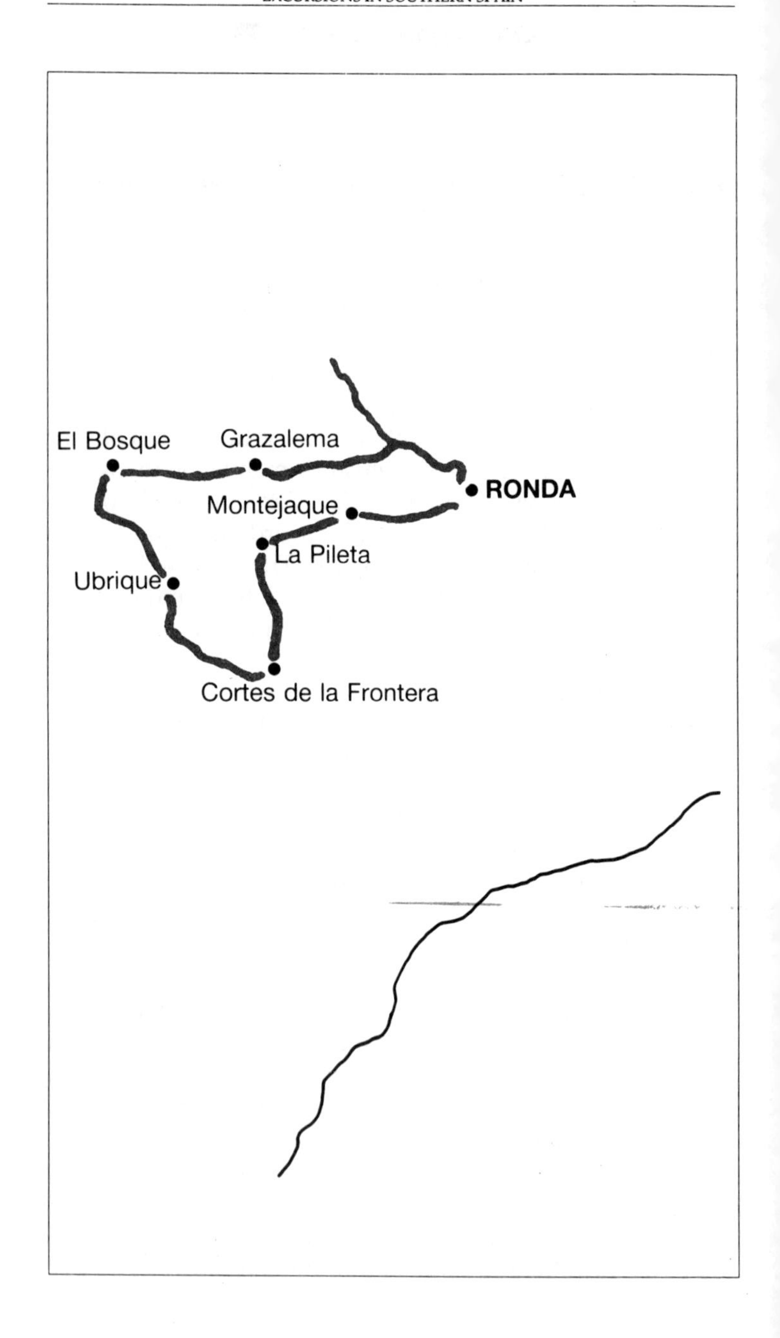
El Bosque
Grazalema
RONDA
Montejaque
La Pileta
Ubrique
Cortes de la Frontera

Otherwise it is a quiet place. A tranquil spot to overnight is the Villa Turística Grazalema (Ctra. Comarcal 344, Grazalema, Cádiz. Tel: 956-13 21 36), facing the pueblo across the valley. Rooms are a little cheaper in the old hotel, to which has been added a village-style development with self-contained apartments.

You can eat at the Villa and also at El Tajo restaurant, with its pool, which overlooks the village on the way up the steep valley to El Boyar pass. From here, 3,500 feet above sea level, you enjoy stupendous mountain vistas. In early summer the slopes blaze yellow with gorse blooms. In the heights grows the pinsapo, the pine unique to this part of Europe.

The road swoops down, passing a picnic area with tables on the right. Benamahoma appears further on. Take the lower entrance. It runs below the village to a hatchery where thousands of trout swarm in pools. You can buy them by the kilo.

A hundred yards or so past the trout farm are a bar, restaurant and municipal swimming pool, benefitting from the clear water gushing from the mountains.

Just below Benamahoma, we reach the junction for El Bosque (pop. 1,700). It also has important fish hatcheries and appropriately its two-star hotel, in traditional Andalusian style, is called Las Truchas (Avda. Diputación, 1. Tel: 956-71 60 62. Usually closed November). Fresh trout is on the menu in the restaurant.

At number 13 on Avenida de la Diputación in El Bosque is the office of the Parque Natural de Grazalema (956-71 60 63).

From El Bosque you can drive 20 miles (32km) to Arcos de la Frontera (see Excursion 17) through a lush valley where corn, tobacco and sunflowers flourish. But today's route is over the mountains in the other direction, 10 miles (16km) south to Ubrique on the CA524. Shortly after crossing the Tavizna river, you will see the ruins of Aznalmara castle up to your left.

Ubrique (pop. 18,000) shelters in the valley at the foot of the Cruz del Tajo mountain. Despite its isolated position, it is renowned for the quality of its handworked leather. The industrious inhabitants began making *petacas* (tobacco pouches) from goat-skin, often trading with the smugglers who brought tobacco from Gibraltar.

In the past Ubrique achieved a certain notoriety for pirating brand names, but of course this no longer occurs. Now Piel de Ubrique is a luxury item, with an international reputation. Dozens of small workshops turn out handbags and wallets for top brand names. If you want to make a purchase, a number of the shops bear the *fabrica propria* (our own make) sign.

The two-star hostal Ocurris (Solis Pascual, 49. Tel. 956-46 39 39) at the beginning of town offers comfortable accommodation. Its four-storeys are built in a modern style that makes it better to be inside looking out than outside looking at it.

Leaving Ubrique on the Cortes de la Frontera road, you can seek refreshment at the Bar Stop, good for fish, and about two miles (3km) out of town the Venta el Chorizo, specialising in sausages, is a typically rustic inn. Try Ubrique's dry, sherry-style wine.

The picturesque road soars upwards to the Monjón de la Víbora crossroads, from where you can enjoy a breath-taking panoramic view of the Sierra de Cádiz. A left turn on the C3331 would take you to Puerto de Galis (see Excursion 12), but we turn left towards Cortes de la Frontera, 10 miles (16km) away). A venta by the crossroads serves snacks.

The road sways and dips downwards, entering Málaga province and passing the Sierra de los Pinos, which rises to 4,500 feet. We dart in and out of the cork-oaks and chestnuts of the Cortes hunting reserve. Keep your eyes open for the deer that roam the woods and eagles and vultures that patrol the skies.

This is one of the wettest parts of Andalusia, producing flourishing vegetation, and Cortes is one of the loneliest villages. But, if the mists have moved in shrouding trees and houses, it is a handy place to stop for a warming coffee and brandy.

From Cortes, take the MA549 up the Guadiaro valley. Six miles away (10km) is the Cueva de la Pileta. It is not the place for claustrophobic types, but it does have some remarkable cave paintings. The entrance is up a rocky hillside in a secluded valley occupied by one farmhouse. One of the Bullón family, who discovered the cave and occupy the house on the flat valley bottom, acts as your guide. Tours are on the hour 9am-1pm, 4-6pm.

There is no fancy lighting in the Pileta cave. Your guide hands you a lamp and you tramp through the dark galleries and the stalactite-and-stalagmite-encrusted caverns, carved out originally by an underground river.

Farmer José Bullón Lobato stumbled over the cave in 1905. He found an opening in the rock and lowered himself on a rope, thinking he might find useful supplies of bat-dung. Instead, he came across innumerable traces of prehistoric man. Skeletons, pottery, and Paleolithic wall paintings were revealed in La Pileta. An archer, a deer, a fish, abstract symbols are among the murals created by early man.

From La Pileta, it is 18 miles (29km) to Ronda. Carry on up the Guadiaro valley to Benaoján. For a stay in a delightful converted old mill, turn right to descend through the village towards the river and railway station to the Molino del Santo (Barriada Estación, tel. 95-216 71 51). A weeping willow dips over the pool in this British-run two-star hotel.

The Benaoján-Montejaque area is famed for its pork products, such as black sausage and cured ham. Continue past Montejaque and soon you wind through a chasm with steep cliffs. To your left a wall blocks part of the valley, an example of man's often vain attempts to control nature.

It is a 200-foot-high dam built in the 1920s. Unfortunately, the project proved a waste of effort for mysteriously the dam never filled. It turned out that the trapped water all leaked away through the innumerable fissures in the rock.

Near the dam is the large entrance to the Cueva del Hundidero. A stream flows into this cave, runs several miles underground then emerges further down the valley in the Cueva del Gato (Cat Cave).

When you reach the Ronda-Seville road, C339, turn right and you reach **RONDA** after nine miles (14km)❑

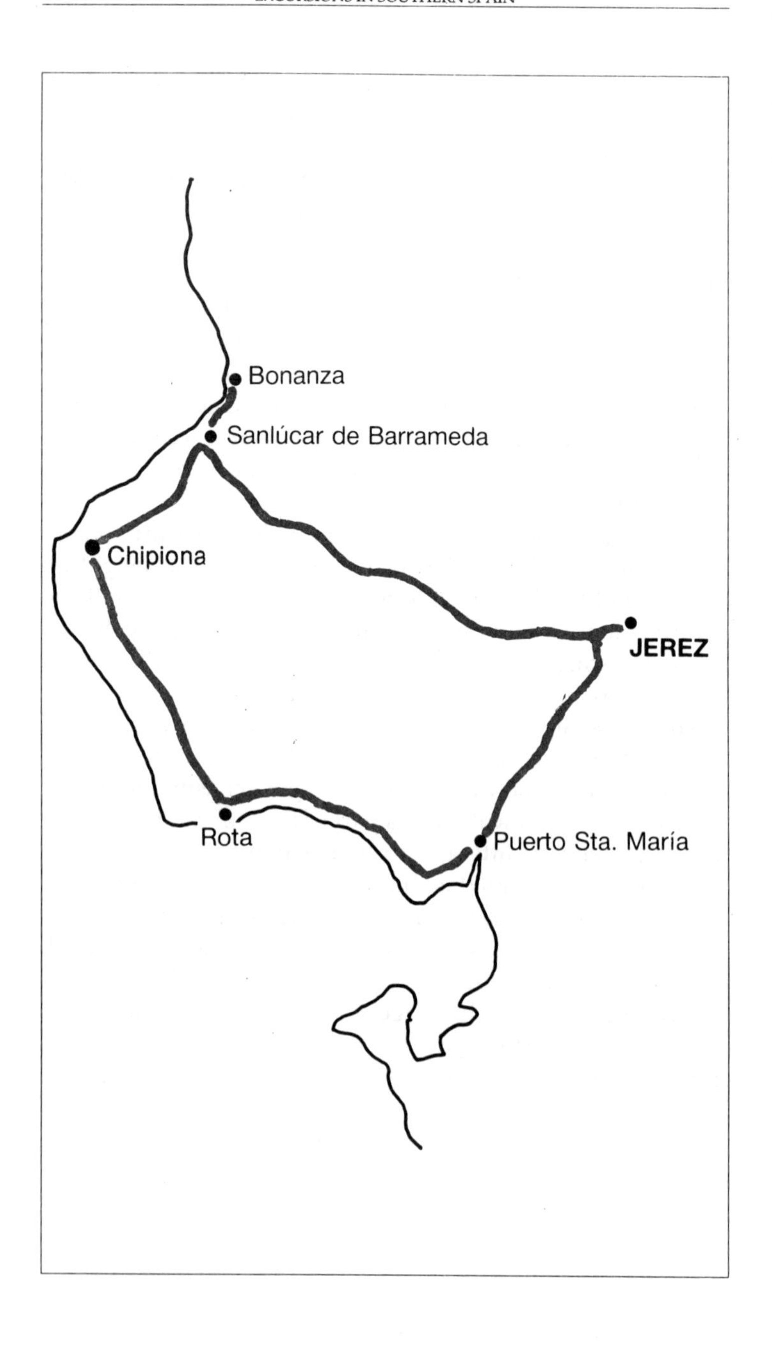
Bonanza
Sanlúcar de Barrameda
Chipiona
JEREZ
Rota
Puerto Sta. María

Excursion 28 - Sherry Triangle:

Jerez-Sanlúcar-El Puerto-Jerez
Distance: 56 miles (90km)

Sherryland is the place where all the stereotypes about Southern Spain seem to fit. Fiery flamenco dancers, land-owning aristocrats, superb horses, fighting bulls, pretty girls and fine wine. . . they are all here.

This excursion starts in Jerez and takes you on a journey through the Sherry Triangle, formed by the towns of Jerez, Puerto de Santa María and Sanlúcar de Barrameda, all in Cádiz province. Atlantic breezes, wet winters, hot summers and the chalky soil combine with centuries of expertise to turn out a wine that was famous even in Shakespeare's time.

At first sight, the apartment blocks and broad boulevards of **JEREZ DE LA FRONTERA** (pop. 176,000) suggest a modern city, but at its core is a pleasant old quarter of narrow streets, palatial dwellings and impressive churches.

It is dominated by the industry that made it famous. You will find bodegas (literally wine cellars but signifying wineries) dotted about the town.

You can visit many of them to see how the wine is made, sample it and carry away bottles at lower-than-shop prices. Visits are usually made in the mornings (details under Jerez at rear of the book).

The Moors called this place "Scheris" and from this came the name "Jerez". The British - traditionally grand topers of the golden liquid - converted the name into "sherry". British names and links abound among the sherry families, although most of the great bodegas are now run by multinational companies.

Modern methods of crushing grapes and fermenting them are in general use, but the bodega guides will explain that the time-honoured method of producing sherry continues. You may also see a demonstration of how to use a *venencia*, a whippy dip-stick used to scoop wine from the barrel.

The *solera* system rules here, guaranteeing that sherry is of consistent quality. Jerez has a million barrels of American oak, each with a capacity of 500 litres. These are piled tier upon tier. Young wine passes down successively over the years from tier to tier, blending with older wines.

Vino fino, dry, pale and best served chilled, usually goes through more blending stages than sherries with more body, such as *amontillados,* nutty-flavoured and deeper-coloured, and *olorosos,* darker still and full-bodied.

One of the city's palaces is Las Cadenas, on the Avenida Duque de Abrantes, where a special arena has been constructed to accommodate the "dancing horses of Andalusia". You can see members of the Real Escuela Andaluza del Arte Ecuestre training every weekday morning and on Thursdays at noon they stage a dazzling, full-blown show of horsemanship.

Jerez has a large gypsy community and strong flamenco tradition. In Pemartín palace, on the Plaza de San Juan, the Andalusian Flamenco Foundation has its centre, which aims to foster the art of flamenco. You can see flamenco every night at the Bar Camino de Rocío or at one of the clubs (consult the tourist office).

Take the C440 from Jerez towards **SANLUCAR DE BARRAMEDA,** 15 miles (23km) away. You pass Venta Antonio, a popular eating spot, and regiments of vines marching over rolling hills. The soil is often a dazzling white. This is albariza, which has a high percentage of chalk, plus clay and sand. It absorbs moisture well, then under the baking sun forms a hard crust to retain it. Palomino grapes predominate in the making of finos and amontillados.

Sanlúcar sprawls at the mouth of the Guadalquivir river. By turns elegant and seedy, it lives from fishing and wine. A plaque on the Ayuntamiento wall records that, of 265 men who sailed from here with Magellan on September 20, 1519, only 18 returned on September 6, 1522, under the command of Juan Sebastián Elcano. About to embark on another epic voyage, Columbus had to delay his ships' departure from Sanlúcar because his crew insisted on joining the pilgrimage to El Rocío.

At Pentecost every year cavalcades of pilgrims cross the Guadalquivir at Sanlúcar en route to that lonely shrine (see Excursion 29).

From Sanlúcar's bodegas comes manzanilla, a light dry sherry with a delicate flavour which the locals claim is caused by the sea breezes wafting over the maturing wine. You can see the production process at one of Sanlúcar's wineries by phoning in advance.

Manzanilla is served from the barrel in the many bars and is ideal to drink with tapas. You will find a number of bars near the palm-shaded central square, the Plaza del Cabildo.

Four brothers, Antonio, Joaquin, Balbino, and Elías, plus the stuffed head of a 475-kilo bull killed by matador Paco Ojeda to mark the opening of Seville's Expo 92, preside over the Bar Balbino which offers everything from stuffed squid to sea snails.

Head towards the Bajo de Guía, the fishermen's district by the river to sample fresh seafood. Once rather shabby, it has been spruced up by a promenade. Langostinos (king prawns) are a speciality in the many eating places. Acedías (small flounder) and pijotas (whiting) are worth trying and a lot cheaper.

On the far shore is the Doñana National Park, but you are not permitted to enter except on a guided tour. A boat, named the Real Fernando after the first steamboat built in Spain which started plying the river in 1817, leaves daily and calls at two points, allowing visitors to make short walks with guides.

Contact the Centro de Interpretación de la Naturaleza at Bajo de Guia (see Town and City Guide). To penetrate deeper into the park, make the long trip via Seville to Huelva province, and arrange for a Land-Rover tour through the Reception Centre, Parque Nacional Doñana, El Acebuche. Tel: 959-43 04 32. Open: 8am-7pm, except Monday. (See Excursion 29).

Sanlúcar is the home of the Duchess of Medina Sidonia. Known as The Red Duchess, because of her courageous championing of the under-privileged, she includes among her ancestors a legendary warrior named Gúzman el Bueno and the duke who commanded the Invincible Armada against England.

Her austere, centuries-old palace at Conde de Niebla, 1, next door to the Iglesia de la O, was once open for guests, but lately the Duchess's big concern has been the future of the family's priceless archives.

Two miles (3km) along the Guadalquivir river bank from Sanlúcar is Bonanza, once a port much used for trade with the Indies. Now, if you arrive around 4 or 5pm, you will see vast catches of fish being unloaded and auctioned.

The C441 from Sanlúcar runs six miles (9km) to Chipiona, a nondescript town with fine beaches which attracts thousands of holidaymakers in summer. Its other claim to fame is that Rocío Jurado, queen of Spanish popular song, was born here - look for her statue near the fishing harbour. A pleasant place to watch the sun sink into the Atlantic is the esplanade by the Chipiona lighthouse. Continue south along the coast, featureless but with good beaches.

Rota is notable mainly for the adjacent naval base (officially under Spanish control but bestknown for the big U.S. presence). However it has some claims as a resort, with an excellent beach. The Castillo de Luna has been restored to house the town hall. On a wall is a plaque to Bartolomé Pérez, of Rota, who was one of the crew in Columbus's first voyage.

On the same small square as the castle is a beautiful Gothic church, Santa María de la O. Dry years are nothing new around here as you will see from an inscription on the church wall which reads: "In the prolonged drought of 1917 the Rota people, distressed by the prospect of tremendous misery, implored the clemency of Jesus with ardent prayer and on the night of December 21 they took his venerated image out in procession, when the sky immediately darkened and a copious rain providentially fell during that and succeeding days until the calamity was remedied."

Nearby is the fishing port, at the entrance of which El Embarcadero bar, with a terrace, serves platefuls of fresh seafood. *Urta a la roteña* (sea-bream cooked with brandy, peppers, tomato, thyme and white wine) is a popula dish along this coast.

The road makes a big detour around the perimeter fence of the base before running towards Puerto de Santa María. Large apartment and villa complexes have sprung up by the beaches on this section of the coast, none of which need detain you.

On the outskirts of the Puerto a sign points to Puerto Sherry. This is a huge pleasure port, whose modernistic buildings give it the soulless air of a Brasilia dropped on the Atlantic coast. Television cameras survey the quaysides.

Pass quickly by to **EL PUERTO DE SANTA MARIA** (pop. 70,000), rival to Jerez and famed for its matadors, seafood, and bodegas. It is time for a drink. The town is laid out on a grid pattern with lots of confusing one-way streets, but eventually you will find yourself on the Ribera del Marisco, the Guadalete river waterfront.

This is a popular spot to try the seafood. You know it is going to be ultra-fresh because it is landed early every morning on the quayside across the river. Buy your *gambas* or *centollas* from the vast selection on display at a *cocedero,* a sort of takeaway. Then carry your purchase, wrapped in paper, to a pavement cafe table, where the custom is to order chilled dry sherry to wash the food down.

Nearby, you can take El Vapor, a ferry, across the bay to **CADIZ**. In the Puerto you can also visit several large bodegas, where wine and brandy are produced.

El Puerto is said to have 800 bars. One of the more interesting ones is the Bodega Merello, at Calle Santa Lucía, 29, a step away from El Puerto's century-old Plaza de Toros. Yellowing bullfight posters decorate the barn-like place lined with large barrels and the atmosphere redolent of another age. If you are an aficionado of the toros, Manuel, nearly 40 years behind the bar, is the man to talk to.

From the Puerto the N1V heads northeast towards Jerez and Seville, skirting the vine-covered Sherry Triangle and one or two bull ranches, including that of Osborne whose big black replicas of a fighting bull are silhouetted on hilltops right across Spain. When their removal was decreed in 1994, there was a national outcry and they were reprieved.

Just along this highway is the Casino Bahía de Cádiz (Ctra

Madrid-Cádiz, km 650) where gamblers can try their luck at everything from blackjack to roulette. A road to the right, CA201, meanders over rolling country near the Guadalete river. After El Portal look for a right turn leading to La Cartuja, which lies on the Jerez-Medina Sidonia road, the C440.

This monastery, founded in 1477, is a striking building. The church has a richly-decorated Baroque facade, with carvings showing scenes from the life of San Bruno, and a Gothic interior. Only men are allowed inside the monastery, with special permission, as it is occupied by an enclosed order.

From La Cartuja it is under three miles (4km) to **JEREZ**❑

Excursion 29 - In the Steps of Columbus:

Seville-Coto Doñana-La Rabida-Palos-Moguer-Seville
Distance: 156 miles (250km)

Christopher Columbus gained support for his great voyage of discovery at a monastery in Huelva province and he set sail from a nearby port. This tour takes in the towns where Columbus prepared for his voyage and one of Europe's most important wildlife sanctuaries.

With a very early start it can be covered in one day, but you need two to do it comfortably.

From **SEVILLE** we head west towards **HUELVA**, past the Isla de Cartuja, site of the 1992 world exhibition, and across the Guadalquivir River. We take the fast A49, the four-lane Autopista del Quinto Centenario.

It passes over undulating agricultural country with citrus and olive trees, then after crossing the border into Huelva province into a region of vineyards. Turn left on H612 to Bollullos Par del Condado, 32 miles (51 kilometres) from Seville.

Bollullos (pop. 12,500) is the centre of the Condado wine country. It produces wines very similar to those from the sherry region and indeed, in the past, supplied grapes to Jeréz bodegas. The first wine drunk in the New World by Columbus and his men was almost certainly from here.

Recently, local wine-makers have developed light fruity white wines, which are very pleasant to the palate.

On the main street through Bollullos you will see several bodegas where you can stop to try *mosto* - new wine direct from large barrels - and snack on shellfish. These places are particularly busy on Sunday.

On the way out of town is a small square to the left with a black statue of a local celebrity. Facing the square is the Bar El Cañonazo, recommended for its tapas taken with a glass of cold fino del Condado.

Close by, along the street across the main road, is El Reñiero, a restaurant built around a cockpit. Those with a taste for the

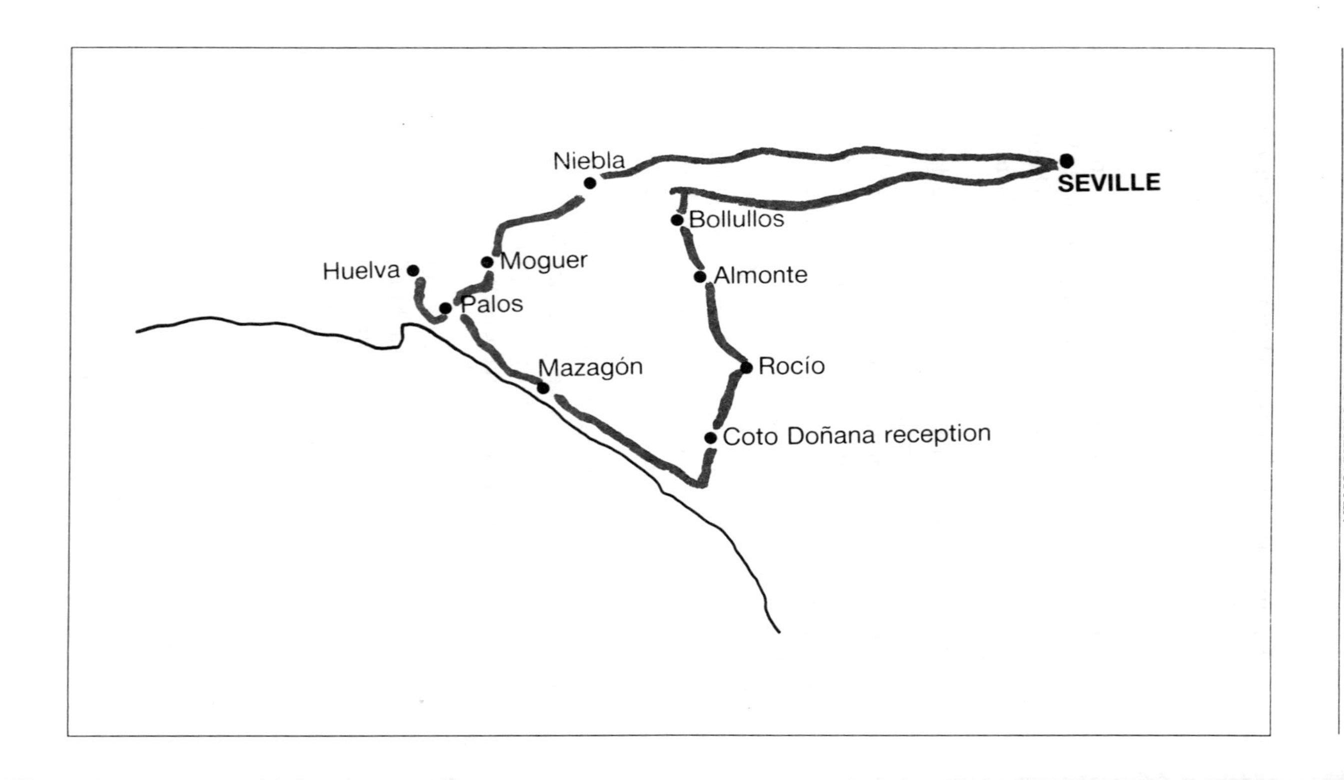
SEVILLE
Bollullos
Almonte
Rocío
Coto Doñana reception
Niebla
Moguer
Palos
Mazagón
Huelva

gruesome or animal rights campaigners looking for a cause can check whether fights are still taking place on Sunday afternoons. In the past, during the season (January to July), diners would tuck into their meals apparently oblivious to the blood splashing about as the cocks clashed in the ring.

Vineyards clothe much of the flat country between Bollullos and Almonte (pop. 15,000). In Almonte's agreeable main square, lined with palms and orange trees, storks nest on top of the church belfry.

South we enter sandy terrain, covered with pines. We are entering Las Marismas, the wilderness of dunes and marshes at the mouth of the Guadalquivir. Ten miles (15 kilometres from Almonte) is the bizarre deserted township of El Rocío. With its single-storey dwellings, hitching posts and wide streets of sand, it resembles a Wild West ghost town.

Once a year, however, at Pentecost (usually in May), El Rocío is crammed with up to a million pilgrims. Most arrive by motor vehicle, but many trek on foot and horseback across marshes and dunes to pay tribute to the Virgin of Rocío, also known as the Blanca Paloma (the white dove) and the Queen of the Marshes. She stirs intense emotions and tumultous scenes occur when the Virgin is finally carried out of her temple, a large white structure, in the early hours of the Monday morning, to be paraded around for 12 hours or so.

According to legend, the image was found by a shepherd in the hollow of a tree six centuries ago. It mysteriously returned to the tree when he tried to carry it to Almonte, so a shrine was built here.

Just outside El Rocío, on the right, you come to La Rocina information centre (open: 9.30am-1.30pm, 4-7pm. Tel: 959-44 23 40) for the Doñana National Park. The park, embracing altogether 190,000 acres (76,000 hectares), is an important sanctuary for such endangered species as the imperial eagle and the lynx, and a vital breeding ground and stopover for thousands of water fowl. The centre can inform you about non-guided visits to areas near the park where you can observe the wildlife.

To enter the park itself you must go on a guided tour,

starting from the El Acebuche reception centre, further along the Almonte-Matalascañas road near the park entrance. Four-wheel-drive vehicles make four-hour trips twice a day, usually departing at 8.30am and 3pm, except Mondays. Places should be reserved in advance through the Reception Centre, Parque Nacional Doñana, El Acebuche (tel: 959-43 04 32. Open: 8am-7pm, except Monday).

As hours of visits can change according to the season, check beforehand by calling 959-43 02 11 or 44 23 40.

A mansion built by Doña Ana, a Duchess of Medina Sidonia, stands in the park, giving it the name. Legend has it that, while dallying there with Goya, an 18th-century Duchess of Alba posed for his famous picture La Maja Desnuda (The Naked Woman), apparently not noticing the sabre-toothed mosquitoes in the marshes.

Meanwhile, nature-lovers are fighting to save the park from further damage. You can see what they are up against at Matalascañas, a chaotic eruption of villas and high-rise apartments on the sea-shore at the park edge.

Turn right on C442, which runs through pinewoods 30 miles (48 kilometres) to Huelva. Halfway along, a left turn leads through the pines to a clifftop. Below run miles of good sandy beach lapped by the Atlantic. And on the clifftop is the Parador Cristobal Colón (Ctra. Matalascañas. Tel: 959-37 60 00). Lawns lead down to a swimming pool. This is an ideal place to overnight.

Four miles (6 kilometres) west lies Mazagón, a summer resort with a fine beach. The first street on the left after turning off the C442 has several bars, some specializing in fresh fish.

Near **HUELVA** the coast has been blighted by petro-chemical plants. On the Punta del Sebo, a peninsula created by the Odiel and Tinto rivers, stands a massive monument dedicated to Christopher Columbus (known as Cristobal Colón to Spaniards). The sculpture by Gertrude Vanderbilt Whitney was a gift from the United States in 1929.

Columbus came this way when he was seeking support for his project to find a new way to the Indies. When you leave the Columbus monument, go back across the Tinto bridge and take the first left.

Orange trees blossom on the approach to La Rábida monastery, where Columbus once sought for food for his son Diego. According to legend, he told the friars: "I am called Cristóbal Colón. I am a sea captain from Genoa, and I must beg my bread because kings will not accept the empires that I offer them." He won over the prior and a friar-astronomer who helped convince Spain's monarchs. In the chapel, Columbus prayed to the Virgin of the Miracles before sailing into the unknown.

One of the Franciscan monks shows visitors around the 14th-century Mudejar-style monastery, refurbished for Expo 92 (open 10am-1pm, 4-6.15pm, closed Monday).

Next to the monastery stands the Hostería de la Rábida (Tel: 959-35 03 12), a small, two-star hotel with restaurant. Below stands a large auditorium, where functions of the Hispano-American University are held, and nearby, on the Tinto river, are three replicas of Columbus's ships.

At the Muelle de la Reina a statue of a winged man, erected by Argentina, pays tribute to four fliers, including General Franco's brother Ramón, who "with their glorious flight opened over Columbus's sea a new route between mother Spain and her American daughter." The pioneer flight to Buenos Aires took place in 1926.

Strawberry fields stretch for ever on the sandy soils as you approach Palos de la Frontera and Moguer. This fruit ripens as early as February here and thousands of tons are transported to European markets.

A palm-lined avenue leads into Palos (pop. 6,500), the launch-point for the epic Columbus voyage of 1492. Follow it past the Ayuntamiento in the town centre and it becomes Calle Colón (Columbus Street). At what by logic should be number 34, but carries a "24", is the Casa de los Pinzón, the house of the Pinzón brothers who provided and crewed Columbus's ships.

The facade is adorned with a coat of arms, two columns, tiles and a plaque claiming that the discovery of the Americas was organized here. To see inside, ask for the key at the Ayuntamiento. Further along, where the street curves and dips stands San Jorge Church (open during services). Columbus and his crew prayed here before starting their epic voyage and drew water for their ships from La Fontanilla, a brick-roofed well in gardens below the church.

Trees struggle to grow in the bare park created between here and the Tinto river, but you will look in vain for the quayside from where the Pinta, the Niña and the Santa María set sail. The river long ago became too silted for use at this point.

At the neighbouring town of Moguer (pop. 11,000), five miles (7 km) from Palos, a wander through labyrinthine streets brings you to the 14th-century Gothic-Mudejar convent of Santa Clara. Columbus and his men gave thanks here for safely riding out a terrible storm (open 10.30am-2.30pm, 4.30-8pm, closed Sunday).

Just across from the convent is La Parrala (Plaza Monjas, 22. Tel: 959-37 04 52. Open: 11am-5pm, 7-12am. No cards), a traditional-style family-run restaurant with very reasonable prices. La Parrala was a cafe singer in Huelva's mining areas who lived passionately and died violently.

Among the many tapa bars in the centre of town you will find the Café Puerto Rico, on the Plaza del Marqués. The two-star hostal Platero (Aceña, 4, tel. 959-37 21 59) offers agreeable budget accommodation.

Wall plaques all over Moguer quote lines from the town's Nobel prize-winning poet Juan Ramón Jiménez (1881-1958). The house where he spent his early years has been converted into the Casa-Museo de Zenobia y Juan Ramón (Juan Ramón Jiménez, 10. Open: 10am-2pm, 4.30-8pm, Closed Sun afternoon). Zenobia was his wife.

The fine old house accommodates a library and displays many of the poet's possessions, including 4,000 books.

Opposite the Nuestra Señora de Granada church, a plaque quotes Jiménez's popular children's book Platero and I (translated into 50 languages): "The tower of Moguer, from nearby it looks like the Giralda seen from a distance."

And indeed the church tower, around which wheel a pair of storks, does look like Seville's Giralda in miniature.

From Moguer drive north to the N431 highway, which

parallels the faster A49, and turn right towards Seville. After 10 miles (16 kilometres) you will see the glowering, 50-foot-thick walls built by the Moors around Niebla (pop. 4,000). It was the capital of a kingdom for a while.

When Christian forces besieged the town for nine months in 1257, they used gunpowder, the first time it had been employed on the Iberian peninsula. Today a peace symbol stands in the park below the ochre walls, a giant metal statue of a dove with an olive branch in its beak.

Just out of Niebla, the road crosses the dark red waters of the Río Tinto by a Roman bridge.

Seven miles (12km) before **SEVILLE** the N431 passes by Sanlúcar la Mayor in the Aljarafe, the Moorish name for this area of fertile high ground above the Guadalquivir. It used to be said that "five rivers flow from the Aljarafe, of water, milk, wine, olive oil and honey".

Several churches show Moorish influence. Santa María has three naves with horseshoe arches on square pillars and a tower from the Almohad era, while San Pedro has a similar tower and windows with horseshoe arches❑

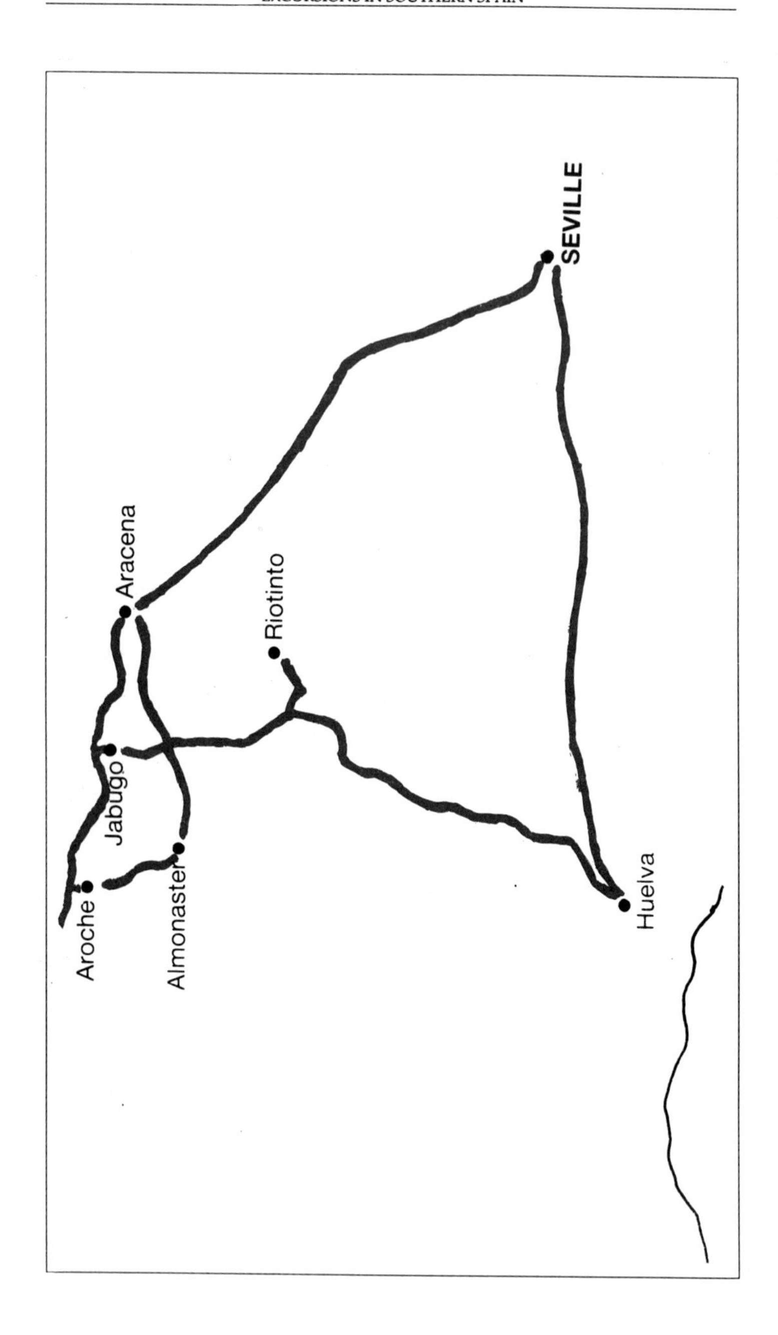
SEVILLE
Aracena
Riotinto
Jabugo
Almonaster
Aroche
Huelva

Excursion 30 - Land of Hams and Silver:

Seville-Huelva-Riotinto-Cortegana-Jabugo-Aracena-Seville
Distance: 212 miles (340km)

Behind the Huelva coast, in thickly-forested uplands lie mines that have fed men's need and greed since ancient times. There too are castle-studded sierras, noted for cured ham and for subterranean wonders.

From **SEVILLE**, take the main four-lane highway, the A49, to **HUELVA**. Near Huelva, turn north on route N435 towards Valverde del Camino and Aracena. At first you pass fertile farmland and vineyards, then increasing numbers of eucalypts and holm oaks.

Valverde, 28 miles (45km) from Huelva, spreads up a rise to your left. It is noted for its leatherwork, particularly sturdy boots. You climb into wilder forested country. Just after Zalamea la Real, the C421 forks right to Minas de Riotinto and Nerva.

Around these communities the earth has been gouged and riven since ancient times in the hunt for minerals. The fabled kingdom of Tartessos is said to have enriched itself from these mines.

British interests bought the mines last century and left behind them Riotinto's Bella Vista suburb. With its leafy avenues, gabled villas and social club, it retains a very English air.

Lately the mines have run into financial troubles so to recoup they have been converted into a tourist attraction. Visits can be made (entrance fee) through the Museo Minero, Carretera de Sevilla, Minas de Riotinto (tel. 959-59 00 25). The visit includes Bella Vista, a Roman acropolis, and the vast open-cast mines - one cut goes down 2,000 feet - from where copper, silver, gold and pyrites are extracted. In addition, you can buy tickets at the museum for a trip on the old mines railway, but it only runs on weekends and holidays or on special trips.

Further north on the N435, an endless vista of rolling hills clothed in evergreens presents itself. Chestnut, apple and pear trees, elms and poplars flourish in the well-watered valleys.

This is the extreme west of the Sierra Morena and forms part of the Sierra de Aracena y Picos de Aroche nature park, which reaches heights of around 3,000 feet.

Among the rust-red trunks of cork oaks dotting the hills root thousands of Iberian pigs. They are brown-coloured but their feet are black, which is why the ham that comes from them is known as *pata negra*. It is highly prized, and expensive. Its special flavour comes from the breed of pig, its acorn diet and the long months of curing.

You can visit one of the ham-curing companies to learn more about the process and buy some of their products. Call in at Sánchez Romero Carvajal (open 10am-1pm) at Jabugo (pop. 2,600). The name Jabugo, once notorious for its tobacco smugglers, has become synonymous with good ham, but many other villages also turn out hams and sausages.

Before reaching Jabugo a left turn leads towards Cortegana, and eventually to the Portuguese frontier. The road winds about the hills until you reach Almonaster la Real, 2,000 feet above sea level.

On a hill above the village are the battlements of a mighty Moorish castle and above them, next to a bullring constructed in 1891, is a church with a square tower. Closer examination reveals that the building is a splendid 1,000-year-old mosque.

A fountain bubbles at the entrance and in the gloomy interior you can make out four naves with 17 columns, plus a mihrab (prayer niche). Traces of Roman and Visigothic settlement can also be found in this national monument. (Inquire at the town hall if the access gate is closed).

Sleepy Almonaster (pop. 2,300) has some fine old buildings, including the Mudéjar church of San Martín and houses dating from medieval times. From a nearby hilltop there are good views of the sierras.

Four miles (6km) west of Almonaster a restored 13th-century castle (ask at the Ayuntamiento if you want to visit) recalls the warlike past of Cortegana (Corticata to the Romans). Penetrate this town of 5,000 people and you come to the parish church with white doves fluttering about its lichen-crusted roof and small tiled spire. Divino Salvador church is a fortress-like, Mudéjar-style building of the 16th century, with three ornate iron pulpits.

A plaque on the church wall pays homage to Fray Alonso Giraldo de Terreros, "intrepid pioneer of the faith in North America". He founded the mission Río de San Sabas de los Apaches, but alas he was destined to be a "martyr of Christ" for he was killed by Comanche Indians in 1758.

Medieval castles stand guard over the sierra fastnesses. If you drive 10 miles (16km) west of Cortegana on N433 you come to Aroche, a walled town perched high above the forest and pastureland. Sancho 11 of Portugal ousted the Moors from here in 1236. Its Moorish fortress now accommodates a bullring and also an acheological museum (key at the town hall). Aroche also has the unique Museo del Santo Rosario, in a 16th century house on Calle Alférez Carlos Lobo. Its owner has collected more than 1,300 rosaries, presented by all manner of celebrities, including Mother Teresa, Archbishop Makarios, Richard Nixon and J.F. Kennedy.

Retracing our steps, we drive east towards Aracena. Wander along the main street of orchard-girdled Galaroza and you encounter a monument to children splashing water. This is a reference to the annual Fiesta de los Jarritos. On September 6 the villagers run riot dousing everybody in sight with water.

Water gushes abundantly too from the fountains of the picturesque neighbouring village, Fuenteheridos. In late autumn, you will see mushroom collectors bringing in heavy baskets to the bars in this and all the villages.

Many of these exotic fungi end up as expensive titbits for French gourmets, but the local bars serve them as delicious, bargain-priced snacks.

Along the N433 between Fuenteheridos and Aracena a track to the left takes you to Finca Buen Vino (Los Marines, tel. 959-12 40 34), a three-storey white-shuttered, pink mansion apparently transported from England. Set in 187 acres (75 hectares) of chestnut and olive trees, this is a four-bedroom, English-run hotel where guests enjoy gourmet meals, a cosy country house atmosphere and rural tranquillity. Not for the 10-dollars-a-day traveller.

At Aracena (pop. 6,500), the pleasant centre of the sierra, the big attraction is the Gruta de las Maravillas (Cave of Marvels, open 10.30am-1.30pm, 3-6pm, hours may vary with the season). A guided tour conducts you nearly a mile along the galleries, past vividly coloured rock formations, 12 large chambers and six lakes. Look out for the fleshy curves in the Sala de los Desnudos.

Local pottery is on sale near the cave and several restaurants cater for visitors. Casas (Pozo de la Nieve, 41. Tel: 959-11 00 44. Open 12am-5pm. Visa) is famed for its regional ham and pork dishes. Its prices have climbed, however, and local residents recommend the Sierra restaurant, at Avenida Andalucía, 51, where you can also sample the best ham.

The 13th-century church of the Knights Templar, a Mudejar tower at one corner, is silhouetted against the skyline above Aracena. On Holy Thursday evening, a religious brotherhood bears the images out of the church and carries them down to the town in solemn procession.

Opposite Aracena's crumbling former town hall on Plaza Alta rises the massive Renaissance facade of Nuestra Señora de la Asunción. It appears to be abandoned, but actually part of the church is in use. Work on restoring the whole edifice halted when a wealthy patron died.

The two-star Hotel Sierra de Aracena (Gran Vía, 21. Tel: 959-12 61 75) offers comfortable lodging in the town. Aracena has a tourist information office on the Plaza de San Pedro (tel. 959-11 03 55) and also an office for the Parque Natural de la Sierra de Aracena on the Plaza de Santa Lucía, 23 (tel. 959-11 04 75).

For an exceptional view over the sierras, drive seven miles (11km) to Alájar, where the sanctuary of the Virgin of Los Angeles is built atop the Arias Montano hill. This summit is named after a theologian and philosopher who lived many years here and was visited by King Philip 11. A colourful romería to the shrine is held annually on September 6.

From Aracena the N433, much improved in recent years, heads southeast through the forested hills, descending into Seville province where it joins the N630. The distance from Aracena to **SEVILLE** is 56 miles (90km)❑

Excursion 31 - Across the Frontier:

Huelva-El Rompido-Lepe-Ayamonte-Vila Real (Portugal)-Tavira-Huelva
Distance: 106 miles (170km)

Portugal, with its distinctive culture and cuisine, is only a step away from Huelva. An easy day-trip takes you along the Atlantic coast and across the frontier to the beautiful beaches of the Algarve.

In Huelva, look for the signs for Punta Umbria and Ayamonte. The road, H414, leaves town via a long bridge over the Río Odiel, with docks on your left. You pass over marshes, known as the Marismas de Odiel. Some 200 species of birds are found here, including spoonbills and herons.

Soon you are running past mile upon mile of pines. When you reach the sea, a left turn takes you to Punta Umbria, a summer and weekend resort popular with Spaniards. The beach is good, but the unimaginative high-rise apartment blocks hardly make it worth a detour. Turning right, you drive past dunes and pines and miles of sandy beach. The Laguna de El Portil, just off the road to the right, is a nature reserve where you can observe a rich variety of water fowl.

At El Rompido, a small fishing settlement 15 miles (25 km) from Huelva, head for the waterfront. Just below the lighthouse are rows of single-storey houses. Right on the water's edge, near boats rocking at anchor is Caribe 11, a simple but reliable fish restaurant. The fish is ultra-fresh and goes down well with a bottle of Odiel, one of the fruity white wines produced in the province.

North of El Rompido, the road meets the N431 highway. Heading west, you bypass the thriving, workaday community of Lepe (pop. 16,000).

The local inhabitants, the *leperos,* are famous in Spain but not for the reasons they would like. Just as the English tell their Irish jokes, the Dutch tell their Belgian jokes and so on, Spaniards tell jokes against the *leperos.*

A sample: A detective investigating a bank robbery an-

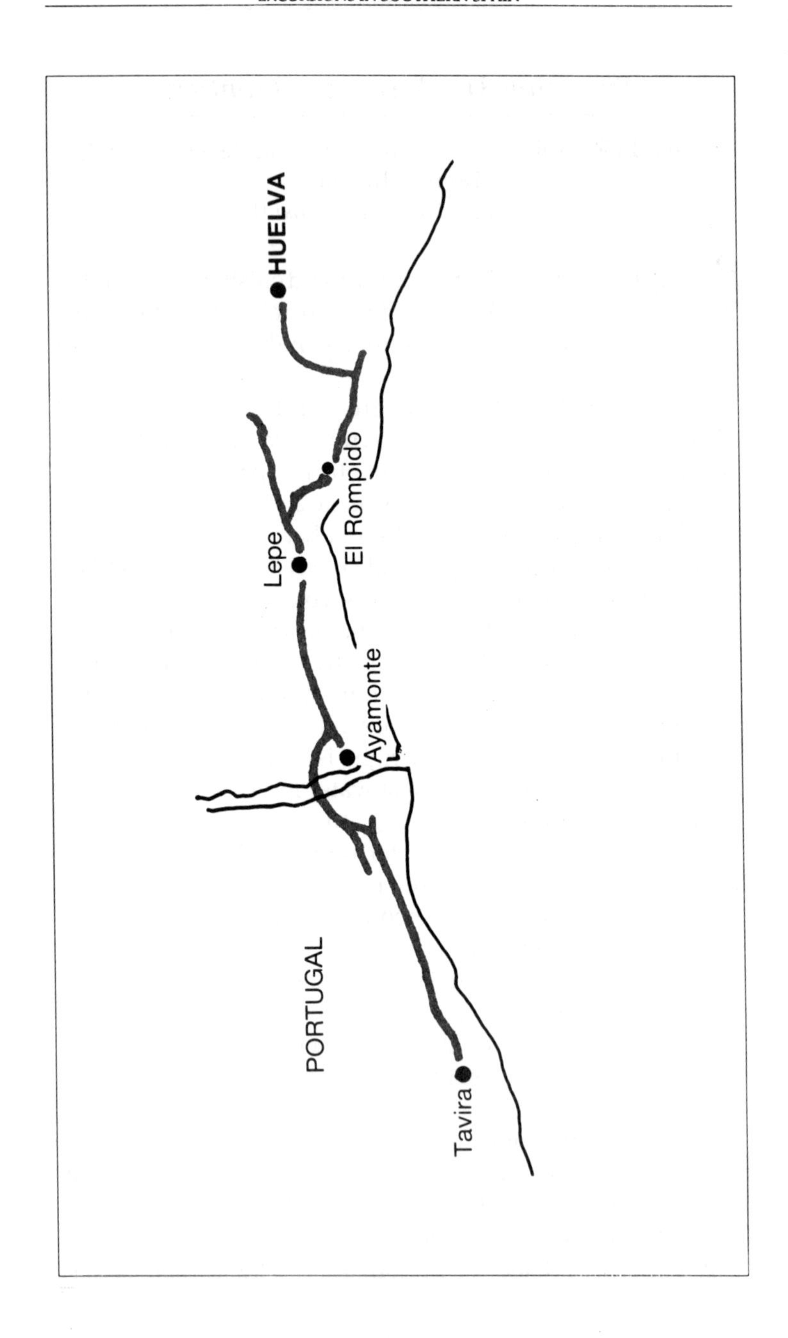
HUELVA
El Rompido
Lepe
Ayamonte
PORTUGAL
Tavira

nounced: "The thief must be a lepero - he made two holes, one to get in and one to get out."

Actually the hardworking people of Lepe are laughing all the way to the bank. Vast plantations of strawberries and citrus fruit, which you will glimpse from the road, have made them prosperous.

At El Empalme, you can take a left and visit Isla Cristina, so low-lying on its sandspit that it seems about to disappear beneath the waves. Thousands of Spaniards flock to the new apartment blocks and brown themselves on the sandy beaches here in summer, but otherwise it is important for its fishing fleet.

Ayamonte (pop. 17,000), 32 miles (52 km) from Huelva, used to have a shabby, end-of-the-road air about it, but it has spruced itself up. Smart shops and new bars and restaurants have opened. A tourist development with hotels and apartments is mushrooming at Isla Canela, a few minutes from town, where there is an excellent beach.

The best place to stay in Ayamonte is the Parador Costa de la Luz (El Castillito. Tel: 959-32 07 00). Commanding beautiful hilltop views over town and estuary, it has undergone a major expansion. If it is closed, try the Don Diego, a comfortable, modern three-star hotel near Ayamonte centre (Ramon y Cajal, 21. Tel: 959-47 02 50).

A handy place to enjoy good tapas or a meal is Manuel Rodríguez's two-fork La Casona, one street back from the waterfront park (Lusitania, 2. Tel: 959-32 10 25. Amex, Diners, Master, Visa. Closed Sun in winter, end September). Brick arches, wooden beams and tiled walls give a pleasant atmosphere to the long bar and dining room. Try the acedías (small flounder). They are excellent value.

A bypass runs around Ayamonte to give access to a 2,200-foot-long bridge, opened in 1991, linking Spain and Portugal across the Guadiana River. Within minutes you are in the Algarve, Portugal's southern corner where the Arab influence is most evident.

Nostalgic types can take the *transbordador*, or ferry, which continues to carry both vehicles and passengers across the

Guadiana. The river crossing has always been a pleasant leisurely way to enter Portugal and within 15 minutes you step ashore in the border town of Vila Real de Santo Antonio (remember your licence, Green Card and car documents).

Vila Real, laid out on a gridiron pattern, holds little of interest. Close by lies the resort of Monte Gordo, modern and mushrooming. For an enjoyable day trip along part of the Algarve coast, the best place to head for is Tavira, 15 miles (23 kilometres) away.

This is a delightful old port, presided over by castle walls and the church of Santa Maria del Castillo, built on the site of a mosque. The tourist office is in the main square, the Praca da República.

Spain seems fast-moving and noisy compared to this easy-going town with meandering cobbled streets. Several shops sell good quality pottery and other crafts at bargain prices.

Sand silted up Tavira's river so that it lost its importance as a port. A mile or so out of town (head south along the water-front), past a series of fish-breeding pools, you find a jetty from where a ferry crosses to an island with fine beaches.

Stroll along the riverside, take a look at the market, gauge the subtly different atmosphere of Portugal, and enjoy a meal at one of the waterfront restaurants.

They offer very good value. Try O Galeao near the market, for friendly service (Visa, Mastercard). Their rice with shellfish goes down well with a bottle of chilled Vinho Verde.

Basic decor and hearty food at basic prices is available at Restaurante Bica, at Rua Almirante Candido dos Reis, 22. Try *Bife de Peru com delicias do mar* (turkey stuffed with seafood).

If you are tempted to stay the night, there are several hostals. Two of the best bets are out of town. As you approach Tavira on the main highway, turn right by a ceramics shop on the right to reach the Pensao Almargem (tel. 081-23386), a budget-priced establishment with a small pool. The restaurant is popular, the speciality being steak grilled on a slab of slate.

Further along, the Eurotel Tavira (Quinta das Oliveiras, Tavira, tel. 081-22041/23071) stands above the highway just over a mile (2km) from Tavira. It boasts two swimming pools, tennis courts and riding facilities, and has a sister hotel on the beach and is priced accordingly.

Remember that during July and August the Algarve coast's popularity means that it can be difficult to find a room❑

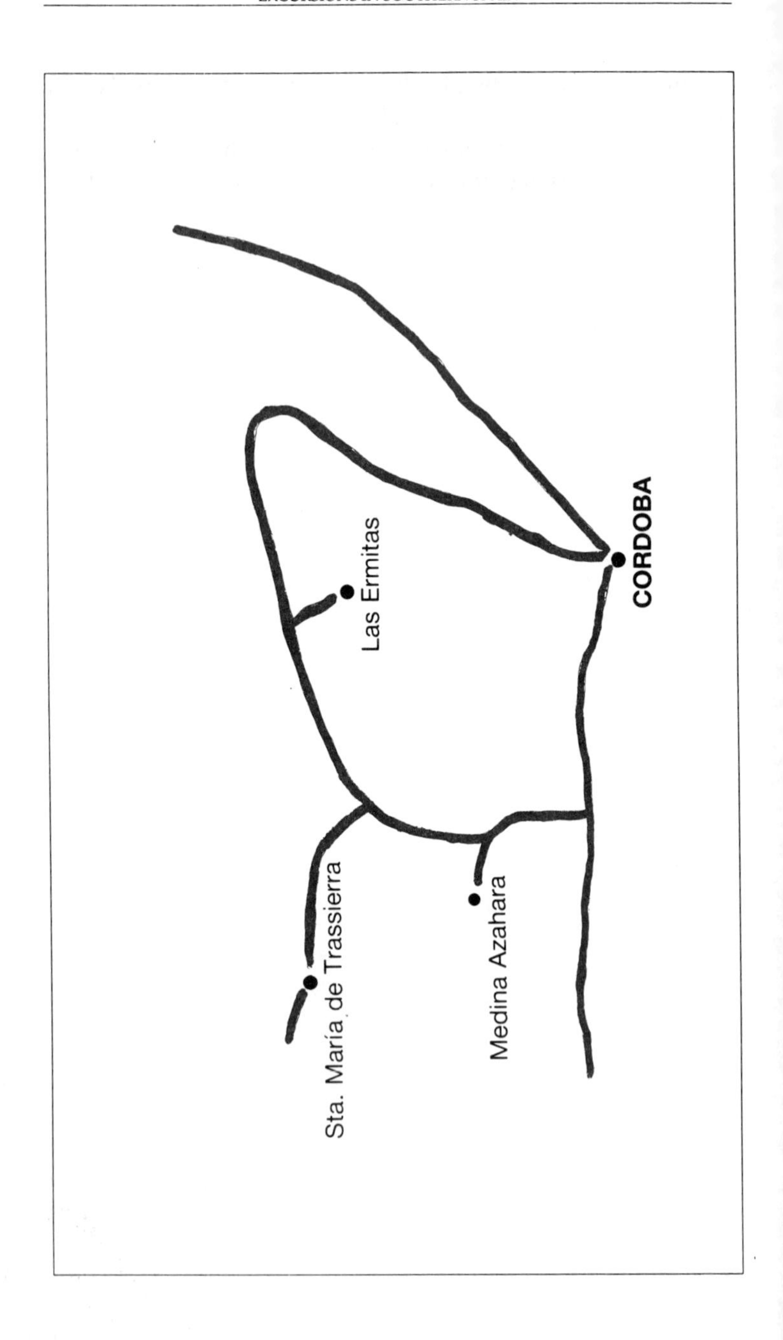
CORDOBA
Las Ermitas
Sta. María de Trassierra
Medina Azahara

Excursion 32 - Sierra Sanctuaries:

Córdoba-Medina Azahara-Las Ermitas-Córdoba
Distance: 40 miles (64km)

When the sun bakes down on **CORDOBA** and the tourists desperately seek relief in the cafes around the Mosque, sensible cordobeses head for the hills. The Sierra Morena runs right up to the city's edge and its breezy heights and thick woods are only a few minutes away.

This is a half-day trip to pleasant picnic spots, wayside restaurants, a potentate's dream palace, and the ancient sanctuaries of medieval mystics.

Take the C431 from Córdoba, which heads west along the Guadalquivir valley towards Almódovar del Río and Seville. After three miles (5km) turn right to Medina Azahara. It is two miles (3km) to the sumptuous residence created by the Caliph of Córdoba, Abd al-Rahman 111, in the 10th century, and named after his favourite wife.

Keep left at the first junction to reach Medina Azahara (open: mid-Sept to April 10am-2pm, 4-6.30pm, May to mid-June 10am-2pm, 6-8.30pm, mid-June to mid-Sept 10am-1.30pm, 6-8.30pm. Closed Mon, Sun afternoon).

More than 10,000 men built the palace, employing 15,000 mules and 4,000 camels to haul up the material to a point overlooking the fertile valley. The palace was on three levels, including gardens, a mosque and the caliph's residence. The Caliph retired here with his concubines, slaves and dancing girls, listening to the tinkling fountains and taking his ease amid halls of marble and jasper, decorated by leading craftsmen from Córdoba, at that time Europe's largest city.

Sumptuous receptions were held, at which awed visitors walked over precious carpets between lines of slaves and soldiers and admired a shimmering pool of quicksilver in the great reception chamber. But the palace endured only a few years. In 1010 Berber invaders sacked it and over the centuries it was ransacked for building materials. Now it is being pieced together from the ruins.

After strolling through this amazing example of Arab sophistication, go back to the junction and fork left towards Santa María de Trassierra and Las Ermitas (CV19).

You glimpse the San Jerónimo monastery to the left as you climb into the sierras past oak-dotted slopes. At a cross-roads, the Restaurant El Cruce offers refreshment and shade under the trees.

Three miles (5km) to the left lies the dozy settlement of Santa María de la Trasierra. The drive takes you past ventas and private houses sheltering amid cork oaks, eucalypts and umbrella pines.

Following the sign to the Ermitas from the crossroads, you pass over a pleasant wooded plateau. A mile from the crossroads a short detour takes you to a mirador (lookout point).

Continuing, you know you are approaching the hermitages as roadside granite crosses mark the way.

Las Ermitas are a closed world of meditation, harking back to early times. Christian hermits are said to have established themselves in caves in these mountains in 400AD. In the 16th century the Council of Trent formed them into a single community near the San Jeronimo monastery.

Around 1700, the community moved to the present site, remaining there until 1957, when it finally died out. Since then the Carmelites have looked after the hermitages and four monks are in residence.

It is a tranquil spot, on a rocky promontory studded with pines, cypresses and cedars. High above Córdoba and the Guadalquivir, you can enjoy the clear air and magnificent views over the city.

After parking your car, you pass through an entrance hall - a donation is expected (visiting times 10am-1pm, summer 4-7.45pm, winter 3-6pm). Over a door are the words *¡Bendita Soledad! Tu mueves a penitencia/O sola felicidad!/Inspira austeridad, contemplación y abstinencia.* (Blessed Solitude! You move one to penitence. Oh, happiness alone! It inspires austerity, contemplation and abstinence.)

Explanatory pamphlets are available in Spanish and tortured English. A cypress-lined path leads first to a cross to the memory of the Conde de Torres Cabrera, "remarkable protector of this venerable desert".

Further on is an example of the 13 hermits' cells, where the recluses enjoyed the comfort of wooden beds covered only with esparto mattresses. A sign exhorts the faithful: "Punish your body but castigate your will more."

The adjacent cemetery features two niches occupied by skulls and nearby palm-trees stand outside the church, dating from 1732. A wall plaque records that Queen Isabel 11 visited with her son Alfonso, the future king, on September 16, 1862.

Inside the church, insert a coin near the entrance and lights flick on to reveal the richly decorated interior, with sculptures, oil paintings, tiles, and - says the brochure - a crucifix made of cinnamon.

Behind a grill sits another skull. This was used by Brother Juan de Dios Aguayo, Marques de Santaella y Villaverde, as a plate and drinking vessel. The English pamphlet explains why: "Doing so penitence for his before licentious life."

Back in the shady gardens, you will find steps leading down to an esplanade from where you can feel the breeze and contemplate the Guadalquivir valley and the Campiña (the Córdoba plain), a patchwork of green, yellow and brown. Above the esplanade stands a huge statue of Christ.

Beyond Las Ermitas, the road continues to a junction with the Córdoba to Villaviciosa road, the CO110. Close by is the Barbacoa La Cabaña, with a big swimming pool and four hundred yards to the left down a side road is Las Dos Columnas, a restaurant with another pool.

On summer weekends half of Córdoba seeks the coolness of this area, cooking vast paellas in the many picnic spots. The ventas do roaring business. During the week they are usually quiet and most are closed on Mondays.

Crossing the Villaviciosa road, we carry on eastwards to a T-junction. To the right the road corkscrews steeply down to **CORDOBA**. A mile or so to the left, amid beautiful open, pine-dotted country lies the former Los Villares golf club, closed for the moment.

If you return to the CO110 at Barbacoa La Cabaña, it is six

miles (9km) from here back to the city. The road winds down, then straightens to pass through some of Córdoba's best residential areas with large houses in extensive grounds. The wide road and spaciousness of this section have an almost Californian air.

As you enter the city itself, the road surface becomes cobbled and surprisingly soon you are amid heavy traffic❑

Excursion 33 - Renaissance Riches:

Granada-Jaén-Baeza-Ubeda-Granada
Distance: 172 miles (274km)

Two of Andalusia's best-preserved historic towns lie on this route, which takes you through the sierras and olive groves of Jaén province and gives you the opportunity to spend a night in medieval splendour.

Leave **GRANADA** on the N323. It curves past the pine-shaded banks of the Cubillas reservoir. This is popular with Granada folk as a place for picnics and outdoor recreation. A clay pigeon-shooting club and the university sailing club are located here.

The Jaén road climbs steadily past olive groves. Near the junction for Iznalloz two large truck-stops, the cafes 402 and La Nava, attract heavy custom. We continue into the mountains, finally reaching the Carretero pass, more than 3,500 feet above sea-level, and entering Jaén province.

From here the road descends along the wooded valley of the Guadalbullón river as it cuts through the craggy Sierra de Alta Coloma. There are no towns or settlements of any size on this route, but the scenery is spectacular in places.

If you do not wish to visit **JAEN**, look for the turn-off to Pegalajar and Mancha Real. This splits off to the right 10 miles (15km) before Jaén and rambles over the sierras by a scenic route to join the Jaén-Ubeda road. Mancha Real, once a textile centre, has one or two interesting buildings, including the Renaissance San Juan Bautista church. From here it is only a mile or so north to the N321.

The mighty Santa Catalina fortress dominates Jaén and, if you want to spend a night in a castle, this is as good a spot as any. The restored building houses a parador. Hannibal is said to have built a tower on this hilltop. Later the Moors established a strongpoint to hold back the Christians, until in 1246 King Ferdinand ejected them.

After you have done your sightseeing in Jaén, take the Ubeda and Albacete road, N321, which heads northwest past

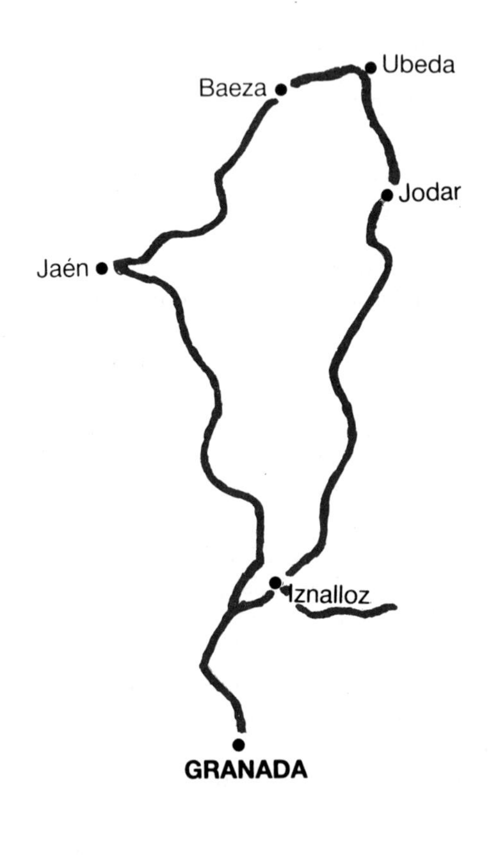
Ubeda
Baeza
Jodar
Jaén
Iznalloz
GRANADA

endless plantations of olive trees. Normally you do not see much activity in this countryside, except during harvest time from about December to February. Jaén province is famed for its olives and harvests around one million tons every year.

Often families work together, spreading sheets to collect the ripe fruit as it is shaken from the trees. Olives must be crushed while fresh or a higher acid content results. Jaén's oil is renowned for quality. Remember that the purest oil is aceite virgen, which has no additives or special treatment.

After 30 miles (48km) you approach Baeza, a town of monuments, with an atmosphere - like its neighbour Ubeda - closer to that of sober Castile than flamenco-dancing Andalusia.

Beatia was the name of the Roman settlement here. Baeza flourished under the Visigoths and later ruled a Moorish mini-kingdom. Its most striking buildings, however, date from the prosperous 16th century.

You enter town along the Camino Real and immediately encounter the Plaza del Pópulo, a museum in itself. Here is the tourism office (953-74 04 44), housed in a fine Plateresque building. From its small projecting balcony the first mass was pronounced after the Moors were ousted, so tradition has it. In the centre of the square is the fountain of Los Leones. The Iberian-Roman statue of a woman above the fountain is said to be Imilce, wife of Hannibal.

In one corner of the plaza is the Villalar Arch, which was built in 1521 to mark a victory over the Comuneros, a rebel movement in Castile.

Baeza's quiet streets retain a medieval feeling, but don't be alarmed at the number of Civil Guards wandering about, especially at weekends - they are off-duty trainees from the local encampment.

Penetrating further into town, you come across the cathedral, a rich mixture of Gothic, Italian Renaissance and Mudejar styles (open during services, usually 1.30am-1pm, 5-7pm). Do not miss the ornate silver monstrance, revealed only after depositing a coin in a slot.

Just down the street is the Jabalquinto palace, a fine piece of 15th-century Gothic civil architecture with a beautiful patio and staircase (open mornings). Close by is a building which housed a university for 300 years. Converted into a high school last century (open 10am-2pm, enter through the college), it still has the old classroom where the great Andalusian poet Antonio Machado taught French from 1912 to 1919.

Opposite the Ayuntamiento (the Andalusian Plateresque town hall, once a jail) on Plaza Cardenal Benavides, a wall plaque on a corner house records that Machado lived there.

Near the centre of town is the Baeza (Concepción, 3, tel. 953-74 43 61) a modern three-star hotel and its associated restaurant, Palacio Andrés de Vandelvira (San Francisco, 14, tel. 953-74 81 30. DC, MC, V. Closed Sun night) a former convent, with a vast, glassed-in cloister.

An interesting new establishment is the Hospedería Fuentenueva (Paseo Arca del Agua. Tel. 953-74 31 00), a 12-room hotel located in the former women's prison. Stonework, marble and timber create a welcome atmosphere and the restaurant specializes in local dishes.

Restaurante Juanito, on the Ubeda road (Paseo Arca del Agua, s/n. Tel: 953-74 00 40. Open 1-4pm, 8-11pm. Closed Sun and Mon nights. No cards. M-E) has achieved a reputation for its use of local produce. If you are a celebrity, your picture may end up on Juanito's crowded wall of fame.

Up the road lies **UBEDA**, where you can stay in the splendid medieval surroundings of the Parador. This 400-year-old palace once accommodated Don Fernando Ortega Salido, Dean of Málaga and first chaplain of the adjacent El Salvador chapel.

The Parador is a good place to stay because you are in the heart of the *zona monumental*. Many of Ubeda's modern buildings are, to put it mildly, undistinguished and it is a dull town, but the architectural magnificence of the past justifies a leisurely visit.

Ubeda owes much of this rich heritage to Francisco de los Cobos, an ambitious 16th-century operator who became the Emperor Charles V's secretary. He grabbed as many other remunerative posts as he could.

But his greed led to his downfall, and a relation, Juan Vázquez de Molina, replaced him. The Parador and several fine Renaissance buildings are located on a square called, no surprise, Plaza Vázquez de Molina.

A notable architect named Andrés de Vandelvira, was responsible for Vázquez's simple little abode, now the town hall, as he was for the Hospital de Santiago, an austere building sometimes compared to the Escorial, Felipe 11's bleak palace near Madrid.

It is advisable to park your car and walk around Ubeda, as negotiating the labyrinth of narrow, one-way streets can be a frustrating experience. Inevitably, you will come across shops selling local handicrafts, including green pottery and esparto weavings, a tradition that goes back to Moorish times.

To return to Granada, head south on the C325. Partridges and lapwings may flutter up as you cross the Guadalquivir and and the Baeza-Almería railway line and drive through open country sown with barley, rye and wheat.

The road bypasses Jódar, bleached and brown on its hillside, with the towers visible of church and old castle. Olive-treed valleys stretch to the distance between the lumpy outlines of bare mountains. Walls of rock reflect the heat in this rugged, sparsely-populated area.

As you traverse the stretch of green offered by the long valley of the Río Jandulilla, a sign to your left tries to lure you to visit a religious shrine on the road to lonely Cabra del Cristo. Up goes the road into the heights, reaching 3,800 feet at Cuesta Los Gallardos before running down steeply to Guadahortuna, sheltering in a hollow, in Granada province.

A grain silo competes for attention with the sandstone-coloured church tower, topped with a tiled belfry. Turn right here, sticking to the C325. One or two bars and restaurants offer refreshment.

You pass through the Montes de Granada, fertile rolling country covered with cornfields. After a right turn to join the C336, you run along a new road down the flat, irrigated valley. Iznalloz sprawls over a rock on the left, boasting of its Arab castle, Los Almendros, and in a few minutes you reach a T-junction on the N323. **GRANADA** is 19 miles (30km) away❑

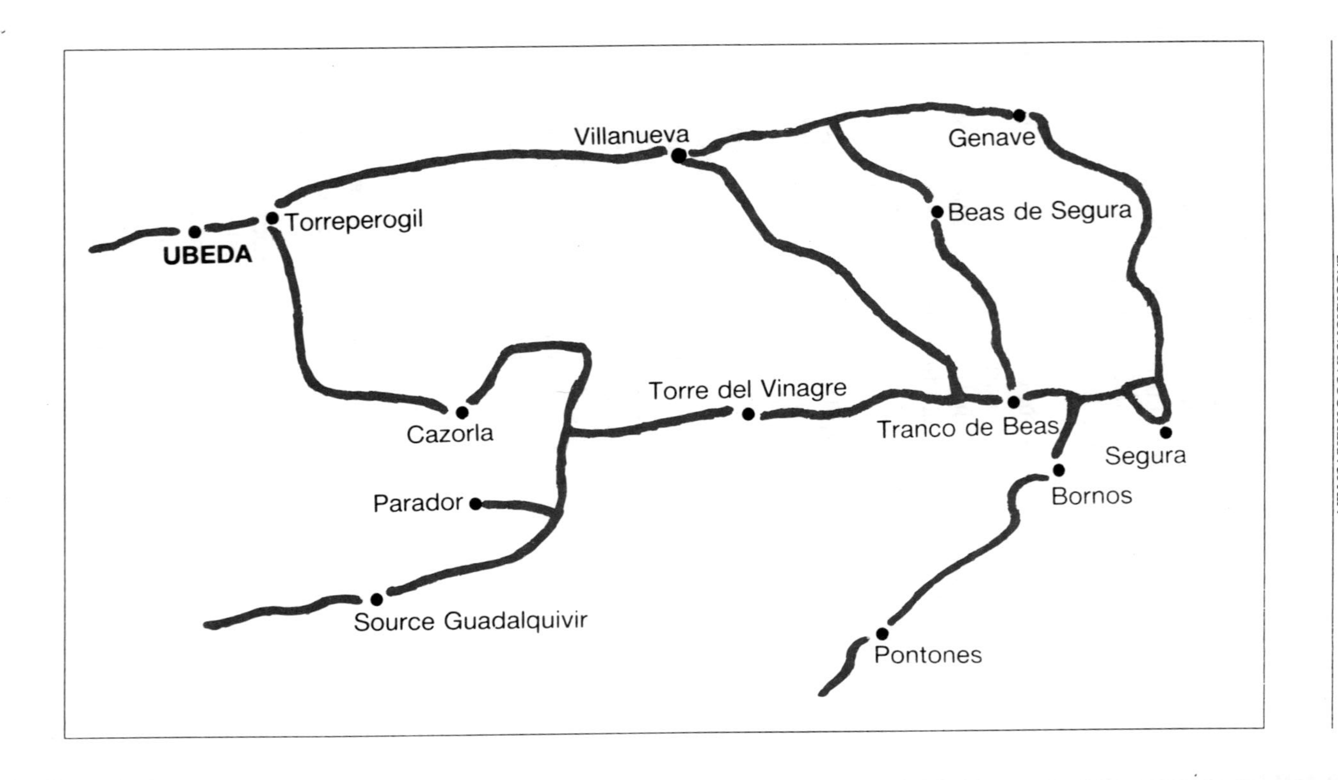
Villanueva
Genave
Beas de Segura
Torreperogil
UBEDA
Torre del Vinagre
Cazorla
Tranco de Beas
Segura
Bornos
Parador
Source Guadalquivir
Pontones

Excursion 34 - To Trout Streams and Eagles:

Ubeda-Cazorla-El Tranco-Segura-Ubeda
Distance: 180 miles (290km)

Hidden away in Andalusia's northeast corner is a wilderness treasure-house of tumbling waterfalls, soaring crags, abundant wildlife, and remote villages, where you really can get away from it all.

Plan a minimum of two to three days to visit the town of Cazorla and the 535,000-acre (214,000-hectare) Parque Natural de Cazorla, Segura y Las Villas. It is ideal camping country, but there are comfortable hotels too. Bring your binoculars.

From **UBEDA**, the N322 runs northwest along a ridge looking out over regiments of olive trees marching away to the sierras.

At Torreperogil, five miles (8km) from Ubeda, you can pay a visit to the cooperative, Nuestra Señora de la Misericordia, which makes both wine and olive oil. The wine is a hearty, drinkable beverage, though hardly likely to figure in any gourmet guide.

Leaving Torreperogil, take the J314 to the right, which rolls past cornfields and olive groves, crossing the Guadalquivir River where it is dammed to form a reservoir, the Embalse del Puente de la Cerrada.

At Peal de Becerro, 20 miles (33km) from Ubeda, veer left on the C328 to Cazorla. The Sierra de Cazorla rears up ahead and as the road dips you catch your first glimpse of Cazorla, with its square watch-tower standing guard above the huddled dwellings.

Cazorla (pop. 9,000), the gateway to the nature park, rambles up and down ridges at the foot of a crag called Los Halcones (the falcons).

Leave your car near the Plaza de la Constitución (or in the area below, except on Mondays when the countryfolk flock in for market day). Doctor Muñoz street (pedestrians only in the evenings) leads to the heart of Cazorla, the Plaza de la Corredera.

Between the parish church at one corner and the town hall

at another lies the Bar Monterrey, where nothing much has changed in decades, except that the domino players have acquired a few more grey hairs.

Verses on the wall pay tribute to this bar as "a jewel which is pure gold". It is written by one Juan Luis Amador, whose poetic achievements grace the walls of several other Cazorla establishments.

For excellent tapas, try the more modern Bar Las Vegas just across the square. Squeezing down the older quarter's narrow streets and dodging traffic on José Salcedo street, you arrive at the Plaza de Santa Maria. Above is the Castillo de la Yedra, with a folklore museum.

Near the ruins of Santa María church is the Cueva de Juan Pedro (Tel: 953-72 12 25), a restaurant of beams and mighty stone walls which looks ancient enough to have welcomed Don Quixote for dinner. Mercedes, the spritely owner, grills chicken and lamb over an open fire. Good value and lots of atmosphere.

Cazorla has several basic pensions and a Villa Turística (Ladera de San Isicio, tel. 953-71 01 00. Three star price rate). Accommodation in this village complex, built in traditional style, includes a fireplace and cooking facilities.

A mile beyond Cazorla en route to the natural park is another excellent overnight spot, the two-star Hotel Sierra de Cazorla 11 (Ctra de la Sierra, km2, La Iruela. Tel: 953-72 00 15) with swimming pool and restaurant. It perches below the melodramatic Knights Templar castle, which clings to a crag at La Iruela, and enjoys breath-taking views over the olive groves.

For information about the natural park, Andalusia's largest, call at the office of the AMA (Agencia del Medio Ambiente), the regional environmental agency. You will find it on the Cazorla street leading to the sierras, at Martinez Falero, 11 (953-72 01 25). It is open 11am-2pm on weekdays, except Mondays.

If you are interested in a guided tour through the park, contact Quercus, Guías de la Naturaleza. They have an office just off Cazorla's Plaza de la Constitución at Juan Domingo, 2 (Tel: 953-72 01 15) and an office inside the park at the Torre del Vinagre information centre.

Quercus takes up to five passengers in Land-Rovers along tracks closed to other traffic. Their guides are knowledgeable about the flora and fauna of the park and some speak French and English.

From Cazorla the road runs past La Iruela, dwellings wedged perilously on the mountainside below castle and crag, and passes the park control point at Burunchel. Any weapons you are carrying must be declared (permits are necessary to fish or hunt).

Zigzagging upwards, with vistas of olive-clad hills rolling to the horizon, you enter a pine and fir forest and at 3,900 feet cross La Paloma Pass. If you stop at the first lookout point on the left, you will get an idea of the extent of this corner of the park.

The Guadalquivir valley runs northwards, bounded by thick forest and bare mountain-tops. The lookout point was known as the Mirador del Caudillo, recalling the time when the whole valley was sealed off so that General Franco could spend a few days hunting here.

Ten miles from Cazorla, you reach the Empalme del Valle. This is a crossroads, with a large ceramic map of the natural park. A left turn leads 27 miles (43km) to El Tranco, a mighty dam across the Guadalquivir.

Continue straight ahead and you reach a turn to the right. It is a scenic three-mile (5km) drive up this road to the Parador El Adelantado (Sierra de Cazorla. Tel: 953-72 10 75). Across the thickly-wooded valley you see Poyos de las Mesas, a mighty flat-topped buttress.

The Parador is magnificently situated in a secluded spot above crags. Green lawns lead down to a swimming pool in this tranquil hideaway. This is favoured hunting territory and, in season, venison is on the menu in the restaurant.

Continuing past the turn to the Parador, the road curves down to the Guadalquivir River, passing on the right the Vadillo timber mill and forestry centre. The settlement of neat stone houses has two bars.

Just before the road crosses the river, a path leads to the left. Follow this down the Guadalquivir chasm, past water foaming over a dam, to reach the Linarejos waterfall, a fine sight in years of good rains as it tumbles over a rock face. Continue on this path and you circle around to meet the road again, a pleasant walk of 30 to 40 minutes.

Crossing over the river bridge at Vadillo, turn immediately right towards the source of the Guadalquivir. After two miles (3km), just after a privately-run camp-ground, you cross the Puente de las Herrerías. Legend has it that this bridge was built in one night so that Queen Isabel could speed past en route to conquer the Moorish Kingdom of Granada.

From the bridge, an unpaved track winds seven miles (11km) up the valley to La Cañada de las Fuentes, where the Guadalquivir bubbles from beneath a rock and begins its 410-mile (660km) journey to the Atlantic.

A right turn near the source takes you to Quesada while a left leads to Pozo Alcón. If you follow the Pozo Alcón track, you pass a shady picnic spot with stone benches and flowing water.

The road winds up and up through the pines until at more than 5,000 feet above sea-level you reach a pass marked by four stone cairns. A hut crowns the summit of Cabañas, a bare 6,650-feet peak above the pass, from where you have stirring views of the hills and mountains to the west.

You don't have to be an expert ornithologist to pick out circling eagles and hawks in the park. Peonies, lupins, orchids and the unique Cazorla violet are among the flowers to be seen in springtime. Fallow and red deer, *muflón* (mountain sheep), wild goats, boar, fox and badger are common. Be careful driving at night as deer often stray on to the roads.

The easiest way to view the larger animals is to visit the Parque Cinegético, before 10am and after 6pm. Fodder and water are provided at that point to attract the animals.

To reach the Parque, return to the Empalme del Valle and take the Tranco road down the valley. The animals' feeding-point is about 20 miles (32km) from the Empalme.

Before that you will reach the Centro de Interpretación (open 11am-2pm, 4-7pm, possibly later in summer, closed Monday), housed in a stone building at Torre del Vinagre. This has interesting information on the geology, plants and animals of the park. Next door is a hunting museum, with a daunting range of trophies. Among these are the interlocked horns of stags which died of starvation when they became trapped during the autumn battles for supremacy.

Previously one of Franco's record trophies was displayed, but his name has mysteriously disappeared. When he came to fish and shoot, he stayed at the solid stone lodge next to the museum. Nearby is a botanic garden.

The centre can inform you on possible walks. One of the most enjoyable starts nearby. Take the road opposite the Torre del Vinagre down to the river.

Continue to the Piscifactoria. This is a trout farm (open 12am-2pm, 5-7pm, closed Monday). Just beyond is a parking spot and a track, closed to the public, runs alongside the Borosa River to a hydro-electric station.

Follow the track for a delightful walk up the valley. Trout frolic in the clear tumbling river. Lizards skitter away at your approach. If you trek three to four hours, the last section up a steep gulch of tumbled rocks, you reach the lakes of Aguas Negras and Valdeazores.

Less energetic types can limit themselves to a three-hour round trip. Where the track veers away from the river, stick to the path. It crosses foot-bridges over cascading water, then reaches a spectacular narrow gorge, where wooden planks are pinned to the rock face. Shortly after, the path meets the track again.

Campsites, picnic spots and ventas dot the road to El Tranco. One hotel with an ideal location is the three star Noguera de la Sierpe (Km 13, Ctra de la Sierra, Coto Ríos. Tel: 953-72 16 01). Attractively converted from a farmhouse, it features a view over the wooded valley of the Guadalquivir, with heating and television in the rooms and a swimming pool.

Simpler accommodation is available at the one-star Hostal Mirasierra (Ctra del Tranco Km 20. Tel: 953-72 05 00), near Coto Ríos. You can eat grilled trout at the Mirasierra restaurant, although this has lost some of its rustic charm thanks to "modernisation" and expansion. If you are lucky you may see the boar that wanders down to rummage among the rubbish bins outside.

Away from the road in a tranquil spot is La Hortizuela (Ctra del Tranco, km18.5, tel. 953-71 31 50), comfortable and reasonably priced. It has a restaurant and pool.

El Tranco dam is designed to hold up to 500 million cubic metres of water. You pass over the top of the 300-foot-high barrier and can make a sharp left turn with the river to descend westwards towards Villanueva del Arzobispo and cut short the trip.

Alternatively, continue on J704 until Hornos and its ruined castle appear high on a crag. Drive into this hamlet (pop. 800) and park by the town hall and the medieval Asunción parish church. A doorway alongside the town hall (undergoing major renovation) leads to the Mirador El Aguilón, a breezy balcony from where you gaze down on the valley and El Tranco reservoir.

It is possible to make a detour from Hornos to the source of another important Spanish river, but allow at least three hours. Take the road to Pontones, which corkscrews up through pinewoods before emerging on a ridge with tremendous vistas of cliffs, crags and distant lake.

The road descends between rock faces to the dozing settlement of Pontones, above which are some odd rock formations. Turn right just after the village to Fuente Segura. A potholed track runs three miles (5km) to a picnic spot and a point where chill, transparent water surges out of a blue grotto. This is the Segura River, which eventually empties into the Mediterranean in Murcia.

From Pontones the road continues through wild, uninhabited country to lost and lonely Santiago de la Espada and then into a remote corner of Granada province.

Retracking, if you continue on the route that runs below Hornos from El Tranco towards Puente de Genave, take a road to the right to the fortress village of Segura de la Sierra (pop. 2,600). Climb up the ramparts of Segura's restored castle, look out at the cultivated slopes and sierras fading into purple distance, and reflect how difficult it must have been to conquer this 4,000-foot-high stronghold when it was under the sway of

Córdoba's Caliphs.

Segura has a an unusual plaza de toros. Partly chipped out of rock, it is rectangular instead of round.

From Segura it is 15 miles (24 km) via Orcera and la Puerta de Segura to Puente de Genave on the N322, the Jaén-Albacete highway. A left takes you past rolling seas of those ubiquitous olives and a succession of small towns. Detour up to hilltop Iznatoraf for panoramic views. Continue on to Villacarrillo and **UBEDA**, 48 miles (77km) from Puente de Genave.

Note: The most detailed map of Cazorla park is published by Libros Penthalon. It combines several large-scale military maps on a scale of 1:50,000, produced by the Servicio Geográfico del Ejército❑

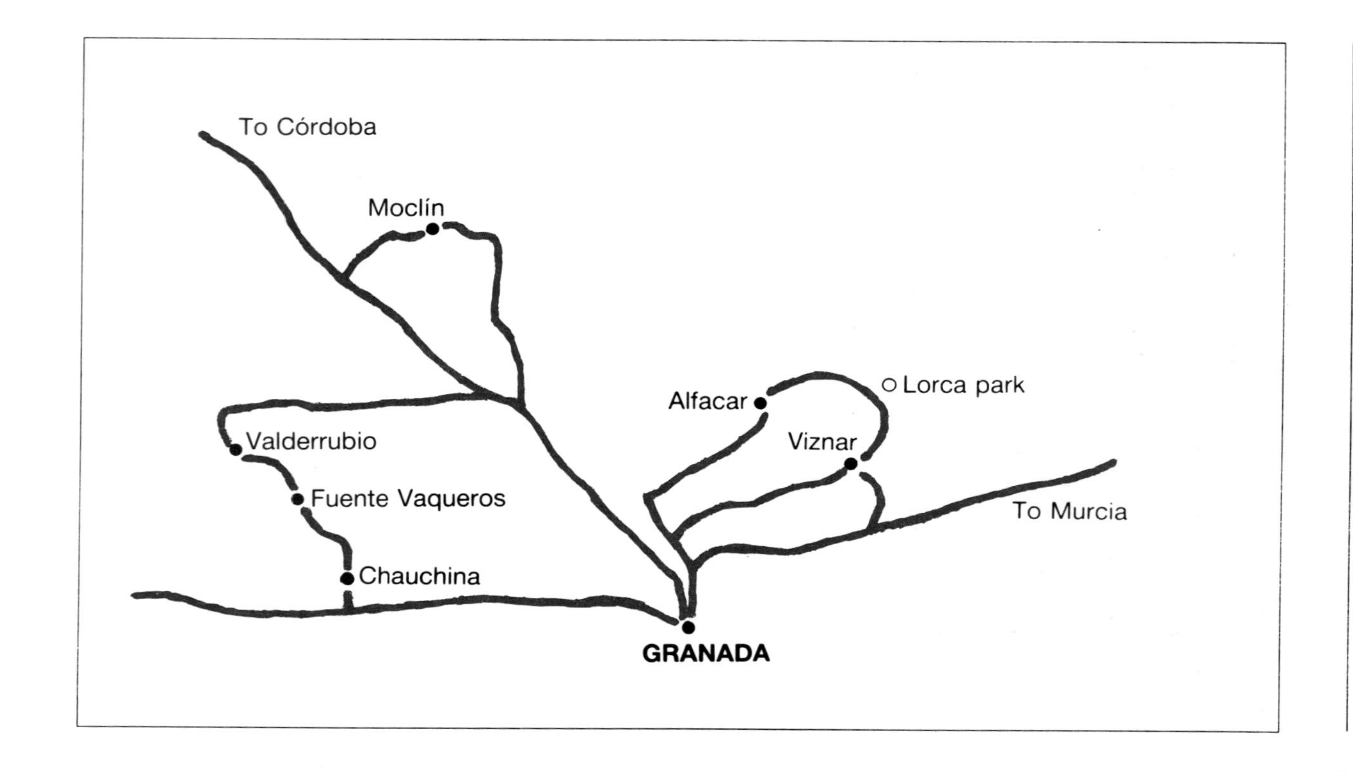
To Córdoba
Moclín
Alfacar
Lorca park
Valderrubio
Viznar
Fuente Vaqueros
To Murcia
Chauchina
GRANADA

Excursion 35 - A Poet's Journey:

Granada-Fuente Vaqueros-Valderrubio-Moclín-Viznar-Granada

Distance: 60 miles (96km)

Federico García Lorca, one of the greatest Spanish poets and dramatists of this century, was profoundly influenced by his childhood and life as a young man in **GRANADA**.

He hated some aspects of the city, but he also loved it - "the hours are longer and sweeter there than in any other Spanish town," he once commented. He himself was loved and hated, as it turned out when he was killed at the start of the Spanish Civil War.

This route takes you to Lorca's birthplace outside Granada and some of the places he frequented in the city, from where he drew inspiration for a number of his most famous works.

Head west on the Malaga and Seville road, the N342. You pass Santa Fe and Granada airport on the left. The Catholic Monarchs camped at Santa Fe with their army in 1491, when they were laying siege to Granada. A royal maid is said to have left a candle too close to a curtain in Queen Isabel's tent and flames destroyed the campground. King Fernando thereupon ordered a proper town built and Isabela chose the name, which means "holy faith". The capitulation of Granada was signed there in November, 1491.

Nine miles (14km) from Granada, turn right to Chauchina. Follow the signs for Fuente Vaqueros as the road zig-zags through Chauchina, a farming community with trundling tractors holding up faster traffic. Fuente Vaqueros is two miles (3km) from Chauchina across the Genil river and through typical scenery in the Vega, the fertile plain which spreads out from the hills of Granada and which a Moorish historian likened to "a silver bowl filled with emeralds and precious stones".

Large plantations of poplars dot the landscape. In between them everything from maize to melons grows in the well-watered soil. Here and there are barns with openwork brick walls, which allow breezes to flow through and dry the tobacco leaves when they are harvested in autumn.

Fuente Vaqueros has an English connection, since it once formed part of a latifundio or vast estate, known as Soto de Roma. This was donated by Spain in 1813 to the Duke of Wellington in gratitude for his part in ousting Napoleon from the peninsula. The Duke never bothered to visit and these lands no longer belong to his descendants, although the family still owns the Molino del Rey estate to the north, near Illora.

Fuente Vaqueros (pop. 3,700) itself is an unremarkable place, although Lorca recalled it lyrically - "surrounded with poplars, which laugh and sing and are palaces of birds, and elders and blackberries, which in summer give fruit that is sweet and difficult to pick".

Off the long main square, with its cafes, shady trees and an ugly modern monument to the poet, lies the Casa-Museo Fedrico García Lorca, where he was born. Buy your ticket in Manuel de Falla street, opposite the school Lorca once attended. Then walk around into the next street, once Trinidad street, now - surprise, surprise - Calle Poeta García Lorca.

A guide shows visitors around Number 4, a simple, two-storey building (visits 10am-1pm, 4-6pm, on the hour, later afternoon hours in summer. Closed Monday. Tel: 958-44 64 53).

To the left of the entrance is the room where Lorca's parents slept and there is the wooden and brass bed in which he was born on June 11, 1898. Photographs, copies of first editions, childhood sketches, letters by the poet to Dalí's sister Ana María and the piano where he played are among the carefully arranged contents of the house. The first floor, formerly a granary, has been converted into a hall where exhibitions on Lorca-related themes are held.

Continue the journey to the neighbouring village, Valderrubio, some three miles (4km) to the northwest of Fuente Vaqueros. When Lorca was nine, the family moved here. At that time it bore the unfortunate name Asquerosa (meaning "disgusting"). No doubt weary of neighbours' gibes, the village leaders changed the name to Valderrubio in 1943.

The Lorcas spent two to three years here before moving to Granada. Near their first house, in Calle Real, was the home of

Frasquita Alba, a woman of strong character on whom Lorca based his play "The House of Bernarda Alba". For most of their stay, the family lived at Number 20 on Calle de la Iglesia.

Hot on the trail of the inspiration for some of Lorca's most famous works, we head north from Valderrubio towards Illora, turning right at a T-junction towards Zujaira and Pinos Puente. We pass through olive groves and reach the N432, the Granada-Córdoba highway. Turn right, then left on a minor road to Moclín. The road follows the Frailes river, then loops upwards to Moclín (pop. 5,100), squatting on its hilltop.

Queen Isabel and King Fernando spent some time at the castle here while they tightened the screws on the Kingdom of Granada. After Granada's fall in 1492, they gave Moclín a standard used in the campaign. This canvas, depicting Christ shouldering the Cross, was installed in the church and over the centuries a cult grew up around it. The Santo Cristo del Paño, as it came to be known, was credited with curative powers and, in particular, it was said to work miracles on infertile women.

Apparently hearing about the Cristo and the bizarre scenes accompanying the annual pilgrimage to Moclín sowed the seeds in Lorca's imagination which led him to write the play *Yerma.* You can see the famous canvas in the sanctuary inside the castle walls and, if you turn up on October 5, you can witness it being carried in the romeria, which is still held every year.

From Moclín it is 22 miles (36km) back to **GRANADA**, via Puerto López to the west and down the N432.

Within the city itself there are many spots recalling the poet's life there. Opposite the Correos (post office) on the Puerto Real, in the heart of the city, is the facade of an old building which housed El Suizo, a famous Granada cafe and meeting place. The interior has been totally rebuilt since the days when García Lorca frequently sat at one of the marble tables of El Suizo, joking and discussing with his friends.

Not far away along the Acera del Darro, which leads to the Genil river, is the house the Lorca family first occupied in Granada. Today it is part of the Hotel Montecarlo.

From there it is a few steps to the Plaza del Campillo and a cafe now called the Chikito. It is much changed from the days in the early 1920s when it was known as the Cafe Alameda and a rendezvous of writers, artists, musicians, young idealists, all eager and ambitious. Lorca was a leading light and no doubt enjoyed excited conversations with composer Manuel de Falla here. The two helped to organise a legendary *cante jondo* (flamenco-singing) festival in the Alhambra in 1922.

Lorca's interest in flamenco was encouraged by his wanderings over Sacromonte and his contacts with the large community of gypsies inhabiting the caves. This helped inspire one of his most popular poetic works, *Romancero Gitano.*

From 1925 the Lorca family spent their summers at the Huerta de San Vicente, an enchanting old farmhouse on the Vega with views of the Alhambra. Here Lorca wrote some of his most famous works, including Blood Wedding.

To reach the Huerta, go west from Puerto Real along Recogidas street, turn right on the Camino de Ronda and then left along Virgen Blanca. The city has invaded the once-tranquil farmland. Ghastly modern apartment blocks reach almost to the Huerta and on its western side a new bypass carries heavy traffic.

But the old house survives, surrounded now by a rather bleak municipal park. Granada town hall has created the Casa-Museo de Lorca there, restoring the farmhouse to its original state. The poet's bed, piano and other belongings have been donated by his family.

This was where Lorca returned to from Madrid at the start of the Spanish Civil War in 1936, ill-advisedly, for he had antagonised fanatical rightwingers who supported Franco's uprising.

On August 9, Lorca took refuge in the house of friends in the city. A few days later he was arrested by the Nationalist rebels, who had taken over the city, and conducted to the offices of the Civil Governor, now the Law Faculty of Granada University, on Calle Duquesa.

From here we can follow Lorca's route after it had been decided that he must die. Follow the signs on the Gran Vía and the Avenida de la Constitución that point to the Murcia road.

This takes you up a steep, one-way street. At the junction at the top, the Murcia road swings right. Follow the sign to the left to La Cartuja and Alfacar.

You pass the magnificent Baroque church of La Cartuja and a rather dismal suburb of high-rise blocks. Take the road to the right to Viznar. It runs up along a ridge planted with olive trees and with fine views of the mountains, city and Vega.

We pass through the narrow streets of Viznar (pop. 680), with its old church and archbishop's palace, and follow the road which curves around the hillside to Alfacar. Just outside Viznar, below the road, barely visible, are the ruins of a building where Lorca and his fellow-prisoners spent their last hours.

From here hundreds of prisoners - nobody knows exactly how many - were taken at dawn to the nearby Barranco de Viznar, where they were shot. Lorca, however, apparently got special treatment. Carry on along the Alfacar road. Beyond a modern block of apartments is the Lorca memorial park. Inside, a granite block marks the spot where he is believed to have been shot. His remains were apparently buried by the olive tree standing alongside.

A brick entrance and iron gates lead to the park, surrounded by poplars and cedars and dedicated to Lorca and all victims of the Civil War. Ceramic plaques on the walls record some of the poet's verses. Although it was only opened in April 27, 1986, weeds are already sprouting in the park, the water channels are dry and the gates are often closed.

A little beyond the park, on the left, is a pool of clear water. This is the Fuente Grande, from which water has been channelled to Granada since Arab times. Appropriately, the Moors gave it the name "Spring of Tears".

It is possible to return to Granada by continuing on this road to Alfacar. Near the old village church with its square stone tower is a bakery, recalling the fame this village has always had for the quality of its bread. From Alfacar it is five miles (8km) back to the city.

Alternatively, retrace your steps from the Lorca park and on reaching Viznar, fork left above the village. A good road winds through pinewoods with good picnic spots to the Murcia highway, just one mile (2km) away. Turn right and it is eight miles (13km) to Granada, passing over the Puerto Lobo (wolf pass) before winding down to the city, with magnificent views along the way.

Note: Aficionados of Lorca and his work can enter deeper into his world by reading Lorca's Granada: A practical guide (Faber & Faber 1992) or the Spanish version, *Guía a la Granada de Federico García Lorca* (Plaza & Janes 1989). This book is written by Ian Gibson, the poet's acclaimed biographer, whose painstaking investigations finally uncovered the truth about his death❑

Excursion 36 - Europe's Highest Road:

Granada-Pinos Puente-Pradollano-La Veleta-Río Genil-Güéjar-Sierra-Granada
Distance: 60 miles (95km)

Andalusia's ice cube, the Sierra Nevada, has a grandeur all its own. Its glittering snows can be seen from parched, far-off olive groves and vineyards and its waters help to keep much of the region alive.

Running from Granada province into Almeria, the sierra was formed 20 million years ago during the terciary folding, and glacial action has carved out 40 lagoons. To protect the area and its varied botany and animal life, 340,000 acres have been declared a nature park.

The sierra has 14 peaks over 9,500 feet (3,000 metres), one of which, Mulhacén at 11,400 feet (3,482 metres), is the highest point on mainland Spain. In the summer months, it is possible to climb the 14 peaks in a tough three-day hike and there are other fine walking opportunities. However, nobody should venture on the mountain unless they are fit and properly equipped. Consult the Federación Andaluza de Montañismo, Reyes Católicos, 1, Granada. Several refuges exist to shelter walkers and climbers.

The highway that runs to the top of the Sierra Nevada is claimed to be Europe's highest, but the driving is fairly simple as there are no really steep gradients or hair-raising bends. The road as far as the ski resort at Pradollano underwent costly improvements in the early 1990s.

Only in winter can the road be difficult and then all motorists are advised to carry chains.

Leaving **GRANADA** on the Paseo de la Bomba, you pass in the park two yellow tramcars, recalling the days when trams rattled and rolled through the city and out to distant points in the country. They continued to run until the early 1970s.

Fill up before leaving town, as once out of Granada there is only one petrol station on the route. The GR420 road runs along the Genil valley, passing orchards and stands of poplar trees.

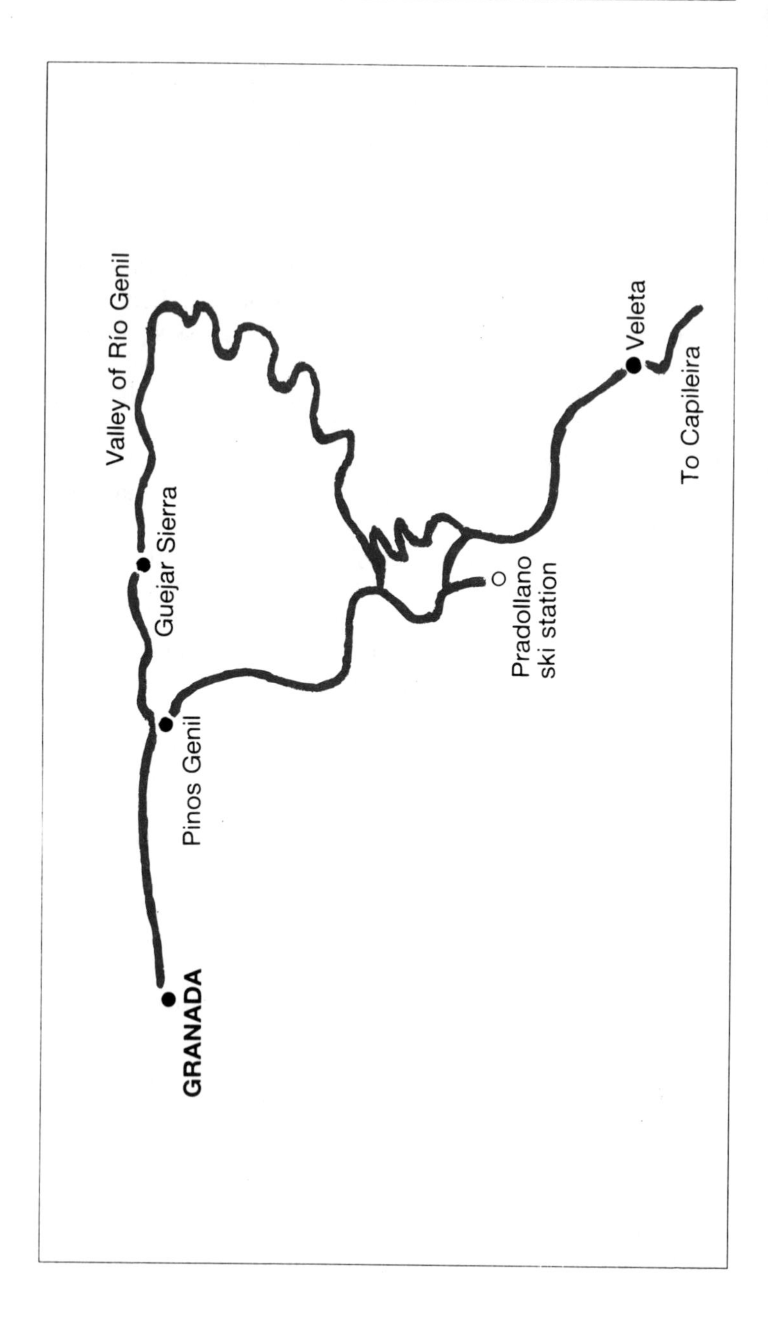
Valley of Río Genil
Guejar Sierra
Pinos Genil
GRANADA
Pradollano
ski station
Veleta
To Capileira

At Cenes de la Vega a building frenzy has transformed the village and a wall of concrete rises up the valley-side.

At Pinos Genil, the road begins to climb upwards and you glimpse a colossal stone wall blocking the valley, a dam creating the Embalse de Canales. There is a viewing point on the left.

Just past La Higuera hostal and restaurant a narrow, potholed side road to the right shins up the mountainside towards El Purche, a 5,000-foot high peak. There are excellent views.

You cross an old track known as the Camino de los Neveros. This was the route taken by muleteers descending from the mountains with loads of ice and snow. From Moorish times the *neveros* (from *nieve,* snow) earned a living bringing a breath of coolness to those granadinos who could afford the luxury.

Thirteen miles (21km) from Granada, the red roof of El Nogal, a two-star hotel and restaurant, appears (Ctra Sierra Nevada, km 21. Tel: 958-48 48 36). This is a pleasant spot to eat, take refreshment or to stay and take off on hiking expedititions.

Continuing, you see the Campsa petrol station and below it a surprisingly bright patch of emerald-green, a football pitch. Retrieving a ball kicked out of play must require mountaineering skills as the pitch is perched high on the mountainside, with the village of Güéjar-Sierra visible far below.

Nearby is the three-star Hotel Santa Cruz (Ctra Sierra Nevada km 23. Tel: 958-447 08 00), named after Juan José Santa Cruz, the engineer responsible for the road to the Sierra Nevada.

Virtually the last building before the final haul to the ski station is the one-star hostal El Desvío (958-34 01 83), a useful point to stop for a snack or a meal of rabbit with mushrooms. Local honey is on sale here and at other points.

Past the Mirador Las Víboras, the road climbs steadily, but without any excessive gradients, entering the upper levels of the Monachil river valley. Great ridges run upwards, planted here and there with conifers, but the country is generally eroded and rounded without any spectacular peaks as you would find in the Alps. The grey rocks definitely look more attractive under a layer of snow.

Even the snow cannot do much to soften the jarring outlines of the hotel and apartment blocks at Pradollano, the centre of the Solynieve skiing area at 6,800 feet above sea-level. They look as though they have been picked up from a city suburb and planted down on the mountainside by mistake.

Twenty miles (33km) from Granada, the resort underwent huge expansion for world ski championships in 1995, only for these to be postponed for lack of snow in the driest winter on record. Nineteen lifts carry skiers up the slopes where they can career down more than 30 miles (50km) of marked runs from as high as 11,000 feet (3390 metres) above sea level. There is also cross-country skiing. If you intend skiing here, double your usual skin protection, as this is Europe's southernmost ski slope and in spring the sun shines with African intensity.

In season (December to late April), Pradollano's bars, restaurants and hotels buzz with life. Off-season, only one or two cafes and hotels are open. For ski resort information (weather, snow reports, buses to Pradollano from Granada) see Granada under Town and City Guide.

Above the ski resort, the highway runs past crags known as the Peñones de San Francisco and continues zigzagging upwards. High on a ridge to the right, the white bowl of a radio telescope scans the heavens.

We pass a monument to the Virgen de las Nieves. Every August 5 people of the sierras pay homage to this Virgin, in the Romería Blanca. Her small image is carried up by torchlight from Pradollano to a lofty spot near the Veleta peak, and just after dawn a priest conducts a mass, often watched from adjacent rocky slopes by wild goats.

A cable car runs in winter to the top of the Veleta, 11,130 feet high, from which you have magnificent views of the mountains and possibly a glimpse of the Mediterranean and Africa.

The paved road runs right to this peak, 31 miles (46km) from Granada. If you are in adventurous mood, you can continue over the sierras to the Alpujarras region on a dirt track that commences just below the Veleta. This route is only open in summer and autumn - usually from mid-July. Check with the Civil Guard (tel. 958-48 03 51) and also check weather reports as from October on there can be snowfalls.

Despite the height, the track does not present any serious difficulties and can be negotiated by car without problems, if you drive carefully. From the Veleta to Capileira is about 15 miles (25km). The track runs past a series of chilly lagoons - Aguas Verdes, Rio Seco, La Caldera - and jagged, slate-grey crags. Initially, the scenery is bleak and with little vegetation.

Because these mountains have a unique mix of high altitude and Mediterranean climate, a rich diversity of flora and fauna exists. Wild goats, rare butterflies, hawks and eagles patrol the glaciated slopes and 40 species of plants are found only in this nature park. Wild flowers abound.

You skirt the western edge of the great bulk of Mulhacén, then a bumpy side-track to the left doubles back towards this peak, at 11,300 feet (3,482 metres) the highest in the Iberian peninsula. Park your car and walk the last few hundred yards over a rocky path to the summit, where there is a religious shrine, and gaze down on the cliffs and chasms falling away below you. Mulhacén gets its name from one of the last Moorish kings of Granada.

Nature-lovers went to war over Mulhacén in 1994 to protest a Defence Ministry attempt to build a satellite-tracking station on the summit.

The track continues over open moorland some 9,000 feet above sea-level as it follows the Piedra Blanca ridge. You glimpse Trevélez in the valley to your left. Then the route weaves downwards past grazing flocks of sheep and plantations of pines, executing a series of hairpins as it approaches Capileira in the Poqueira valley (see Excursion 23).

Retracing your steps from the Veleta, some way after passing the Albergue Universitario you come to a junction. The main road to Pradollano and Granada curves left. Keep straight on and you are on the original road to the sierra. It wiggles down and, shortly before rejoining the newer road at Mirador La Víbora, you see a sharp right turn. A signpost points to "Seminario Sierra Nevada".

This is a narrow, twisting road which takes you down to the Genil river. It is marked *"Camino estrecho y muy peligroso"* (narrow, dangerous road). However, if you drive slowly with due precaution, there is no danger, although it should be avoided in winter and early spring when it could be icy.

In parts this route is like an English country lane. Cherry and chestnut trees flourish on the hillside, in sharp contrast to the bare slopes on the other side of the Genil valley.

There are no signs to the seminary, a religious retreat located in a large building known as the Hotel del Duque. This property, once a gambling casino, was built by the Duque de San Pedro Galatino, a colourful entrepreneur who was responsible for the construction of the Hotel Alhambra Palace in Granada and of the city's tram services.

On the last stretch as the road dips down through leafy shade, it zigs and zags in dizzy fashion, finally, emerging above the Genil river. El Charcón restaurant and several other establishments offers refreshments in this shady valley, where the breeze rustles through the trees and the translucent Genil river splashes cheerfully along.

A path known as La Vereda de la Estrella follows the river upstream and if you have the time it makes a wonderful walk.

The road follows the old track of the tranvías (trams). The stone structure of the Maitena station still stands. There are roses over the doorway, flowering bushes and geraniums in profusion. Today it is a bar and restaurant. You can enjoy a drink under shady trees and look down at a swimming hole in the river below.

The road along the tramway plunges through tunnels at several points, finally emerging in the village of Güéjar-Sierra (pop. 2,500). Flowers adorn the narrow back-streets and old men gossip around the fountain in the square, belying a turbulent past.

After the 16th century Morisco rebellion, Guéjar's inhabitants were expelled and their property shared out between 100 Christian families. When it was placed under Granada's jurisdiction, the new residents kicked up a storm until Guéjar was ceded to them. One condition was that every year they donated rushes and other greenery to decorate Granada's streets for the Corpus Christi procession.

After Güéjar the road widens, passing cherry and plum orchards and climbing above the flooded valley floor. The Canales reservoir, to your left, holds the waters of the Genil between steep rock walls. Soon the road is running above the village of Pinos Genil. It meets the GR420 and we turn right to return to **GRANADA**.

Note: A good map of the Sierra Nevada is published by the Instituto Geográfico Nacional on a scale of 1:50,000❑

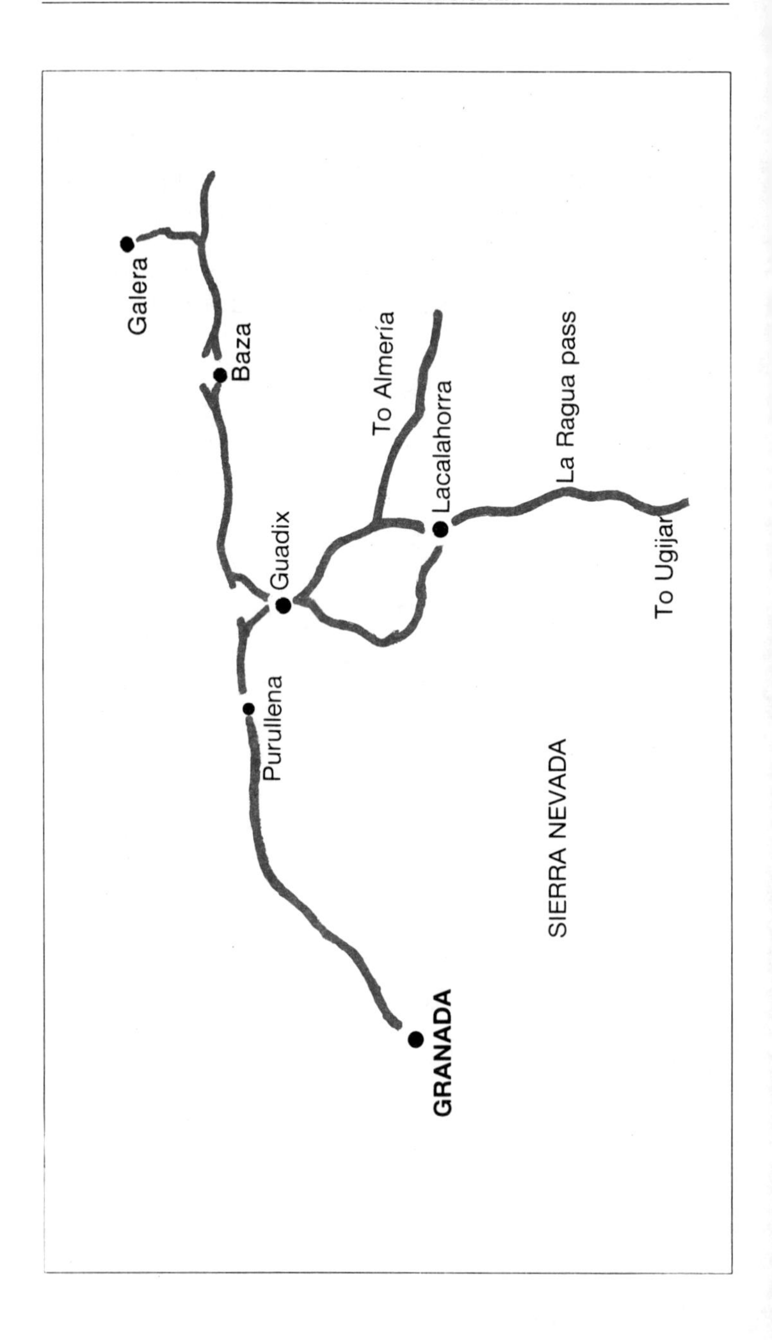
Galera
Baza
To Almería
Lacalahorra
La Ragua pass
Guadix
To Ugijar
Purullena
SIERRA NEVADA
GRANADA

Excursion 37 - Land of the Troglodytes:

Granada-Purullena-Guadix-Lacalahorra-Granada
Distance: 100 miles (160km)

This trip is recommended for some spectacular mountain scenery and a glimpse of the unusual world of the troglodytes.

Take the Murcia road, the N342, out of **GRANADA**. It hairpins upwards out of town, curving around the upper edge of the Albaicín quarter and offering magnificent views over the city towards the Alhambra and the Sierra Nevada.

You climb to the Puerto Lobo, 3,640 feet above sea level and merge with the four-lane A92, bypassing Huétor Santillán, then climb the Puerto de la Mora, altitude 4,500 feet. It is wild mountainous country, with large tracts of pine forest and lumpy hills rising to the south towards the snowy heights of the sierras.

When you approach Purullena, bypassed by the A92, the scenery changes. Strange undulating hills appear, eroded into odd shapes. Purullena's main street is bounded by a string of shops selling a vast array of pottery. But virtually none of that on display is made in Purullena. It is all imported from other regions, much of it from Valencia.

The hills are honeycombed with caves, each with a white-washed facade and a whitewashed chimney sticking out of the hillside above. A television antenna is usually attached to the chimney. You expect a Hobbit or a talkative gnome to pop out his head at any moment.

At least a third of the population lives underground. In fact in this area of Granada province, more than 20,000 people inhabit man-made caves. Don't imagine that these are gypsies or that they are necessarily deprived citizens. Most are ordinary working-class Spaniards who like cave life. The temperature inside remains a steady 18 degrees summer or winter, electricity and modern plumbing have been installed in many of these dwellings, and if another child arrives it is a simple matter to hack out another room.

Because the hills are of hard, compacted clay - part of the

Guadix-Baza post-pliocene deposit if you want to get technical - they are easy to excavate and remain impermeable to rain. Inside, they are whitewashed and kept as clean as any house. The troglodytes are extremely cave-proud.

Many Moriscos (Moorish converts to Christianity) are believed to have moved underground in the 17th century to escape Felipe 11's persecution.

Just back from the highway through Purullena, you can rock with the cavemen in one of Europe's most unusual discos, located inside a hillock hollowed out like a Gruyere cheese. Once this two-storey cave was an inn welcoming weary muleteers.

Purullena is renowned for its luscious peaches. Try some if they are in season.

To the south a road runs into the foothills of the Sierra Nevada, following a well-watered valley to end at Lugros, a small village remote from everyday life, with the massive mountain barrier soaring behind it.

Carry on to **GUADIX** (pop. 20,000), a town famous in ancient times for its silver, iron and copper riches. The Emperor Augustus founded a colony here to guard an important crossroads on the route from Cartago to Nova Hispalis.

It is not Andalusia's most exciting town and do not expect any gourmet treats. But it does have some impressive monuments and, behind the Arab fortress, lies a large troglodyte quarter, known variously as the Barrio de Santiago and Ermita Nueva.

You can inspect a cave-museum. One or two caves are available for rent. Some have all mod cons, including a telephone. But they are not for claustrophobic types.

Guadix inhabitants are known as *accitanos*, from Acci, the ancient name of the settlement.

One of the best-known pieces of Spanish music has connections with Guadix. The Three-Cornered Hat, a ballet for which Manuel de Falla composed the music, was based on a short story by Pedro Antonio Alarcón, born here.

Nineteen miles (30km) to the north of Guadix, up the valley of the Río Fardes along which fat melons ripen, are the Baños de Alicún de las Torres, a spa with hot springs. This is a good place to relax or make use of the curative waters, which are said to help with breathing, nervous and rheumatic conditions. Steam-baths, saunas and massage are available. There is a two-star hotel, the Reina Isabel (tel: 958-69 40 22). The balneario and hotel are open from April to November.

To the south of Guadix stands a unique Italian Renaissance palace, concealed inside grim castle walls. Follow the Almería road, the N324, and after nine miles (15km) turn right to the Castillo de Lacalahorra. You cannot miss the rectangular castle, with its circular towers. It stands proudly austere atop a hillock commanding the plain.

The castle is open on Wednesdays, 10am-1pm, 4-6pm, although you may be able to gain access on other days if you can find the guardian Antonino Tribaldoz, who was actually born in the castle. The proud structure was built by Rodrigo de Mendoza, son of Cardinal Mendoza, between 1509 and 1512, with the aid of Italian craftsmen. Rodrigo, Marquis of Zenete, was given this area, with its six villages, by the Catholic Monarchs.

The patio is graced by columns and a staircase of Carrara marble and there are some fine coffered ceilings in bedrooms. The women's prison is a grim slit between the walls.

In Lacalahorra's Bar Labella, basic but cheap, you can enjoy a meal of stewed kid.

South of the village, the C331 scales the 6,500-foot-high La Ragua pass, leading to the southern flank of the Sierra Nevada and the region known as the Alpujarras, the last stronghold of the Moors after the Kingdom of Granada was crushed in 1492.

You can return to Granada via this beautiful region. It is some 25 miles (40km) from La Calahorra to Ugíjar, and from there 75 miles (120km) over spectacular but twisting mountain roads to Granada. See Excursion 23 for more details about the Alpujarras.

Ice and snow can make La Ragua pass hazardous. In winter, when it rains in Guadix it is probably snowing higher up, so inquire about conditions from the Civil Guard. Cross country skiing is planned in the area and European taxpayers will be interested to see that development funds from Brussels have financed a timber refuge and information point at the top next to a picnic area.

A pleasant way to return to Guadix is to drive west from Lacalahorra across the Marquesado de Zenete, one of the highest plateaus in Spain at a height of more than 3,500 feet. Iron is mined at Alquife and shipped by train to Almeria. From Lacalahorra the road winds along via a series of villages. Jeres del Marquesado is a pretty place with quaint houses. An imposing iron-studded door gives access to the 16th century Jeres church, which features Moorish-style brickwork, massive pillars, and a beautiful altarpiece.

You reach the N324 again close to Guadix. If you turn right on the N324, you can drive 60 miles (98km) to **ALMERIA**, joining the N340 and Excursion 40 near Tabernas, with its Wild West villages.

An interesting tour extension from Guadix takes you 26 miles (42km) east along the N342 through austere, steppe-like country to Baza. The first week of every September Guadix despatches a volunteer, known as El Cascamorras, to Baza to bring back a coveted image of the Virgin from the Franciscan convent of La Merced. But the youths of Baza, in a riotous fiesta, drench him with dirty oil and send him back empty-handed.

Ancient cultures existed around Baza and in 1971 a large seated figure, believed to be a 2,400-year-old Iberian goddess was discovered in a necropolis. The Dama de Baza can be seen in the Museo Arqueológico in Madrid, but Baza has a copy in its museum.

Baza (Basti to the Romans) has some handsome buildings, including the Gothic Colegiata de Santa María, with an entrance attributed to Diego de Siloé and a fine tower built in 1764, and the Mudéjar-style Palacio de los Enriquez. In the old Jewish quarter are some 10th century Arab baths. The one-star Hotel Baza (Travesía Ctra de Granada, tel. 958-70 07 50) has comfortable rooms.

Or for something a little different head for Galera, 26 miles (42km) to the northeast, via N342 and the C3329. Here you can spend the night in a cave-home. Abandoned hillside caves have been tastefully converted and furnished, with bathrooms and fully-equipped kitchens, by an enterprising local couple (Minimum stay two days, contact Miguel and Dolores Rodríguez at 958-73 90 68).

Galera is a strange little place, which experiences extremes of heat and cold. It produces its own wine, using methods long abandoned elsewhere. And it has another point of interest - more than 130 tombs and an alabaster image of a fertility goddess have been discovered in the Tutugi necropolis, from the pre-Christian era.

Return to highway N342 and, via Guadix, to **GRANADA**❑

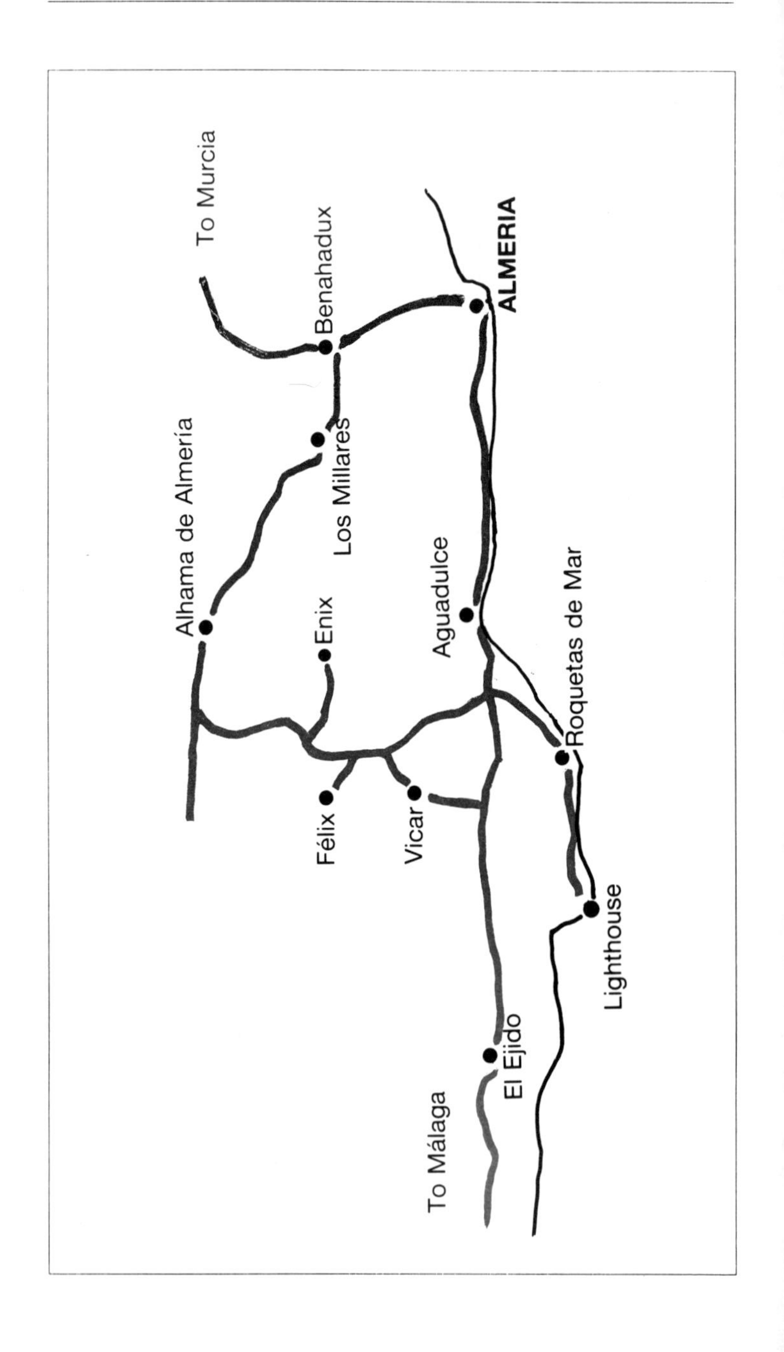
To Murcia
Benahadux
ALMERIA
Alhama de Almería
Los Millares
Enix
Aguadulce
Roquetas de Mar
Félix
Vicar
Lighthouse
El Ejido
To Málaga

Excursion 38 - To Enix and Felix:

Almería-Los Millares-Alhama de Almería-Enix-Vicar-Roquetas del Mar-Aguadulce-Almería
Round trip: 56 miles (90km)

A visit to a Bronze Age community, vineyards where some of Spain's most delicious eating grapes are grown, and spectacular coast views lie along this half-day excursion from Almería.

Head north from **ALMERIA** through the dusty suburbs and along the N340 towards Murcia.

At Benahadux, turn left on the Guadix road, N324. The road winds upwards, crossing the Guadix rail line several times.

Shortly before a turn-off to the hamlet of Santa Fe de Mondújar, you will see a white low building on the right. This is the reception centre for Los Millares, a significant relic of human endeavour dating back more than 4,000 years (open: winter, 9.30am-2pm, 4-6pm, Sun 9.30am-2.30pm; summer, 9am-1pm Tuesday-Sunday, 6.30-9pm Tues, Thurs, Sat. Closed Mon).

Archeologists are still excavating the site, where it is believed a community of some 2,000 people flourished in the Copper and Bronze Ages. Remains of houses, workshops, mills, defensive walls, and a hundred or so tombs have been uncovered.

Just beyond the Santa Fe turn, the C332 branches left. As this twists upwards, look back for fine views of the badlands of Almería, the deeply-eroded valleys and hills beyond the Andarax valley and the Rambla de Tabernas.

You pass terraces clothed in vines. Note the way the plants are trained to grow tall, unlike vines producing grapes for wine-making which are pruned back near ground level every autumn. The juicy eating grapes from these vineyards have long been exported to the tables of distant European countries.

Alhama de Almería (pop. 3,105) offers relief for sufferers from rheumatics and nervous complaints. Its mineral-rich waters have been famous for their curative properties since early times. A three-star hotel, the San Nicolas (Baños s/n. Tel:

951-10 01 01. Closed last week of December to mid-March) stands next to the spa.

Leaving Alhama keep a sharp eye out for a left turn to Roquetas de Mar. The AL 412 spirals up through dramatic rocky scenery, climbing over the Sierra de Gador, where little grows beyond esparto grass. You pass the hamlet of El Marchal de Antón López with red-roofed church and a breath-taking panorama over the sea opens up to your view.

A left turn takes you one-and-a-half miles (2.7 km) to Enix. A chipped sign at the entrance declares: "Enix salutes its visitors." But mostly the whitewashed village of only 240 inhabitants sleeps. Perched on slopes covered with almond trees, it has a grandstand view of the Almería coast.

Behind the old stone church with its square tower you will find a handy bar for refreshments.

Downhill, you will see a right turn to Enix's twin, Felix, another cluster of white-washed cubes with fine views. You can veer left here for a run down towards Roquetas or continue towards Vícar.

The narrow Vícar road is not recommended for nervous drivers or vertigo-sufferers and should be avoided in darkness. It twists around the mountainside with alarming drops below your wheels and no safety barriers.

But the views are magnificent, particularly at evening when the setting sun turns to gold the vast fields of plastic that cover the coastal plain.

The old village of Vícar, dozing in a fold in the mountains, has only a few hundred inhabitants. But the boom in agriculture on what was a barren desert has lured thousands of new settlers to the area, including high-priced girls eager to help the farmers spend their cash.

Flowers bloom and tomatoes, peppers, and melons ripen whatever the season in the plastic-covered greenhouses.

After negotiating the plastic sea you reach the N340, 17 miles (27 km) after leaving the highway near Alhama de Almería. Turn left towards **ALMERIA**.

Feeling hungry? Detour to the right to Roquetas del Mar (pop. 29,000). Once little more than a fishing village, it has developed rapidly as a package holiday resort.

Sample some stylish Andalusian-Catalan cooking at the Albaida restaurant (Avenida de Las Gaviotas, s/n. Urbanización Roquetas de Mar. Tel: 950-33 38 21. Open 12am-4pm, 7-12pm. Closed Mon, two weeks Jan, two weeks Feb. Amex, Diners, Master, Visa. M-E).

If you venture west of Roquetas, past Playa Serena, towards the Punta Sabinar lighthouse, you may see flocks of flamingoes and other wild birds paddling in the salt lagoons❑

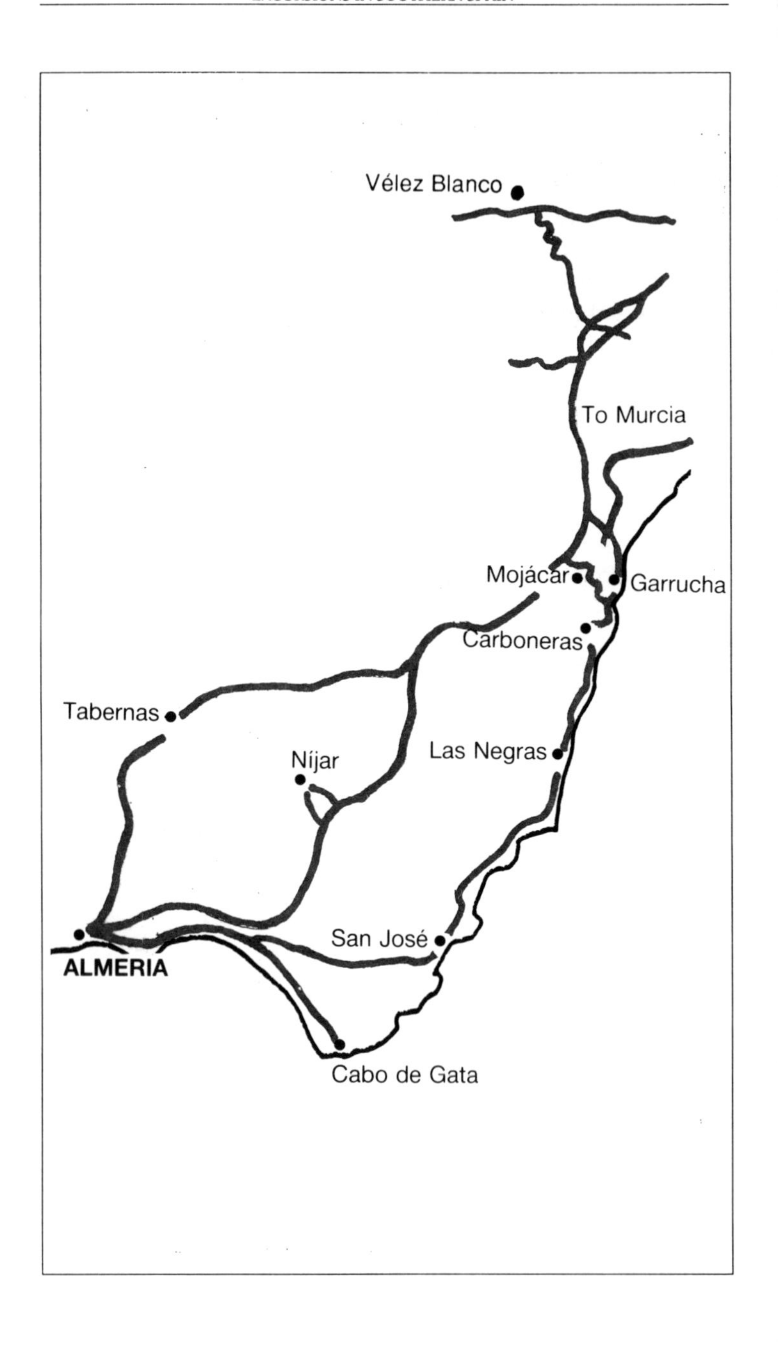
Vélez Blanco
To Murcia
Mojácar
Garrucha
Carboneras
Tabernas
Níjar
Las Negras
San José
ALMERIA
Cabo de Gata

Excursion 39 - Snorkelling Heaven:

Almería-Cabo de Gata-San José-Las Negras-Carboneras-Mojácar-Garrucha-Almería
Round trip: 130 miles (210km)

Cliffs plunging into clear blue waters, lonely beaches, desert landscapes... these are to be found within easy reach of the city of **ALMERIA**. This route takes you to the Cabo de Gata-Níjar nature park and along a still-untamed coast where tarmac occasionally gives way to dirt.

From Almería, the provincial capital, follow the signs for the airport and Níjar. You drive through shabby suburbs with a distinctly African look about them before crossing the wide dry bed of the Andarax river. Nine miles (14 km) out, branch right towards the sea and Retamar, then left to Cabo de Gata.

Crossing flat scrubby country, you enter the nature park, which covers 29,000 hectares and includes a stretch of seabed about two kilometres wide.

Thousands of birds flying between Europe and Africa touch down amid the dunes, saltpans, and thorny jujube trees between San Miguel beach and the cape. Among the 170 bird species recorded in the park are flamingoes, Dupont's larks, griffon vultures and avocets.

The fishing hamlet of Cabo de Gata is a down-at-heel, sun-bleached huddle of dwellings, struggling to convert itself into a holiday resort. It has a way to go. Drive on along the coast and you will pass desolate salt flats and dazzling piles of salt, ready for loading.

The road climbs up towards the Cabo de Gata itself. At the tip of the rocky headland stands a lighthouse marking the end of the cape, near the Arrecife de las Sirenas (Sirens' Reef).

Northeast of here the track is closed to traffic so you must retrace your route to pick up the road to San José. Energetic types can walk along the coast to San José through rugged country with no sign of human habitation, although it is not advisable in high summer as there is no shade.

Only lizards, cactus and esparto grass can scrape a living

here. Steep cliffs plunge into the foaming sea and from secluded beaches snorkellers launch themselves into the transparent waters. Attempts are being made to re-introduce the monk seal, which died out in the 1970s.

After trudging across a dusty plain dotted with cactus, which runs inland from the long beach of Los Genoveses, hikers hit tarmac again at San José, still a small resort but growing fast with a 200-berth pleasure port.

Overlooking the bay with its sandy beach is the comfortable little one-star Hotel San José (Barriada San José, Níjar. Tel: 950-38 01 16. Closed January15-February 15). For cheaper accommodation, try Hostal Las Gaviotas 1 and 11 (Tel: 950-38 00 10).

Inland from San José, 16 miles (26 km) from Retamar by the direct inland route, lies El Pozo de los Frailes. Near here turn towards Rodalquilar to follow the coast. Eroded hills, old windmills and cactus border the road as it winds down to lonely Los Escullos.

Just beyond, rocks like stranded whales jut out into the sea by the primitive fishing hamlet of La Isleta del Moro. Fish dry in the sun, women pound clothing at the communal wash-house, dogs sprawl in the dust.

If you like the end-of-the-world feeling, you can stay at the Hostal Isleta (950-38 97 13) right by the water. Fresh fish is on the menu.

From here the road climbs steeply upwards. Stop at the Mirador de la Amatista to enjoy the fine views along the coast. Then continue to Rodalquilar. Entering, you will see rows of abandoned houses, where employees lived when the local gold mines were being worked.

Leaving the village, you will see a track to the right which leads to a fine beach, dominated by an old fort and a backdrop of mighty cliffs. A little further on, a right fork will take you to Las Negras, with its cluster of houses (some for rent), fishing boats and gravel beach.

The left fork runs up to Fernán Pérez. A right turn here, easily missed, takes you towards Carboneras. The road quickly becomes dirt, but it is in good condition and after six miles (9 km) joins a paved road to Agua Amarga.

This village on a beautiful bay with a sandy beach and good snorkelling off the rocks is expanding fast. Flats are available for rent and by the beach La Palmera restaurant offers food at reasonable prices. Try the *arroz de marisco.*

Until recently Agua Amarga was virtually isolated, but now an excellent road scales the hills to the north. A side road leads to the Roldán lighthouse, which looks down on a cormorants' fishing area and Punta de los Muertos (Dead Man's Point), where the bodies of shipwrecked sailors sometimes washed ashore.

The first sight of Carboneras, five miles (8 km) from Agua Amarga, comes as a shock. The Philistines have been at work, with their usual shortsighted ideas of "progress". A massive cement works and a power station have been built slap on the beach, with a port to serve them.

Fortunately it is a long beach and at the far end you will find the two-star Hotel El Dorado (Playa de Carboneras. Tel: 950-45 40 50). Note the ornate front door and the pillars in reception - you may have glimpsed them before in the film Nicholas and Alexander.

The phone booth and the statues on the stairs figured in Dr Zhivago and the elegant tasselled chairs about the hotel were props in The Three Musketeers (the musketeers' swords are there too).

Photos of international stars on the cafeteria wall offer an explanation. They are dedicated to Eddie Fowlie, owner of the hotel. Eddie is an English film set decorator and location researcher. Parts of the films mentioned were made here, as was Lawrence of Arabia, the flat roofs of Carboneras doubling for Aqaba on the Red Sea.

The town (pop. 5,000) has spruced itself up considerably since those days, although eating possibilities are still limited. Several bars offer reasonable tapas, however.

The coast road to Mojácar imitates a mountain goat as it skips along the clifftops, with the Sierra Cabrera rearing to the left. After 14 miles (22 km) you reach burgeoning **MOJACAR**, approximately 50 miles (80km) from Almería by the direct inland route.

Atop its hill, it looks like a mirage of white cubes, but in its sinuous streets, all whitewash and flower-decked balconies, you can hear every language under the sun. Most of the population had emigrated when the mayor started luring the rich and influential back in the 50s and 60s; now it has become a package resort, with hotels, gift shops, boutiques, bars and a big parking lot, while villa developments have mushroomed along the coast.

According to local legend, Walt Disney was born in Mojácar, but for some inscrutable reason his family does not seem inclined to admit it.

Summer nightlife happens mostly along the beach with its bars and discos. There are reasonably priced hotels here too, likely to be full in season.

North along the coast from Mojácar lies the fishing port of Garrucha with several miles of well-maintained beach. Once pretty scruffy, the town now has a fine promenade and several good fish restaurants.

Right on the port is the deservedly popular El Almejero (Explanada del Puerto, tel. 950-46 04 05, open 1-4pm, 8-11.30pm, Amex, Visa) with a terrace, and large-windowed dining room with timber ceiling. The shrimps are particularly renowned and there is a good wine list. For dessert, how about *tocino del cielo,* translated here as "sky custard"?

Just up the coast from Garrucha is Palomares, where in 1965 a United States aircraft carrying an atom bomb crashed. Now the beaches are rapidly being developed for tourism. Some campsites cater for nudists, as does the three-star Hotel Vera Playa Club (Ctra Garrucha-Palomares, s/n, tel. 950-46 74 75).

If you are in the mood to explore more of eastern Almería, head north to Vélez Rubio and **VELEZ BLANCO**, 48 miles (76km) from Garrucha, via Vera and the N340 and C321 (see Town and City Guide).

To return to **ALMERIA**, drive inland from Garrucha along the AL152 to join the N340 autovia. That becomes the N344 to speed you to Almería. Or you can branch right off the autovía and follow the old N340 to Almería via Sorbas. Near Tabernas you will pass spaghetti Western film sets, described in Excursion 40❑

Excursion 40 - Wild West:

Almería-Tabernas-Níjar-Almería
Round trip: 80 miles (130km)

Clint Eastwood and Raquel Welch once hammed it up in blood-and-passion epics in the Almería desert. This is a day trip to the bleakly spectacular land of spaghetti Westerns and to a town where a violent real-life drama was once played out, to be later immortalised on stage.

Drive north from Almería on the main Murcia highway, N340. You follow the Andarax valley with its palms and citrus orchards.

To make a detour to some hot springs and remains of Roman baths, turn right after about six miles (10km), following signs for El Chuche and Pechina, then for the Balneario de Sierra Alhamilla. Amid dessicated hills you encounter an oasis where water gushes from the rock at 57 degrees C.

You can plunge into the waters at the Balneario, a hotel with modern spa facilities (three to four star prices, tel. 950-31 74 13) and an island of calm amid the desert. Two hundred years ago the Bishop of Almería constructed a spa here, following in the steps of Iberians, Romans and Moors.

The old-style building, with its arches and tilework, has been restored and bubble baths and mudbaths are some of the treatments offered for rheumatism, nerves, digestion, obesity and other problems.

Back on the N340, a narrow bridge takes you across the Andarax riverbed and into badlands territory. The resemblance to Arizona and other desert regions attracted film-makers here during the 1960s.

After 15 miles (24 km), amid increasingly arid, harshly-scoured terrain, the highway swings right over a bridge. You can make a short detour to film-making territory by taking the road to the left towards Guadix.

There are no signs to help you and recent roadbuilding makes matters more difficult, but a few miles up this highway, off to the left near the old road, a "Mexican pueblo" slowly

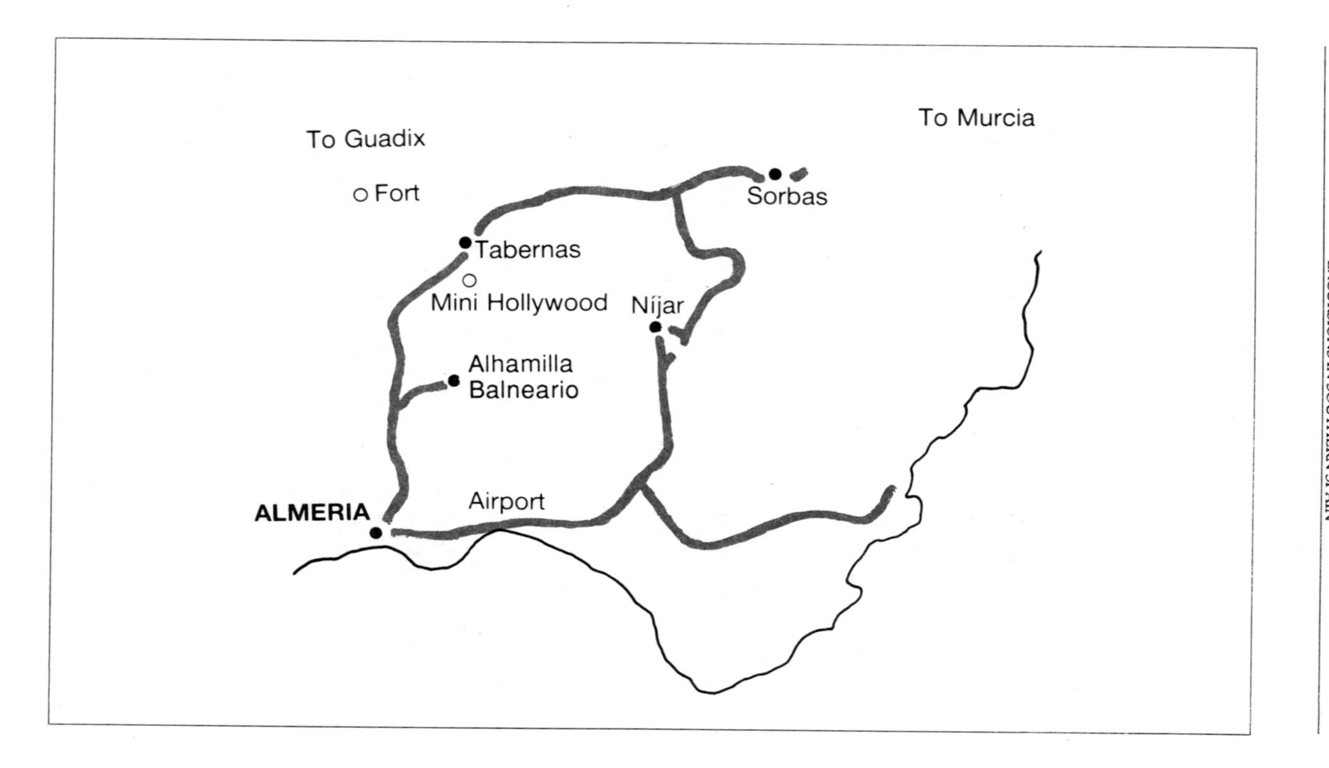
To Guadix
To Murcia
Fort
Sorbas
Tabernas
Mini Hollywood
Níjar
Alhamilla
Balneario
ALMERIA
Airport

crumbles into dust. To the right of the Guadix road, a track leads to the ranch built by Sergio Leone when he was directing such films as" The Good, the Bad and the Ugly" and" For a Fistful of Dollars".

Deeper into the rocky, cactus-dotted desert stands a grim, high-walled fort, used in many a celluloid epic. Commercials and television series are still made in the area so, if there are some vehicles around, filming may be in progress.

Return to the N340 and turn left towards Murcia and Tabernas. Soon you will see signs on the right for Mini Hollywood, otherwise known as Yucca City.

More than 100 films were made on this dusty replica of a Western township, complete with saloons, hardware stores, saddleries and a wide main street just made for High Noon encounters. Local gypsies played Indians and Mexicans and did horse-riding stunts during the boom years.

Today tourists have taken over. They come in groups and pay to watch Wild West shootouts. In winter months these are usually staged only at weekends, but from Easter onwards every two hours daily.

Bank raids, saloon brawls, riding stunts form part of the action provided by an enthusiastic young bunch of desperados who dream of making it in films. Afterwards anybody can briefly imagine they are Lee Van Cleef or Clint Eastwood as they pace the creaking sidewalks and push open the saloon's batwing doors, or have themselves immortalised in a "Wanted" poster.

Driving on, you encounter another film-set open to visitors. A track dips to the left into the Rambla de Tabernas, a dry riverbed, then climbs to Texas. This features a township, a Mexican village, Indian tepees, horses, ponies and camels.

A bypass runs around the village of Tabernas and its ruined castle atop a hill. Two miles (three km) beyond, a side-road to the left leads to the Plataforma Solar de Almería, a solar energy research centre.

Three miles (five km) from the N340, a tower juts up from the scrubby plain. Near it hundreds of heliostats (large mirrors) bounce the sun's rays into receptors, creating solar energy. You can visit the Plataforma Solar research station, but call 950-27 48 00 beforehand.

Good eating places are few and far between on this route, so it may be as well to bring a picnic with you. Between Tabernas and Los Yesos there are a number of truck stops, where you can get basic meals and refreshment.

The road flattens out after Tabernas and after 16 miles (26km) you reach Sorbas, spectacularly situated on a bend of the Río Aguas, with its houses teetering nervously on the chasm's edge.

To the east of Sorbas is an area honeycombed with caves, the Karst en Yeso de Sorbas. You can visit the caves, guided by a member of the Federación Andaluza de Espeleología, the fee including equipment but not boots (tel 950-47 85 65/46 72 27).

From Sorbas, retrace your steps for five miles to turn to Níjar on the AL 102. This road passes Lucainena de las Torres, shadowed by a jagged buttress, then corkscrews over rugged hills. Only at Rambla Honda is there sign of human habitation amid the bare rock, cacti and occasional almond trees.

Níjar comes as a relief, orange and lemon trees and palms flourishing in this oasis in the desert. The town is renowned for its rustic, hand-painted pottery and you will find the street leading towards the Almería highway lined with workshops and displays. Locally made handwoven blankets known as *jarapas* are also good buys.

Federico García Lorca was inspired to write one of his most famous plays, Blood Wedding, after reading of an incident near Níjar in 1928. Just before a girl named Paquita La Coja (Paquita the Lame One) was due to get married, she eloped with her cousin. Relatives chased them and in a bloody act of vengeance the cousin was shot dead. Paquita's prospective groom felt so humiliated that not only did the marriage fall through but ever after he refused even to look at her photograph. She never married.

From Níjar a good road leads 23 miles (37 km) to Carboneras on the coast to join Excursion 39.

Alternatively, it is an easy 21-mile run over the arid plain to Almería on the N334 autovía❑

SEVEN-DAY TOUR

To see all that Andalusia has to offer would take months. To see the major sights, you require at least a week. Using this book, you should be able to put together your own tour, allowing adequate time for driving and visiting the most interesting towns and cities.

If you are pressed for time, this is our suggestion for a seven-day tour, which takes in some of the most spectacular scenery, the three historical cities of Seville, Córdoba and Granada, and lets you visit a sherry bodega too. Full information on places in bold type is given in the Town and City Guide. Total distance: approximately 500 miles (800km).

Day one: *Excursion 17:* Málaga-Marbella-Ronda-Arcos de la Frontera-Jerez de la Frontera. Overnight in Arcos-Jerez area.

Day two: Morning visit to Jerez bodega, lunch in Jerez or Puerto de Santa María *(see Excursion 28).* Afternoon, to Seville. Two nights in Seville.

Day three: Visiting Seville

Day four (afternoon): *Excursion 24,* Seville-Carmona-Ecija-Córdoba. One night in Córdoba

Day five (afternoon): *Excursion 26,* Córdoba-Baena-Priego de Córdoba-Granada. Two nights in Granada.

Day six: Visit Granada, possible side-trip *Excursion 35* or *36.*

Day seven: Return to the coast by *Excursion 21,* Granada-Loja-Riofrío-Alfarnate-Málaga or by picking up *Excursion 16,* Granada-Otivar-Almuñecar-Nerja-Málaga.

■ TOWN AND CITY GUIDE ■

Telephone calls

The eight provinces in Andalusia have different telephone area codes. These are: Almería 950, Cádiz 956, Córdoba 957, Granada 958, Huelva 959, Jaén 953, Málaga 95, Seville 95.

When telephoning from one province to another, use the appropriate code. When calling within a province, no codes are necessary. When calling from outside Spain, drop the digit 9 from the area code. To call outside Spain, first dial 07, wait for the tone, then dial the foreign country code and number.

Emergencies

Note that in all major centres the National Police emergency number is 091. In smaller localities, where there is no National Police station, contact the Civil Guard or Municipal Police.

Addresses

Street numbers follow the name of the street, as in the Spanish style. Note that Ctra signifies Carretera (highway). The letters s/n signify *sin número* (no number).

Eating Out

The letters B, M, and E give a rough guide to the price of a three-course á la carte meal, not including wine. B (budget) under 1,500 pesetas. M (moderate) 1,500 to 4,000 pesetas. E (expensive) more than 4,000. VE (very expensive) VERY expensive. Many restaurants offer a menu del día, a three-course meal at an inclusive price under 1,500 pesetas.

Hotels

Expect to pay for a double room: Pension and one-star hostal, between 2,500 and 4,000 pesetas. Two-star hostals, up to 5,000 pesetas. One-star hotels, between 4,000 and 6,000 pesetas. Two-star hotels, up to 8,000 pesetas. Three-star hotels, 6,000 to 10,000. Four-star hotels, 12,000 upwards. Five-star hotels, from 15,000 pesetas. Paradors (state-run hotels), from 10,000 pesetas.

ALGECIRAS, in Cadiz province (pop. 100,000). Cádiz 120km. Malaga 133km. Madrid 712km. Telephone area code 956.

Tourist information, Avda de la Marina, s/n. 57 26 36.

Strategically placed on the Strait of Gibraltar with magnificent views of the Rock, this busy port (pronounce it Al-heth-eerass) has regular ferry services to North Africa. Ferries and hydrofoils leave for Tangier and Ceuta, the Spanish enclave on the coast of Morocco. There is a raffish air about the town, befitting a cosmopolitan crossroads and a notorious entry point for drugs. Customs controls of arrivals from Morocco are rigorous. The old quarter, particularly the Plaza Alta, retains some appeal but has been submerged beneath characterless modern buildings. Avoid taking the ferries at the end of June and the first weeks of July and August, when you will compete with thousands of returning Moroccan migrants queuing to cross the Strait.

PLACES TO STAY

Reina Cristina, Paseo de la Conferencia. Tel: 60 26 22. Four stars. Stately old hotel with tropical gardens, built to accommodate passengers using the British-built Algeciras-Ronda railway line, now part of the Trusthouse Forte chain. Library, tennis courts, tea on the terrace.

Alarde, Alfonso X1, 4. Tel: 66 04 08. Three-star hotel in central location.

EATING OUT

Reina Cristina restaurant. Amex, Diners, Master, Visa. A touch of old world elegance. International cuisine. (M-E)

Marea Baja, Trafalgar, 2. Tel. 66 36 54. Closed Sun. Amex, Master, Diners, Visa. Seafood. (M-E)

At Los Barrios, 8km from town: *Mesón El Copo,* Palmones. Tel: 67 77 10. Open 1-4.30pm, 8pm-12.30am. Closed Sunday. Amex, Diners, Master, Visa. Although located in a dismal area, El Copo is claimed to be Andalusia's best fish restaurant. First-rate fresh seafood and shellfish. (E)

SERVICES

Buses: Portillo, Virgen del Carmen,15, 65 10 55; Comes, San Bernardo, 1, 65 34 56; La Valenciana, Avda de la Marina, 60 11 89.

RENFE 63 02 02. Isnasa ferries, 65 20 00.

Trasmediterránea ferries, 65 17 11.

Radio taxis 65 55 12.

Post office, Ruis Zorrilla, s/n.

Telephones, Prim,5.

CONSULATES

Britain - contact British Consulate in Málaga.

Denmark, Paseo de la Conferencia, 11. Tel: 57 25 45.

Netherlands, Calle Teniente Maroto, 2-3rd floor. Tel: 65 60 00.

Norway, Virgen del Carmen, 29. Tel: 66 75 11.

Sweden, Alfonso X1, 10. Tel: 66 05 66.

EMERGENCIES

National police 091. *Municipal police,* 66 01 55. *Civil Guard* 66 11 00. *First aid* 66 20 54. *Cruz Roja* 66 41 51.

• • • • • • • • • • • • • • • • • •

ALHAMA DE GRANADA, in Granada province (pop. 6,000). Granada 53km, Málaga 85km. Telephone area code 958.

Tourist information, Plaza de los Presos, tel. 36 02 71.

Magnificently situated below the bulk of the Maroma mountain, often snowcapped in winter, Alhama balances above a precipitous gorge. In Andalusia's great earthquake of Christmas Day, 1884, several houses tumbled into the chasm. A plaque outside the Encarnación parish church relates that the tremor affected 106 towns and killed altogether 745 people. The Moors' loss of the town in 1482 was an important blow to the Kingdom of Granada. The town has a picturesque old quarter with a number of interesting sights. Alhama was given its name by the Arabs, Al-hamma meaning thermal waters, and you can still see their baths at the Balneario hotel.

DON'T MISS

Iglesia del Carmen: 16th century. Recently restored after being ravaged by fire in the Civil War. Fine stonework and Baroque paintings on the dome and arches. Open daily. Rafael, the caretaker, acts as guide.

Tajo (gorge): Beautiful views. Pleasant walk down to the river, where ancient water-mills stand.

Encarnación: Gothic-Renaissance parish church founded by the Catholic Monarchs. Open Tuesday-Friday 12am-1pm (or whenever you can find the priest).

Casa de la Inquisición: Once used by the Inquisition, the house has an interesting facade in the Isabelline style.

Hospital de la Reina: Dating from the 15th century, this was a royal hospital and later a convent. Now a library. Fine coffered ceiling.

WHERE TO STAY

Balneario Alhama de Granada. Tel: 35 00 11. Open June to early October. Three stars. Spa hotel at thermal springs, with medical supervision for visitors.

San José, Plaza de la Constitución, 27. Tel: 35 01 56. Basic one star pension.

EATING OUT/TAPAS

Alhama has a number of tapa bars around the Plaza de la Constitución (try *Mesón de Diego*) and around the petrol station and main highway. Meals are served at *Balneario* and *Pension San José.*

SERVICES

Post office, Adarve Remedios, s/n.

EMERGENCIES

Local police 35 01 61. *Guardia Civil* 35 00 33. *First aid* 36 00 33.

• •

ALMERIA Pop. (capital) 150,000. Málaga 219km. Granada 171km. Madrid 550km. Telephone area code 950.

Tourist information, Corner Parque Nicolás Salmerón & Martínez Campos, tel. 27 43 55.

Almería, hot and dusty in summer, has an African air about it. Parts of the province resemble Morocco or the badlands of Arizona. The city was known as Portus Magnus by the Romans. An important port during the Caliphate of Córdoba, Al-Miriya (Mirror of the Sea) later became capital of an independent emirate. It was noted for its cultural pursuits and exports of fine silk. In the Spanish Civil War Almería was badly damaged and for a long time it presided over Spain's poorest province, but is enjoying unusual prosperity since the boom in cultivation under plastic in the adjacent desert. Almería eating grapes have long been famous. The dramatic desert landscape and the 3,100 hours of sunshine annually attracted film-makers in the 60s and hundreds of spaghetti Westerns were churned out here. Today the same factors encourage the growth of tourism. Ferries ply between Almería and Melilla and Nador, on the African coast.

DON'T MISS

Alcazaba: Built 1,000 years ago by Abd al-Rahman 111, Caliph of Córdoba, this fortress towers above the city. Covering more than 25,000 square metres, it could shelter 20,000 men. La Ventana de la Odalisca (The Concubine's Window) is called thus because an emir's favourite threw herself from it after her Christian lover was put to death. Cacti and flowers now grow inside the walls. Wandering about the Alcazaba area after dark is not wise. Open 10am-1.30pm, 4-7.30pm, winter 9am-1pm, 3-7pm.

Cathedral: Built like a fortress to withstand pirate attacks. It replaces a mosque destroyed in an earthquake and combines 16th century Gothic with Renaissance and Neoclassical style. Renaissance facade by Juan de Orea, who was also responsible for the sacristy and the choir-stalls carved from walnut. Three paintings by Alonso Cano were saved from Civil War damage. Open 10.30-12am, 5.30-6.30pm.

Iglesia San Juan, Calle San Juan: The church incorporates parts of Almería's most important mosque, dating from the 10th century. In the Moorish south wall is a *mihrab,* a prayer niche with cupola. Seriously damaged in the Spanish Civil War, the church was abandoned but has recently been restored.

Open Sat-Sun services and by arrangement (tel. 23 20 46).

Plaza Vieja (Plaza de la Constitución): Fine old porticoed square with the town hall on one side.

Centro de Rescate de la Fauna Sahariana. This centre, located behind the Alcazaba, shelters and breeds endangered Sahara species (antelopes, gazelles, vultures, foxes). A number have been returned to African nature parks. To visit call 27 64 00 in advance.

La Chanca: Hillside gypsy quarter, with cave dwellings. Street market on Mondays.

PLACES TO STAY

Costasol, Paseo Almería, 58. Tel 23 40 11. Three stars. TV in rooms. Central.

Torreluz, Plaza Flores, 1, 3 & 5; tel. 23 47 99. A modern, comfortable three-hotel complex, graded two, three and four stars. In the heart of the city. Parking. Sun terrace and pool available for four-star guests..

EATING OUT

You will find several seafood restaurants in Tenor Iribarne street, off the Paseo de Almería. Off this street at Fructuoso Pérez, 3, the Bodega *Las Botas* has a traditional atmosphere and serves good tapas.

Anfora, González Galbín, 23. Tel: 23 13 74. Open 1.30-3.45pm, 9-11.45pm. Closed Sunday, holidays, mid-July to mid-August. Amex, Diners, Master, Visa. Excellent regional, international food, in discreet surroundings. Good range of wines. (M)

Bellavista, Llanos de Alquián, Urb. Bellavista. Tel: 29 71 56. Open 12am-4pm, 8-12pm. Closed Sunday night, Monday, two weeks in October. Amex, Diners, Master, Visa. Unprepossessing approach, past plastic-covered fields. Carefully-prepared regional dishes, such as avocadoes with anchovies, wine cellar with more than 12,000 bottles. (E)

Club de Mar, Muelle, 1. Tel: 23 50 48. Open 1-4pm, 8-11pm. Closed Mon. Amex, Diners, Master, Visa. Fresh seafood by the port. (M)

La Gruta, Ctra 340, km 436 (towards Aguadulce). Tel. 23 93 35. Open 9pm-1am. Closed Sun & Nov. Amex, Diners, Master, Visa. Partly located in a cave, rustic decor. Roast and grilled meat. (M)

SERVICES

Bus station, Plaza de Barcelona, 21 00 29.
RENFE station, Plaza de la Estación, 25 11 22.
Airport, 22 19 54. Iberia information 23 09 33. Aucona
Trasmediterránea (ferry), Parque Nicolás Salmerón, 23 63 56.
Taxis 25 11 11, 22 61 61.
Post office, Plaza Casinello, Paseo de Almería.

CONSULATES

Denmark, Alvarez de Castro 34. 23 64 29.
Germany, Centro Comercial Satélite Park, Aguadulce. 34 05 55.
Netherlands, Reyes Católicos, 26. 26 85 04.
Sweden, Doctor Aráez Pacheco 2. 25 00 33.

EMERGENCIES

National police 091.
Municipal police 092.
Ambulance 23 48 79.
First aid: 23 07 12.
Red Cross, Parque Nicolás Salmerón, 14, tel: 22 22 22.
Mojácar municipal police 47 83 50.

• • • • • • • • • • • • • • • •

ALMUÑÉCAR, in Granada province (pop. 20,000), Málaga 70km. Granada 73km. Telephone area code 958.

Tourist information: Palacete La Najarra, Avda de Europa, tel. 63 11 25.

Squeezed between mountains and sea, this is the centre of the Costa Tropical, important both for tourism and agriculture. The sheltered climate allows the growth of custard apples, avocadoes and other tropical fruits. The Phoenicians knew the settlement here as Sexi, the Romans called it Julium Firmium and the Moors named it Al-Munakkab. A bronze statue marks the landing here in 755 of Abd al-Rahman 1, later to become Emir of Córdoba. Near another monument, to the Phoenicians, a plaque refers to English writer Laurie Lee, who ended his trek across Spain here in 1936. Modern apartment blocks line the beaches, but the old town is an attractive labyrinth of narrow streets rising up towards the castle walls.

DON'T MISS

Castillo San Miguel: Built on Moorish ruins over Roman fortifications, with a cemetery inside. Its Mazmorra tower dominates the bay.

Museo Arqueológico, Cueva de Siete Palacios. Roman galleries house relics from a Phoenician necropolis and a 4,000-year-old amphora, said to have belonged to an Egyptian Pharaoh. Open 6.30-8.30pm, Saturday 11am-1pm. Closed Sunday.

Roman fish-salting factory: In El Majuelo park.

Parque Ornitológico, Playa de San Cristóbal: Tropical bird park. Open 11am-2pm, 5-8pm.

Peñon del Santo: A lookout point at the top of this rock jutting into the sea offers views of town and beaches.

Roman aqueduct: On the edge of town, it was in use until the presentday.

Weekly market: Friday.

Fiesta: August 15, Virgen de la Antigua, maritime procession.

PLACES TO STAY

Goya, Avenida de Europa, 2. Tel: 63 05 50. Comfortable, unpretentious one-star hotel a block or so from the beach.

Helios, Paseo de San Cristobal, s/n. Tel: 63 44 59. Large, modern three-star hotel. Mirrors and marble. On San Cristóbal beach.

La Tartana, Ctra de Málaga, km 308, La Herradura. Tel: 64 05 35. Cosy little hotel, country house style, with oil paintings, fire-places, flagged floors, brick-arched patio, sunny terraces, English owner. Restaurant (see below).

EATING OUT

La Ultima Ola, Puerta del Mar, 17. Tel. 63 00 18. Open: 1-

4.30pm, 7.30-12pm. Closed: Mon & Jan to mid-March. Amex, Diners, Master, Visa. On the seafront. Good fish dishes. (M)

El Cotobro, Bajada del Mar, l. Tel: 63 18 02. On a small bay west of Almuñécar. Open 1-4pm, 7.30-11pm. Closed Monday (except June 15-Sept 30) & mid-November to early December. Amex, Master, Visa. Excellent French cuisine, delightfully presented. Gastronomic menu highly recommended. Choice of 19 desserts. Spanish and French wines. Booking advisable. (M-E)

La Tartana (see hotel for address). Open: 2-4pm, 8-11pm. Closed three weeks in November. Master, Visa. Chef Giancarlo Rompato cooks Spanish, French, Italian dishes. Outdoor eating in summer. Try the risotto frutto di mare. (M)

SERVICES

Bus station, Alsina Graells, Avda Juan Carlos 1, 1. tel. 63 01 40.
Taxis, 63 00 17.
Post office, Plaza Livry Gargan.

EMERGENCIES

Municipal police 83 86 14.
Civil Guard, 63 11 13.
First aid 63 11 25.
Municipal hospital, Ctra de Málaga, La Paloma, 63 05 16.

• • • • • • • • • • • • • • • • •

ANTEQUERA, in Málaga province (pop 38,000). Málaga 57km. Madrid 512km. Telephone area code 95.

Tourist information, Palacio de Najera, tel. 270 40 51. Also office on Infante Don Fernando, opposite hospital, tel. 270 04 05.

Commanding a fertile plain, Antequera has been an important crossroads since ancient times. The Romans established the settlement of Antikaria here and the fortress was a stronghold of the Moorish Kingdom of Granada, falling to the Christian forces in 1410. The town, at 1,800 feet above sea level, has an easy-going pace. It has 24 churches and a number of monasteries. Relics of early man abound in the area, the most fascinating and mysterious being the dolmens, used as burial tombs more than 4,000 years ago.

DON'T MISS

Dolmens (see Excursion 14): Cueva de Menga and Cueva de Viera, 1km from town centre on Granada road. Romeral, at 6km, turn left at junction of Granada road & old bypass, follow signs. Open: 10am-2pm, 4-6pm (5-7pm May-Sept, 10am-2pm Sat & Sun, closed Mon, admission free.

Municipal Museum, Palacio de Najera, Plaza Coso Viejo: Paintings, sculptures, Roman statue of Efebo. Open 10am-1.30pm, Sat 10am-1pm, Sun 11am-1pm, closed Mon.

Puerta de Arco de los Gigantes: Arch erected 1585.

Colegiata de Santa Maria la Mayor, Plaza Santa Maria: Renaissance monument, 10am-3pm, Sun closed.

Alcazaba: Castle and old walls offering excellent views.

Iglesia de Los Remedios: 17th century, national monument. Open: 7pm daily.

Monasterio San Zoilo, Gothic church dating from 16th century. Open: 4.30-8.3-pm, Sat-Sun 11am-1pm.

Belén: Baroque church. Open: daily to 8pm.

Iglesia del Carmen: 16th century Mudejar church. Open: midday Sun.

PLACES TO STAY

Parador, Paseo Garcia del Olmo, s/n. Tel: 284 00 51. Modern building in tranquil spot amid gardens.

Nuevo Infante, Infante D. Fernando, 5. Tel. 270 02 93. Good value, modern one-star hotel, in centre but quiet. TV, garage.

EATING OUT

La Espuela, Plaza de Toros, Paseo María Cristina. Tel. 270 26 76. Open: 12am-12pm. Amex, Diners, Master, Visa. Agreeable spot under the bullring. Imaginative local cuisine, well priced. Recommended: aubergine with ham and molasses, rabbit with mushrooms. Budget menu del día. (M)

Lozano, Polígono Industrial. Tel: 284 03 96. Open: 1-4.30pm, 8.30-11.30pm. Amex, Diners, Visa. Edge of town, modern building. Regional dishes. (B-M)

SERVICES

Bus station, Campillo Alto, s/n. Alsina Graells 284 13 65.
RENFE, Divina Pastora, 8. 284 32 26.
Taxis, 284 10 76.
Post Office, Najera, 23.

EMERGENCIES

Police 091.
Civil Guard 284 01 06.
Municipal police 284 11 91.
First aid, Picadero. Tel: 284 44 11.

• • • • • • • • • • • • • • • • •

ARCOS DE LA FRONTERA, in Cádiz province (pop. 27,000). Jerez 30km, Ronda 85km. Telephone area code 956

Tourist information, Cuesta de Belén, s/n. 70 22 64.

Magnificently situated on a cliff above the Guadalete river, Arcos typifies the Pueblos Blancos, with its narrow, cobbled streets and ancient castle. According to legend it was founded by a grandson of Noah. As a Moorish fortress, it ruled a small kingdom. It fell to Fernando 111 in 1250, but the Moorish inhabitants rose against Alfonso X who crushed the rebellion in 1264 and expelled them. Arcos has notable churches and some palatial buildings.

DON'T MISS

Plaza del Cabildo: Views over Guadalete gorge and surrounding country.

Castillo: Rebuilt in the 15th century on Arab foundations. The private residence of the Marqués de Tamarón.

Santa Maria: Built in 15th century over site of a mosque. Gothic-Plateresque facade, star vaulting, murals and carved choir-stalls.

San Pedro, Gothic church with fine baptismal chapel, and

San Agustín, sheltering venerated image of Jesus, carved in 1600.

WHERE TO STAY

Parador Casa del Corregidor, Plaza Cabildo. Tel: 70 05 00. Beautiful views. Restaurant with regional dishes.

Los Olivos, San Miguel, 2. Tel: 70 08 11. Friendly, three-star establishment in a carefully restored old Andalusian house.

El Lago, Ctra Jerez-Cartagena, km 31.5. Tel. 70 04 67. Functional two stars.

Mesón La Molinera, Ctra. Arcos-El Bosque, Km 6. Tel: 956-70 05 11. Two star hostal and restaurant by the lake.

Cortijo Fain, Ctra de Algar, km 3. Tel: 70 11 67. Beautiful old cortijo in an olive grove 5km from Arcos. Four star price range.

WHERE TO EAT

El Convento, Marqués de Torresoto, 7. Tel. 70 32 22. Open 1-4pm, 7-10.30pm. Amex, Master, Visa. In an old palace with tiled walls, arched patio. Faisan al paraiso, pheasant cooked with wine in a casserole, is a speciality. (M).

Bar Alcaraván, Calle Nueva. Stone vaulted dungeon under castle ramparts, offers excellent tapas and good flamenco music. Closed Mon.

SERVICES

Bus station, Alcaldes s/n, 70 02 57 and Corregidores, 70 20 15.
Post office, Paseo de Boliche, 24.

EMERGENCIES

Local police, 70 16 52.
Civil Guard 70 00 52.
First aid, Cruz Roja, 70 03 55.

• •

BENALMADENA, in Málaga province (pop. 21,000). Málaga 20 km. Telephone area code 95.

Tourist information, Avda Antonio Machado, 14. Tel. 244 24 94.

A modern resort has sprouted along the coast, below the old

whitewashed pueblo high on a ridge inland. Benalmadena-Costa has a large pleasure port and noisy night life in season.

DON'T MISS

Old quarter: Immaculate streets, fine views.

Museo Municipal de Arte Pre-Colombino, Avda Juan L. Peralta, s/n, old town: Pre-Colombian exhibits. Open 10am-2pm, 4-7pm, closed Sat, Sun.

Puerto Deportivo: Pleasure port.

Sea-Life marine centre with 2000 specimens, Puerto Marina Benalmadena. Open from 10am to midnight.

Casino Torrequebrada, Ctra N340 km 226, open 9pm-5am, winter 8pm-4am (passport or identity card required).

Castillo El Bill-Bill: Moorish-style castle of recent construction, concert and exhibition hall.

Tivoli World, Arroyo de la Miel (tel. 244-28 48): Large amusement park with restaurants and live shows with star names in summer. Open: 4pm-12pm or 6pm-3am May-Sept, 1-10pm winter weekends and holidays.

Weekly market, in the pueblo: Friday.

Fiesta: Virgen de la Cruz, August 14-18.

PLACES TO STAY

Torrequebrada, Ctra Cádiz km 220. Tel: 244 60 00. Five-star seaside luxury. Casino, night-club, tennis, golf, disco.

Los Patos Sol, Ctra Cadiz, km227. Tel: 244 19 90. Three stars. Well-run, geared to tour groups, as are most larger hotels on the coast.

Villasol, Ctra Cadiz, km228. Tel: 244 19 96. Smaller, three-star establishment.

EATING OUT

Mar de Alborán, Avda de Alay, 5. Tel. 244 64 27.Open 1.30-4pm, 8.30-12pm. Closed Sun night, Mon, Jan. Amex, Diners, Master, Visa. Upmarket dining in the Hotel Alay. Imaginative dishes prepared by a Basque chef. (E)

Ventorillo de la Perra, Avenida de la Constitución s/n, Arroyo de la Miel. Tel: 244 19 66. Open: 1-4pm, 8-12pm. Closed Monday and November. All cards. Traditional local and national dishes served in an old country house. Try the pickled partridge. (M).

SERVICES

Taxis, 244 15 45.
Post Office, Ctra de Cádiz.

EMERGENCIES

National police, 091.
Municipal police, 244 88 44.
First aid, 244 35 45.

• • • • • • • • • • • • • • • • •

CADIZ Pop. 154,000. Málaga 260km. Seville 123km. Madrid 633 km. Telephone area code 956.

Tourist information, Calderón de la Barca, 1. Tel: 21 13 13.

Gaditanos (natives of Cádiz) have a reputation for being witty, easygoing and exuberant and they best demonstrate this during Carnival in February. The elongated city packed into a narrow peninsula is claimed to be the oldest in the Western world. Gadir, as it was originally known, was founded by the Phoenicians in 1100 BC. After the discovery of America, it became the headquarters of the Spanish treasure fleets. Sir Francis Drake singed the king of Spain's beard here and Nelson's fleet bombarded the city in 1797. During the Napoleonic Wars it briefly was capital of all Spain not under French control. Loss of the colonies in the New World and the disastrous War of Cuba in 1898 led to decline. An important port, it has large shipyards. The dark narrow streets of the old quarter have a medieval air. In summer, youngsters flock to the long beach, unfortunately marred by high-rise mania. Fish farming is the growth industry around the Bay of Cádiz while the province is noted for wine, fishing, fine horses and fighting bulls. Much of the coast is bordered by magnificent pine-fringed, sandy beaches.

DON'T MISS

Cathedral: Constructed in Greco-Roman style, it was begun in 1702 and finished in 1838. The stalls, the crypt and the treasury are worth seeing. Composer Manuel de Falla is buried in the cathedral. Open: During services, usually 6.30-7.30pm. Also access via Cathedral museum, open 10am-1pm, closed Sundays and holidays.

San Felipe Neri church, Santa Inés: a shrine to Spanish liberals as the country's first constitution was signed here in 1812. Painting of Immaculate Conception by Murillo. Open: 8.30-10am, 7.30-9.30pm.

Oratorio de la Santa Cueva: paintings by Goya. Open: 10am-1pm, closed Saturdays, Sundays and holidays.

Museo de Cádiz (Fine Arts and Archeological Museum), Plaza de Mina: Open: 9.30am-2pm. Closed Mon and holidays. In a magnificent mansion. Roman statuary, Phoenician sarcophagi, paintings by Murillo, Zurbarán.

Torre Tavira: This 107-foot (33m) high watch-tower is one of 113 built in the 18th century to check shipping movements. Part of a palace of the Marqueses de Recaño. View Cádiz through a *camara oscura.* Open: May-Sept 9.30am-8.30pm, Oct-April 10am-6pm.

Boat trip, 45 minutes, to Puerto de Santa Maria: Ferry known as El Vapor leaves from quay near port entrance from 10am. Two-hour night cruises in summer.

PLACES TO STAY

Atlántico, Parque Genovés 9. Four stars. Tel: 21 23 01. Modern state-run hotel, beautifully located on the bay. Totally refurbished. Pool.

Francia y París, Plaza San Francisco,2. Tel. 22 23 48. Old three-star hotel recently renovated, well situated for the sights.

Meliá La Caleta, Amílcar Barca, s/n; tel. 27 94 11. New four-star hotel on the beach.

Regio 11, Avda. Andalucía, 79. Tel: 25 30 09. Two stars. Modern. Near the beach.

Colón, Marqués de Cádiz, 6. Tel. 28 53 51. One star hostal. Central, basic, cheap.

EATING OUT

El Faro, San Felix, 15. Tel: 21 10 68. Open: 1-4pm, 8.30-

12.30pm. Amex, Diners, Master, Visa. Regarded as one of Spain's top seafood restaurants. Discreet service in an upmarket atmosphere. Try the rape al amontillado. (M-E)

Ventorillo El Chato, Ctra de San Fernando, km 647. Tel: 25 00 25. Open: 1-5pm, 8-12pm. Closed: Sunday, in winter Sunday night. Amex, Diners, Master, Visa. The first owner of this 200-year-old inn was a bandit who smuggled salt through a passage under the building to waiting vessels. Fernando VII dined here. Stews, bull's tail and fish are specialities. (M-E)

Achuri, Plocia, 15. Tel: 25 36 13. Open: 1-4pm, 7-12pm. Closed: evenings of Sunday, Tues, Wed. Master, Visa. Atmospheric traditional spot, near the waterfront and old tobacco factory. Try the *cocochas en salsa verde* (hake chunks in green sauce). (M)

El Sardinero, Plaza San Juan de Dios, 4. Tel: 28 25 05. Open: 1-4.30pm, 8-12pm. Closed Sun night. Amex, Diners, Master, Visa. Unpretentious. Good value Andalusian dishes. (B-M)

TAPAS

Among a multitude of tapa bars worth trying are: *Bahía,* Avda Ramón de Carranza, 29, spare ribs; *Casa Manteca,* Corralón de los Carros, 66, *erizos de mar* and sherry; *Taberna La Manzanilla,* Feduchy, 18, old bodega serving manzanilla; and *El Moderno,* Plaza Libertad, seafood. Specialities are *ostiones* (large oysters) and *erizos* (sea urchins).

SERVICES

Bus station Comes, Plaza Independencia, 22 42 71. *Bus station Los Amarillos,* Avda. Ramón de Carranza, 31, 28 58 52. *RENFE,* Plaza de Sevilla, 25 43 01. *Compañia Trasmediterránea,* 28 43 11. *Taxi* 22 10 06, 28 69 69. *Post office,* Plaza de Topete, 21 39 45.

CONSULATES

Denmark, Finland, Norway, Sweden, Alameda Apodaca 21. Tel: 22 13 64.

Italy, Ancha 8, entresuelo izquierda. Tel: 21 17 15.

Netherlands, Plaza Tres Caravelas 5. Tel: 27 63 26.

EMERGENCIES

National police 091.

Municipal police 092.

First aid 21 10 53.

Red Cross, Santa Maria de la Soledad 10. Tel: 25 42 70.

Residencia Sanitaria (social security hospital), Avda Ana de Viya, 21. Tel: 27 90 11.

• • • • • • • • • • • • • • • • • •

CARMONA, in Seville province (pop. 24,000). Seville 33km. Telephone area code 95.

Tourist information, Plaza de las Descalzas s/n. Tel: 414 22 00.

Bulging with noble residences, churches and convents, Carmona - declared a national monument - was a fortress back in Carthaginian times when it was named Kar-Hammon (city of the god Hammon, a sun deity). Under Roman rule it sided with Caesar in his war with Pompey. Later it dominated a small Moorish kingdom. Roman walls reinforced by the Moors protect the old quarter.

DON'T MISS

Roman Necropolis and Museum: More than 900 tombs, some of them very elaborate. Open 10am-2pm, 4-6pm. Monday and holidays closed.

Alcázar de la Puerta de Sevilla: Access to the battlements 11am-2pm, daily. Closed holidays. Entry charge.

Puerta de Córdoba: Entrance gate dating back to Roman times.

Santa Maria: Gothic church, designed by the architect of Seville Cathedral, with the patio from the mosque which stood here.

San Felipe: 14th century Mudéjar church with artesonado ceiling.

Plaza Mayor: Fine old houses.

Ayuntamiento, large Roman mosaic in the patio.

WHERE TO STAY

Parador Nacional Alcázar del Rey Don Pedro. Tel: 414 10 10.

Located in a much-restored castle, first built by the Almohades, rebuilt by Mudéjar craftsmen in the 14th century. Handsome patio, views, swimming pool.

Comercio, Torre del Oro, 30. Tel. 414 0018. One-star hostal at entrance to the old quarter.

WHERE TO EAT

San Fernando, Sacramento, 3. Tel. 414 35 56. Open 1.30-4pm, 9-11.30pm. Closed Sun night, Mon & Aug. Master, Visa. Imaginative dishes served in an old house overlooking main square. (M-E)

SERVICES

Buses, San Pedro, 31, 414 05 19. *Taxi* 414 13 59. *Post office,* Prim, 29.

EMERGENCIES

Local police 414 00 08. *Cruz Roja* 414 07 51.

• •

CORDOBA Pop. 300,000. Málaga 176 km. Granada 166 km. Seville 138 km. Madrid 400 km. Telephone area code: 957.

Tourist information, Oficina municipal, Plaza Judá Leví, s/n. Tel: 20 05 22, and Junta de Andalucía, Palacio Congresos, Torrijos, 10. Tel. 47 12 35.

One thousand years ago Córdoba was Europe´s largest city with up to one million inhabitants and a byword for culture, crafts and wealth. A settlement existed here on the banks of the Guadalquivir in early times. Córdoba's name is believed to come from Kartuba, Phoenician for "rich and precious city". More than 150 years before Christ was born, the Romans granted it the status of "patrician colony" and made it capital of the province of Baetica. Moslem invaders conquered the city in 711. Abd al-Rahman 1, of the Umayyad dynasty, founded the Great Mosque, expanded by his successors. Córdoba experienced its golden age in the 10th century under Abd al-Rahman 111, who broke with Baghdad and declared himself Caliph of the West. Christians, Jews and Moslems lived together. Civil war destroyed the caliphate in the 11th century and

Córdoba fell under the rule of the Almoravid and Almohad sects. Maimónides, the Jewish sage and physician, was born in Córdoba in the 12th century, when the Talmudic school was ranked one of the great centres of Hebrew scholarship. Ferdinand 111 ousted the Moors from the city in 1236 and it became a military base in the war against Granada. Later Córdoba lost its eminence and declined into a quiet provincial city. Famous *cordobeses* include Seneca the Roman philosopher, the philosophers Averroes and Maimonides, poets Juan de Mena and Luis de Gongora, and the matador Manolete. The city is still wellknown for its excellent quality embossed leatherwork, for its silversmiths, and for its bullfighters. The cordobeses are generally considered to be more reserved and serious than frivolous Málaga types.

DON'T MISS

Mezquita: With the Alhambra, the Mosque is one of the great Moorish architectural masterpieces. Founded in the 8th century, with many later additions. The Torre del Alminar bell-tower is built on top of a minaret. More than 850 marble, jasper and granite columns, many rescued from Roman and Visigothic buildings, are topped by two tiers of red and white arches. The mihrab, or prayer niche, is magnificently decorated. A 16th-century cathedral with an Italianate dome is slotted into the mosque's centre. Open: 10am-5.30pm Oct-March, 10am-7pm April-Sept, Sun mornings for services & 3.30-5.30pm, later in summer.

Alcázar: 14th-century fortress where the Catholic Monarchs planned the reconquest of Granada. Later it became a prison. Striking Roman mosaics and sarcophagus. Climb the towers for good views. Beautiful gardens, floodlit May-September, 10-12pm. Open: 9.30am-1.30pm, 4-7pm, from May 1, 5-8pm. Sun 9.30am-1.30pm.

Judería: Old Jewish quarter, with many echoses of the past in its narrow, whitewashed streets, grilled windows, cool patios.

Sinagoga, Calle Judio. 14th century synagoue, one of three remaining in Spain. Open: 10am-2pm, 3.30-5.30pm. Sunday &

holidays, 10am-1.30pm. Closed Mon.

Museo Taurino (bullfight museum), Plaza Maimonides, 5: In the Judería (old Jewish quarter). Relics of the corrida and especially of Córdoba's big names. Open: 9.30am-1.30pm, 4-7pm, May-Sept 5-8pm. Closed Mon, Sun afternoon.

Puente Romano: Bridge across the Guadalquivir, on Roman foundations, often rebuilt and restored. Nearby is replica of giant Moorish waterwheel.

Torre de La Calahorra: Tower built in 14th century to guard river. Multivision show on city's history and the impact of Islamic, Christian and Jewish cultures. Open daily, 10am-6pm, in winter 10am-2pm, 5.30-8.30pm.

Palacio de Viana, Plaza Don Gome, 2. Valuable collections of paintings, tapestries, porcelain in beautiful old palace. October-May 10am-1pm, 4-6pm, June-September 9am-2pm. Sunday & holidays, 10am-2pm. Closed Wed.

Posada del Potro, Plaza del Potro. Old inn mentioned by Cervantes. Exhibitions. Open: 9am-2pm, 6-9pm. Closed Saturday and Sunday.

Museo Julio Romero de Torres Museum, Pl. Potro. Works varying from the erotic to the macabre by popular local painter. Open: 9.30am-1.30pm, 4-7pm, May-Sept 5-8pm. Closed Mon.

Museo Bellas Artes, Plaza del Potro: Works by Murillo, Valdés Leal, and Zurbarán. Open:10am-2pm, 5-7pm, summer 10am-1.30pm, 6-8pm, Sun 10am-1.30pm. Closed Mon.

Museo Arqueológico, Plaza de Jéronimo Páez, 7: Iberian, Roman and Moorish artefacts exhibited in a Renaissance mansion. Open: 10am-2pm, 5-7pm, summer 10am-1.30pm, 6-8pm, sun 10am-1.30pm. Closed Mon.

Jardín Botánico: Botanic Gardens: 10.30am-2.30pm, 4.30-6.30pm, April-July 5.30-7.30pm. Closed Mon & July 18-Sept 12.

Plaza Corredera: Handsome arcaded square, built in the 17th century, once the scene of bullfights. Daily market.

Patios: Five traditional patios, tiled and flower-filled, can be seen in Martín de Roa and San Basilio streets. During the Festival de los Patios (second week of May) more than 50 patios are open for the admiration of the public.

Medina Azahar, five miles (8km) from city: Caliph Abd al-

Rahman 111 built a sumptuous palace in the 10th century, employing marble, jasper, ebony and alabaster. Berber invaders later sacked it. Restoration work is proceeding. See Excursion 32. Open: mid-Sept to April 10am-2pm, 4-6.30pm, May to mid-June 10am-2pm, 6-8.30pm, mid-June to mid-Sept 10am-1.30pm, 6-8.30pm. Closed Mon, Sun afternoon

Along the Guadalquivir:

Montoro, 26 miles (42km) east via N1V: Montoro's steep, crooked streets straggle picturesquely over five hills on a bend of the Guadalquivir. The river bridge, started in the time of the Catholic Monarchs, was called the Puente de las Donadas (Bridge of the Lay Sisters) because the townswomen contributed by selling their jewellery. On the Plaza de España are the pink sandstone Ayuntamiento, former seat of the ruling dukes, with a Plateresque facade, and the Gothic-Mudéjar church of San Bartolomé.

PLACES TO STAY

Parador Nacional Arruzafa, Avda de la Arruzafa, 33. Tel: 27 59 00. On the edge of town towards the sierras. Fine views. Swimming pool. Airconditioning.

Amistad Córdoba, Plaza Maimonides, 3. Tel. 42 03 35. Two 18th century mansions converted into a four-star hotel, next to the city wall in the Judería. Mudéjar patio, luxury installations.

Albucasis, Buen Pastor, 11. Tel: 47 86 25. Small, two star hotel. Converted from an old house near the Mosque. Large patio.

Andalucía, José Zorilla, 3. Tel: 47 60 00. Two stars. Near the Gran Capitán. Functional and comfortable, at a reasonable price.

Maestre, Romero Barros, 4. Tel. 47 24 10. Value for money, friendly one-star hotel near Plaza de Potro. Under same ownership, the two-star hostal Maestre next door, tel. 47 53 95. Parking facilities.

EATING OUT

El Caballo Rojo, Cardenal Herrero, 28. Tel: 47 53 75. Open: 1-4.30pm, 8.30-12pm. Amex, Diners, Master, Visa. Córdoban and Mozarabic dishes. The *cordero a la miel* is worth trying, but this restaurant may be too popular with tourists for its own good. (E)

El Churrasco, Romero, 16. Tel: 29 08 19. Open: 1-4pm, 8-12pm. Closed Aug. Amex, Diners, Master, Visa. Justifiably popular. Attractive Andalusian patio. Excellent Córdoba dishes. Try the *berenjenas fritas* (fried eggplant) and stuffed bull's tail. More than 12,000 bottles of wine are stored in an adjacent bodega. (M-E)

El Blasón, José Zorrilla, 11. Tel. 48 06 25. Open: 1-4.30pm, 8-12pm. Amex, Diners, Master, Visa. Same family as El Caballo Rojo, but they try harder here. Imaginative dishes in Andalusian atmosphere. (E)

BARS

Córdoba has numerous bars with character, serving Montilla wine and good tapas. A sample: *Taberna San Miguel* (El Pisto), Plaza San Miguel, 1. A popular spot, with inner patio with bullfight posters and wall tiles, good tapas; *Mesón del Arco Bajo,* Plaza Corredera. A true antique, black barrels, uneven tiled floor; *Mesón de la Luna,* Puerta de la Luna. Founded in 1846 and embedded in the city wall, the bar being made from the massive former entrance gate. Cured ham and fried mushrooms.

Near the Mosque: *Casa Rafaé,* corner Deanes and Buen Pastor, and tiny *La Mezquita,* Cardenal Herrero, 24, where *boquerones en vinagre* are the speciality.

For a journey into the past, step into *Mesón de las Cabezas,* Cabezas, 17, near the mosque, with its tiled tables, pot plants and prehistoric air. Over the arches of the crumbling house opposite the heads of seven executed princelings were once arrayed, hence *Cabezas.*

SERVICES

Bus: Alsina Graells 23 64 74, Priego 29 01 58, Ureña 47 23 52.
RENFE 49 02 02. Iberia 47 26 95.
Taxi 45 00 00.
Post office, Cruz Conde, 15. Tel: 47 82 67.

EMERGENCIES

National police 091.
Municipal police, 092.
Red Cross 22 22 22.

First aid 061.

• • • • • • • • • • • • • • • • •

ESTEPONA, in Málaga province (pop. 35,000). Málaga 82 km. Gibraltar 43 km. Telephone area code 95.

Tourist information, Paseo Marítimo Pedro Manrique, s/n. Tel: 280 09 13.

Believed to have Roman origins, Estepona's name probably comes from the Moorish Estebbuna. Long important as a fishing and agricultural centre, it is fast growing as a tourist resort but retains its Spanish atmosphere. The port is the centre for yachtsmen, fishermen and night life. Costa Natura, Spain´s first nudist village, is close by.

DON'T MISS

Old quarter, with remains of a castle.

Nuestra Señora de los Remedios: 18th century church in Baroque style.

Fishing and pleasure port: Bars and restaurants.

Sierra Bermeja, scenic route through the mountains behind the town.

Weekly market: Wednesday.

Fiestas: San Isidro, colourful pilgrimage to Los Pedregales shrine; annual fair, first week July; Virgen del Carmen, July 16.

WHERE TO STAY

Atalaya Park, Ctra N340 km 168. Tel: 288 48 01. Four stars. Extensive sports facilities. On beach.

El Paraiso, Ctra N340 km 167. Tel: 288 30 00. Four stars. Between sea and mountain. Golf course.

Caracas, Avda San Lorenzo, 50. Tel: 280 08 00. Two stars. In town.

EATING OUT

Costa del Sol, San Roque, 23. Tel: 280 11 01. Open: : 12-4pm, 7-12pm. Closed: midday Sunday & Monday. Amex, Visa, Master. Try the bouillabaise and soufflés at this friendly French bistro. First-rate-value menu of the day. (M)

La Rada, Avda España, s/n. Tel. 279 10 36. 12am-12pm. Closed Tues. Visa. Bargain-priced fish restaurant. (B)

Robby's, Ubrique, 11. Tel: 280 21 21. Open 8-11pm. Closed Monday, and last three weeks of August and February. Amex, Master, Visa. Pleasantly intimate atmosphere in converted old house. Imaginative international dishes, excellent puddings. Booking recommended. (M-E)

Macues, Puerto de La Duquesa. Tel. 289 03 95. Open 8-11.30pm, also 1-4pm Sat & Sun. Closed Mon, last two weeks Feb. Amex, Diners, Master, Visa. Overlooking the port. International dishes. (M)

SERVICES

Bus station, Avenida de España, 287 22 62. *Radio taxi* 280 29 00. *Post office,* Paseo Marítimo.

EMERGENCIES

National police 091. *Municipal police* 280 02 43. *Civil Guard* 280 10 87. *First aid* 280 10 84.

• •

FUENGIROLA, in Málaga province (Pop. 37,000). Málaga 29 km. Telephone area code 95.

Tourist information, Avda Jesus Santos Rein, 6. Tel: 246 74 57.

Densely-packed high rises have replaced the little fishing village that once existed here. Fuengirola's long beach and promenade attract numerous foreign and Spanish families in summer. Retirees take over in winter. The Phoenician settlement here was called Suel and the Moorish name was Sohail. Abd al-Rahman 111, Caliph of Córdoba, ordered the castle built in 956. Around 1400 a community of fishermen from Genoa settled in the area known as Los Boliches.

DON'T MISS

Castillo de Sohail: Castle dating back 1,000 years, rebuilt in the 18th century, renovated to serve as cultural centre.

Pórtico romano: Roman gateway reconstructed at Los

Boliches.

Parque zoológico, Camilo José Cela. Open 10am-2pm, 5-9pm. Winter hours 9am-1pm, 3-7pm.

Salon Varietes, Calle Emancipación. Tel. 247 45 42. English-language theatre productions, amateur and professional.

Weekly market, on Tuesday mornings, one of the largest on the coast. Fiestas: Virgen del Carmen, July 16; annual fair, Oct 6-12, with romería before the fiesta.

PLACES TO STAY

Byblos Andaluz, Mijas Golf, Apartado 138. (near Fuengirola). Tel: 247 30 50. Luxury five-star hotel on golf course. Expensive.

Las Palmeras Sol, Paseo Marítimo, s/n. Tel: 247 27 00. Four stars. Vast complex on the seafront.

Florida, Paseo Marítimo, s/n. Tel: 247 61 00. Three stars. Relaxed seafront establishment with tropical garden.

In Mijas: *Hotel Mijas,* Urb. Tamisa. Tel: 248 58 00. Three stars. Beautiful views. Garden. Pool.

EATING OUT

El Bote, Paseo Marítimo s/n, Torreblanca. Tel: 266 02 96. Open: 12-4.30pm, 7.30-11.30pm. Closed: Monday. Amex, Master, Visa. Longtime favourite on the beach, with large terrace. Excellent fresh seafood. (M)

Méson El Castellano, Camino de Coín, 5. Tel: 246 27 36. Open: 12-4pm, 7-11.30pm. Closed: Saturday lunch. Amex, Master, Visa. Good-value Castilian cooking. No frills but pleasant atmosphere. (M)

Portofino, Edificio Perla, 1, Paseo Marítimo, 29. Tel: 247 06 43. Open: 1-4pm, 7-11pm. Closed: Mon & two weeks in July. Amex, Diners, Master, Visa. Good service and an extensive, Italian-influenced menu at this seafront restaurant. (M-E)

SERVICES

Bus station, Avenida Ramón y Cajal, 247 50 66.

RENFE 247 85 40.

Taxis, 247 10 00.

Post office, Calle España.

EMERGENCIES

National police, 091.
Municipal police, 258 93 21.
First aid, 247 86 53.

• • • • • • • • • • • • • • • • • •

GIBRALTAR (pop. 30,000). Malaga 116km. Cadiz 150km. Madrid 804km. Telephone area code 9567.

Tourist information, Gibraltar Museum, Bomb House Lane, at The Piazza, and at kiosks, tel. 74289/74950.

One of Britain's last colonies, Gibraltar - a limestone peninsula jutting from the Spanish coast into the Mediterranean - is a fascinating anachronism. A walk along Main Street with its busy shops reveals a cosmopolitan community of Spanish, British, Moroccan, Jewish, Maltese, and Genoese origin. English is the official language, but many inhabitants mix English and Spanish in their conversation. They go to English pubs but watch Spanish television. Measuring little more than two square miles (5.8 sq km) - reclaimed land is increasing its area - and rising 1,396 feet (426 metres), the Rock has a population of 30,000, of whom 20,000 are Gibraltarians. The House of Assembly led by a Chief Minister rules the colony. The Berber warrior Tarik landed on the Rock in 711, whence the name Gibraltar, from Jebel Tarik (Mount Tarik). In 1704, during the War of the Spanish Succession, an Anglo-Dutch fleet captured Gibraltar and the Treaty of Utrecht ceded it to Britain. Ever since Spain has been trying to get it back. General Franco tried to force the issue by closing the frontier. The blockade, started in 1966 when vehicle traffic was banned and lasting until 1983, was a failure. As Britain reduces its military presence, the stubbornly British Gibraltarians are seeking to convert the colony into a self-sufficient community, through tourism and establishing an off-shore financial centre. Costa-dwellers flock to Gib to buy cheaper British-made foodstuffs, such as biscuits and marmalade. Visitors often buy jewellery, electrical goods, perfume, watches, quality clothing, tobacco, and spirits. Price differences with Spain, however, have narrowed. Hotel and restaurant charges are higher than for equivalent standard in Spain. There is only land access with Spain, but ferries run to Tangier.

Note: Leave your car in La Linea. Gibraltar drives on the right. Petrol is cheap, but roads are crowded and parking is difficult. Also there can be big delays when leaving.

DON'T MISS

Apes' Den: Take the cable car from the lower station in Grand Parade. The cheeky tail-less monkeys, the only breed living wild in Europe, are now confined to a park (open 10am-7pm, entrance fee). From the top of the Rock, great views of Africa and the Bay of Gibraltar. Cable car goes every 10 mins, Monday to Saturday.

Europa Point: Look across Strait to Africa from the 144-year-old lighthouse at Gib's most southerly point. Nearby there is a shrine to Our Lady of Europa, venerated by sailors.

Upper Galleries: These were hacked out of solid rock in 1782 to make gun emplacements during the Great Siege,. Excellent views. Upper galleries open 10am-7pm summer, 10am-5.30 pm winter.

St Michaels Cave: Son et lumiére show twice daily. Lower cave has an underground lake, tours of which can be arranged through the Tourist Office.

Gibraltar Museum: History and natural history of Gibraltar from Stone Age to today. Open 10am-1pm, 3-6pm Monday-Friday, 10am-2pm Saturday, closed Sunday.

Trafalgar Cemetery: Has interesting head stones, among them those of men killed in Nelson's famous sea battle off the Spanish coast.

International Club, 7 Europa Road: Gaming casino. Entry fee, passport required. Men must wear ties.

Dolphins: Trips leave from Sheppards Marina to spot dolphins in the Strait. Contact Dolphin Safari, tel. 71914.

PLACES TO STAY

Holiday Inn, 2 Governor's Parade. Tel: 70500. Modern

building, handy for Main Street. Similar tariffs to a five-star Spanish hotel.

Rock Hotel, Europa Road. Tel: 73000. Located in nine acres of gardens. Four to five star price range.

Bristol Hotel, 10 Cathedral Square. Tel: 76800. Old hotel, near the centre. Prices equivalent to Spanish three or four stars.

EATING OUT

For pub grub at reasonable prices: *Royal Calpe,* 176 Main Street. Tel: 75980. Closed: Sun. No credit cards. Good pub grub; and *The Clipper,* 78B Irish Town. Tel: 79791. Nautical themes. British fare.

La Bayuca, 21, Turnbull's Lane. Tel. 75119. Open: 1-3pm, 8pm-midnight. Closed Tues. No credit cards. Gib's oldest restaurant. Irish and Scottish beef. (M)

Strings, 44 Cornwall Lane. Tel: 78800. Open: 1-3pm Tues-Fri & 8-11pm Mon-Sat. Dishes range from English to Moroccan. No credit cards. Booking advisable. (M)

EVENTS

Changing of the Guard: Military pomp, once a month in front of the Governor's Residence on Main Street. *Ceremony of the Keys:* Celebrates the traditional locking of the Fortress Gates at Landport and the return of the keys to the safe custody of the Governor. Held three times a year in Casemates Square. For security reasons details of both these events are published in the local press only one week before the event. Every July an *International Festival of Music and Performing Arts* is staged. A highlight is the gala night in the auditorium in St Michael's Cave.

CROSSING THE BORDER

A valid passport is necessary. The Gibraltar pound, on a par with Sterling, is the official currency. UK and Gibraltar notes circulate freely, but Gibraltar notes are not exchangeable outside Gibraltar. UK coinage is legal tender and Spanish pesetas are accepted. Most banks (generally open 9am-3.30pm Monday-Thursday, and 9am-3.30pm, 4-6pm Friday) are centred around Main Street or Line Wall Road. Check with banks re use of British cashpoint cards and current account cheque books.

People entering Gibraltar, who have not entered the colony in the previous 24 hours, have a duty free allowance of 200 cigarettes or equivalent, 1 litre of spirits or 2 litres of still wine, 50 grammes of perfume and 0.25 litres of toilet water. Those returning to Spain are allowed the same, plus 35,000 pesetas worth of goods, provided they do not reside in Gibraltar or the Campo de Gibraltar area and make only one visit per month.

TELEPHONES

To call Gibraltar from Spain, dial the area code 9567, except when you are in Cádiz province when you only need to dial 7 followed by the subscribers' number. To phone Spain, dial the province code, then the subscribers' number, e.g. to Málaga 952 + number.

SERVICES

Airport (Gibraltar Airways) Tel 75984. *Taxis* Tel 70027. *Post Office,* 104 Main Street.

CONSULATES

Belgium, 47 Irish Town. Tel 78353.

Denmark, Cloister Building, Market Lane. Tel 72735.

Finland, 20 Line Wall Road. Tel 75149.

France (Consular Office), 209 Main Street , 2nd floor. Tel 78830.

Israel, 3 City Mill Lane. Tel 75955.

Italy, 12 College Lane. Tel 78123.

Netherlands, Suite 9, 1 International Commercial Centre, Main Street. Tel 79220.

Norway, 315 Main Street. Tel 74427.

Sweden, Cloister Building, Irish Town. Tel 78456.

EMERGENCIES

Police Tel 72500, emergency calls 199.

St Bernards Hospital Tel 79700. Health Centre, Casemates Square Tel 77003. Ambulance 199.

• •

GRANADA, capital (Pop. 255,000). Málaga 126km. Seville 256km. Madrid 432km. Telephone area code 958.

Municipal tourist office: Libreros 2. Tel: 22 59 90, also Plaza Mariana Pineda 10, bajo. Tel: 22 66 88.

Although modern apartments ring the city, the glories of yesterday do live on in Granada, for the Moors left a dazzling heritage. Granadinos are alleged by fellow-Andalusians to be mean and a little dour, but that image does not seem to worry them. The last stronghold of the Moors in Spain, their city has a magnificent situation. It meanders over three hills, which have been compared to the opened quarters of a pomegranate (in Spanish a *granada*). The fruit appears on the city coat of arms. With an altitude of 2,260 feet, the city has a pleasantly brisk climate except in summer when it can be very hot. Behind rises the great bulk of the Sierra Nevada, snow-capped for much of the year. After the Christian army took Córdoba in the 13th century, thousands of people sought refuge in Granada. For 250 years under the Nasrid dynasty, Granada was a brilliant centre of civilisation, with some 100,000 inhabitants. But finally, after months of siege, the conquering forces of the Catholic Monarchs, Fernando and Isabel, entered the city in 1492. Expulsion of Jews, Moslems and Moriscos (Moslems converted to Christianity) impoverished Granada and its province, but the later developments produced many fine examples of Renaissance architecture. The university was founded by a decree of the Emperor Charles V in 1526. Granada is important as a judicial and religious centre and as the commercial focus for a large province.

DON'T MISS

Alhambra and Generalife: One of the top sights in all Spain. A glorious reminder of the climax of Moslem sophistication here. Delicate stuccowork and geometric tiles decorate the airy halls of this palace. It dates from the period of the Nazrid dynasty (mid-13th century to 1492), while the adjacent Alcazaba (fortress) was constructed between the 9th and 12th centuries. The sultans Ismail 1, Yusuf 1 and Muhammad V were the most important builders of the Alhambra (literally, the red fort), a royal city that once included many streets and at least six palaces. The Generalife with its terraced water gardens was the summer palace. Open: 9am-6pm (winter), 9am-8pm (summer). Interior floodlit, summer - Tuesday, Thursday & Saturday, 10-12pm, winter- Saturday 8-10pm. Note: More than two million people visit annually so a quota system operates. You can only enter at the time marked on your ticket. At peak times waiting period can be an hour or more. Vehicle access is by a road that bypasses the city centre (look for the signs). Pedestrians can take a tram service from the Plaza Nueva up the Cuesta de Gomérez, due to be closed to motor traffic.

Museo de Bellas Artes & *Museo Hispano Musulmán*, Palacio de Carlos V, Alhambra: Fine collection of Hispano-Moorish art, including the superb 15th century Alhambra Vase, beautifully decorated in blue and gold. Open 10am-2pm, Saturdays 10am-1pm. Closed Sundays, holidays.

Cathedral: A Gothic-Renaissance masterpiece, begun in 1523. Maestros such as Enrique Egas and Diego de Siloé participated in its construction. Siloé's domed Capilla Mayor is a highlight. Alonso Cano, born in Granada, who designed the western facade, is buried in the cathedral. Open: 10.30am-1pm, Sunday mornings closed, 3.30-6pm (winter), 4-7pm (summer).

Capilla Real (Royal Chapel): Magnificently carved images in Carrara marble of Ferdinand and Isabel and Philip the Fair and Juana la Loca. In crypt beneath are their lead coffins and that of Miguel, the Catholic Monarchs' grandson. In the sacristy look for Isabel's crown and sceptre - and embroidery - and Ferdinand's sword. Open: 10.30am-1pm, Sunday mornings & holidays 11am-1pm, 3.30-6pm (winter), 4-7pm (summer).

La Cartuja Monastery: Founded in 1516. Baroque grandeur. Sumptuously decorated sacristy is a highlight. Open:10am-1pm, Sundays 10am-12pm, 4-7pm (summer), 10.30am-1pm, 3.30-6pm (winter).

San Jeronimo Monastery, on Gran Capitán: Renaissance splendour. Contains the remains of the Gran Capitán, a famous 16th century warrior) and his wife. Open: 10am-1pm, 3-6.30pm (winter), 4-7pm (summer).

Albaicín (Arab for Falconers´ Quarter): The old Moorish

quarter, narrow crookback streets straggling over a hillside. For the finest views of the Alhambra and the Sierra Nevada, visit the terrace of San Nicolas Church.

Museo Arqueológico, Carrera del Darro, 41: Open 10am-2pm. Closed Monday, holidays.

El Bañuelo, Carrera del Darro, 31: Arab baths from the 11th century. Open: 10am-2pm. Closed Sunday, Monday, holidays.

Corral del Carbón, Mariana Pineda, near Reyes Católicos: The oldest Moorish building in the city. Once a caravanserai, then a theatre. Now a showplace for handicrafts. Open: 10am-1.30pm, 5-8pm. Closed Saturday afternoon, Sunday.

Casa-Museo Federico García Lorca, Huerta de San Vicente, off Camino de Ronda: Manuscripts and personal items of the poet are displayed in the old family farmhouse where he wrote some of his bestknown works. Inquire at tourism office for opening hours.

Casa Museo Manuel de Falla, Antequeruela Alta, 11 (near Alhambra Palace hotel): Carmen (typical Granada house in a garden) where the famous composer lived. Original furnishings with his piano, desk, pictures. Open 10.15am-2.45pm. Closed Sunday, Monday, holidays.

Palacio de la Madraza, Calle Oficios, opposite Royal Chapel: Once a Moorish university, now a cultural centre. Open mornings, also evenings when exhibitions are held.

Abadía del Sacromonte: Benedictine monastery. Church contains ashes of Granada patron saint, San Cecilio, and venerated image of Cristo de los Gitanos. Catacumbs, where remains of Christian martyrs found, can be visited. Open 11am-1pm, 4-6pm. Closed Monday.

PLACES TO STAY

Parador Nacional de San Francisco, Recinto de la Alhambra. Tel: 22 14 40. This former Franciscan convent is located within the Alhambra. Not cheap and booked for months ahead, but late vacancies do occur.

Alhambra Palace, Peña Partida, 2. Tel: 22 14 68. Four stars. Recently renovated. Elaborate Moorish-style decor. Views over city.

Washington Irving, Paseo Generalife, 2. Tel: 22 75 50. Three stars. Also in the area of the Alhambra. Old style and a bit faded.

América, Real de la Alhambra, 53. Tel: 22 74 71. Intimate and unrivalled position within Alhambra walls, but somewhat pricey for a one-star hotel. Closed November-February.

Suecia, Huerta Los Angeles, 8. (off Calle Molinos) Tel: 22 50 44. Tranquil, two-star hostal. Rooms with bathrooms are cramped, parking is handy.

Niza, Navas, 16. Tel. 22 54 30. Small, one star hotel, in centre.

California, Cuesta de Gomérez, 37. Tel. 22 40 56. Two star hostal on route to Alhambra. For budget travellers

EATING OUT

Los Manueles, Zaragoza, 2. Tel: 22 34 15. Open: 1-4.30pm, 7.30-12pm. Typical Granada dishes served in a traditional setting, tiled walls, near the Ayuntamiento. (M)

Mesón Antonio, Ecce Homo, 6. Tel: 22 95 99. Open: 2-3.30pm, 9-10.30pm. Closed: Sunday & July-August. In a back street near the Campo de Principe. Guarded by an iron gate. Ring for home cooking in an intimate atmosphere. (M)

Mirador de Morayma, Pianista García Carrillo. Tel: 22 82 90. Open: 1.30-3.30 pm, 8.30-11.30pm. Closed Sunday night (winter), Sunday night and Monday (summer). Amex, Master, Visa. Well-prepared Granada dishes in a beautifully-located old house in the Albaicin. (M)

Sevilla, Oficios, 12. Tel: 22 12 23. Open: 1-4.30pm, 8-11.30pm. Closed: Sunday night. Amex, Master, 6,000, Visa. Where Lorca and other intellectuals used to meet. Wood ovens. Regional. (M)

For cheaper eating head for Calle Elvira, on or near which such restaurants as *Mesón Andaluz, Boabdil* and *La Nueva Bodega* offer budget meals.

EVENTS

Granada has several cultural events of note during the year. The big one is the *International Music and Dance Festival,* from mid-June to the first week of July. Featuring some of the world's top performers, it is staged in several in locations such as the Generalife gardens, the Palacio de Carlos V and the San

Jeronimo Monastery. Tickets are usually on sale at the Corral del Carbón, but for latest information inquire at the tourist office or at the festival office, Gracia, 21 (4th floor), tel. 26 74 42/3/4. An international theatre festival is held in May and an international jazz festival in November.

AFTER DARK

Gypsies offer flamenco shows nightly in the caves of Sacromonte. Establish the price first, as complaints of rip-offs are common. The touristy El Corral del Principe restaurant (tel. 22 80 88) has nightly flamenco shows. It is located on the Campo del Príncipe, a lively square with a number of tapa bars and restaurants, including Lago de Como, at Number 8 (tel. 22 61 54. Master, Visa, B-M), an Italian restaurant with 32 different pizzas.

Bars offering tapas and ambiente include: *Casa Enrique,* Acera del Darro, 8. Also known as El Elefante. Superior wines; *Bar Castañeda* or *La Gran Taberna,* on Calle Elvira. Due to a family dispute it has been split into two bars, both as old as time. Wood counter, barrels, beams, bull´s head, traditional local pottery, cracked stained glass, Granada characters; Ca´ Fernando, Plaza Cuchilleros, 11. The sign outside says Bar La Trastienda. Go through the bar to intimate inner room. Ham, sausage tapas, vino de la costa.

SERVICES

Taxis: 20 14 61.

Post office, Puerta Real. Tel: 22 48 53.

Sierra Nevada ski resort, weather information, snow report (December to May): 48 01 53 or 24 91 19. Bus to ski slopes: 9am daily from Bar Ventorillo near the Palacio de Congresos in Granada, returning at 5pm (Autobuses Bonal, 27 24 97).

CONSULATES

Belgium, Recogidas 66, 1-A. Tel: 25 16 31.

France, Pinto López Mezquita, 6-3C. Tel: 27 25 93.

Italy, Dr Martin Lagos 6-3C. Tel: 26 13 61.

West Germany, Avenida de la Constitución 20-2, Edificio

Piramide. Tel: 29 33 52.

EMERGENCY

National police: 091.
Municipal police: 092.
Civil Guard: 25 11 00.
First aid: 22 12 63.
Red Cross, Cuesta Escoriaza 8. Tel: 22 20 24.
Hospital Clínico, Avda Dr. Oloriz, s/n. 27 02 00.

• • • • • • • • • • • • • • • •

GUADIX, Granada province (pop. 20,000). Granada 57km. Málaga 185km. Almería 113km. Madrid 472km. Telephone area code 958.

Tourist information, Ctra Granada, tel. 66 26 65.

More than 3,000 feet above sea-level, the ancient town of Guadix commands a fertile plain on one side while at its back rise strangely-eroded hills where thousands of people still live in caves. Silver, iron and copper were extracted from this region before the birth of Christ, and a Roman colony was founded here in the time of Julius Caesar. In the Moorish era it was a crossroads on the route from the Caliphate of Córdoba to the port of Almería. One of Guadix's sons, Pedro de Mendoza, founded Buenos Aires. Saint Torcuato, sent by St. Paul as part of an evangelising team, established Spain's first Christian bishopric here. Torcuato died a martyr but there is still a Bishop of Guadix.

DON'T MISS

Troglodyte quarter: With Cueva-Museo (museum in a typical cave), Barrio Ermita Nueva. Open 10am-2pm, 4-6pm (3-5pm Sat & Sun). Closed Mon.

Cathedral, impressive Baroque-Renaissance, partly designed by Diego de Siloé. The Cathedral museum holds relics of Torcuato and other precious religious artefacts. Open 11am-1pm, 4-7pm.

Plaza Mayor: Arcaded, Castilian-style square with town hall.

Iglesia de Santiago, Placeta de Santiago: Mudéjar church

with fine Plateresqure facade. Open 6-8pm.

Alcazaba: Arab fortress. Open 9.30am-1.30pm, 3.30-6.30pm. Closed Saturday afternoon, Sunday.

Palacio de los Marqueses de Peñaflor: Built between the 16 and 18th centuries, being restored.

PLACES TO STAY

Hotel Comercio, Mira de Amezcua, 3. Tel: 66 05 00. Old one-star establishment, with restaurant.

SERVICES

Bus station, Urb. Santa Rosa, 66 06 57. *RENFE* 66 06 25. Correos, Plaza Onésimo Redondo, 13.

EMERGENCIES

Municipal police 66 02 50. *Civil Guard:* 66 08 17. *First aid* 66 00 60/66 01 99.

• •

HUELVA, capital (Pop.142,000). Seville 92km. Málaga 299km. Madrid 635km. Telephone area code 959.

Tourist information, Avda de Alemania, 12. Tel: 25 74 03.

Columbus's Voyage of Discovery was planned in the Huelva area and from the Tinto river at Palos de la Frontera his three ships set out on the epic voyage. This sprawling, workaday city at the junction of the Odiel and Tinto rivers is a useful base for visiting sites associated with Columbus, but otherwise it usually does not detain visitors for long. In ancient times its province was noted for its mineral wealth and the legendary kingdom of Tartessus flourished in this area. Here the Phoenicians founded a settlement called Onuba, which is why today's inhabitants are known as *onubenses*. Alfonso the Wise recaptured Ghelbah (thus Huelva) from the Moors in 1257 and from 1468 it belonged to the Dukes of Medina Sidonia. Huelva was long dominated by Seville, but last century it was made the capital of a separate province, which embraces long, pine-fringed beaches, wild marshland, forested mountains and vast strawberry fields.

British interest took over the Rio Tinto mines last century, exporting copper, silver and gold through the port of Huelva. Another link with Britain is an unusual grave in the city cemetery. It contains The Man Who Never Was, an officer named "William Martin", whose body was found floating off Huelva in April, 1943. Apparently the victim of a plane crash, he carried secret documents which German agents were able to examine. In fact, the British had carefully prepared false documents to trick the Germans into expecting an Allied landing in Greece instead of Sicily.

DON'T MISS

Christopher Columbus Monument, Punta del Sebo, junction of Odiel and Tinto rivers: Dedicated to the navigator, this sculpture by Gertrude Vanderbilt Whitney was a gift from the United States in 1929.

Barrio Reina Victoria: Suburb of neat English-style houses, a quaint relic built in 1917 by British owners of the Río Tinto mining company for their employees.

San Pedro: Built in the 15th and 16th century over a mosque.

Museo Provincial, Alameda Sundheim, 17: Fine arts and archaeology, including large collection of objects related to the kingdom of Tartessus. Open: 8.30am-2.30pm, Sat 9.30am-1.30pm. Sun closed.

Fiestas Colombinas (Columbus fiesta), first week of August.

PLACES TO STAY

Huelva: Tartessos, Avda Martín Alonso Pinzón, 13. Tel: 24 56 11. Three stars. Centrally located.

Costa de la Luz, José María Amo, 8. Tel. 25 64 22. Two-star hotel in the centre.

Hosteria de la Rábida, next to La Rábida monastery, across the river. Tel: 37 60 00. Small, three-star hotel.

EATING OUT

La Cazuela, Garcí Fernández, 5. Tel: 25 80 96. Open: 1-4pm, 8-12pm. Closed: Sun night and last two weeks of June. Amex, Master, Visa. Andalusian and Basque dishes at reasonable prices. (M)

Los Encinares, Avenida Alonso Pinzón, 20, excellent tapas of ham and grilled pork. Traditional atmosphere, with barrels and woodwork.

Las Candelas, Ctra Punta Umbria, Aljaraque crossroads. Tel: 31 83 01. Open: 1-4pm, 8-12pm. Closed: Sun. Amex, Master, Visa. An old venta, much modernized. Fresh seafood and meat dishes. (M)

SERVICES

Bus station, Avda de Portugal, 25 69 00.
RENFE, Avda de Italia, 24 66 66.
Teletaxi 25 20 20.
Post Office, Avda de Italia s/n. 24 91 84.

CONSULATES

Finland, Avenida Martin Alonso Pinzon,18. Tel: 24 95 83.
France, Rico 53, 1. Tel: 225 77 00.
Netherlands, Marina, 19. Tel: 25 17 06.
Norway, Sweden and *Denmark,* Santo Domingo de la Calzada. Tel: 24 61 78.

EMERGENCIES

National police 091.
Municipal police 24 51 35.
First Aid 25 38 00.
Red Cross 26 12 11.

JAÉN, capital (pop. 100,000). Málaga 213km. Córdoba, 108km. Granada, 93km. Madrid, 335km. Telephone area code 953.

Tourist information: Arquitecto Berges, 1, Jaén. Tel: 22 27 37.

Even Jaén natives say their city is not exactly exciting. The main Madrid-Granada highway sweeps most tourists straight past, but the sheer provincialism of the place could charm you. And you will never find a more impressive overnight stop than in the parador, located in the hilltop Santa Catalina fortress, which dominates the whole city. Jaén was important in early times. Hasdrubal fortified it and the Romans, who knew it as Auringis, prized its silver mines. Under the Moors, who called it Geen, the city became the capital of a small kingdom. After falling to Fernando the King Saint in 1246, it became a spearhead for the Christian Reconquest. In 1466, a Royal Charter granted by Henry 1V gave the city the title "Very Noble, Renowned and Very Loyal City of Jaén, Rampart and Defence of the Kingdom of Castile". Standing 1,865 feet above sea-level, Jaén looks out on rugged mountains and vast olive groves. The province, mainly agricultural except for some mining areas, is noted for the quality of its olive oil. In the shadow of the frowning Sierra de Jabalcuz, a modern city has grown up, but the old quarters of Magdalena and San Juan in the upper town still retain the charm of the past.

DON'T MISS

Castillo de Santa Catalina: Perched above the city, the much-restored Arab castle has mighty ramparts and magnificent views. It now houses a parador (state-owned hotel).

Baños Arabes, Palacio de Villardompardo, Plaza Luisa de Marillac: The most important Arab baths surviving in Spain, said to be where Ali, a king of Jaén, was slain. Below street level, the baths date from the 11th century. The palace contains an arts and crafts museum. Open 10am-2pm, 4-7pm Tuesday to Friday, 10.30am-2pm Saturday and Sunday. Closed Mon.

Cathedral: Renaissance-style, planned by the maestro Andrés de Vandelvira, but not finished until 1802. Richly sculptured choir stalls. On Fridays, between 11.30am and 12.45pm, visitors are allowed to see the relic of the Santo Rostro (Holy Face), a veil used by St. Veronica to wipe Christ's face. Open 8.30am-1pm, 4.30-7pm. Cathedral museum open 11am-1pm, Sat, Sun.

Museo Provincial, Paseo de la Estación, 29: Roman mosaics, Iberian ceramics, ancient sarcophagi. Open 10am-2pm, 4-7.30pm, Sat, Sun 10am-2pm. Closed Mon, holidays.

Capilla de San Andrés: Mudéjar chapel founded in the 16th century, possibly on the site of a synagogue, by Gutierrez González, treasurer to Pope León X. A magnificent gilded iron screen by Maestro Bartolomé is the highlight. Visits by arrangement, tel. 25 52 22.

Real Monasterio de Santa Clara: Founded in the 13th century. Fine cloister. The church has a bamboo image of Christ. The nuns sell sweet cakes. To visit call 22 79 57

San Ildefonso: Church with facades in three different styles, Gothic, another partly Plateresque, and the third, designed by Ventura Rodríguez, Neo-Classical. Open: 8.30am-12pm, 6-9pm. The Virgen de la Capilla, Jaén's patron, has a *casa-museo* (house-museum) next door, open mornings, Mon-Sat.

Convento de Carmelitas: The manuscript *Cántico Espiritual*, by the mystic San Juan de la Cruz, is guarded in this convent. Visits not permitted. The nuns are famed for their *magdalenas* (sweet cakes), sold via a *torno* (revolving door).

Fiesta: Feria de San Lucas, in week of October 18.

Northern Jaén province: Strategically situated Andújar, with a 14-arched Roman bridge over the Guadalquivir, lies 28 miles (45km) northwest of Jaén. Its churches include the Gothic San Miguel and Santa María, with a Renaissance facade and a Mudéjar tower. In the Sierra Morena (20 miles, 32km, north of Andújar by J501), the Virgen de la Cabeza sanctuary (open daily) shelters a much-venerated Virgin. The original image and building were destroyed in a Civil War siege. On the last Sunday in April thousands make a pilgrimage to the sanctuary. At Baños de la Encina (7miles, 11km, north of Bailén on the N1V) stands a fortess built by Caliph al-Hakam 11 in 967. It has 15 towers (open daily, key at Calle Santa María, 12). Northeast of Bailén is La Carolina, founded in 1767 by settlers from Germany and Flanders, where a monument commemorates Alfonso V111's historic victory over the Moors at Las Navas de Tolosa in 1212. Beyond, along the N1V, is the Desfiladero de Despeñaperros, a spectacular cleft in the mountains, the gateway to Andalusia from Castile.

PLACES TO STAY

Parador Castillo de Santa Catalina. Tel: 26 44 11. Castle with magnificent views over city and sierra.

Xauen, Plaza Dean Mazas, 3. Tel. 26 40 11. Modern, three stars. Centre city.

EATING OUT

Calle Nueva concentrates many tapa bars. *La Gamba de Oro* specializes in seafood.

Bodegón de Pepe, Nueva, 7. Tel: 25 36 45. Open 1-4pm, 8.30-11pm. Closed Sun. Amex, Master, Visa. Andalusian dishes, specialising in leg of lamb. (M)

Casa Vicente, Maestra, 8. Tel: 23 28 16. Open: 12.30-4.30pm, 8.30-12pm. Closed: Sun night in winter, all Sun June-Aug. Master, Visa. Popular for its tasty local dishes, such as rabbit casserole. (M)

SERVICES

Bus station, Plaza Coca de la Piñera, 25 01 06. *RENFE* 27 02 02. *Taxis* 22 00 20, 22 00 21, 26 50 17. *Post office* Plaza de los Jardinillos.

EMERGENCIES

National police, 091.
Civil Guard, Jaén 21 91 00.
Municipal police, 092.
First aid: 25 90 31.
Red Cross, Carmelo Torres, 1. Tel: 25 15 40.

• • • • • • • • • • • • • • • • •

JEREZ DE LA FRONTERA, in Cádiz province (pop. 180,000). Cádiz 36 km. Málaga 222km. Madrid 601km. Telephone area code 956.

Tourist information, Alameda Cristina, 7. Tel. 33 11 50.

Wine, fine horses, fighting bulls, beautiful women and flamenco symbolize Jerez. The settlement was known as Ceret to the Romans, Scheris to the Moors. It was a frontier fortress during the long wars between Moors and Christians, the "de la Frontera" being conferred on it by Juan 1 in 1380. It was already renowned in Shakespeare's time for its wine and for the past 200 years its fortunes have largely depended on sherry exports. The sherry companies have many British connections through business and inter-marriage, although multinationals now control most of the great bodegas (literally wine cellars but meaning wine-makers). Jerez is at its most colourful during the

Feria del Caballo (end April-beginning of May). September 24 is the Día de la Merced, fiesta honouring the patron saint. An international horse week is held early October with races and a spectacular equestrian parade.

DON'T MISS

Sherry bodegas: Open mornings, Mon-Fri, visits by prior arrangement, entry charge. Gonzalez Byass, 34 00 00. John Harvey, 48 34 00. Pedro Domecq (gratis), 33 18 00. Williams and Humbert, 34 65 39. Wisdom & Warter, 18 43 06.

Escuela Andaluza de Arte Ecuestre, Recreo de las Cadenas, Avenidad Duque de Abrantes (tel. 31 11 11): training sessions Monday, Tuesday, Wednesday, Friday, 11am-1pm, dazzling show by the "dancing horses" on Thursdays at 12am.

Centro Andaluz de Flamenco, Palacio Pemartín, Plaza San Juan, 1. Tel. 34 92 65. Open: Mon-Fri 10am-2pm, Tues 5-7pm. View flamenco practice, audiovisual show. Exhibitions, library, language laboratory.

Alcázar: 12th century fortress, with mosque converted into chapel. Open: Mon-Fri 10am-2pm, 4-6pm, Sat 10am-1.30pm.

Museo de Relojes La Atalaya, Cervantes s/n. Open: 10am-2pm, Mon-Sat. Unique collection of 300 clocks.

Cathedral: Gothic, Baroque, Neo-classical. Mon-Sat 6-8pm. Sun 11am-2pm, 6.30-8.30pm.

Churches of San Dionisio (Mudéjar), Santiago (Gothic 15th century), and San Miguel (Elizabethan Gothic).

La Cartuja, three miles (4km) from town, magnificent Gothic monastery founded in 1477, with Baroque facade. Tues, Thurs, Sat, 5-6.30pm, exterior only.

PLACES TO STAY

Don Tico, Ctra N1V, km7. Tel. 18 59 06. Four star hotel in style of a cortijo, amid gardens, near airport.

Guadalete, Duque de Abrantes, 50. Tel. 18 22 88. Luxury ultra-modern, with gardens. Four stars.

Jerez, Avenida Alvaro Domecq, 35. Tel: 30 06 00. Stylish four star. Pool, tropical gardens.

Torres, Arcos, 29. Tel: 32 34 00. Two stars. Well-priced. Old style with inner patio.

High season rates are charged in Jerez during April and May. Accommodation is difficult the first two weeks of May during the horse fair and motor-cycling championships. Mid-season is in summer.

EATING OUT

Tendido 6, Circo, 10. Tel: 34 48 35. 12.30-4pm, 8.30-11.30pm. Closed Sunday. Amex, Master and Visa. Andalusian farmhouse decor. Wood oven. (M).

El Bosque, Avenida Alvaro Domecq s/n. Tel: 30 70 30. Open 1.30-5pm, 9-12pm. Closed Sunday. Amex, Master, Visa. Popular with the sherry crowd. Vast wine cellar. (M).

La Mesa Redonda, Manuel de la Quintana, 3. Tel: 34 00 69. Open 1-4pm, 9.30-12pm. Closed Sunday, holidays and August. Amex, Master, Visa. Pleasant, intimate atmosphere. Good meat dishes. (M).

Venta Antonio, Carretera de Sanlúcar (5 km from Jerez). Tel: 14 05 35. Open 12am-12pm. Closed Monday from October to March. Amex, Master, Diners, Visa. Very popular. Seafood. (M).

TAPAS

Excellent tapas served in bars on Pescadería Vieja, off Plaza Arenal, particularly *Bar Juanito,* presided over by joke-swapping Faustino. Also worth trying *Bodeguita Las Botas,* on Santo Domingo s/n, La Solera, Divina Pastora, and *La Venencia,* Larga, 3.

FLAMENCO: After 10.30pm Bar El Camino del Rocío, Muro s/n. Also consult tourism office.

SERVICES

Bus station, Calle Medina, 34 52 07.
RENFE 34 23 19.
Airport 15 00 83.
Taxi 34 48 60.
Post office, Vera Cruz. Tel: 34 22 95.

EMERGENCIES

National Police 091.
Municipal police 092.

Red Cross Hospital 30 74 54.

• • • • • • • • • • • • • • • • •

MALAGA, capital (pop. 550,000). Córdoba 176km. Granada 126km. Seville 207km. Madrid 576km. Telephone area code: 95.

Tourist information: Marques de Larios, 5. Tel 221 34 45. Tourist information at airport, 231 20 44.

Life is for living, according to the malagueños, and they carry out that policy to the hilt. The city is renowned for its wine, fried seafood, flamenco singers, and light-hearted people. Europe's mildest climate allows figs, grapes, avocados, oranges and lemons to flourish in Málaga province and has encouraged year-round tourism. This has brought a new era of prosperity to a city founded by the Phoenicians 3,000 years ago. They called it Malaca, probably derived from malac (to salt) as it was a depot for salting fish. Then came the Greeks, who named it Mainake, followed by the Romans and Visigoths. Under the Moors it became one of Andalusia´s major cities and at one time ruled an independent emirate. Málaga and Almeria were the ports for the Kingdom of Granada, but the ousting of the Moors brought sharp decline. Always a centre of liberal ideas, Málaga was the scene of a revolt in 1831, crushed when General Torrijos and 52 companions were executed on San Andrés beach. Last century Málaga staged a revival as a leading industrial centre, with textile mills, sugar refineries, blast furnaces and shipyards. Sweet Málaga wine was the rage. But a variety of factors led to another decline. The city suffered severe damage in the Spanish Civil War before it fell to the rebel Franco forces in 1937. Modern Málaga has breweries, service industries and a growing number of high-tech production plants. The large number of visitors to the Costa del Sol make its airport one of the busiest in Europe.

DON'T MISS

Cathedral: Built to the plans of Diego de Siloé on the ruins of a mosque, the Renaissance-style structure has a magnificently spacious interior. Work began in the 16th century but did not finish until 1769. The cathedral is nicknamed La Manquita (the cripple) because its second tower was never finished. Pedro de Mena carved the 40 superbly executed statues of saints above the choir stalls, also the polychrome sculptures of the Catholic Kings in the chapel of Nuestra Señora de los Reyes. Open: 10am-1pm, 4-5.50pm.

Alcazaba: A Moorish construction on Roman foundations, it was a residence for governors of the city. To left of the entrance is a Roman theatre. Open: 9.30am-1.30pm, 4-7pm, Sat 10am-1pm, Sun 10am-3pm. Closed Mon. On same premises interesting Archeological Museum. Open: Summer, 11am-1pm, 5-8pm; winter, 10am-1pm, 4-7pm. Sun, 10am-2pm. Closed Sun.

Gibralfaro Castle: Connected by walls to the Alcazaba, this fortress is of Phoenician origin but was rebuilt in the 14th century by Yusuf 1, sultan of Granada. It stands 426 feet above sea-level and offers fine views of city and Mediterranean.

Museo de Bellas Artes, San Agustín, 6. Roman mosaics, Mudéjar window arches, works by Alonso Cano, Ribera, Murillo, Zurbaran etc in old palace. Open: 10am-1.30pm, 5-8pm (summer), 4-7pm (winter). Closed: Sun afternoon and Mon. Information: 225 2148.

Museo de Artes Populares, Pasillo de Santa Isabel, 7: This museum, housed in a 17th century inn, gives an idea of past Málaga life-styles, crafts and traditions. Open: 10am-1.30pm, 5-8pm (summer), 4-7pm (winter). Closed Sun afternoon, Mon and holidays.

Plaza de la Constitución. The hub of city life. A handsome fountain is the focal point. On the square are an exhibition hall, Casa Paez (selling fans and once "visited by the Kings of Spain"), and the Café Central a traditional meeting place (note the wall tiles with information on different orders for coffee). In the narrow alleys off the square are ancient bars, printers, shoe shops, ironmongers, knife-grinders, barbers and buskers.

Pablo Picasso Foundation, Plaza de la Merced, 16: This centre for Picasso research, in the house where the painter was born, promotes contemporary art and organizes lectures on aspects of Picasso's life and work. Entry free. Open: 10am-2pm, 5-8pm.

Tel: 28 39 00.

English Cemetery and St. George's Church, Paseo de Reding: The hillside site was ceded to the British Crown last century. Before that non-Catholics were buried in the sand on Málaga beaches. People of many nationalities are interred here.

La Concepción, botanic gardens: Just north of the city. Follow arrows as you leave Málaga on the Antequera road. Guided tours take you around a three-hectare garden planted with exotic tropical plants. Open: 9.30am-7pm, 9.30am-5.30pm in winter. Closed Mon.

PLACES TO STAY

Parador Nacional Gibralfaro, Monte de Gibralfaro. Tel: 222 19 02. Next to the old Moorish fortress, overlooking city and sea.

Parador del Golf, Ctra de Málaga. Tel: 238 12 55. Off road to Torremolinos. By the sea, surrounded by golf course and near Málaga airport.

Larios, Larios, 2. Tel. 222 22 00. Four stars. Luxury hotel in the heart of the city. Bedrooms soundproofed. Cheaper rates at weekends.

Guadalmar, Ctra Cádiz, km 238. Tel: 231 90 00. Four stars. 10km from centre, near sea and airport.

Derby, San Juan de Dios, 1. Tel: 222 13 01. Two star hostal. Overlooking the port.

EATING OUT

Cafe de Paris, Vélez-Málaga s/n, La Malagueta. Tel: 222 50 43. Open 1.30-pm, 8.30-midnight. Closed Sunday & mid-June to mid-July. Amex, Diners, Master, Visa. French cooking in a trendy spot. Booking advisable. (E)

Casa Pedro, Quitapenas 4, Playa El Palo. Tel: 229 00 13. Open: 1-4.15pm, 8-11.45pm. Closed: Monday night and November. Amex, Diners, Master, Visa. Huge, popular beach eating place. Paella, sardines. (B-M)

La Villa, Avda Juan Sebastián Elcano, 130, Pedregalejo. Tel. 220 01 94. Amex, Master, Visa. Open: 1.30-4pm, 8-12pm. Closed Sun & Aug. Stonework gives a pleasant feeling to this stylish old house. Traditional cuisine with modern touches. (M-E).

Antonio, Fernando de Lesseps, 7. Tel. 222 33 97. Amex, Diners, Master, Visa. Open: 1-4pm, 8.30-12pm. Closed: Sun. A lively tapa bar and restaurant off the pedestrian street Calle Nueva. Try the lamb in almond sauce (M).

Málaga has scores of cheap eating places. For pizzas, try *Pizzeria La Romántica* on Calle Carcer, near Cervantes theatre, and in other locations.

TAPA BARS

Three chains, La Campana, Jimenez Barceló, and Casa Flores, are among bars offering Málaga wine from the barrel. Popular drinks are the *pintao* (Pedro Ximénez wine mixed with a dry white) and *secopedro* (mix of Pedro Ximénez with Seco Añejo).

Antigua Casa Guardia, Alameda, 18. Founded 1840. Lined with barrels and pungent with oldtime atmosphere. Seafood tapas.

Casa Flores, Ancha del Carmen, El Perchel district. Seafood.

Las Garrafas, Mendez Nuñez, 5. Cavernous, with barrels and glass casks.

Jimenez Barceló, Pozo Dulces (near market). Cod, broth.

Lo Gueño, Martín García, 11. Between Calle Larios and the central market. Narrow, always crowded. Ham, tripe.

La Tasca, Martín García, 12. Sherry, Montilla, ham, cheese.

EVENTS

Numerous publications, some free, offer information about what's on in Málaga and along the Costa del Sol.

AFTER DARK

Recitals and drama are staged at impressively refurbished *Teatro Cervantes.*

Pop concerts sometimes held in the bullring, La Malagueta area. Bars with live music include the *Café Teatro,* next door to the house where sculptor Pedro de Mena lived, in Afligidos, a cul-de-sac near the Cathedral, and the *Ragtime Cafe Bar,* at Reding, 12, La Malagueta, with jazz, salsa, and flamenco. Centre town, north of the Plaza de la Constitución, has interesting bars, some with live music, but take care in this area after shop hours. Tacky gay bars around Plaza de la Merced and Calle Madre de Dios. Youngsters flock to Pedregalejo beach area on eastern edge of city, which hums after midnight with music, disco bars.

SERVICES

Airport, information, 224 63 24. Iberia, information 213 61 66, domestic flight reservations 901-33 31 11, international reservations 901-33 32 22. Aviaco, 223 08 63. Viva, 224 38 87. British Airways, 223 06 23.

Railway (RENFE) information 236 02 02/233 33 33. Tel: 31 25 00; information, tickets, Strachan, 2. Tel: 21 31 22.

Bus station, Paseo de los Tilos. Tel: 235 00 61.

Radio taxis, 232 79 50.

Post Office, Avda de Andalucía.

Telephone office with operator service, Molina Larios.

CONSULATES

Austria, Occidente,1, Benalmadena-Costa. Tel: 244 39 52.

Belgium, Compositor Lehmberg Ruiz, 5. Tel: 239 99 07.

Canada, Cervantes, Edif. Horizonte. Tel: 222 33 46.

Denmark, Blasco de Garay, 7. Tel: 222 63 73.

Finland, Blasco de Garay, 3. Tel: 221 24 35.

France, Duquesa de Parcent, 8. Tel: 222 65 90.

Great Britain, Duquesa de Parcent, 8. Tel: 221 75 71.

Ireland, Avda Los Boliches, Fuengirola. Tel: 247 51 08.

Italy, Palestina, 3. Tel: 230 61 50.

Morocco, Avda de Andalucía, 15. Tel: 232 99 62.

Netherlands, Alameda Colón, Pasaje Linaje 3, portal 2, 4°D. Tel: 260 02 60.

Norway, Blasco de Garay, 7. Tel: 221 03 31.

Sweden, San Antonio, 7, Fuengirola. Tel: 246 71 95.

Switzerland, San Lorenzo, 4, 6°. Tel: 221 72 66.

U.S.A., Centro Las Rampas, fase 2, 1, Fuengirola. Tel: 247 48 91.

West Germany, Paseo del Limonar, 28. Tel: 222 78 66.

EMERGENCIES

National Police 091.

Municipal Police 092.

Civil Guard 239 19 00.

Red Cross 225 04 50.

Carlos Haya Hospital, 239 04 00.

Lost property, Ayuntamiento, Paseo del Parque, 222 86 00.

• • • • • • • • • • • • • • • • •

MARBELLA, in Málaga province (pop. 80,000). Málaga 57km. Telephone area code 95.

Tourist information, Glorieta de La Fontanilla. Tel. 277 14 42. Also Plaza de los Naranjos, tel. 282 35 50, and El Arco, arch on N340, tel. 282 28 18. In San Pedro de Alcántara, Conjunto San Luis, Bloque 3 bajo, tel. 278 52 52.

A flood of foreign and Spanish cash has made Marbella possibly Spain's richest community and surrounded it with luxury hotels, millionaires' villas, marinas and golf courses. Bullfighters, film stars, pop stars and oil-rich Arabs have expensive properties. Behind the flash and glitter, the old town remains, with the Plaza de los Naranjos a focal point. Jetsetters and hangers flock to Puerto Banús, which throbs with life all night in summer.

DON'T MISS

Old town: Partly surrounded by Moorish walls, narrow streets, pretty squares.

Plaza de Los Naranjos: Outdoor cafés in square with 16th century Ayuntamiento.

Puerto Banús: pleasure port, with luxury yachts, restaurants and piano bars.

Casino Nueva Andalucía, Hotel Andalucía Plaza. Open: 8pm-5am. Indentification required. Entry fee.

Museo de Bonsai, Parque Arroyo de la Represa, Avda del Dr. Maiz Viñal: The one thing Marbella was missing - an exhibition of mini-trees. Open morning and afternoon.

Museo del Grabado Español Contemporáneo, Hospital Bazán, s/n. Exhibits of contemporary engravings. Open: 11am-2pm, 5.30-8.15pm. Closed Sun & Mon afternoon, Sat.

Ancient remains near San Pedro de Alcántara, west of Marbella: Las Bovedas Roman bath house on beach, Vega del Mar Visigothic Christian basilica, and mosaics at Río Verde Roman villa.

Weekly market: Monday. Flea market by Puerto Banús

bullring on Saturday morning.

Fiestas: San Bernabé, June 7-14; Virgen del Carmen, July 16. San Pedro annual fair, Oct 18-23.

PLACES TO STAY

Meliá Don Pepe, Finca Las Marinas. Tel: 277 03 00. Classic five stars, amid large gardens and near beach.

Marbella Club, Boulevard Prince A. de Hohenlohe. Tel: 277 13 00. Four stars. Pioneer of Marbella's jetset image. Luxury low-rise accommodation, amid gardens.

El Fuerte, Avenida El Fuerte s/n. Tel: 286 15 00. Comfortable four-star hotel in the centre of town near beach.

El Castillo, Plaza San Bernabé, 2. Tel: 277 17 39. Modest, clean two-star hostal in old town, for those on a budget.

EATING OUT

Hostería del Mar, Avenida Cánovas del Castillo, 1-A. Tel: 277 02 18. Open 7.30pm-midnight. Closed Sun, Jan. Amex, Master, Visa. High-quality Spanish cooking in intimate surroundings. Terrace for outdoor dining. (E)

La Meridiana, Camino de la Cruz. Tel. 277 61 90. Dinner only mid-June to mid-Sept. Closed Mon, Tues & mid-Jan to mid-Feb. Amex, Diners, Master, Visa. Rated the best restaurant on the Costa del Sol. Sophisticated cuisine at very sophisticated prices. Immaculate service and decor. (VE)

Mesón del Conde, Avenida del Mar, 18. Tel: 277 10 57. Open 1-4pm, 8-12pm. Closed Mon, Tues, Nov. Amex, Diners, Master, Visa. Swiss and international dishes amid rustic atmosphere. (M)

Taberna del Alabardero, Muelle Benabola, Puerto Banús. Tel. 281 27 94. Open: 1-4pm, 8-12pm. Closed Sun, except mid-June to mid-Sept. Amex, Diners, Master, Visa. Stylish spot on the port. Basque dishes. (E)

Triana, Gloria, 11. Tel. 277 99 62. Open: 1.30-4pm, 7.30-12pm. Amex, Diners, Master, Visa. Pleasant house in town. Mediterranean cooking. (M)

SERVICES

Bus station, Avda Ricardo Soriano, 21, 277 21 92.

Taxi 277 44 88/278 38 39.
Post office, Alonso Bazan, 1.

EMERGENCIES

National police 091.
Municipal police 092 and 277 31 94.
Traffic police 277 25 49.
Civil Guard 277 03 44 and (San Pedro) 278 00 37.

• • • • • • • • • • • • • • • •

MOJACAR, in Almería province (pop. 5,000). Almería 78km. Madrid 518km.

Telephone area code 950.

Tourist information, Plaza Nueva, s/n. Tel. 47 51 62.

From a distance Mojácar still looks like a Moorish citadel, its houses flat-roofed houses cascading over a hilltop. In fact, the Moors were conquered here in 1453 and the Christians massacred the inhabitants. Mixed fortunes continued and earlier this century the village was virtually abandoned. But in the 1960s Mojácar was discovered and a new era of prosperity began. Bars, souvenir shops, and restaurants abound. Below the village, the coast is lined with villa developments and apartments.

DON'T MISS

Streets of the old town, with many picturesque corners.

Puerta de la Ciudad: Old entrance through the walls. Virtually all that remains of Arab domination.

Wednesday market.

Fiesta, last week August, San Agustín.

WHERE TO STAY

Moresco, Horizonte s/n. Tel: 47 80 25, clinging to the hillside, this three-star hotel enjoys fine views.

Parador Reyes Católicos, Playa de Mojácar. Tel: 47 82 50. Four stars. Comfortable accommodation near the beach.

Finca Listonero, Cortijo Grande, Turre (10km east of Mojácar). Tel. 47 90 94. Five bedrooms in carefully renovated farmhouse.

Gourmet meals. Australian host. Near nine-hole golf course. Three-star price rate.

WHERE TO EAT

Tapa bars, beach restaurants, and excellent seafood restaurants at Garrucha *(see Excursion 39)*

SERVICES

Taxi 47 81 29.
Post office, Plaza Nueva.

EMERGENCIES

Municipal police 47 51 29.
First aid 47 51 13.

• • • • • • • • • • • • • • • • • •

NERJA, in Málaga province (pop. 14,000). 53km from Málaga. Telephone area code 95.

Tourist information: Puerta del Mar, 4. Tel: 252 15 31.

This former fishing village has developed into the most flourishing resort on the Costa del Sol Oriental. Traces of Phoenician, Roman and Moorish settlement abound in surrounding areas. The old town near the Balcón de Europa retains its charm and there are several good beaches. Nerja was put on the tourist map by the discovery in 1959 of spectacular caves behind the neighbouring hamlet of Maro.

DON'T MISS

Cueva de Nerja: Cave inhabited 20,000 years ago. The Cave of the Cataclysms has the world's largest stalactite, 60 metres high and 18 metres in diameter. An international music and dance festival is held in the cave in July. Open : 10.30am-2pm, 3.30-6pm. Tel. 252 95 20.

Balcón de Europa: Promenade jutting into sea, offering splendid views.

Paseo de los Carabineros: Spectacular walkway through rocks at foot of the cliffs, between Calahonda and Burriana beaches.

Hermita de las Angustias: 17th century chapel with frescos

attributed to Granada maestro Alonso Cano on the cupola.

Weekly market, Tuesday.

Fiestas: February, Carnival. San Isidro, May 15. Annual fair, October 8-12.

PLACES TO STAY

Parador, El Tablazo, s/n. Tel: 252 00 50. Splendidly located above Burriana Beach. Gardens, pool.

Balcón de Europa, Paseo Balcón de Europa, 1. Tel. 252 08 00. Three-star hotel with its own beach.

Nerja Club, Ctra Almería km 293. Tel. 252 01 00. Well-appointed two-star hotel. Tennis courts.

Cala Bella, Puerta del Mar, 10. Tel: 252 07 00. Small, reasonably-priced one-star hotel near Balcón de Europa.

Alhambra, Antonio Millón, 12. Tel. 252 21 74. One-star hostal, about the cheapest in town.

EATING OUT

Haveli, Cristo, 44. Tel: 252 42 97. Open: 7-12pm, also Sun & Tues 1-3pm. Closed Mon. Master, Visa. Well-prepared Indian Tandoori. (M)

Mesón Gallego, Manuel Marín, 12. Tel. 252 41 30. Open: 12am-4pm, 7pm-1am. Closed Tues lunch. Master, Visa. Tapa bar and restaurant serving Galician dishes and wines. (M)

Mesón Patanegra, Plaza de la Marina, Edificio Tomé 1. Tel. 252 02 22. Open: 1-4pm, 7-12pm. Closed Tues & two weeks in Feb. Amex, Master, Visa. Agreeable bar-restaurant, specializing in cured ham, roast lamb and other typical Spanish dishes. A good range of wine, including gran reservas. (M)

SERVICES

Alsina Graells bus station, Avda Pescia, s/n. Tel: 252 15 04.

Taxi rank: 252 05 37.

Post office, Almirante Ferrándiz, 6.

EMERGENCIES

Municipal police, 252 15 45.

Civil Guard, 252 00 91.

First aid, 252 24 50.

Ambulance, 252 09 35.

• • • • • • • • • • • • • • • • • •

OSUNA, in Seville province (pop. 17,000). Málaga 125km. Seville 86km. Telephone area code 95.

Tourist information, Ayuntamiento, Plaza Mayor s/n. Tel: 481 00 50.

One of the best-preserved old towns in Andalusia, with fine old mansions and some splendid monuments to past days of glory. Bears (*osos*) once roamed this area, from which the town's name is derived. In 1562 Philip 11 created the title Duke of Osuna. The Osunas became one of Spain's most powerful families in the 17th and 18th centuries, accumulating more than 50 titles and vast land holdings. Their patronage enriched Osuna with architectural treasures.

DON'T MISS

La Colegiata de Santa María de la Asunción, 16th century Renaissance architecture, with its Sepulcro Ducal, the crypt containing the remains of the dukes. Guided visits 10.30am-1.30pm, 3.30-6.30pm, closed Mon.

La Encarnación Monastery: Many treasures and a beautiful patio. Open: 10am-1.30pm, 4.30-7.30pm.

Renaissance mansions, especially on Calle San Pedro.

Old University, 16th century, now a a school.

Museo Archeológico, Plaza de la Duquesa: Open 10am-1.30pm, 3.30-6.30pm.

PLACES TO STAY

Caballo Blanco, Granada, 1. Tel: 481 01 84. An ancient two-star hostal recently renovated.

EATING OUT

Doña Guadalupe, Plaza Guadalupe, 6. Tel: 481 05 58. Open: 2-4.30pm, 8-12pm. Closed Tues & last two weeks Aug. Amex, Visa. A touch of elegance in a small arcaded square. (M)

Mesón del Duque, Plaza de la Duquesa, 2 (opposite the Museo Arqueológico). Tel: 481 31 01. Visa. Open: 10am,-11pm, closed Mon, first fortnight in May & Sept. Typical local dishes. (B-M)

SERVICES

Bus station, Plaza de San Agustín, 481 01 46.
Taxi 481 02 89.
RENFE 481 03 08.

EMERGENCIES

Local police 092.
Civil Guard 481 0913.
First aid 481 00 27.

• • • • • • • • • • • • • • • •

PRIEGO DE CORDOBA, in Córdoba province (pop. 21,000). Córdoba 100km. Granada 78km. Telephone area code 957.

Tourism office, Río, 33. Tel. 70 06 25. To gain access to churches and tourist sights, contact José Mateo at tourism office.

Once a capital of a Moorish province, Priego reached a high level of prosperity in the 18th century through its silk industry. Its taffeta and velvet were sold in France and the Indies. Many of its finest mansions and magnificent Baroque churches were constructed then. Not for nothing has it been called the Capital of Córdoba Baroque. That industry faded but today manufacturing clothing is important and the town breathes an unusual air of contentment. Ironwork and wood-carving are local crafts. Priego's Fiestas de Mayo, with processions, take place every weekend in that month.

DON'T MISS

Calle del Río: Street of fine mansions.

Fuente del Rey: Magnificent fountain with 139 water spouts.

Castillo: Originally an Arab fortress with later additions.

Asunción: Church founded in 1525, remodelled in Baroque style in the 18th century. The sacristy is a masterpiece of Spanish Baroque.

Barrio de la Villa: Medieval quarter of narrow, whitewashed streets similar to the Judería of Córdoba.

Carnicerías Reales: Market and slaughterhouse, 16th century, with fine patio.

WHERE TO STAY

Hostal Rafi, Isabel La Católica, 4. Tel. 54 07 49, Immaculate, reasonably priced, two star hostal near the centre of town. Parking is difficult.

Río-Piscina, Ctra Monturque-Alcalá la Real, km 44. Tel. 54 08 16. Two star hostal outside town with pools, gardens, restaurant.

Villa Turística, Aldea de Zagrilla (8km from Priego). A tourist village due to open in 1995.

WHERE TO EAT

Priego has few restaurants, but many tapa bars. Two that are recommended: *Los Pinos,* Calle Republica Argentina, 12, excellent grilled prawns, and *Los Pinchos,* on Calle Real in the old quarter. *Hostal Rafi* has a restaurant (Amex, Master, Visa. Open 2-4.30pm, 8.30-11pm).

SERVICES

Bus station, Calle Fuenclara, 54 03 42.
Taxis, 54 12 76.
Post office, Calle Lozano Sidro, 54 09 51.

EMERGENCIES

Municipal police 54 01 34.
Civil Guard 54 01 15.
First aid 54 01 10.

• • • • • • • • • • • • • • • • • •

PUERTO DE SANTA MARIA, in Cádiz province (pop. 70,000). Cádiz 22km. Jerez 11km. Málaga (via Tarifa) 252km. Telephone area code 956.

Tourist information, Guadalete s/n. Tel: 86 31 45.

El Puerto reached its greatest splendour during the colonising of the Americas. Columbus spent the years 1483 to 1486 here, when the local lord, the Duke of Medinaceli, showed interest in his plans for a voyage of discovery, and here he met

Juan de la Cosa, owner of the ship the Santa María. Basques, Navarrese, Flemish, Italians and others flocked to share in the flourishing trade with the Indies. The splendid structures built by merchants and adventurers caused it to be called The City of 100 Palaces. These often had lookout towers so that watchmen could check shipping movements. A few remain, with their coats of arms on the facades. Important military expeditions set off from the port from the 16th to 18th centuries when it was the base for the royal galleys. Buried in the labyrinth of narrow streets are important sherry bodegas and El Puerto is famed for its ultra-fresh seafood. There is considerable tourist development in its beach areas and in summer the population triples.

DON'T MISS

Castillo de San Marcos: castle built on site of a 12th century Moorish mosque and fortress. Guided visits. Open Saturday 11am-1pm.

Plaza de Toros: century-old bullring. Open 11am-2pm, 5.30-7.30pm, closed Monday.

Fuente de las Galeras, on the waterfront: naval vessels filled their casks with water at this fountain in the 16th and 17th centuries.

El Vapor: Ferry runs regularly across the bay to Cádiz, departing 9am, 11am, 1pm, 3.30pm and (summer only) 7.30pm.

Sherry bodegas: Osborne, Calle de los Moros. Tel: 85 52 11; Terry, Cielo, 1. Tel: 48 30 00 00. Both open 9am-1pm Monday to Friday. By prior arrangement.

Casino Bahía de Cádiz: Ctra. Madrid-Cádiz, km 650. Tel. 887 10 42. From 7pm. Passport or other identification required. Entry fee.

PLACES TO STAY

Monasterio de San Miguel, Calle Larga, 27. Tel: 54 04 40. Four-star hotel in a former monastery. Marble, antiques and stonework. Swimming pool. The restaurant Las Bóvedas in a vaulted dining-room wins praise.

Los Cántaros, Curva, 6. Tel: 54 02 40. Three stars. Central and comfortable.

EATING OUT

Casa Flores, Ribera del Rio, 9. Tel: 54 35 12. Open 1-11pm. Amex, Master, Visa. Excellent seafood. (M).

El Patio, Misericordia, 1. Tel. 54 05 06. Open 1-5pm, 8-12pm. Closed Mon. Amex, Diners, Master, Visa. Dining in an Andalusian patio. Seafood. (M)

La Goleta, Ctra Rota km 0.75. Tel: 85 42 32. Open 11am-5pm, 7pm-12.30am. Closed Mon except summer, Nov 1-15. Amex, Diners, Master, Visa. Seafood such as *urta* (sea bream) *al brandy*. (M).

TAPA BARS

Hundreds of bars serve excellent seafood tapas. On the Ribera del Marisco: Takeaways known as cocederos offer a vast selection of fresh shellfish and fried fish, Cervecería Romerijo being one of the best known. *Echate Paya,* a tiny bar with bullfight reports papering walls, has excellent *tortillitas de camarones* (shrimp pancakes). On Calle Misericordia, try *El Betis*, for bull's tail and *ajo caliente,* a tasty dish served only Sat and Sun am, *La Bodeguilla* for ham, and *El Patio* for its pleasant setting. *Ortiguillas* (sea anenome) and *cazón* (shark) are among local specialities.

SERVICES

Bus station, Plaza Elías Ahuja, 54 24 13.
RENFE, 54 25 85.
Taxis 87 25 55.
Post office, Plaza del Polvorista, 3.

EMERGENCIES

National police 091.
Municipal police 092.
Civil Guard 87 13 32.
First aid 85 72 05.

• • • • • • • • • • • • • • • • • •

RONDA, in Málaga province (pop 34,000). Málaga 122km. San Pedro 49km. Telephone area code 95.

Tourist information, Plaza de España,1, Ronda. Tel: 287 12 72.

Smugglers and outlaws no longer roam the surrounding mountains, but Ronda - teetering on the edge of a 600-feet deep chasm - still has a special flavour. For a time Ronda was the capital of a small Moorish kingdom. The town is regarded as the birthplace of modern bullfighting, thanks to the 18th-century exploits of the Romero family. Pedro Romero (died 1839), who fought in the classic, sober style of Ronda, is regarded as one of the greatest-ever matadors. Antonio Ordoñez, hailed as one of the greats of recent times, runs the 200-year-old bullring. The old town has many fine buildings. A modern highway, the C339, connects Ronda with San Pedro de Alcántara on the Costa del Sol.

DON'T MISS

Plaza de Toros and Bullfight Museum. Open 10am-6pm, in summer 10am-8pm.

Espiritu Santo, 15th century church built on site of Moorish tower. Byzantine-style painting on Baroque altar. Open: 10am-7.30pm

Puente Nuevo and El Tajo: The chasm, 600 feet deep, is spanned by a two-centuries-old bridge.

La Ciudad, old quarter with narrow streets and fine buildings.

Colegiata de Santa María la Mayor, church built over mosque on King Fernando the Catholic's orders. Open 10am-7pm.

Casa de Mondragón: Built in 1314, contains Museo Arqueológico. Open 10am-6pm.

Palacio del Marqués de Salvatierra: Unusual Renaissance mansion. Guided visits on the hour, 11am-2pm, 4-7pm. Closed Thurs, Sun afternoon.

Casa del Rey Moro: 18th century mansion on site of Moorish palace with steps to river up which Christian slaves humped water. Closed to public.

Arab Baths: Open10am-1pm, 4-7pm, closed Sun afternoon and Mon. May be closed for repairs.

Acinipo (Ronda Vieja): Roman ruins. Open 10am-6pm, Fri-Sun 9am-7pm. Closed Mon pm.

PLACES TO STAY

Parador, Plaza de España. Tel: 287 75 00. In a magnificent situation on the site of the old town hall and market on the edge of the gorge, the three-storey parador opened in 1994.

Reina Victoria, Jerez 25. Tel: 287 12 40. Four stars. Spacious old hotel with majestic views. Recently refurbished.

Posada Real, Real, 42. Tel. 287 71 76. Stone arches, pillars, carved wooden doors distinguish this small hotel converted by a local architect from an old house. Four star price range.

Royal, Virgen de la Paz, 42. Tel: 287 11 41. Two-star hostal in modern block, near bullring.

EATING OUT

Don Miguel, Villanueva, 4, Ronda. Tel: 287 10 90. Open 12.30-4pm, 8-11pm. Closed Sun June-Sept, evenings Nov-Dec. Major cards. Traditional dishes, terrace looking over the gorge. (M)

Pedro Romero, Virgen de la Paz, 18. Tel. 287 11 10. Open: 12-4.30pm, 8-11pm. Amex, Diners, Master, Visa. Facing the historic bullring. Many mementoes of the bullfight scene. No better place to try oxtail. Eat downstairs as the groups are shuffled upstairs. (M)

TAPAS

Tapas are a good alternative to restaurant eating in Ronda. On the alley Pedro Romero, near the bullring, are several bars, particularly *Bodega La Verdad,* with barrels of sherry and Málaga wine and such tapas as *flamenquines* (deep-fried ham and cheese rolls) and *cangrejo rebozada* (crayfish in batter).

SERVICES

Bus station, Plaza Concepción García Redondo, 2. Bus lines: Amarillo 287 22 64, Gómez 287 19 92, Portillo 287 22 62.

RENFE, Infantes, 20, 287 16 62.

Taxis 287 23 16.

Post office, Virgen de la Paz, 20.

EMERGENCIES

National Police 091.

Civil Guard 287 14 61.

Municipal police 287 13 69.

First aid 287 58 82.
Red Cross 287 14 64.

• • • • • • • • • • • • • • • • • •

SANLUCAR DE BARRAMEDA, in Cádiz province (pop. 56,000). Cádiz 54km. Madrid 640km. Telephone area code: 956.

Tourism office, Calzada del Ejército, s/n. Tel. 36 61 10.

Strategically located at the mouth of the Guadalquivir, Sanlúcar is famed for its seafood and its manzanilla wine. Columbus and Magellan set sail from here. Under the Duques de Medina Sidonia it prospered, but an attempt by the ninth duke to make himself king of Andalucía resulted in the Spanish crown taking over the town in 1645. A highlight of the year is the Fiesta de Exaltación al Río Guadalquivir in the third week of August when horse races are held along the beach.

DON'T MISS

Bajo de Guía: Old fishermen's district on Guadalquivir river.

Santa María de la O: 14th century church with Mudéjar portal and artesonado ceiling.

Castillo de Santiago, square-towered 15th century castle overlooking town and river.

Sherry bodegas (visits by prior arrangement, usually Thursday mornings): Barbadillo, Luis de Eguilaz, 11. tel. 36 08 94; Herederos de Argüeso, Mar, 8. tel 36 01 12; Hidalgo, Banda Playa, 28 (call tourism office).

Coto Doñana visit: Boat trip and guided tour on foot, reserve tickets at Centro de Interpretación de la Naturaleza, Bajo de Guía, tel. 36 38 13. Two tours a day in summer, one a day September-April, except Mon.

Bonanza: fishing quay two miles (3km) from Sanlúcar, fish auctions 4-5pm daily except Sundays.

PLACES TO STAY

Los Helechos, Plaza Madre de Díos, 9. tel 36 13 49. Two star hotel in a traditional house with pleasant patio.

Posada del Palacio, Caballeros, 11. Tel. 36 48 40. Two stars. In a 19th century mansion with a beautiful patio.

EATING OUT

A string of restaurants along the Bajo de Guía offer views of the Guadalquivir and fresh seafood. Fish stews are particularly recommended. The restaurants include *Secundino, Joselito,* and *Casa Juan.* You can eat more cheaply by ordering plates of fish in the restaurant bars. The most noted are:

Casa Bigote, Bajo de Guía, s/n. Tel. 36 26 96. Open 12am-4pm, 8-12pm. Closed Sun. Amex, Diners, Master, Visa. King prawns are one of the specialities. (M-E).

Mirador de Doñana, Bajo de Guía. Tel. 36 42 05. Open 1-5pm, 8-12pm. Amex, Diners, Master, Visa. (M)

TAPAS

Apart from the bars of the Bajo de Guía, the *Bar Balbino* and *Casa Martínez* on the Plaza del Cabildo are recommended, plus bars *(Los Caracoles, Taberna Viruta)* around the Plaza de la Paz in the Barrio Alto. Specialities include *tortillitas de camarones* (shrimp pancakes), *puntillitas* (baby squid), and *galeras* (large crunchy shrimps). For roast meat, try the *Mesón del Asador,* Calle Bolsa, its interior timbered like a barrel.

SERVICES

Bus station, Plaza la Salle, s/n. 36 04 66.
Taxis, 36 00 04.
First Aid, 36 02 69.
Post office, Cerro Falón, 6.

EMERGENCIES

National police 091.
Municipal police 36 01 02.
Civil Guard 36 09 25.
First aid,,Casa de Socorro, Calzada del Ejército, s/n. 36 20 07.

• • • • • • • • • • • • • • • • • • • •

SEVILLE, capital (pop. 700,000). Málaga 207km. Córdoba 154km. Madrid 538km. Telephone area code: 95.

Tourist information, Avda de la Constitución, 21. Tel: 422 14 04. Municipal tourism office, Paseo de las Delicias. Tel: 423 44 65.

Guitar-twanging Don Juans, secluded jasmine-scented plazas, myth and folklore, plus a number of operas, have helped create a romantic legend about Seville. The exuberant inhabitants do their best to live up to it. Verses engraved on the Jerez gate - now gone - summed up Seville's early history: "Hercules built me; Julius Caesar surrounded me with walls and high towers; and the King Saint took me with the aid of Garci Pérez de Vargas." The fabled kingdom of Tartessus is believed to have been located somewhere near present-day Seville. An early settlement was known as Hispalis and Phoenicians, Greeks, Carthaginians, Romans and Vandals invaded. It became capital of the Visigoth kingdom, was taken by the Moors in 712 and by the 10th century rivalled Córdoba in importance. In the 11th century, the city became capital of the Almohad kingdom, under Al Mansur, who built the Giralda. On November 19, 1248, King Fernando 111 of Castile ousted the Moors. Seville entered its most prosperous times with the discovery of the New World, monopolising trade with America until 1717. Amerigo Vespucci and Magellan were among the navigators who sailed from its port. Those were days when Seville earned the name "Great Babylon". Its streets were crowded with merchants and mountebanks, all eager for a share in the riches carried in by galleon from the Americas - storms and English pirates allowing. But the Guadalquivir silted up and Seville's fortunes declined when the monopoly was transferred to Cádiz. Colossal investments in infrastructure for Expo 92, the world fair celebrating Columbus´s epic voyage 500 years ago, have awakened Seville from its narcissistic slumber, cleaned up its finest buildings, and reshaped the riverside. A high-speed train, the AVE, makes it possible to reach Madrid in two-and-a-half hours. Spain´s fourth largest city has sprawling suburbs, an important port and such industries as food processing and aircraft manufacture. As capital of the Andalusian autonomous region, it is the seat of the Andalusian parliament. Seville´s famous sons include the painters Murillo, Velázquez and Zurbarán, and the poets Becquer and the Machado brothers.

Important note: Security has improved in downtown Seville but tourists and their cars are a favourite target for thieves. Don't stray into dark side streets at night and leave valuables and documents in the hotel safe. The area around the Alameda de Hércules and the Macarena Basilica should be avoided at night.

DON'T MISS

Cathedral: Europe's third largest cathedral and largest Gothic church in the world contains numerous art treasures. "Let us build a cathedral so immense that everyone on beholding it will take us for madmen," declared its 15th century builders. Impressive Columbus tomb, though his remains are actually believed to be in Santo Domingo. In Royal Chapel, tombs of King Ferdinand and Pedro the Cruel. Open: 11am-5pm Mon-Sat, 2-4pm Sun.

Giralda: The symbol of Seville, this is a 12th century Arab minaret. In 1568 the belfry by Hernán Ruiz and the windvane (giraldillo), the bronze figure of Faith, were added. It is 322 feet (94m) high, with walls eight feet thick. Climb it for fine views. Open: similar hours to Cathedral, also Sun 10am-2pm.

Reales Alcazares: A Moorish fortress-palace, originating in the 8th century. Pedro the Cruel in the 14th century employed Moorish craftsmen to adorn the palace with intricate plasterwork, tiles and coffered ceilings. Beautiful gardens. Open: 10.30am-5pm, Sun 10am-1pm. Mon closed.

Barrio de Santa Cruz: Romantic old Jewish quarter, near the Cathedral. Narrow streets, intimate squares, wrought ironwork.

Torre del Oro/Maritime Museum, Paseo Colón: The Tower of Gold was built by the Moors to guard the River Guadalquivir. Open: 10am-2pm, Sun & holidays, 10am-1pm. Closed Mon.

Archives of the Indies, Avda de la Constitución: Formerly the Mercantile Exchange, housing unique collection of documents relating to discovery and settlement of New World. Open: 10am-1pm, Monday-Friday. Researchers, 8am-3pm, Monday to Friday. Tel: 421 12 34.

Casa Pilatos, Plaza Pilatos: Mansion, supposedly a copy of Pontius Pilate's house in Jerusalem, with a remarkable mixture of Renaissance, Gothic and Mudéjar styles. Open: 9am-6pm.

Maria Luisa Park: Redesigned for Seville's 1929 Iberoamerican Exhibition. Impressive buildings remain, some in use as museums, including the Museo Arqueológico, open 9am-2pm, closed Mon, and the Museo de Arte y Costumbres Populares (Popular Art and Customs), open 9am-2.30pm, closed Mon. The semi-circular Plaza de España has fine tilework and a boating channel.

Museo de Bellas Artes (Fine Arts Museum), Plaza del Museo, 9. Housed in a recently remodelled former convent. Magnificent collection of paintings, second only to the Prado. Works by Murillo, Zurbarán, Valdés Leal. Open: 9am-3pm. Closed: Mon.

Antigua Fábrica de Tabacos: The former Tobacco Factory where thousands of women manufactured cigars and snuff was immortalised in Bizet's Carmen. The huge building with its Baroque facade is now part of Seville University.

La Macarena: Church containing one of Seville´s most venerated Virgins. Open: 9am-1pm, 5-9pm.

Hospital de La Caridad, behind Maestranza opera house: Miguel de Mañara, notorious for his dissolute ways, who reformed and devoted his life to charity after a nightmare vision of his own funeral, founded the hospital in 1674 to help the needy dying. Important collection of paintings by Murillo and Valdés Leal. Open: 10am-1pm, 3.30-6pm. Closed Sun.

Ayuntamiento (City Hall): Striking Renaissance-style building. Interior open: Tues & Thurs 6-8pm.

Calle Sierpes: Pedestrian shopping street, which is the hub of Seville life.

Plaza de Toros (Real Maestranza): No matador has reached the top until he has triumphed in this 14,000-seat bullring. The season begins on Easter Sunday (Domingo de Resurrección) and ends in October. Open: 10am-1.30pm. Closed Sun.

Parque de los Descubrimientos (Discoveries Park): Science and theme park on Expo 92 site on the Isla de La Cartuja. Pavilions devoted to nature, the environment, and voyages of discovery, audiovisual spectacles, funfair, pop concerts, discos and laser shows. Open: year-round 11.30am-12pm Fri, Sat, Sun, in summer also Tues, Wed, Thurs evenings, closed Mon. Information 446 16 16.

Monasterio de La Cartuja: Historic monument, restored for Expo 92. Columbus was buried in the crypt of the Santa Ana chapel, before his remains were shipped to the Caribbean. Open: 11am-7pm. Closed Mon.

Itálica, six miles (9km) from Seville at Santiponce: Ruins of an important Roman settlement, where the emperors Hadrian and Trajan were born. Mosaics. Open: 9am-5pm (later in summer). Sundays 10am-4pm. Closed: Mon.

Events: Holy Week processions and the Feria de Abril.

PLACES TO STAY

Alvarez Quintero, Alvarez Quintero, 9-13. Tel. 422 12 98. Elegant modern three star hotel, near the Ayuntamiento.

Atenas, Caballerizas, 1. Tel. 421 80 47. Two-star hostal with traditional patio and decor.

Córdoba, Farnesio, 12. Tel: 422 74 98. One star hostal. Santa Cruz area.

Doña Maria, Don Remondo, 19. Tel: 422 49 90. Old world style in a four star hotel. Close to the Cathedral and Santa Cruz quarter.

Goya, Mateos Gago, 31. Tel: 421 11 70. Two star hostal. Good value in the Santa Cruz area.

Los Seises, Segovia, s/n. Tel. 422 94 95. A four-star hotel in a 16th century palace, part of the Archbishop of Seville's residence. Roman mosaics, Arab tiles and a view of the Giralda tower from the rooftop pool

Simon, García de Vinuesa, 19. Tel: 422 66 60. One star. An 18th century house around a charming patio. Central.

Outside the city:

Hacienda Benazuza, Sanlúcar la Mayor, west of Seville, off the N431 Seville-Huelva highway. Tel. 570 33 44. An aristocratic mansion converted into an expensive luxury hotel, with patios, fountains, palms, tennis courts, swimming pools, antique furnishings. Three restaurants.

Hacienda San Ignacio, Real, 194, Castilleja de la Cuesta (off the A49, 8km W of Seville) Tel. 416 04 30. Once a Jesuit retreat, a 300-year-old whitewashed mansion has been converted into a four-star hotel.

EATING OUT

El Ancora, Virgen de las Huertas, s/n, Los Remedios. Tel: 427 38 49. Open: 1-5pm, 8.30-12pm. Closed Mon in summer. Amex, Master, Visa. Excellent fresh fish at reasonable prices. (M)

Don Raimundo, Argote de Molina, 26. Tel: 422 33 55. Open: 12-4, 7-12pm. Closed: Sun nights. Amex, Diners, Master, Visa. Andalusia dishes served amid antique furnishings in a former convent. Try the perdiz mozárabe. (M)

La Albahaca, Pl. Sta. Cruz, 12. Tel: 422 07 14. Open: 12-4, 8-12pm. Closed: Sun. Amex, Diners, Master, Visa. Nouvelle cuisine, chandeliers and old tiles in a beautiful house built by an architect of Seville's 1929 Iberoamerican exhibition. Open-air dining in summer. (E).

Río Grande, Betis s/n. Tel: 427 39 56. Open: 1-5, 8-12pm. Amex, Diners, Master, Visa. Traditional meeting place. Terrace with views across the river. Paella, bull's tail. (M)

BARS

Those on a tight budget should stick to tapas as Sevilla is a bar-hoppers' paradise. Beer or manzanilla (a light sherry) are the favoured drinks. Good tapas are available at establishments ranging from Yuppy Elegant to Splendid Prehistoric. A selection:

Casa Morales, Garcia de Vinuesa, 11. Fine old bodega, with huge barrels.

El Rinconcillo, Gerona, 42. Founded 1670. Tiles, beams, wine from barrel.

Bar Becerra, Recaredo, 13. Mussels, cocido.

Bar Modesto, Cano y Cueto, 5. Speciality: *pajaritos.*

Luis Senra, Becquer, 41-43. Shellfish.

Taberna del Alabardero, Zaragoza, 20. Pricier and upmarket. In an 18th century mansion. Snacks amid pillars and pot plants on ground floor. Elegant dining upstairs.

Abades, Abades, 13 (Santa Cruz). Not a tapa bar but a late-night drinks place in a fine old mansion. Open 5pm, closed Mon.

The Triana quarter, across the river, has some of the best tapa bars. Look for:

Bodega La Albariza, Betis, 6. Pleasant traditional. Shrimp omelette.

Casa Cuesta, Castilla,1. Menudo (tripe & chick-pea stew).

Kiosco Las Flores, Betis, 1. Terrace. Fried fish.

Sol y Sombra, Castilla, 151. Cave-like, genuine old bullfight posters. Prawns with ham.

EVENTS

Jazz, pop, flamenco and classical music are the subject of a series of festivals held during the year. Publications such as El Giraldillo, and the Guía de Ocio give details of theatre, music, jazz, cultural activities. Youngsters flock to art shows, live music etc at *La Carboneria*, Levies, 18. Once a palace, later a coal merchants, now a bar and meeting point. Flamenco: For live music and impromptu dancing by young locals, check out *La Garrocha* and other bars on Calle Salado (in Los Remedios across the river from the city centre). You are more likely to catch the true spirit of flamenco by luck at some impromptu performance than at professional shows, usually aimed at tourists. But colourful flamenco shows can be seen at *Los Gallos*, Pl. de Sta. Cruz, 11. Tel: 421 69 81, Arenal, Rodo, 7. Tel. 421 64 92, and *Puerta de Triana*, Castilla, 137. Tel. 434 22 04.

SERVICES

Bus station, Manuel Vázquez Sagastizabal, Prado San Sebastián, 441 71 11.

Estación Plaza de Armas (for buses for Huelva and Badajoz) 490 80 40.

RENFE 454 02 02.

San Pablo Airport 451 06 77. Iberia information 422 89 01.

River trips: Compañia de Cruceros 456 16 92 and 421 13 96.

Post office, Avda de la Constitución, 32.

CONSULATES

Belgium, Jose Maria de Ibarra y Gomez Rull,4. Tel: 451 43 55.

Britain, Plaza Nueva, 8. Tel: 422 88 75.

Denmark, Norway, Sweden, Avda Reina Mercedes, 25. Tel: 461 14 89.

France, Plaza de Santa Cruz, 1. Tel: 422 28 97.

Netherlands, Gravina, 55. Tel: 422 87 50.

United States, Paseo de las Delicias, 7. Tel: 423 18 85.

West Germany, Ramon de Carranza, 22. Tel: 445 78 11.

EMERGENCIES

National police 091.

Municipal police: 092.

First aid: Casa de Socorro, Jesús del Gran Poder, 34, tel 438 24 61.

Ambulance: 433 09 33.

Hospital Universitario, Avda Dr Fedriani, 437 84 00.

Lost property, Almansa, 21. Tel: 421 26 28.

• • • • • • • • • • • • • • • •

TARIFA, in Cádiz province (pop. 15,000). Cádiz 101km. Málaga 154km.

Telephone area code 956

Tourist information, Ayuntamiento, Avda Andalucía, tel. 68 41 86.

Spain's southernmost town, facing across the Straits of Gibraltar, only about eight miles (13km) wide here. The Roman settlement of Julia Traducta was founded here nearly 2,000 years ago with inhabitants from Africa. Tarif Ben Malik landed on the Isla de la Paloma in 710 on a reconnoitring trip that led to the Moorish invasion of the peninsula. The Moors were not ousted until 1292. Until recently Tarifa depended on the military presence and fishing, but the reliable winds and the fine beaches have made it the Windsurf Capital of Europe. Championships are held regularly and it can get very crowded in season.

DON'T MISS

Ancient walls: Enclosing the narrow streets of the old quarter.

Houses and bars are built into the walls.

Puerta de Jerez, the town's entrance gate.

*Castillo de Guzmán el Bueno:*10th century castle.

Plaza de Santa María and *Ayuntamiento.*

San Mateo: Gothic church, with Baroque facade and Ionic door.

Los Lances: magnificent sandy beach.

Fiesta of Virgen de la Luz, start of September.

WHERE TO STAY

Hotel Dos Mares, Ctra N340, km 79. Tel. 68 40 35. Two-star hotel amid pines by the beach. Popular with windsurfers, with its own school.

Hurricane, Ctra N340, Km 77. Tel. 68 49 19. English-run beachside establishment in pleasant gardens, with pool and windsurf school. Two star ranking, but four-star prices to match its airy elegance.

100% Fun, Ctra Cádiz-Málaga, km 76. Tel. 68 03 30, a crazy name but good value in bungalows.

Tarik, San Sebastian, 36. Tel. 68 25 40, a basic pension.

In summer booking essential and some hotels may insist on you taking meals as well as bed.

WHERE TO EAT

Mandragora, Calle Independencia, near church in the old quarter: In an ancient house with a quirky charm - it just says "Bar" outside. Manolo and Gloria serve local delicacies and cous cous.

For excellent tapas and good prices, try *Bar La Rueda,* specialising in seafood (Cardenal Cisnero, 1. Open 11am-4pm, 7pm to late) in the modern part of Tarifa near the beach.

Mesón de Sancho, Ctra N340, km 94 (towards Algeciras). Tel: 68 49 00. Open 12am-5pm, 7-11pm. Amex, Master, Visa. *Urta al brandy* (urta is a type of sea bream) is a speciality. (M)

SERVICES

Bus station 68 40 38.

Taxi 68 42 41.

Post office, Coronel Moscardó, 5.

EMERGENCIES

Local police 68 41 86.
Civil Guard 68 42 63.
First aid 68 48 96.

• • • • • • • • • • • • • • • •

TORREMOLINOS, in Málaga province (pop. 25,000). Málaga 14 km. Telephone area code 952.

Tourist information, Ayuntamiento, Plaza Picasso. Tel: 237 11 25.

Foreign residents' information bureau: Casablanca, 25. Tel: 237 42 31.

Package tours made "Torre," for better or worse, converting it from a one-donkey town into a huge resort with around 100 hotels. It is brash and breezy, with nine kilometres of good beaches and noisy nightlife. Bars cater to all nationalities and a surprising variety of sexes. Discos and nightclubs are thick on the ground. In a few backstreets you may still find a semblance of the simple fishing village Torremolinos used to be. Behind the town, just off the bypass, is the Palacio de Congresos, a conference and exhibition hall. Near it is a large aquapark, the highlight of which is the Kamikaze slide. The town gets its name from *torre* (tower) and *molinos* (water-mills, used to grind corn).

DON'T MISS

San Miguel: Running from the centre of town towards the sea, this is a pedestrians-only street, which provides a continuing side-show. At the seaward end, above steps leading down to the Bajondillo beach, lies a rare relic of the past, a tower from where watch was kept on the coast.

Carihuela beach: Lined with restaurants offering fresh fish at a wide range of prices.

Weekly market, Thursday. Fiestas: San Miguel fair, Sept 24-29, with romeria.

PLACES TO STAY

Don Pedro, Av. Lido, s/n. Tel: 38 68 44. Three stars. Surrounded by gardens, near the main beach.

Lago Rojo, Miami, 1. Tel: 38 76 66. Three-star hotel in Carihuela district, with studio-style rooms.

Melia Torremolinos, Avenida Carlota Alessandri, 109. Tel: 238 05 00. Closed Nov-Feb. Luxury four-star hotel with pleasant garden.

Miami, Aladino, 14. Tel. 238 52 55. Mercedes has ruled over this small, low-priced hotel for 40 years. Designed by a cousin of Picasso. Swimming pool.

Pez Espada, Vía Imperial, 11. Tel. 238 03 00. Four stars. Near the beach at Montemar.

EATING OUT

Frutos, Ctra Cádiz, km235, Urb. Los Alamos. Tel. 238 14 50. Open: 1-4.30pm, 8-12pm. Closed Sun night except in summer. Amex, Master, Visa. Reliable track record. Favoured by business types for lunch. Try the *brocheta de rape* or the roast lamb.

La Carihuela beach is one of the most popular eating areas for both locals and tourists. It is lined with fish restaurants, some basic, some upmarket. They include:

Juan, Paseo Marítimo, 29. Tel. 238 56 56. Closed Tues. Amex, Diners, Master, Visa. (M)

El Roqueo, Carmen, 35, La Carihuela. Tel: 38 49 46. Open: 1-4pm, 8-12pm. Closed: Tuesday and November. Amex, Master, Visa. Often crowded. (M)

SERVICES

Bus station, Calle Hoyo.
RENFE, 238 57 64.
Taxis, 238 06 00/237 29 15.
Post office, Avenida Palma de Mallorca.

EMERGENCIES

National police, 091.
Municipal police, Juan de la Cierva, 238 14 22.
Ambulance, 238 62 66;
First aid, Ctra de Benalmadena, 38 16 86.

• •

UBEDA, in Jaén province (pop. 30,000). Malaga 270km. Jaén 57km. Madrid 319km. Telephone area code 953.

Tourist information, Plaza del Ayuntamiento, 2. Tel: 75 08 97. Also in Hospital de Santiago.

Ubeda, squatting above the surrounding olive groves on its *loma* (ridge), is distinguished by an outstanding collection of 16th-century Renaissance architecture, dating from the time of the Emperor Carlos V when the Cobos family enjoyed great prestige and highly-placed positions. The Moors were ousted from the town by King Fernando 111 in 1234. Continual conflict between local lords resulted in a royal edict in 1506 that the town fortress should be destroyed. Ubeda has some outstanding potters. Olive oil production is the major industry.

DON'T MISS

Plaza de Vázquez Molina: Lined with magnficent Renaissance buildings, several by the architect Andrés de Vandelvira.

El Salvador: 16th century church, built as the personal chapel of Francisco de los Cobos, whose tomb is in the crypt. Vandelvira, Diego de Siloé, and Esteban Jamete worked on the design. Pillaged during the Civil War. Treasures include Bartolomé's choir screen, a carved Christ by Berruguete, and Vandelvira's sacristy. Open: 9am-1pm, 4-8pm, entry through sacristy.

Francisco de los Cobos, secretary of state to Charles V, Holy Roman Emperor;

Palacio de las Cadenas, now the town hall: Classical facade and patio. Built by Vandelvira. Open: mornings.

Santa María de los Reales Alcázares: 13th-century church built on site of a mosque. beautiful cloister. Being restored.

Parador Condestable Dávalos: Built in the 16th century, reformed in the 17th. Former residence of the chaplain of El Salvador church.

Carcel del Obispo: Nuns punished by the bishop were confined here. Now the courthouse.

Hospital de Santiago, Carrera Obispo Cobos: Square towers flank the handsome facade of this Vandelvira building, sometimes called the Escorial of Andalusia. Genoese marble columns support the two-tier patio. Open 8am-10pm.

San Pablo, Plaza Primero de Mayo: Church combining Gothic, Romanesque and Isabelline styles.

Museo Arqueológico, Cervantes, 6: Artefacts from prehistory to Moorish era displayed in Mudéjar mansion. Open: 10am-2pm, 5-7pm. Closed Mon.

Museo de San Juan de la Cruz, Carmen, s/n: Cell where the mystic died is part of museum. Open: 11am-12.45pm, 5-6.45pm. Closed Mon.

Redonda de Miradores: Views of countryside from top of the old walls.

PLACES TO STAY

Parador Condestable Dávalos, Plaza Vázquez de Molina, 1. Tel: 75 03 45. Noble 16th-century palace.

Palacio de la Rambla, Plaza del Marqués, 1. Tel. 75 01 96. Gracious Renaissance palace belonging to an aristocratic family. Alfonso X111 once stayed here. Antiques, TV and mini-bar in the rooms. Four star price range.

La Paz, Andalucia, 1. Tel: 75 21 40. Two-star hotel, in modern part of town.

El Castillo, Avda Ramón y Cajal, 20. Tel. 75 04 30. One star hostal for budget travellers.

EATING OUT

Parador restaurant. Open 1-pm, 9-11pm. Amex, Diners, Master, Visa. Regional dishes in stately surroundings.

El Gallo Rojo, Torrenueva, 3. Tel. 75 20 38. Open: 1-4.30pm, 7-12pm. Closed last fortnight Aug. Visa. Local dishes. (M)

El Castillo, Avda Ramón y Cajal, 20. Tel. 75 04 30. Cheap and cheerful. Good stews. (B)

SERVICES

Bus station, San José, s/n. 75 21 57.
Taxis, Plaza Andalucía, 75 12 13.
Post office, Trinidad, 4.

EMERGENCIES

National Police 091.
Civil Guard 75 01 02.

Municipal police 75 00 23.
First aid 75 11 03.

• • • • • • • • • • • • • • • • • •

VÉLEZ BLANCO in Almería province (pop. 2,400). Almería 145km. Lorca 54km. Granada 170km. Telephone area code 950.

Tourist information: Ayuntamiento, Corredera, 38. Tel. 41 50 01 and Vélez Rubio Ayuntamiento, Mesón, 1. Tel. 41 00 00.

An impressive castle constructed in 1505 by the first Marqués de Los Vélez dominates this village, settled since the Copper Age. Occupied by the Moors for 500 years, the village preserves its medieval style, while its twin, Vélez Rubio on the main highway, has grown faster. The *blanco* is believed to have been attached to the place by the Moors because of the whiteness of the soil in this rather bleak northeast corner of the province.

DON'T MISS

Castillo: The splendid Renaissance interior was sold and removed to New York's Metropolitan Museum early this century. Open from 11am Sat-Sun, on weekdays ask at Bar Sociedad in the village.

Cueva de los Letreros: Prehistoric paintings. Near petrol station outside village rough track runs through pines, then steep, rocky path leads to a shelf of rock under which crude figures are visible. One image depicts the Indalo, a figure holding aloft an arc, thought to be a deity with magical powers and now used as a symbol of Almería.

Moorish walls: Remains of fort where Boabdil, the last king of Granada, stayed.

Magdalena: Mudéjar church built on site of a mosque.

Santiago: Gothic, Renaissance and Mudéjar styles are mixed in the parish church.

Los Vélez nature park: with pine forests and recreation facilities, covers 19,500 hectares in the Sierra de María near Vélez Blanco.

Vélez Rubio (6km from Vélez Blanco): *Encarnación church,* a magnificent Baroque temple built in 1768, is Rubio's outstanding monument. Its cost was borne by the feudal lords, the Marqueses de Los Vélez.

WHERE TO STAY

La Sociedad, Corredera, 14. Tel. 41 50 27. One-star hostal with bar and restaurant, offering excellent value.

Zurich, Plaza de la Libertad, s/n, Vélez Rubio. Tel. 41 03 35. Functional, modern, two star hostal.

WHERE TO EAT

La Sociedad, Corredera, 14. Tel: 41 50 27.

El Molino, Curtidores, 1. tel. 41 50 70. Home cooking.

Mesón La Ribera, Recinto Polideportivo, Vélez Rubio. tel. 41 21 19. Local dishes.

EMERGENCIES

Municipal police 41 50 01.
Civil Guard, Vélez Rubio, 41 00 31.
Red Cross, Vélez Rubio, 41 02 61.

• • • • • • • • • • • • • • • • • •

VÉLEZ-MALAGA, in Málaga province (pop. 50,000). Málaga 36km. Granada 99km. Telephone area code 95.

Tourist information (at Torre del Mar): Avda de Andalucía, 92. Tel: 254 047.

Vélez (as it is known for short) is a pleasant old market town, capital of the Axarquía, the eastern corner of Málaga province. Phoenicians, Carthaginians and Romans left traces of their settlements in or near the fertile Río Vélez valley. A heavily-restored fortress rising above the town recalls its importance to the Moors who knew it as Ballix-Malaca and praised it as "a beautiful city with a fine mosque and an abundance of fruit trees". It fell to the Catholic Monarchs in 1487. Close by is its once-poor relation Torre del Mar, a fishing village converted into a high-rise resort.

FIESTAS & EVENTS

July 15-17 Veladilla del Carmen; September 28-October 1

Feria de San Miguel. Third week of December Juan Breva flamenco festival.

DON'T MISS

Old quarter: Sinuous, narrow streets below the castle.

Murallas and Castillo: Reached on foot from the Plaza de la Constitución. The Puerta Real pierces the old walls (viewing point on the top). Walk up through alleyways to the castle, heavily restored, with a lofty tower, the Torre de Homenaje.

Santa María la Mayor, Calle Santa María: Built on site of the main mosque, this 16th century Mudéjar church overlooking the town has a fine brick tower and coffered ceiling.

San Juan Bautista, Plaza de la Constitución: A Gothic church of the 16th century restored in neo-classic style. Christ Crucified carving by Pedro de Mena.

Casa de Cervantes, Calle San Francisco: A fine old building with a handsome brick-pillared patio and a well in one corner, in which Cervantes who visited Vélez-Málaga to collect taxes apparently stayed.

Palacio del Marqués de Beniel, Plaza Palacio: A noble, 16th century building housing historic archives and the Fundación María Zambrano (she was a distinguished thinker born in Vélez) and hosting cultural exhibitions. Fine patio and carved ceiling above the stairs.

San Francisco convent, Plaza San Francisco: Built in 1495 in the old Jewish quarter, but much modified. The Buen Pastor chapel has Baroque decor.

PLACES TO STAY

Dila, Avda Vivar Téllez, 3. Tel: 250 39 00. Two star modern hotel. On main road, but with quiet rooms at side and rear. TV, phone, heating. Better value off-season, mid-September to June 1.

EATING OUT

El Rincón de Antonio, Conjunto el Carmen. Tel. 250 60 79. Open: 1-4pm, 7.30-12pm. Amex, Master, Visa. Tapa bar and restaurant. Agreeably situated in stone-arched cloister of a former convent. Excellent stews and home-made desserts. (M)

SERVICES

Bus station, Avda Vivar Téllez. Tel. 250 17 31.
Taxis, 250 00 88.
Post office, Calle Capuchinos.

EMERGENCIES

National police 091.
Civil Guard 250 01 48.
Municipal police 250 09 91.
Red Cross 250 03 21.
First aid, Torre del Mar, 254 00 00.
Regional hospital 254 05 62❑

CAMPSITES BY PROVINCES

The camping guide, Guía de Camping, obtainable in tourist information offices, has a full list of campgrounds in Andalusia. Some sites are only open in peak season. Free camping is possible in more isolated areas. It is forbidden on many beaches, although the regulations are often ignored.

ALMERIA

Almería: La Garrofa, Ctra N340 km.435. Tel: 23 57 70.

Adra: La Sirena Loca, Ctra N340 km60, Adra. Tel: 40 09 20; Las Gaviotas, Ctra N340 km58, Adra. Tel: 40 06 60; La Habana, Paraje La Habana, Ctra N340 km64.; Las Vegas, Paraje La Habana, N340 km64.

El Ejido: Balerma Playa, Ctra Guardias Viejas s/n. Tel: 40 70 05; Mar Azul, Urb. Almerimar, Playa San Miguel. Tel:48 18 29.

Los Gallardos: Los Gallardos, La Perulaca, Ctra N340, Km 523. Tel: 46 92 03.

Mojácar: El Cantal de Mojácar, Ctra Garrucha-Carboneras. Tel: 47 82 04.

San José: Tau, Bancalón de Sotillo, Barriada San José, Níjar. Tel: 38 01 66.

Serón: Las Menas, Pueblo Minero, Las Menas. Tel: 42 60 01.

Naturist camping: Las Rozas, Las Herrerías, Cuevas de Almanzora; Camping Almanzora, Playa Vera, Ctra Garrucha-Palomares km 5, Vera. Tel: 46 74 25.

CADIZ:

Algeciras area: Bahía, Playa Rinconcillo, Ctra N340 km 109. Tel: 66 19 58; Costa del Sol, Ctra N340 km 108. Tel: 66 02 19.

Arcos de la Frontera: Arcos, Urb. El Santiscal. Tel: 70 05 14.

Caños de Meca (Barbate): Camaleón, Playa de los Caños, Ctra Vejer-Caños, km13,3. Tel: 65 48 32; Camping Caños, Ctra Vejer-Caños, km 10. Tel: 45 04 05.

Benaocaz: Tavizna, Ctra Com. 3331, km 49. Tel: 46 30 11.

Conil: Pinar Tula, Rincón Juan Arias, Ctra CN340 km 20. Tel: 44 55 00; Cala del Aceite, Roche Viejo, s/n. Tel: 44 09 72; El Faro, Ctra Puerto Pesquera, km2. Tel: 44 01 87; Fuente del Gallo, Urb Fuente del Gallo El Pradillo. Tel: 44 01 37; Los Eucaliptos, Ctra CA-P 2131, km 0.2. Tel: 44 12 72; Roche, Pago del Zorro. Tel: 44 22 16.

Chiclana: La Rana Verde, Pago de la RAna Verde. Tel: 49 50 16; La barrosa, Ctra La Barrosa, km3. Tel: 49 46 05.

Chipiona: El Pinar, Ctra Chipiona-Rota, km3. Tel:37 23 21.

El Bosque: La Torrecilla, Ctra El Bosque-Ubrique, km1.5. Tel: 71 62 54.

El Puerto de Santa María: Las Dunas de San Antón, Rotonda de la Puntilla, s/n. Tel:87 01 12; Guadalete, Ctra. N340 km655. Tel: 56 17 49.

Grazalema: Los Linares, Calle Nacimiento. Tel (Ayuntamiento): 13 20 11; Tajo Rodillo, Ctra Com 344, El Bosque-Grazalema, ikm 49. Tel: 13 20 63.

Prado del Rey: La Jaima, Ctra Prado del Rey-ARcos. Tel: 72 32 35.

Puerto Real: El Pinar, Ctra N1V, km 666. Tel: 83 08 97.

Rota: Punta Candor, Ctra Chipiona-Rota km3. Tel: 81 33 03; Aguadulce, Pago Aguadulce. Tel: 908-85 77 85.

San Roque: La Casita, Ctra N340, km126. Tel:78 00 31; San Roque, Ctra N340 km 124. Tel: 78 01 00.

Tarifa: Bahia de la Plata, Ctra de Atlanterra, s/n. Tel: 43 90 87; El Jardín, Los Algarves, Punta Paloma. Tel: 68 49 49; Paloma, Ctra N340 km72. Tel: 68 42 03; Río Jara, Ctra N340 km80. Tel: 68 42 79; Tarifa, Ctra. N340, km 78. Tel: 68 47 78. Torre de la Peña, Ctra N340 km78. Tel: 68 49 03; Torre de la Peña 11, Ctra N340 km75. Tel: 68 41 74.

Vejer de la Frontera: Vejer, Ctra N340 km39. Tel: 45 00 98; Los Molinos, Ctra N340 km34. Tel: 45 09 88; El Palmar.

Zahara de la Sierra: Arroyomolino. Tel: 12 31 14.

Zahara de los Atunes: Bahía de la Playa. Tel: 43 90 40.

CORDOBA

Córdoba: Campamento Municipal, Avda del Brillante 50.

Tel: 28 21 65.

La Carlota: Carlos 111, Ctra N429. Tel30 06 95.

Santaella: La Campiña, Ctra Aldea Quintana-Santaella km 11. Tel: 31 51 58.

GRANADA

Granada: Sierra Nevada, Avda de Madrid, 107. Tel: 15 00 62; Los Alamos, Ctra N342 km290. Tel: 20 84 79; María Eugenia, Ctra N342 km286. Tel: 20 06 06.

Albolote: Cubillas, Ctra Bailén-Motril, km115. Tel: 45 34 08.

Almuñécar: El Paraiso, Ctra Málaga-Almería km 334. Tel: 63 23 70.

Castell de Ferro: El Cortijo, Paseo Marítimo. Tel: 65 60 83; El Sotillo, Paseo Marítimo. Tel: 65 60 78; Huerta Romero, Paseo Marítimo. Tel: 65 64 53; Las Palmeras, Ctra N353. Tel: 65 61 30.

Güéjar Sierra: Las Lomas. Tel: 47 07 42.

La Herradura: Paseo Marítimo s/n. Tel: 64 00 56.

La Zubia: Reina Isabel, Ctra Granada-La Zubia km4. Tel: 59 00 41.

Motril: Don Cactus, Ctra Motril-Almería km 11, Carchuna. Tel: 62 31 09; Playa Granada, Playa de Poniente. Tel: 82 27 16; Playa Poniente. Tel: 82 03 03.

Otura: El Juncal, Ctra Bailén-Motril km 142. Tel: 57 61 75; Suspiro del Moro, Ctra Bailen-Motril, km 144. Tel: 57 61 05.

Pitres: Balcón de Pitres, Ctra Orgiva-Ugíjar, km51. Tel: 76 61 11.

Polopos: Casillo de Baños, Ctra N340, Playa. Tel: 82 95 28.

Salobreña: El Peñon, Paseo Marítimo. Tel: 61 02 07.

Trévelez: Ctra Trévelez-Orgiva, km1. Tel: 85 85 75.

HUELVA

Aljaraque, near Huelva: Las Vegas, Ctra Huelva-Punta Umbria km 7. Tel: 31 81 41.

Aracena: Aracena-Sierra, Ctra N433.

El Rompido: Catapum, Ctra El Rompido-Punta Umbria km 3. Tel: 39 91 65.

Isla Cristina: Luz, Ctra Isla Cristina-La Antilla, km5, La Redondela. Tel: 34 11 42; Playa Taray, Ctra Isla Cristina-La Antilla, km9, La Redondela. Tel: 34 11 02.

Lepe: Antilla: Ctra La Antilla-El Terrón, km2. Tel: 48 08 49; La Barca, La Barca, s/n. Tel: 39 02 94.

Matalascañas: Rocío Playa, Ctra Huelva-Matalascañas km45. Tel: 43 02 38.

Mazagón: Doñana Playa, Ctra Huelva-Matalascañas km 28,8. Tel: 53 62 81; Fontanilla Playa, Playa Mazagón. Tel: 53 62 37; Playa de Mazagón, Cuesta de la Barca, Ctra Huelva-Matalascañas. Tel: 37 62 08.

Punta Umbria: Derena Mar, Ctra Huelva-Puntra Umbria, Paraje de la Bota. Tel: 31 20 04.

Sanlúcar de Guadiana, Camping Municipal, Nueva, s/n. Tel: 38 80 71

JAÉN

Andújar: Andújar, Bernardo Martínez, 46. Tel: 50 07 00.

Cazorla, Segura y Las Villas Nature Park: Chopera de Coto Ríos, Ctra Cazorla-Coto Ríos km21, Coto Ríos. Tel: 72 19 05; Complejo Los Enebros, Ctra El Tranco, km 7, La Iruela. Tel: 72 16 10; Fuente de la Canalica, Ctra Las Acebeas, km6, Siles. Tel: 49 10 04; Fuente de la Pascuala, Ctra Cazorla-Coto Ríos km 22. Tel: 72 12 28; Garrete Gordo, Paraje Garrete Gordo, Segura de la Sierra; Llanos de Arance, Ctra Cazorla-Coto Ríos km20. Tel: 72 09 39; Montillana, Ctra Tranco-Hornos, km12, Hornos de Segura. Tel: 41 59 19; Puente de las Herrerías, Vadillo de Castril, Cazorla. Tel: 72 06 09; Río Los Molinos, Ctra Las Acebeas, Siles. Tel: 49 10 03.

Pozo Alcón: Hoyo de los Pinos, Ctra de Castril, km8. 73 90 05.

Santa Elena: El Estanque, Ctra NIV, km260. Tel: 62 30 93.

MALAGA

Málaga: Camping: Balnearío del Carmen, Avda Pinto Sorolla, 26. Tel: 229 00 21.

Algatocín: Camping Algatocín, Vega del Río Genal, s/n. Tel: 215 00 00.

Alhaurín de la Torre: Camping Morales, Arroyo Hondo, 15. Tel: 241 02 83.

Ardales: Parque Ardales. Tel: 245 80 87.

Cañete La Real: Al-Jalib, Nueva, s/n. Tel: 218 32 10.

Fuengirola: La Rosaleda, Ctra N340, km211. Tel: 246 01 91;

Fuengirola, Ctra N340, km207. Tel: 247 41 08.

Fuente de Piedra: La Laguna de Fuentepiedra, Camino de la Rábita, s/n. Tel: 273 52 94.

Manilva: Chullera 1 & 11, Ctra N340, km198. Tel: 289 01 96 & 289 03 20.

Marbella: La Buganvilla, Ctra N340 km 188. Tel: 283 19 73; Marbella 191, N340, km184. Tel: 277 83 91; Marbella Playa, Ctra N340. km192. Tel: 283 39 98.

Mijas-Costa: La Debla, Ctra N340 km200; Calazul, N340 km200, La Cala. Tel: 249 32 19; Los Jarales, Ctra N340 km197, Calahonda. Tel: 283 20 35.

Mollina: Saydo, Ctra Sevilla-Málaga, km 146. Tel:274 04 75.

Nerja: Camping de Maro, Ctra N340, km 296.

Ronda: El Sur, Ctra Algeciras, km1.5. Tel: 287 59 39; El Abogao, Ctra Campillos, km7. Tel: 287 58 44.

Torre del Mar & area: Almayate: Almayate-Costa, Ctra N340, km267. Tel: 254 02 72; Torre del Mar, Paseo Marítimo. Tel: 54 02 24; Valle Niza, Ctra N340, km264, Benajarafe. Tel: 251 31 81.

Torremolinos: Torremolinos, Ctra N340 Km 228. Tel: 238 26 02.

SEVILLE

Seville city area: Los Naranjos, Finca Cristina, Vial RV-19, Alcalá de Guadaira. Tel: 908-75 53 81; Sevilla, Ctra. Madrid-Cádiz, km 534 (7km from city). Tel: 451 43 79; Club de Campo, Avda de la Libertad, 13, Dos Hermanas (14km from city). Tel: 472 02 50; Villsom, Ctra. Madrid-Cádiz, km 555, Dos Hermanas. Near Club de Campo. Tel: 472 08 28.

Cazalla de la Sierra: Cortijo Batán de la Monjas, Ctra Estación de Cazallas, km7. Tel: 588 65 98; Reserva Verde del Huéznar, Ctra Estación de Cazalla-San Nicolás, km1. Tel: 488 49 34❑

ON THE ROAD

Driving tips

If driving your own vehicle, bring the car documents, international insurance and a bail bond in case of accident, an international driving licence (although for short stays by EEC visitors your national licence should be sufficient), spare car light bulbs, fanbelt and a red warning triangle.

Driving in Spain - and Gibraltar - is on the right. But, particularly on country routes, expect to encounter vehicles hogging the centre of the road, often on bends. So be extra cautious. Remember Spain has one of Europe's worst accident records.

If stopped by a Civil Guard highway patrol, maintain good humour. *Nobody* in their senses argues with the Civil Guard. They can impose extremely heavy, on-the-spot fines for driving offences. Radar speed traps are common.

Four-lane highways (autovías) now link major cities in Andalusia. A massive road-building programme has transformed communications. Secondary roads, no longer potholed dustbowls except in remoter areas, are usually more agreeable and much less nerve-wracking to drive than main highways. However, when calculating travelling time, remember that many of these are tortuous mountain roads so that progress can be slower than expected.

Motorcycles without lights, mules and other livestock can be hazards at night. The speed limit in urban areas is usually 30mph (50kph). On main roads the limit is usually 50mph (80km) to 62mph (100kph). On autopistas the limit is 75mph (120km). Seat belts must be worn. The law requires motorcyclists to wear crash helmets, although this is often not observed. Traffic from the right has priority unless otherwise signalled.

Petrol stations are much more numerous than a few years

ago, but in country areas are still few and far between and usually closed at night. Petrol prices vary little between different gas stations. Leaded petrol usually comes in one grade, which is Super (three star). Unleaded petrol is sold at most stations, though not in more remote areas. Two brands are available, Euro super (95 octane) and Super plus (98 octane).

Maps

Michelin's map of Southern Spain (number 446) is recommended as a guide to Andalusian roads. It includes an index of places with map coordinates. For a larger scale view of the Costa del Sol and hinterland, use Firestone T-29, which includes maps of Antequera, Fuengirola, Granada, Malaga, Marbella, Ronda and Torremolinos, although it is not always reliable as it badly needs updating. The annual Campsa guide has fold-out maps of all Spain, plus tourist and gastronomic information.

Security

Commonsense safety precautions should be observed. Never leave valuables or documents in an unattended car at any time. When staying overnight, take all baggage into the hotel. If possible, park your car in a garage or a guarded car-park. If you leave your car in the street, expose the boot interior if possible so that it is obvious there is nothing worth taking. This particularly applies to cities such as Málaga and Seville. Unofficial parking attendants - dubbed *gorillas* by the locals - may ask you for money. The safest course is to give them something.

When driving through Seville, do not leave anything of value within view. The *semaforazo* is a local custom; youths smash the windows of out-of-town cars at traffic lights, grab anything in sight, then escape by motorcycle. Avoid badly-lit city streets at night. Leave valuables, your passport and other documents in the hotel safe. Make photocopies if you want to carry identification.

Look for three distinct police forces: the *municipales* (blue uniforms, peaked caps), employed by the local council for minor tasks such as bill collection and controlling traffic; National Police (dark blue uniforms), concerned with crime prevention and investigation; Civil Guards (olive-green uniforms, their distinctive patent leather tricorn hats have been relegated to ceremonial occasions), crime prevention in small towns and rural areas. National police stations *(comisarías)* in tourist areas generally have report forms in several languages.

What to wear

Light clothing is essential in summer when Southern Spain can be very hot, especially in the interior. The pleasantest periods of the year are generally the months of April, May and June and September and October. While the sun often shines strongly in winter, the weather is sometimes colder and wetter than many visitors expect, particularly in mountainous areas, so that it is essential to bring a range of clothing.

Casual dress is acceptable almost anywhere. But when sightseeing dress appropriately. While anything goes in tourist resorts, elsewhere locals have little respect for sun-blistered, half-dressed visitors wandering their streets and scanty gear is definitely out when visiting places of worship. You only require formal dress for better-class restaurants and social occasions such as weddings❑

FIESTAS

There is nothing quite as colourful as an Andalusian festival. If you want to experience one, there are hundreds to choose from. If you can't stand crowds, noise and traffic jams, however, you will want to avoid these exuberant occasions. Fiestas are not the ideal time to do the sights. Shops and public buildings are closed, churches and other monuments difficult to visit. Hotels are fully booked. Also if the fiesta is close to a weekend, many Spaniards take the chance to make excursions so that there may be extra traffic on the roads.

Every town and village has an annual *feria* (fair), several days when little work is done and entertainment usually includes bullfights, fireworks, flamenco dancing and fairground fun, plus a certain amount of drinking. Romerias consist of a trek to a local religious shrine, followed by flamenco, dancing and drinking.

For fiesta fans and seekers after tranquillity, here is a brief rundown of the bigger sprees and some interesting smaller ones. Note: dates can vary so check them with local tourist office or town hall.

Celebrated region-wide

Cabalgata de Reyes, January 5: The Three Kings arrive on this night, bearing gifts for the children. Colourful processions parade through towns and cities, the Kings sometimes mounted on camels.

Carnival, in February, is the excuse for a big party. Fancy dress dances and big parades are held all over Andalusia before and after Ash Wednesday, but Cadiz stands out as the place where the celebrations go over the top. Satirical ditties poking fun at wellknown personalities are sung by competing groups.

Semana Santa: A mixture of solemn pomp and pagan ecstasy

characterises Holy Week, celebrated in every town and village. Processions, the biggest in Seville and Málaga, begin on Palm Sunday and reach a climax on Good Friday.

Corpus Christi (May or June): Many towns decorate the streets for the solemn procession. It is particularly worth seeing in Granada where La Tarasca, a figure mounted on a dragon's back, and bigheads parade through town.

Virgen del Carmen: On July 15 or 16, fishermen pay homage to their patron in numerous towns, including Barbate (Cádiz), Estepona, Málaga, Nerja, Salobreña (Granada) and Garrucha (Almeria). The Virgin's image is taken for a sea voyage amid popular acclamation.

Local fiestas of interest

Almería: Annual fair, last week of August: Homage is paid to the Virgin of the Sea.

Baza (Granada), El Cascamorras, September 6: Annual fair starting with the attempt by the Cascamorras, a representative of neighbouring Guadix, to recover a disputed Virgin. Dirty oil is poured over him and he is chased through the town.

Córdoba Patios Festival, first fortnight of May: Patios are opened to the public for this event which includes concerts and flamenco. The Córdoba fair is held in the second half of May.

El Rocío (Huelva), Pentecost (May or early June): Andalusia's most popular fiesta attracts a million or so people. They trek to this spot near the mouth of the Guadalquivir, to pay homage to the Virgen del Rocío, camping out around the sanctuary until the Virgin is brought out in the early hours of Monday morning.

Granada: Día de la Toma, January 2: Solemn procession through the city streets to celebrate the 1492 victory of the Catholic Monarchs over the Moorish Kingdom of Granada; May 3, Day of the Cross, colourful spring festival. May, International Theatre Festival. End of June, International Music and Dance Festival.

Huelva: Columbus fiesta, first week of August.

Jerez: Feria del Caballo, first week of May: Flamenco, equestrian competitions, bullfights and a certain amount of sherry drinking. Jerez holds its wine festival for two weeks leading up to the Día de la Merced, September 24.

Málaga: Fair, first two weeks of August. Businesses close early as Málaga does its best to outdo the Seville Fair; December 28, Fiesta of the Verdiales, a primitive, driving music dating at least from Moorish times, held just outside town at the Venta de San Cayetano, Puerto de la Torre.

Ronda (Málaga), Pedro Romero Fiesta, first fortnight of September: A Corrida Goyesca is held, bullfighters wearing dress typical of Goya's time.

Sanlúcar de la Barrameda, Manzanilla Wine Fair, mid-May. Exaltación al Río Guadalquivir, mid-August. Horse races on beach, second and fourth week August.

Seville Fair (usually in April): A very public private party in which the sevillanos go on the spree for a whole week. The daily parade through the fairgrounds, from around midday, of horsemen and carriages is worth seeing. Daily bullfights and non-stop dancing of the light-hearted sevillana. Beds are hard to find.

The following are holidays all over Andalusia. In addition, towns have local holidays: New Year's Day; January 6, Día de los Reyes; February 28, Día de Andalucía; Easter Thursday, Good Friday (Easter Monday is not a holiday) : May 1, Labour Day; May/June: Corpus Christi (not observed in all localities); August 15, Assumption of the Virgin; October 12, National Day or Día del Pilar; November 1, All Saints' Day; December 6, Day of the Constitution; December 8, Immaculate Conception; Christmas Day❑

VOCABULARY

USEFUL PHRASES

On the road:

Is there a petrol station near here?
Hay una gasolinera (or estación de servicio) por aqui?
Fill her up, please: *Lleno, por favor*
One thousand pesetas of premium (or diesel): *Mil pesetas de super (orgasoil)*
Where is the road to Seville?: *¿Dónde está la carretera a Sevilla?*
How do I get to the airport, the market?: *¿Como se puede ir al aeropuerto, al mercado?*
left: *izquierda*
right: *derecha*
straight on: *todo recto*
first right/second left: *la primera a la derecha, la segunda a la izquierda*
to turn left: *girar a la izquierda*

Road signs

Aparcamiento: parking
Autovía: four-lane highway
Autopista: motorway, turnpike
Carga o descarga: Loading and unloading zone, no parking
Carretera cortada: road blocked
Ceda el paso: give way
Centro urbano: town centre
Circunvalación, ronda: bypass
Entrada: entrance
Firme en mal estado: poor road surface
Llamamos grua: We call the tow-truck (i.e. no parking)
Peaje: toll to pay
Peatones: pedestrians

Peligro: danger
Prohibido aparcar, no aparcar: parking forbidden
Prohibido el paso: no entry
Salida: exit
Tramo en obras: road works
Vado permanente: always in use
Vado inundable: subject to flooding
Vía única: one way

Breakdowns

I have run out of petrol: *Me he quedado sin gasolina*
I have a puncture (flat battery): *Tengo un neumático pinchado (la batería descargada)*
My car has broken down: *Mi coche esta averiado*
The car will not start: *El coche no arranca*
The lights don't work: *No funcionan los faros*
Where is the nearest garage? *¿Dónde está el taller de coches más próximo?*
Can you fix it? : *¿Puede arreglarlo?*
Do you do repairs?: *¿Hace reparaciones?*

petrol: *gasolina*
petrol station: *gasolinera*
lead-free petrol: *gasolina sin plomo*
diesel: *gasoil*
oil: *aceite*
mechanic: *mecánico*
repair shop: *taller de reparaciones or garaje*
crossroads: *cruce*
puncture: *pinchazo*
tow-truck: *grua*
traffic lights: *semáforo*
driving licence: *carnet de conducir*
insurance certificate: *certificado de seguro*
logbook: *permiso de circulación*

Car parts

battery: *batería*

bulb: *bombilla*
car keys: *llaves del coche*
clutch: *embrague*
distilled water: *agua destilada*
exhaust: *tubo escape*
fan belt: *correa de ventilador*
fuse: *fusible*
gearbox: *caja de cambios*
headlights: *faros*
petrol tank: *depósito de gasolina*
points: *contactos*
radiator: *radiador*
spark plug: *bujía*
tyre: *neumático*
wheel: *rueda* (spare wheel: *rueda de recambio*)
windscreen: *parabrisas*

Emergencies - Look for:
ambulancia: ambulance
casa de socorro, puesto de socorro: first aid post
comisaría de policia: police station
Cruz Roja: Red Cross
cuartel de la Guardia Civil: Civil Guard post
farmácia: chemist, pharmacy
hospital,: hospital
médico: doctor
urgencias: casualty department

I am lost: *Estoy perdido*
There's been an accident: *Ha ocurrido un accidente*
I have been robbed: *He sido robado or me han robado*
Call the police: *Llame a la policia*
I have lost my luggage, my passport, the car keys, my wife: *He perdido mi equipaje, mi pasaporte, las llaves del coche, mi mujer*
I am ill: *Estoy enfermo/a* (feminine adjectives end in"*a* ")
I need a doctor, a dentist, a lawyer: *Necesito un médico, un dentista, un abogado*

I am diabetic, pregnant: *Soy diabético/a, Estoy embarazada*
I have heart trouble: *Padezco del corazón*

Useful basics

Please: *Por favor*
Thank you: *Gracias*
Good morning: *Buenos días*
Good afternoon: *Buenas tardes*
Good night: *Buenas noches*
Goodbye: *Adiós*
Where is the post office, railway station, police station?: *¿Dónde está correos, la estación de ferrocarril, la comisaría?*
Where is the toilet?: *¿Dónde están los servicios* (also *caballeros* and *damas*)?
Where can I buy a film, postcards, cigarettes, stamps, medicine?: *¿Dónde puedo comprar una pelicula, postales, tobaco, sellos, medicina?*
Do you have a room free?: ¿Hay una habitación libre?
I would like a double (single) room: *Querría una habitación doble (individual).*
Can I see the menu?: *¿Puedo ver la carta?*
Me gusta la comida: *I like the food*
Breakfast: *Desayuno*
Lunch: *Almuerzo*
Dinner: *Cena*
How much is it?: *¿Cuánto es?*
The bill, please: *La cuenta, por favor*
What time is it?: *¿Qué hora es?*
It is two o'clock, midnight: *Son las dos, es medianoche.*
When does the bus to Estepona leave?: *¿A qué hora sale el autobús para Estepona?*
What time does the plane from London arrive?: *¿A qué hora llega el vuelo de Londres?*

Commonly used Spanish words:

abierto: open
aficionado: amateur, fan (sport)
autobus or *autocar* (long distance): bus

ayer: yesterday
ayuntamiento, casa consistorial: town hall
balneario: spa
barrio: quarter (of a city)
bodega: wine cellar
calle: street
cama: bed
cambiar: to change
campo: countryside, field
carretera: highway
cerrado: closed
cerveza: beer
ciudad: city
coche: car
comida: meal
corrida: bullfight
cortijo: farmhouse
dinero: money
finca: farm
fino: dry sherry
gitano: gypsy
hoy: today
jamón serrano: mountain-cured ham
mañana: tomorrow
mañana por la mañana: tomorrow morning
mercado: market
mesón: bar-restaurant
mirador: viewpoint
moto: motor-cycle
pan: bread
parador: state-run hotel
playa: beach
plaza: square
pueblo: village, town
tablao: flamenco night club
tapa: snack
venta: inn

Architecture:

alcazaba: castle
alcázar: fortress, royal palace
artesonado: Moorish-style coffered ceiling
azulejo: glazed tile
barroco: Baroque, ornate style
capilla mayor: chapel with high altar
claustro: cloister
churrigueresco: Churrigueresque, highly ornate Baroque art
coro: chancel with choir-stalls
ermita: hermitage
isabelino: Isabelline, Gothic style from era of Queen Isabel
mihrab: prayer niche in a mosque
mozárabe: Mozarab, art developed by Christians under Moslem rule
Mudéjar: Moslem art in Christian-occupied territory
murallas: walls, ramparts
neo-clásico: Neo-classical, imitating sober Greek and Roman styles
plateresco: Plateresque, finely carved early Renaissance style
qibla: mosque wall orientated towards Mecca
reja: iron grille
retablo: decorated altarpiece
torre del homenaje: keep

0, *cero*
1, *uno*
2, *dos*
3, *tres*
4, *cuatro*
5, *cinco*
6, *seis*
7, *siete*
8, *ocho*
9, *nueve*
10, *diez*
20, *veinte*

25, *veinticinco*
50, *cincuenta*
100, *cien*
500, *quinientos*
1,000, *mil*

GEOGRAPHICAL INDEX

MORE GREAT BOOKS ON SPAIN

Excursions in Eastern Spain
by Nick Inman and Clara Villanueva. 272 pages.
This guide takes you on thirty easy-to-follow excursions by car to the most famous sights and the least-known corners of the Costa Blanca, Valencia and beyond, and tells you what's worth seeing, where to stay, where to eat, how to get there, and lots more.

Birds of Iberia
by Clive Finlayson and David Tomlinson. 240 pages (Hardback, large format)
A journey through the different regions of this fascinating peninsula which describes the main habits and birds found there, migration patterns and ornithological sites. Beautifully illustrated throughout with fine line drawings and more than 150 colour photographs, the book is an appreciation of the extraordinarily rich and varied birdlife of Iberia.

The Story of Spain
by Mark Williams. 272 pages
The bold and dramatic history of Spain, from the caves of Altamira to our present day. This is a story of kings and poets, saints and conquistadores, of Torquemada, Picasso, Cervantes, Franco, the Alhambra, the Escorial... Mark Williams has drawn on years of rigorous research to recreate the drama, excitement and pathos of crucial events in the history of the western world. Illustrated in colour.

Gardening in Spain
by Marcelle Pitt. 216 pages
Your most valuable tool for successful gardening in Spain, from the author of Lookout magazine's popular gardening column. How to plan your garden, what to plant, when and how to plant it, how to make the most of flowers, trees, shrubs, herbs. Illustrated with full-colour photographs.

Cooking in Spain
by Janet Mendel. 376 pages
The definitive guide to cooking in Spain, with more than 400 great Spanish recipes. Plus complete information on Spain's regional specialities and culinary history, how to buy the best in the market, a complete English-Spanish glossary with more than 500 culinary terms, handy conversation guide... all of it illustrated with colour photographs.

1. SET THE TUMBLER TO ZERO THEN TURN COUNTER CLOCKWISE (LEFT) FOUR COMPLETE TURNS THEN CONTINUE TO 1ST NO OF COMBINATION IN SAME DIRECTION.

2. TURN TUMBLER ~~ANTI~~- CLOCKWISE (RIGHT) THROUGH THE 1st No TWICE, & CONTINUE ON TO 2ND No

3. TURN TUMBLER ANTI - CLOCKWISE THROUGH 2ND No ~~to~~ 3RD No

4. TURN TUMBLER CLOCKWISE TO 4th No

5. ROTATE KEY & LIFT DOOR USING THE GRIP

TO LOCK :: ROTATE THE KEY & REMOVE
SCRAMBLE TUMBLER

99 - 76 - 6 - 46

TRAVEL NOTES

TRAVEL NOTES